TROUBLE, TRIALS, AND VEXATIONS

T0379110

TROUBLE, TRIALS, AND VEXATIONS

The Journal and Correspondence of Rachel Perry Moores, Texas Plantation Mistress

Edited by THOMAS W. CUTRER

State ✦ House Press

Schreiner University · Kerrville, TX
325-660-1752 · www.mcwhiney.org

Cataloging-in-Publication Data

Names: Moores, Rachel Perry, author.
Title: Trouble, trials, and vexations: the journal and correspondence of Rachel Perry Moores, Texas plantation mistress / Rachel Perry Moores; edited by Thomas W. Cutrer.
Description: First edition. | Kerrville, TX: State House Press, 2024. | Includes bibliographical references, illustrations, and index.
Identifiers: ISBN 9781649670243 (paperback)
Subjects: LCSH: Moores, Rachel Perry – Diaries. | Moores, Rachel Perry – Correspondence. |Texas – History – Civil War, 1861-1865 – Personal narratives. | Texas – History – Civil War, 1861-1865 – Social aspects. | Cutrer, Thomas W.
Classification: LCC E605 (print) | DCC 973.7

First edition 2024

Cover and page design by Allen Griffith of Eye 4 Design

Distributed by Texas A&M University Press Consortium
800-826-8911
www.tamupress.com

For those lost to history, unnamed and forgotten.

CONTENTS

TROUBLE, TRIALS, AND VEXATIONS

TROUBLE, TRIALS, AND VEXATIONS

THE GARDEN SPOT OF TEXAS

O n February 27, 1840, a caravan consisting of Charles and Mary Virginia Moores, their fourteen children and various in-laws, their slaves—including, according to local genealogist Charles A. Steger, Giles Joplin (the father of the famed ragtime composer and musician, Scott Joplin)—and numerous cousins, members of the Rochelle, Harrison, Rosborough, and Whitaker families whom they had induced to join them all began the long, arduous trip from Longtown, Fairfield County, South Carolina, to relocate in "the garden spot" of northeast Texas. The white women made the trip in carriages—Mary's was drawn by four horses—and the men rode on horseback while the enslaved came in ox carts and wagons, bringing the livestock.[1]

Three years earlier, in 1837, Charles Moores, accompanied by his five sons, had scouted the vicinity then known as the Red River District of Texas and began to "set up" a home place. In the winter of 1839, Charles and his three younger sons returned to South Carolina, leaving the two eldest sons, Eli and Reuben, with the family's slaves to clear land, prepare fields for cultivation, and build accommodations. After more than two years the labor was complete, and, as Charles and Mary's fourth surviving son, Anderson Rochelle Moores, recorded, "we left our South Carolina home behind and started to Texas."[2]

Eli Moores, older brother of David H. Moores. Moores Collection, Wilbur Smith Archives, Museum of Regional History, Texarkana, Texas.

Their reasons for relocating were many and varied. The new Republic of Texas, having recently gained its independence from Mexico, offered to settlers free land and plentiful resources. Rainfall was abundant, averaging forty-seven inches a year, and the growing season was long, averaging 235 days annually. With the Red River offering convenient transportation for cotton to downstream markets—most notably New Orleans—and having over the millennia deposited rich layers of silt over the bottomlands—to cotton planters such as the Moores, the region was a natural extension of the cotton kingdom of the Deep South and a place where fortunes were to be made.[3]

Others had reasons of their own. Jane Ross Moores, one of Charles and Mary's daughters, wrote to her brother Reuben Harrison Moores in 1839, "I have not the most distant idea of marrying until I get to Texas."

Although she facetiously claimed that "my external appearance will require a good deal of flattering," she enjoined Reuben to tell their brother, William Henry Harrison Moores, who had accompanied his father and brothers to Texas in 1837, that he was to "select me one of the most magnificent looking gentlemen that Texas affords, and keep him in reserve for me until I emigrate to Texas."[4]

Anderson Rochelle Moores, youngest brother of David H. Moores.

Considering her marriage prospects in South Carolina to be limited, she wrote, "as ladies are not very numerous in Texas, I presume I will stand a pretty good chance. At any rate, I will go to Texas as Miss Moores."[5]

Anderson Rochelle Moores, the family's youngest son, kept a daily log of the three months' trek. Traveling at a rate that varied between one to twenty miles per day depending upon road conditions and other terrain, the caravan crossed the Blue Ridge Mountains and the Cumberland Gap arriving at the home of Uncle John Norvelle in Bell Buckle, Bedford County, Tennessee, in March. There they remained long enough for Charles and Mary's fourth son, Thomas Briggs Moores, to meet and marry his cousin, Sarah Margaret Norvell.[6]

At Memphis on the tenth, the caravan ferried across the Mississippi River into Arkansas. After that, communities became fewer and farther between and roads became increasingly primitive. Averaging only about five miles a day thereafter, the train ferried across the Arkansas River at Little Rock on

May 9. On the nineteenth, tantalizingly near their destination, they reached the Red River but found that they could not continue due to high water. Not until the twenty-first could they cross into Texas, and, at last, on May 24, 1840, came to "our place" after a trek, according to Anderson Moores' calculation, of 1,027 miles.[7]

On August 2, 1841, the General Land Office of the Republic of Texas granted Charles Moores and his sons Reuben, Thomas, Eli, and Anderson each 320 acres of well drained bottomland on what is now the old Redwater Road, extending from the Forest Home community in what is now northern Cass County, across Moores Landing on the Sulphur River into Bowie County. They called their settlement Mooresville—now known as Redwater—and the Republic of Texas established a post office there later that year with Reuben Henry Harrison Moores as its first postmaster.[8]

Charles and Mary built a plantation home for themselves at Mooresville, naming it "Sweet Springs." The enslaved persons dug a lake directly in front of the house, and according to family lore visitors enjoyed boat rides on the lake and hunters shot ducks from the front porch. "Beautiful flowers surrounded the slave quarters behind the plantation home."[9]

Charles and Mary Moores, parents of David H. Moores.

Near "Sweet Springs," at Mary's request, the family built Harrison Chapel, named for her parents. This, the first known church in Bowie County, is said to have been a quaint little building with a balcony in the back for the black congregants, and, although Mary was a Baptist, circuit riders from all Protestant faiths held services there.[10]

David Harrison Moores, Charles and Mary's third son, received a 320-acre grant on September 6, 1841, and his elder brother Reuben Moores settled on adjacent grants on the south bank of the Sulfur River near Forest Home in what was soon to become Cass County.[11]

The land on which the Moores, their extended family, and friends settled was part of what had been a Spanish grant to Arthur Goodall Wavell, a Scottish soldier of fortune, which had given him permission to introduce colonists into present-day Lamar, Red River, Bowie, Fannin, and Hunt counties as well as Miller County, Arkansas. Wavell's efforts to recruit settlers had been hindered, however, by Mexico's hostility to slavery and by the great Red River Raft, a log jam stretching 165 miles from Loggy Bayou to Carolina Bluffs on the Mississippi River, which prevented river transport to and from the colony. In addition, on April 6, 1830, Mexico banned further immigration from the United States and

Margaret Perry Godbold, sister of Rachel Moores. Moores Collection, Wilbur Smith Archives, Museum of Regional History, Texarkana, Texas.

refused to issue land titles to the 140 families that had emigrated to Wavell's colony.[12]

In 1836, however, following its successful war for independence, the newly fledged Republic of Texas established Red River County in the far northeastern corner of Texas. Including all of the territory now in Bowie and Cass counties, it was bordered on the north by the Red River and on the east by Miller County, Arkansas.

Bowie County was carved out of Red River County in December and included all or part of the territories of present Cass, Titus, and Morris counties. On April 25, 1846, the county was reduced to its present boundaries with the establishment of Cass County. Lying on the eastern boundary of Texas and just south of Bowie County, it was named for Michigan Senator Lewis Cass, an early advocate of Texas annexation.

On August 12, 1846, shortly after the outbreak of the United States' war with Mexico, Col. Humphrey Marshall's First Kentucky Cavalry crossed the Arkansas line and entered Texas, en route to Col. Zachary Taylor's army on the Rio Grande. The regiment's major, John Pollard Gaines, recorded in his diary, "was the land for which we are fighting, or rather the land for which we are seeking a fight." On his first night in Texas, Major Gaines described the land as beautiful, "but the soil generally thin, the growth a low, scrubby oak and hickory, and the soil rather sandy."[13]

After a march of twenty miles on the following day, Marshall's regiment arrived at the Moores' settlement where it encamped. Gaines recorded "ticks innumerable, a good plantation and a wealthy man, store, grog shop, handsome women." The country, he described as "beautifully undulating, the same timber, low, scrubby and thin, with the appearance of great antiquity."[14]

The region's inhabitants he characterized as "immigrants from the south, with a few exceptions, generally very poor, who left the bare sandy hills of S. Carolina, Georgia and Alabama to better their condition in Texas, which I have no doubt they have done."[15]

Bowie and Cass counties were, to the largest degree, settled by old stock Anglo-Southerners. The white population built a way of life similar to the one they had known in the older Southern states and an agricultural economy based on cotton as the cash crop and corn and hogs—the so-called "hog and hominy" diet—as primary food sources. From 1849 through 1859, cotton production grew from 1,573 bales to 9,968 bales, and corn production expanded from 167,250 bushels to 289,979 bushels in the same decade. Cass County farmers and planters owned 16,732 hogs in 1849 and 17,432 in 1859.

In common with their fellow emigrants from the Lower South, East Texas planters of the antebellum era valued tradition. The principal characteristics of their culture emphasized an agrarian economy and lifestyle, close kinship ties, an hierarchical social structure, ascribed status, patterns of deference, and a masculine code of honor and chivalry.[16]

Despite its still relatively small population, northeast Texas in the mid-nineteenth century was a close-knit community of family and friends, although decidedly patriarchal and hierarchical, with the planter elite at the top of the economic and social order. As in the rest of the cotton South, slavery was a vitally important institution. The labor force was composed almost entirely of enslaved blacks, and as agricultural production expanded, the slave population grew faster than the free. Throughout the antebellum years, enslaved men and women outnumbered free inhabitants.

In 1850, 1,641 blacks were enumerated in the Bowie County census and 1,271 whites. Of the county's 145 slaveholders in 1850, twenty-two (15 percent) owned more than twenty slaves each, these planters owning more than half of all the slaves in the county. During the ensuing decade, although the white population grew at a slightly faster rate than the black, in 1860 the enslaved still outnumbered the free by 2,651 to 2,401.

During the 1850s slaveholding also became more concentrated. While the free population of the county grew by 89 percent between 1850 and 1860, the number of slaveholders in the county increased by only 30 percent. Within the

slaveholding class the distribution of slaves remained about the same. Roughly 23 percent of the slaveholders living in the county in 1860 were of the planter class—that is, those who owned at least twenty enslaved persons—and they owned 65 percent of the enslaved population.

Cass County, due to its relative distance from the Red River, developed somewhat more slowly, but growth was still robust. By 1847, it was home to a population of 2,949, of whom 943—roughly 31 percent of the total—were enslaved. By 1850, the general population had grown to 4,991, and 1,902 of whom were enslaved. By 1860, the population stood at 8,411, of whom 3,475 were enslaved, constituting 41 percent of the total population. In 1847, only one free black lived in Cass County, and the census of 1860 reported none.

Land use grew in lockstep with population growth, and the two counties became well settled before the Civil War. By 1850, 24,062 of Bowie County's 608,640 acres were under cultivation, and by 1860 that figure had risen to 47,902

Samuel Ananias Godbold, father of Rachel Perry Moores.

acres. Moreover, lands to the west were quickly filled, as well, so that Bowie and Cass were never truly frontier communities in the sense of being on the very edge of settlement. Neither were they isolated from access to larger markets. Jefferson, in Cass County, was a major riverport, serving antebellum Texas as a supply point and shipping center for produce.

To this growing but still largely rural and underdeveloped region, Rachel Perry Moores came as a bride in 1855. Rachel Perry Godbold was born on November 22, 1830, in Monroe County, Alabama, and her mother died on the following day from complications of childbirth. "There was lamentation instead of thanksgiving at my birth," Rachel wrote more than thirty years later, "grief instead of joy, for as I came into the world, my dearest of mothers passed from its checkered scene."

On January 19, 1831, less than two months after the death of his first wife, Samuel Ananias Godbold married Elizabeth Johnson and moved his family to Columbia County, Arkansas. Like the Moores of northeast Texas with whom they were to intermarry, the Godbolds were members of the plantation elite. On March 1, 1855, Rachel's father filed for a homestead grant of forty acres in Nevada County, and on July 1, 1859, he was awarded an additional 320 acres. By 1860, he had amassed real estate valued at $6,000, $25,000 in personal property, and was the owner of nineteen slaves.[17]

Rachel Moores was not a beautiful woman. "For your sake, Love," she wrote to her husband many years later, "I often wish I was prettier and more fascinating. I know everyone most likes pretty women best, but I try to make up for these deficiencies in making you a good wife."

David answered, somewhat tactlessly, that he did not want a prettier wife. "What is beauty? It is nothing. It just makes anyone vain." If Rachel was not beautiful, he continued, she possessed other qualities. "I know I might of married someone that was prettier in the face, but that would be all; no one on earth could make as half as good a wife as you do."

Nevertheless, as a young woman she seems to have enjoyed such social occasions as rural Arkansas offered. She alludes in a letter to a friend to the time "when I was a young lady in society," and among her papers, preserved for more than fifty years at the time of her death, was an invitation to a "Cotillion Party" held on July 9, 1850, at Vaughn's Saloon in nearby Camden, Arkansas.

On a visit to New Orleans with her father in 1853, twenty-four-year-old Rachel Godbold met David Harrison Moores and on February 6, 1855, the couple were married at her parents' Ouachita County home.

Upon their return from their bridal tour, on which they visited Niagara Falls, purchased furniture, and had their portraits painted in New York City, David and Rachel began building their plantation near the community of Forest Home in northern Cass County, across the Sulfur River from Mooresville. Their nearest neighbors were Reuben Moores, David's elder brother, and his wife Jane Godbold Moores, Rachel's younger half-sister.[18]

David and Rachel Moores possessed significant wealth, allowing them entrée into the elite planter class. The 1860 Federal census reveals that they owned more than 200 acres of improved agricultural land and 2,000 acres of unimproved land with an estimated cash value of $7,000 as well as thirty enslaved persons. In addition, the couple owned personal property worth $19,395 including more than $300 in farm equipment and machinery, two horses, five mules, eighty-four head of cattle, forty sheep, and one-hundred hogs valued at $1,600, and stored crops—corn, cotton, and wool—worth an estimated $700.[19]

One uninvited visitor to the Moores' plantation home "declared her intention of surveying the whole house" to learn whether local gossip about the family's "fine house and fine things" was true. Although Rachel assured her that "the house was quite ordinary" but that the furnishings were "as nice as we could get in New York," after assessing the home and its contents the old woman concluded that "she had not heard an exaggerated account."

For that reason, perhaps, the Moores were looked upon as haughty by some of the less well-off of their neighbors. Rachel attributed their unpopularity to the rumor that "we put cup towels (table napkins) on the table and would only drink out of silver goblets." Although she claimed to pity more than condemn such "uncharitable people," Rachel did take great pride and pleasure in fine things, including a set of sterling silver engraved with the monogram "DRM" and her carriage horses—"noble looking steeds, matched well"—that pulled her carriage at "almost at lightning speed."

But besides wealth, the Victorian lady possessed such traits as leisure, prestigious family connections, and skills and social graces. Speaking of a group of people who she had recently met on a visit to Arkansas, Rachel opined that "They all are cultivated people, very nice. The ladies performed excellently on the piano, and the gentleman talked theology."

Her letters to and from her husband and her journal entries during the Civil War era, 1858–1865, provide a remarkably clear window into the life and times of the planter class, and especially the Victorian "lady," on the western fringe of the slave-owning frontier. They reveal significant insights into social attitudes and familial relationships, travel, hospitality, foodways, farming techniques, impressions of and attitudes toward the North and Northerners in general and Abolitionists in particular, the seeming barbarity of mid-nineteenth century medical care and, more important, the impact of the Civil War on a relatively isolated and remote community. The dominate motif of her writings, however, is the bitter daily relationships between master and slave and the interplay between a plantation mistress and her "servants"—one that was almost invariably fraught with mutual hostility and violence.

Following the Victorian axiom that a lady's name should appear in print only three times—in announcements of her birth, her marriage, and her death—of Rachel Moores' early life and education we know almost nothing. "I was so frail as a child," she wrote. "I was early learned to sew, and when not engaged with my lessons, was closely—too closely—confined for any child, whether invalid or robust, and to this day do I feel the consequences and never shall I grow over it."

Nevertheless, hers seems to have been a happy childhood, for she remembered "sporting amid the flowers, chasing the butterflies, and looking for birds' nests, my favorite sport." In the fields of her family plantation, "covered with nature's greenest velvet," Rachel made garlands of jasmine and "grasped at the tiny hummingbirds," while her brother "would ascend to the topmost boughs of the overspreading oaks in quest of the merry warbler who had just poured forth his sweetest strains."

In many ways, Rachel Perry Moores exemplified the Victorian ideal of the perfect woman, wife, housekeeper, and ministering angel. She was devoted and submissive to her husband, passive and seemingly powerless, meek, charming, graceful, sympathetic, self-sacrificing, and devout. Typical of the women of her class, Rachel wrote, the "only real satisfaction I have ever felt through life has been in regard to my conduct as wife and daughter."

A prime indicator of high-status Southern women was their focus on the wellbeing of others. The lady was ideally self-negating and other-oriented, performing acts of sympathy and selflessness. She was by nature a nurturer. Recounting the qualities that she admired in one of her nieces, Rachel wrote that "She is all sympathy for suffering humanity. Her heart is overflowing with affection for her friends and relatives." [20]

Rachel's journal reveals how lovingly she nursed her pet lamb, "it's maternal parent refusing to acknowledge it." But more important, she remembered "what a dear privilege it has ever been to me to serve him in sickness," she wrote of her invalid father, "and how sweet the reflection that I did everything in my power to lessen his suffering." Typically, as well, when her husband returned home one evening, "hungry, weary, and dispirited," a lawsuit "having unjustly gone against him," she put away her handwork and "tried to soothe his perplexed mind."

Writing of a neighbor whose companionship she enjoyed, Rachel explained that she "is so ladylike, genteel, and refined, so respectful of other people's rights." Rachel herself was educated, refined, and accomplished, a cultured lady, a gifted musician, and was steeped in literature. "I can enter into, appreciate, enjoy, the beautiful lines I read," she lamented, "and yet I am not able to compose one line of decent poetry" despite the "burning, bright thoughts [that] crowd through my head to my very soul."

Nothing is known of Rachel's formal education, but in keeping with the gendered expectations of the era, she became proficient only in those subjects which prepared her to converse and write pleasantly and well, and to appreciate classic literature and current novels. She was also proficient in music and such domestic arts and crafts as tatting and sewing.

Rachel played both the piano and the organ and often sang for her guests. "I played and sung so long tonight for the young ladies," she recorded in her journal, "my throat hurts me much and I am not a little weary."

Florence Hartley, a mid-nineteenth century maven of upper-class decorum, saw skill in needlework as "essential to a lady's education, with implications for her overall happiness and for her usefulness to, and acceptance within, society." Such handwork as sewing, knitting, spinning, weaving, and dying, both for decorative and ornamental purposes and to keep her household clothed, occupied a great deal of Rachel's time, and descriptions of her hours dedicated to needle and loom fill many pages of her journal.[21]

She was also widely traveled, often to fashionable spas and clinics where she journeyed to recover her health, and her writings contain vivid descriptions of the horrors of travel by steamboat and stagecoach, but also of the delights of New Orleans, New York, New England, Louisville, and Havana.

Rachel Moores possessed in full measure the delicate sensibilities of the Victorian era, although the tone of her journal varies sharply between passages of sentimental, romantic idealization and stark—even harsh—reality. As she confessed in one of her many letters to her husband, "I have a heart keenly attuned to all tender situations, either of joy or grief. Too sensitive, impulsive, I know." She displayed a flair for the melodramatic and was perhaps inclined to overstatement.

Many times, her rhetoric is highly reminiscent of Mark Twain's Emmeline Grangerford in *Huckleberry Finn* and her mawkish elegies of deceased friends and relatives. Twain's creation entitles her maudlin crayon drawing of a young woman weeping over a dead bird, "I Shall Never Hear Thy Sweet Chirrup More Alas." Rachel is repeatedly guilty of such literary offenses, as when she apostrophizes her dead father, "can it be that I never, no never in this world, can see you more? . . . Can I ever feel thus again? No, never."

Rachel waxed poetic over the passage of time and the loss of youth. "Alas! Has the May of life deserted me?" she asked rhetorically at the age of thirty-two. "And is the summer here? So soon! Why, it seems but yesterday I was a little child. . . . But now those blissful days are over, and my joys are subdued."

She was finely attuned to the charms of nature. Following a long ramble about the plantation with her husband she wrote in her journal, "such a scene of a rural enchantment was presented that all else was for the time forgotten in my admiration for nature, animate and inanimate. The gentle zephyr swaying the green oak boughs and apple limbs which almost breaking beneath their treasures, and the birds, blue, red, and mockingbird singing, chirping, twittering, and hopping from tree to tree and from branch to branch."

She loved what she called "melancholy sweetness." On one beautiful Sunday morning, she wrote, "there is something in it of melancholy acuteness. Something that accords with my sadness, sadness of feelings. The very hum of the insect and song of the birds is now soft and soothing to my ear. It seems to be in accordance with my mood."

Not remarkably, she claimed to "love the Autumn better than any other season," despite—or perhaps because of—the gloom that it foretold and because it "forcibly impresses me with a certainty of death and the brevity of human existence." She felt, she wrote to her husband, "a melancholy pleasure in watching the falling leaves and listening to the 'wailing winds.'"

In a culture in which weeping was identified with femininity, Rachel quite frequently and candidly admits to spells of melancholy. More than once she confesses to having "indulged in a bath of tears," and, she wrote to her husband, "You know I do cry of pain at times, of sickness and other such foolish things."

Her nature was also sensitive to slights. "How illy my spirit brooks the harsh censures I oft times have to bear, unmerited reproaches, how they chafe me," she moaned. Aware of her susceptibility, she resolved to "bear the petty vexations of my life with more fortitude, be more resigned to that which I could not control," but continued all her life "to feel all the poignancy such a spirit must feel when wronged or insulted."

She was especially "chaffed" by what she perceived as her ill-treatment by other members of her family. Her relationship with her sisters, half-sisters, and sisters-in-law seems to have been fraught with tensions if not absolute enmity—a circumstance that she greatly deplored—but she was emotionally close to her father, her step-mother, her brothers, and her nieces and nephews. And she adored her husband.

In his vastly popular 1854 poem, "The Angel in the House," Coventry Patmore expresses the ideal romantic love a woman should feel for her husband:

Man must be pleased: but him to please

Is woman's pleasure; down the gulf

Of his condoled necessities

She casts her best. she flings herself.

How often flings for nought. and yokes

Her heart to an icicle or whim,

Whose each impatient word provokes

Another. not from her. but him;

While she. too gentle even to force

His penitence by kind replies,

Waits by. expecting his remorse.

With pardon in her pitying eyes;

And if he once. by shame oppress'd.

A comfortable word confers,

She leans and weeps against his breast.

And seems to think the sin was hers;

Or any eye to see her charms.

At any time. she's still his wife.

Dearly devoted to his arms;

She loves with love that cannot tire.

Her letters to David are overflowing with terms of endearment and express a longing to be reunited with him, and dozens of her journal entries express her concern for his health and safety. While on a visit to her father in Arkansas, Rachel wrote to her husband, "I long to be with you, to attend to your little wants. What a pleasure to sew on buttons for you—to do anything for you—except cut your hair."

Rachel admired her husband's "indefatigable energy and perseverance, his daring coolness and not-too-be-out-done spirit in trying moments—in great perplexities—his independent, defiant spirit doing homage to nothing but true merit or genius, regardless of what the world may say, and it is that which still keeps the flower alive. . . . I want to look up to my husband and admire as well as love him, and I want him to respect as well as pet me. I cannot be happy without either."

As the code prescribed, Rachel was charitable to the poor, giving gifts of clothing and food to the community's indigent. "God only knows how much I strive to be charitable to the distressed and afflicted," she told her journal. She was not, however, without a certain degree of scorn for those who did not help themselves, and she did not attempt to conceal her condescension toward those beneath her on the socio-economic scale.

In common with Fanny Kemble Butler, who described Georgia's poor whites of the same era as "the most degraded race of human being claiming an Anglo-Saxon origin that can be found on the face of the earth—filthy, lazy, ignorant, brutal, proud, penniless savages," Rachel Moores viewed her poor neighbors to whom she dispensed largess with condescension if not outright contempt.

When she delivered a shoulder of meat to one such family, she perceived that "the old woman" interpreted her act of kindness as an act of conciliation, because when she had recently donated to her husband some clothes, Rachel had "reprimanded him severely about rearing a family of such ungrateful, indolent children" who allowed him "to suffer for all the comforts and most of the necessities of life."

During the Civil War, when the home of a Confederate soldier burned, Rachel took to his wife "a satchel of clothes" and on the same day sent to another neighbor, whose husband was away in the army, eighteen pounds of "soap grease" and one and a half bushels of sweet potatoes. Shortly thereafter she gave another impoverished neighbor cloth to make each of her two little boys a pair of pants, but admonished her to say nothing of her charity. "If it is known," Rachel feared, she would be overwhelmed with similar requests. This woman, however, "says she works very hard," and, Rachel added, she "has a female disease, and that always melts my heart."

Although she felt pity for another such "poor old creature," this woman appeared to Rachel "as if she was encrusted in sediment that would surpass the bottom in which she dwelt in growing vegetables," and the "smoked hut" in which she lived was "a hovel of filth and poverty" in which dwelt "loathsome . . . little dirty-faced, matted-haired ignorant children!" Always betraying a weakness for the young, however, she softened her attitude toward them somewhat. "Poor untended little ones," she wrote.

No doubt because of her own childless condition, when a young neighbor asked her to cut out and sew a dress for her, Rachel commented that "she is an orphan, and I will never refuse assistance in anything reasonable," but she did wonder if it were reasonable "to make a dress for her when I hire the most of mine made."

The custom of hospitality also played a central role in the Southern family's life and stood as a test of elite status. Historian Bertram Wyatt-Brown defines hospitality as "the relationship of an individual and family to outsiders," and when strangers and visitors arrived, Southerners felt duty-bound to make welcome whomever sought food or lodging.[22]

Entertaining company was "generally a pleasure," Rachel wrote. Although frequently a generous hostess, with friends, family, and assorted travelers spending extended visits at the Moores' plantation, her hospitality was conditioned by the state of her health, her patience, and her kitchen staff. "What a martyr one is to household duties when one hasn't trained servants," she lamented.

But "home is so much nicer" when she and David were there alone, "unless a visitor comes who is pleasant." She "should dislike to live where company would be coming in often at unreasonable hours," she related to her journal. "It is so fatiguing." Worse, she did not suffer fools gladly. "What an affliction, to be compelled to listen to and entertain people who have neither cultivated heads nor hearts."

In an era that idealized the romantic love a woman should feel for her husband, Rachel declared that she loved hers "almost to idolatry." Their correspondence indicates that the two were, indeed, totally dedicated to one another and she depended upon him for emotional support. "One frown from you," she wrote, "and I am undone."

The concept of separate spheres—a strict division of labor and social roles along gender lines—was central to the construction of traditional order, and the era enforced a strong dichotomy between physical (male) and spiritual (female) . . . purity of womanhood and dependence upon supposedly superior male physical and intellectual power.[23]

As Alfred, Lord Tennyson, a favorite poet of Rachel's, and also of Queen Victoria's, wrote,

Man for the field and woman for the hearth:
Man for the sword and for the needle she:
Man with the head and woman with the heart:
Man to command and woman to obey.
All else confusion.

In a culture that strictly observed the norm of separate spheres of work for men and women, Rachel's husband tended the crops, the cattle and hogs, the maintenance of outbuildings and roads, and all else away from the home, he and bore the family's sole responsibility for decision making on all questions of finance. "David teased me no little," Rachel wrote, trying to coax her into saying whether he should employ a new overseer. "Of course, I did not tell him what to do as that is out of the line of business."

Only once did Rachel seem to willfully exceed the boundaries of her sphere when, during the Civil War, she sought to "exercise that influence over my husband which I think is just and right" when she attempted, "more by insinuation than anything else," to induce him to sell his surplus pork to the

Confederate commissary at half its value on the open market. But, she wrote, "he never gave me much satisfaction," instead, selling five or six thousand pounds of meat to a wealthy Red River planter. "It made me heartsick when he told me of it," Rachel bemoaned. "What in the name of humanity is the army to do?"

Even so, David did write to his wife that "you could make me do anything in the world that you wanted to," and vowed that "nothing gives me more pleasure than for you to advise me." While she was away seeking treatment for her chronically poor health, David wrote to Rachel that he missed her so much "that I don't half attend to my business. If you was here to advise me, I know things would be much better," but Rachel's advice centered almost exclusively around his diet, his drinking habits, his lack of religious faith, and his profane language and admonishing him to "bathe often."

The proper Victorian lady not only kept an orderly home but also set the religious tenor of her family. She was "most bitterly disappointed," Rachel wrote one Sunday when rain prevented her from attending church. A woman of great piety, she believed that her "greatest sin" consisted in taxing her mind "too much with the cares of this world," and was constantly coaxing her husband toward Christian faith and commitment. "Oh, that I could be that means of his conversion," she wrote in her journal. "I would be so proud to have you read the Good Book much," she wrote to David from a clinic in Brandon, Mississippi, where she was being treated for various maladies. "I'm sure you would profit by it." And from a revival meeting in Atlanta, Texas, just down the road from their plantation, she wrote to him in 1888 that she felt "mean and selfish" to be attending religious services while her husband, still having not "gotten religion," was at home. "Don't let all my prayers be a witness against me at the Judgment Day. Heaven and Hell are each all around you. Can I say more?"

For David's part, he thought "if we had a good Baptist Church in this neighborhood that I would try to get religion and join." He pledged, at least, "to lead a different life," but Rachel believed that he was "too doubtful" and thought that "if he could not be the best Christian, he could not be one at all."

The Southern construction of femininity also included the idealization of at least perceived leisure and inactivity. A Northern friend of Rachel's remarked that she "would enjoy being lazy and waited upon like the Southern ladies," and opined that she "would like a little darkey to trot after her." Rachel's activities to a degree exemplify this attribute. A typical entry in her diary reveals that she "spent the day reading, eating fruit, and this evening my husband took me on a long drive down to the river."

Yet, despite her chronic ill health and despite her wealth and numerous enslaved women kept as kitchen help and chambermaids, Rachel belied the stereotypical image of the Southern belle as indolent and pampered. From the clinic in Brandon, Rachel sent her husband detailed instructions for the care and maintenance of the household. "Ain't it too bad for me to make such requirements of you," she wrote, "when I ought to be there and tend to it myself."

She was a hard-working woman, seemingly constantly curing meats, cleaning, cooking, baking, preserving fruit, knitting and sewing—both for herself and for the plantation's enslaved laborers—making starch, dyes, and lye soap—often until her hands were chapped and cracked—making cheese and butter, working in her yard, in her gardens of vegetables and flowers, and in the dairy and in the fowl yards with her beloved poultry. She participated in the weekly washing—"that nuisance of housekeepers"—ironing, rendering lard, and caring for her often-ill husband and their chattels. Even her husband admitted, when she was away, that he "never knew before how much a lady had to attend to housekeeping. It's a very laborious work for me," and "I will be so happy when the time comes when you are to come home."

For all of her industry, however, the domesticity and leisure of the Victorian ideal correlated femininity with whiteness and privilege and required the labor of less-privileged women, particularly enslaved black women. The most frustrating of all of Rachel's efforts were her attempts to train manifestly unwilling "house servants," as she called them, as cooks, maids, spinners, weavers, and seamstresses, and her letters and journal entries give us some remarkable insights into the conditions of slavery and the racial attitudes of the South's elite on what was then the western frontier of the slave-owning culture.

Rachel's efforts to teach domestic skills to the members of her household staff were often met with minor acts of defiance and sabotage: reluctance, tardiness, spoiled dinners, petty thefts, and occasional temporary absence without permission, especially during the Civil War when many of the men of the community were in the army, making punishment unlikely. "Oh, I shall never speak again of cruelty to disobedient servants. They know I can't and won't whip them, and thus they treat me," she complained in her journal. On one particularly trying occasion, she vowed that "I shall never try to get any more work out of that worthless no-account Mary. It wears out my life to make her take the exercise that is essential to keep her alive!"

On another occasion, with company arriving, her cook, Nancy, intentionally burned the biscuits, and although "on such occasions she always puts on a long face and at the same time a serious air, and assumes a pitiful accent—yet I could see from the workings of the corners of her mouth that she was trying to conceal the delight she experienced in trying to annoy me."

This, Rachel said, "was more than I could bear," and although a show of temper was regarded as a flaw among elite women, the mistress "picked up the pot hooks and pelted her shoulders, and smart. She was so surprised, it being the first time I ever struck her or any other grown woman, that she performed all the feats, I think, the most skillful actress or tragedienne."

Historian Kenneth M. Stampp famously observed that "the whip was the most common instrument of punishment" on the plantation and served as "the emblem of the master's authority."[24] But even the lash sometimes failed to engender his desired level of subordination. Apologizing for failing to enforce proper discipline in the past, David pledged to "try the cowhide and see if that don't have a better effect." In the future, he vowed, "if any of them don't walk a line, just let me know and I will make them dance up, if the rod will do it." Some weeks later he again promised that "if the servants don't toe the mark all I will ask of you is to let me know and that shall be all the trouble that you shall have. They shall respect you or I will wear all the cowhide out that is in the store."

But even David Moores, ostensibly the dispenser of discipline and the final authority on the plantation, admitted defeat. Rachel had written to her husband that she "would not have half the trouble housekeeping" when she returned from Brandon that she had before, because she was sure that he would have Louisa well trained. "I am sorry to inform you that she won't be well trained," he replied. "She is the most annoying piece of flesh that I ever had anything to do with. She is the most negligent and forgetful black hussy that I ever had anything to do with. I have to whip her two or three times every week."

Such views were, of course, not uncommon. Even the outspoken opponent of slavery, writer Frances Anne Kemble, the English bride of Georgia planter Pierce Mease Butler, often referred to her husband's laborers as stupid, lazy,

Rachel Perry Moores.

filthy, and ugly. With reference to one of them, she wrote, he "does speak and therefore I presume he is not an ape, orangoutang [sic], chimpanzee, or gorilla." But the well-known Abolitionist could not, "I confess, have conceived it possible that the presence of articulate sounds, and the absence of an articulate tail, should make, externally at least, so completely the only appreciable difference between man and monkey."[25]

Nevertheless, frequent mentions of whippings in the Moores papers, combined with multiple and casual references to the liquidation of slave children to raise needed cash—"If I can sell a Negro, I will have money a plenty"—and the implications of self-induced abortions among enslaved women in order to avoid bearing children into the horrors of the slave system, reveal an utter disregard for the basic humanity of their enslaved persons and do much to belie the old apologies for slavery as a benign institution.

Whether from a sense of guilt or, perhaps, from a genuine sense of Christian responsibility, or in order to take advantage of the Pauline admonition to Roman slaves to "be obedient to your human masters with fear and trembling," the master class not infrequently claimed a sense of concern with the souls of those who worked their lands.

Louisa is specifically mentioned seventeen times in Rachel Moores' letters and journal and, in common with the rest of her numerous "house servants," she often complains of her bitterly, claiming that she "she was possessed with an evil spirit," and on at least one occasion banishing her from the kitchen to the cotton fields. Louisa is, however, one of only two former slaves to whom Rachel left a bequest in her will, calling her "my faithful old servant."[26]

Francis Le Jan, a missionary in Goosecreek, South Carolina, wondered, "Is it possible that any of my slaves could go to Heaven and must I see them there?"[27] Although those who defended slavery often made the claim that the institution introduced their chattels to Christianity, thereby saving their souls, the religious instruction of enslaved men and women seems to have been more often honored in the breach than in the observance. Commenting on the conditions

on her husband's Georgia estate, Fanny Kemble wrote, "the spiritual interests of the slaves were about as little regarded as their physical necessities." Whatever "appearance of religious instruction" that slave-owners allowed their chattels, Kemble attributed solely to the growing power of the Abolitionist movement and ostensibly as an attempt to ameliorate, at least in the eyes of outside world, the condition of the enslaved people of the South. Rachel Moores, however, expressed genuine concern for the spiritual wellbeing of her slaves, attempting to induce them to read—or at least listen to—chapters from the Bible and to heed the Ten Commandments. When she failed to lead her charges to what she believed to be a minimum standard for Christian behavior and salvation she lamented, "Oh, I shudder when I think of our responsibility as slaveholders!"[28]

Unlike Mary Boykin Chesnut, who hated slavery as evil—"God forgive us, but ours is a monstrous system and wrong and iniquity," as she famously wrote—Rachel seems to have had no moral qualm against the South's "peculiar institution" but blamed its faults on the supposed laziness and lack of cooperation of people whom she and her neighbors enslaved, and she expressed her wish that "the set of slaves I have belonged to some abolitionist." A year after the commencement of the Civil War she confided to her journal that "if this war should result only in the emancipation of the Negros, I should take delight at the trophy, provided they were to be sent off for colonization. They are little else than a nuisance."

In two significant respects, however, Rachel deviated from the norm of ideal Victorian womanhood. First, woman's task in a world of separate spheres was to bear children, to mold the spiritual life of the nation, and to shield men and children from the gross material world outside the home. Between man's role as breadwinner and woman's as homemaker and "angel of the house," hers was the more important task, for to the Victorian mind, the hand that rocked the cradle quite literally ruled the world.

Shortly after their marriage, while Rachel was away seeking a cure for her many maladies, she wrote to her husband that she had dreamed of him "and something else. Guess what it was. Oh, I thought we had a beautiful little flower in our own little home of which we were very fond. You may guess, Darling, to what class it belonged, since I thought it the one I wish for more than all others." In response to her dream of "one sweet little rose," David hoped that "when you come home you will have one for us to play with." Throughout her life, Rachel Moores felt "an inordinate desire for that greatest of blessings . . . an affectionate child."

However, she was never able to bear children, a circumstance that largely blighted her life. At last realizing that however much she may have wished for a child, it was not to be, she told David that "I care not so much for anything else if you are only spared to me. We will be all to each other."

For a time, Rachel took in a foster child, but the willful teenage girl proved to be too great a drain on her emotional and physical resources, and after some months she returned her to her aged grandparents.

But Rachel doted on her nieces and nephews and viewed them as surrogate children. One niece lived with her and her husband after the death of her parents and returned to live with Rachel after David Moores' death.

Second, her health was chronically ill—so much so that she was in and out of various hospitals and sanatoria from New York to New Orleans throughout her married life, seeking a cure—and this is a dominate theme of her letters and journal.

The universal remark of travelers visiting the United States during the nineteenth century, as well as the universal complaint of Americans themselves, related to the ill health of its women. "Look where you will," wrote Florence Hartley, "go to any city in the vast Union, the remark and complaint will be made everywhere. With every natural advantage of climate, yet from North to South, East to West the cry resounds.

Foreigners, admiring the dark-eyed girls of the southern states or the blondes of the northern ones, will remark, with comments upon beauty:—'But she looks delicate, poor thing!—Not strong? Ah! I thought not, none of the American women are, and how soon these young beauties fade!'"[29]

As late as 1872, novelist, literary critic, and playwright William Dean Howells observed that American society "seems little better than a hospital for invalid women."[30] The editor of the *Harper's New Monthly Magazine* concurred. In America, he wrote in 1857, "woman has a peculiar delicacy of physical constitution that makes her especially sensitive to external influences, even when in tolerable health, and renders it very difficult for her to keep herself in full health. Whether it is the climate, or our way of living, or whatever may be the cause, the fact is certain that the American girl is a very delicate plant; beautiful, indeed, in comparison with others; more exquisitely organized than the English and German girl, and more self-relying than the Italian or French, yet not generally strong in nerve and muscle, and too ready to fade before her true mid-summer has come." He declared that "persons who might be expected to know what they say" could "hardly name a single instance of perfect health among the young women of their acquaintance," and claimed that physicians "not seldom lose their patience in setting forth the miseries of feminine invalidism, with its shattered nerves and morbid circulations."[31]

Teacher, writer, and women's rights advocate Catherine Esther Beecher, herself suffering from chronic ill health, wrote in 1855 that "The more I traveled, and the more I resided in health establishments, the more the conviction was pressed upon my attention that there was a terrible decay of female health all over the land, and that this evil was . . . increasing in a most alarming ratio."

Female illness was increasing so rapidly, she wrote, that "ere long, there will be no healthy women in the country," and this evil was bringing with it "an incredible extent of individual, domestic, and social suffering."[32] Beecher's women friends and former students, although "united to the most congenial and most devoted husbands," almost universally expressed the hope that their daughters would never marry.

In April 1856, shortly after her marriage, Rachel wrote to her absent husband that "I regret to say my Dear, that I'm afraid your hopes won't be realized, for I shan't be well when you get home. I don't improve any as yet. Have a sick headache now." This was the first of a myriad of comments on her health in her correspondence and in her journal.

Two months later she wrote from her father's home in Arkansas that her old family physician, a Doctor Harris, had examined her and recommended that she consult Dr. Henry J. Holmes, Sr., in Brandon, Mississippi. "He thinks if my disease isn't arrested it will run into consumption as well as into the most loathsome of female diseases and in premature decay and death." Unless she received a cure, he said, "life is bound to be a burden," but believed that her health could be entirely restored.

Consequently, by mid-July Rachel had become an in-patient at the Holmes Clinic, the first in a series of treatment centers at which she vainly sought to have her health repaired. There, although she made friends with the "bon ton," dined with two of the state's most powerful politicians—Senator Albert Gallatin Brown and Congressman Otho Robards Singleton—and called on the ladies of Brandon's "Silk Stockings Street," she underwent shocking surgical procedures that left her no better, but bitterly disillusioned with the medical profession.

Although she entered the clinic with the highest of hopes for full recovery, by the time she left Doctor Holmes' care she could only say of Brandon that "a more hateful den . . . man or beast never wallowed in."[33]

Although no evidence exists that she read Keats's "Ode to a Nightingale," Rachel seemed to have been at least "half in love with easeful death." Believing her own demise to be imminent, she confided to her journal that she sometimes felt it "pleasant—Oh, so pleasant to die! To lay down all pain and care. Oh, what is an invalid's life?" Only her tie to her husband, she wrote, kept her alive. "Everyone else is just so well off without me, and I often think he would be the same. But I have the infinite pleasure—thank God—of feeling that my little stay with him has been and will be productive of good results. Who is there that lives who doesn't exert a good influence on someone?"

Rachel often complained of migraine headaches, "boils, risings, carbuncles, etc.," dyspepsia, neuralgia, erysipelas, cholera morbus, "inflammation of the womb," a "torpid liver," and "uterine colic," and endured anxiety and deep depression. "My diseased liver is affecting my spirits, my vision, and other diseased organs," was a typical journal entry.

These maladies her doctors treated with such barbarous medicines as arsenic, mercury, laudanum, and opium, and with horrific surgical procedures, further evidence of physician and medical reformer Oliver Wendell Holmes, Sr.'s, well-founded opinion that "if the whole materia medica as now used could be sunk to the bottom of the sea, it would be all the better for mankind-and all the worse for the fishes."[34]

Exotic illnesses were often associated with the life of the Victorian lady, and Elizabeth Barrett Browning, perhaps the most famous invalid of her generation, published *Sonnets from the Portuguese* in 1850, making the image of the helpless, suffering, neurasthenic woman even more popular.

Much of Rachel's lamentation does indeed smack of hyperbole for romantic, dramatic effect, and, much to her distress, her sisters accused her of exaggerating her maladies in order to draw attention to herself. "Woman! Mine own sex!" she retorted indignantly in her journal. "To say I imagine that I am sick—imagine I have diseases that do not exist!"

Rachel was not entirely a victim of psychosomatic illness or of hypochondria. She was a life-long invalid, suffering various severe gynecological maladies which she discusses with her husband in unusually candid terms.

Her "female weaknesses" she attributed to the ill-effects of tight corseting in her youth. "Oh, could I but recall that one error of my girlhood. How much suffering I would have been spared. But alas! for the follies of youth, which nothing less than a bitter experience can cure in the most of us."

Internal evidence suggests that she might, however, have suffered from a sexually transmitted disease contracted from her husband. "Oh, if I could bear some of the pain and relieve you of it I would," he often wrote to her. "If it would of not been for me, you never would of had that disease that you now have," he admitted, and again, "If it had not been for me, you never would of been in that fix."

Alexandre Dumas *fils'* widely popular *La Dame aux Camélias* (translated into English as *Camille*) was published in 1848. In Dumas' novel, the life of the heroine, Marguerite Gautier, is described as an unending agony. The argument has been cogently made that Marguerite's illness, "consumption," was a euphemism for syphilis, rather than the more commonly accepted tuberculosis.[35] This book, like Browning's *Sonnets*, contributed to the romanticization of physical incapacity that helped to define the genteel female of the mid-nineteenth century, and by temperament as well as by such cultural influences, Rachel Moores was susceptible to the notion of herself as helpless victim.

Editorial Method

The editor transcribed the letters of Rachel Perry Moores and David Harrison Moores from the originals, which had lain undisturbed for half a century in a small trunk in the attic of the Pryor home before they were donated to the Museum of Regional History, Texarkana, Texas. The letters were at that time in the possession of Minerva Watts Pryor, a double grandniece of Rachel and David Moores. They were, according to Margret Talbot Kittrell of Texarkana, "neatly contained in two little red cloth bags, hand sewn, with draw strings of grosgrain ribbon and each bearing its penciled identification 'Letters of Rachel Moores' and 'Letters of D. H. Moores.'"

These letters, as Mrs. Kittrell wrote, "are in a remarkable state of preservation, only the envelopes in which they were contained having become yellowed and brittle with age."[36]

Also in the trunk was Rachel's journal. "You have most of my thoughts, dear old Journal," she wrote in 1864, and, with her husband away on military duty, "I've no one else to talk to now." The journal came into the possession of the descendants of Nancy Moores Watts "Nannie" Jennings, and is not now available for examination, but Margaret Talbot Kittrell transcribed it in 1949, and copies of her typescript are to be found in Texarkana's Museum of Regional History, in the Texarkana Public Library, and in the University of Texas's Barker Texas History Center in Austin.[37]

Although he was not so well read or cultured, David H. Moores' penmanship is far more legible than that of his wife, which, due no doubt to her many physical ailments and the fact that she often wrote while lying in bed, is often nearly indecipherable. As she wrote in 1860 from a hospital in Louisville, Kentucky, "I'm flat of my back with the limber sheet before me in my hands, and I have to write without looking at it." As Rachel confessed, "my writing is dreadful."

Many words, therefore, are totally unreadable and the editor offered frequent emendations based upon his best educated guess. The editor has also regularized, to some degree, the writers' spelling, capitalization, punctuation, and paragraph structure, David Moores' letters being almost entirely innocent of paragraph breaks.

NOTES

[1]   H. Loring White, *Ragging It: Getting Ragtime into History (and Some History into Ragtime)* (Bloomington, IN: iUnivesrse, 2005); "Genealogist Traces Joplin's Cass County Roots," *Texarkana Gazette,* February 19, 2020, 7C.

[2]   Charles Moores was born on April 4, 1776, in Lincoln County, North Carolina, the oldest son of Jean (or Jane) Brown Ross and Henry Moores, Jr. He and Mary Virginia Harrison were married in about 1807 and the couple established their home in Longtown, Fairfield County, South Carolina. Charles Moores died on March 9, 1852, in Bowie County, and is buried in the Harrison Chapel Cemetery, Redwater, Texas.

Anderson Rochelle Moores, Rachel's brother-in-law, was born on April 29, 1822, in Fairfield County, South Carolina, the son of Charles and Mary Harrison Moores. In 1841, he was married to Pauline Tucker Jarrett (1822–1861) and was the father of Mary Jane, David Andrew, Alexander Ross, Elizabeth Wade, Virginia, Mattie Lee, Perlina A., and Francis H., Martha M., and Adelia Moores. The family plantation was located near Mooresville, Texas, and from July 5 through August 7, 1841, he served in Capt. William

Lane's company of Col. Robert S. Hamilton's regiment of Texas Mounted Volunteers, and for this service on January 5, 1846, he received an additional 320 acres in Bowie County.

During the Civil War he served as a corporal in Company E of Col. Julius A. Andrews' Thirty-Second Texas Cavalry (Crump's Battalion, Mounted Volunteers). The regiment was soon dismounted and ordered east of the Mississippi River. After taking part in the Battle of Richmond, Kentucky, it was assigned to Brig. Gen. Mathew Ector's Brigade of the Army of Tennessee. It participated in the campaigns of the army from Murfreesboro to Nashville, then aided in the defense of Mobile. He died on March 5, 1873, and is buried in the Harrison Chapel Cemetery. Annie May Turner, "Direct Descendants of Charles Moores and Allied Families to Have Gay Reunion Sunday," *Texarkana Daily News*, June 26, 1958.

[3] Bowie County Historical Commission, *Bowie County, Texas, Historical Handbook* (Texarkana, TX: Smart Printing Company, 1976); Barbara S. Overton Chandler, "A History of Bowie County" (M.A. thesis, University of Texas, 1937); Barbara Overton Chandler and J. E. Howe, *History of Texarkana and Bowie and Miller Counties, Texas–Arkansas* (Texarkana, Texas–Arkansas, 1939); Emma Lou Meadows, *DeKalb and Bowie County* (DeKalb, TX: DeKalb News, 1968); Rex W. Strickland, *Anglo–American Activities in Northeastern Texas, 1803–1845* (Ph.D. dissertation, University of Texas, 1937); Tom Wagy, comp., *An Historical Bibliography of Bowie County, Texas and Miller County, Arkansas* (East Texas State University at Texarkana, 1987); Francis White Johnson, *A History of Texas and Texans*, vol. 2 (Chicago, IL: American Historical Society, 1914).

[4] William Henry Harrison Moores married Mary Lunsford Douglass (May 5, 1833–October 12, 1900), the daughter of Dr. John Douglass and Mary Letherd Lunsford of Blacksford, South Carolina, before the family's move to Texas. Mary's niece and namesake, Mary Lunsford Thorn (April 7, 1867–August 19, 1952), the daughter of William Turner Thorn and Frances Petrena Douglass, married William Henry Harrison "Willie" Moores, Jr., the elder Moores' son by a previous marriage and also moved to Texarkana. The correspondence from these two Marys to their kinfolk in Blackstock is preserved in the Papers of the Douglass, Thorn, and Moores Families, Graniteville Room, University of South Carolina Library, Columbia, South Carolina.

[5] Jane Ross Moores to Reuben Moores, December 16, 1838, quoted in Turner, "Direct Descendants of Charles Moores," *Texarkana Daily News*, January 26, 1958.

[6] Thomas Briggs Moores was born on August 16, 1820, in Fairfield County, South Carolina. He and Sarah Norvell were married on February 18, 1840, and became the parents of Margaret Moores. He died on December 25, 1852, and is buried in the Harrison Chapel Cemetery, Redwater, Texas.

[7] "A true and exact copy of the log of the journey kept by Anderson Rochelle Moores," transcribed by Ken Moore, Fresno, California. The original was, as of 1911, in the possession of Mrs. Wiley Linn Murie, of Clarksville, Arkansas. Annie Julia Mims ("Mrs. W. R.") Wright, *A Record of the Descendants of Isaac Ross and Jean Brown*, (Jackson, MS: Consumers Stationery and Printing Co., 1911), 86–87.

[8] Gifford White, comp., *First Settlers of Bowie and Cass Counties Texas, from the Originals in the General Land Office and the Texas State Archives* (St. Louis, MO: Ingmire Publications, 1983), 11, 12.

[9] Nancy Moores Watts Jennings, comp., *Texarkana Pioneer Family Histories: Texarkana, Arkansas, Texas* (Texarkana Pioneer Association, 1961), 4.

[10] Harrison Chapel was located about three miles east of the present community of Redwater on the north side of US Highway 67. Only the cemetery and a state historical marker now mark the spot. Cass County Park today occupies the site of the old settlement of Mooresville.

[11] David Harrison Moores was born in Longtown, Fairfield, South Carolina on January 18, 1827. He died in Texarkana, Texas, on January 18, 1892, and is buried there in the Rose Hill Cemetery.

[12] Robert W. Amsler, "General Arthur G. Wavell: A Soldier of Fortune in Texas," *Southwestern Historical Quarterly* 69 (July 1965); Eugene C. Barker, "General Arthur Goodall Wavell and Wavell's Colony in Texas," *Southwestern Historical Quarterly* 47 (January 1944).

[13] Winfrey, Dorman H., ed., "Diary of Major John Pollard Gaines: March of First Regiment of Kentucky Volunteer Cavalry, from Memphis, Tennessee, to Mexico, During the War with Mexico in 1836," *Texana* 1 (Winter 1963), 25.

[14] Winfrey, ed., "Diary of Major John Pollard Gaines," 26. Notwithstanding Major Gaines's somewhat negative assessment, Cass, like Bowie, was heavily timbered, with short-leaf pine and a varied assortment of hard woods, and lumbering became an important part of its economy.

[15] Winfrey, ed., "Diary of Major John Pollard Gaines," 26.

[16] David Potter, *The South and the Sectional Conflict* (Baton Rouge: Louisiana State University Press, 1968), 15–16, and Potter, *The Impending Crisis, 1858–1861* (New York: Harper and Row, 1967), 451–57.

[17] US Federal Census, 1850, Slave Schedules for Ouachita County, Arkansas.

[18] Neil Abeles, "Plantation Gives Peek at Past," *Texarkana Gazette*, July 27, 2016.

[19] US Selected Federal Census, Non-Population Schedule, 1860, Beat Number Five, Cass County, Courtland Post Office, page 23.

[20] Glenn Hendler, *Public Sentiments: Structures of Feeling in 19th-Century American Literature* (Chapel Hill: University North Carolina Press, 2001), 118.

[21] Florence Hartley, *The Ladies' Hand Book of Fancy and Ornamental Work* (Philadelphia, PA: J. W. Bradley, 1859), 239. For cloth production in Texas, see Paula Mitchell Marks, *Hands to the Spindle: Texas Women and Home Textile Production, 1822–1880* (College Station: Texas A&M University Press, 1996).

[22] Bertram Wyatt-Brown, *Southern Honor: Ethics and Behavior in the Old South* (New York: Oxford University Press, 1982), 332. For a less positive interpretation of this tradition, see Anthony Szczesiul, *The Southern Hospitality Myth: Ethics, Politics, Race, and American Memory* (Athens: University of Georgia Press, 2017).

[23] Mary P. Ryan, *Cradle of the Middle Class: The Family in Oneida County, New York, 1790–1865* (New York: Cambridge University Press, 1981), 189.

[24] Kenneth M. Stampp, *Peculiar Institution: Slavery in the Ante-Bellum South* (New York: Alfred A. Knopf, 1956), 174.

[25] Frances Anne Kemble, *Journal of a Residence on a Georgian Plantation in 1838–1839* (New York: Harper and Brothers, 1863), 260; Catherine Clinton, *Fanny Kemble's Civil Wars* (New York: Simon and Schuster, 2000); Deirdre David, *Fanny Kemble: A Performed Life* (Philadelphia: University of Pennsylvania Press, 2007).

[26] By 1870, Louisa had married a Cass County farmer named Jerry Walker and in 1880 she was widowed and working as a laundress in Atlanta, Texas. She was the mother of eight children, only six of whom were living.

[27] Letter from Francis Le Jan quoted in *Classified Digest of the Records of the Society for the Propagation of the Gospel in Foreign Parts, 1701–1892* (London: 1898), 15.

[28] Kemble, *Journal of a Residence on a Georgian Plantation*, 57.

[29] Florence Hartley, *The Ladies' Book of Etiquette, and Manual of Politeness: A Complete Hand Book for the Use of the Lady in Polite Society* (Boston, MA: G. W. Cottrell, 1860), 265.

[30] Quoted in William Wasserstrom, *Heiress of All Ages*, 135.

[31] "Our Daughters," *Harper's New Monthly Magazine* 16:91 (1857), 73.

[32] Catherine E. Beecher, *Letters to the People on Health and Happiness* (New York: Harper and Brothers, 1855), 9, 21.

[33] James B. Ranck, *Albert Gallatin Brown: Radical Southern Nationalist* (New York: D. Appleton Century Company, 1937).

[34] "Currents and Counter-currents in Medical Science," *The American Journal of the Medical Sciences*, 40 (1860), 467.

35 Bernadette C. Lintz, "Concocting La Dame aux camélias: Blood, Tears, and Other Fluids," *Nineteenth-Century French Studies*, (2005), 33 (3–4): 287–307.

36 The Pryor home, located at what is now 1609 New Boston Road, was built by Eli Harrison Moores, and later became the home of his daughter Nannie and her husband, John C. Watts. Following their deaths, the home became the property and home of their daughter, Minerva Watts and her husband, Judson Pryor.

37 When Nancy Moores Watts "Nannie" Jennings, the daughter of Thomas Jefferson Watts and Latona Bruce McGill, died in 1989, her heirs destroyed her personal papers, which presumably included Rachel Moores' journal.

chapter one

OH, WOMEN, WHAT A SUFFERING LOT IS THINE

1858–1859

In the winter of 1858–1859, while in Charles Town, Virginia, John Brown was awaiting execution for leading the raid on Harpers Ferry, an event that as much as any sparked Southern session and made inevitable the American Civil War, Rachel Moores was occupying her time "as usual, tending to my domestic affairs, reading, sewing, toasting before the fire, planting shrubbery, riding to the river with David, and helping him get the turkeys out of the pen."

Her journal, in fact, presents a detailed inventory of the daily activities of a plantation mistress: "working in my shrubbery, looking after my garden, cuttings and fixing work for Harrit," one of the plantation's enslaved women who worked as a domestic.

Rachel plied her needle "more diligently than usual," she wrote, for she had in contemplation a trip to New Orleans in the spring, although she had to do most of her work lying down, "not being able to sit up much."

Among her reading material was an article in *Harper's New Monthly Magazine* on cheerfulness, which, she wrote, pleased her much, "Though it is much easier to recommend cheerfulness than practice it when one has ill health, the cares of housekeeping, and disobedient servants, etc., etc."[1]

The New Orleans trip, taken March 21 through April 3 of that year, was characterized by uncomfortable and slow steamboat accommodations, difficulty in finding lodgings to her standards, outings to the theater, museums, and art galleries, a dental appointment, and shopping excursions to furniture dealers, dress makers, and jewelers. Rachel found "Goods of every description are exceedingly high" and "Clerks are extremely impudent." "Weary, happy, and hungry" she and her husband "left the Crescent City after a stay of only five days."

Although she found much to complain of, her trip to New Orleans seems to have been in general a pleasure. Back at home, however, her journal again becomes a catalogue of ailments and her estimation of the futility of her existence. "I feel to be nearer hopelessly diseased than ever before," she complained. "I can't say when I've been worse in health, spirits, etc."

Rachel's diary also details the endless resistance that she encountered from the enslaved women who worked in her kitchen, living quarters, dairy, and gardens, and ascribes "this multiplicity of trials" to her ongoing health struggle. "Disobedience makes me the creature of affliction I am." Evidence, perhaps, of the effectiveness of the campaign of passive resistance carried on by those enslaved on southern plantations, "never again in life," Rachel wrote, "shall I wonder at a woman's health declining without any apparent cause if she has an African on the premises."

XXX

[from the Journal of Rachel P. Moores]

[February 21, 1858] *I never felt sadder than when seeing my husband drive off this morning. An indescribable gloom settled over me as he ordered his buggy, though he left only for two days, then at the outside. I think ladies who have no children are more foolish about their husbands and they like their husbands to be more foolish about them.*

I've not spent this Holy Sabbath as I ought. Instead of reading my Bible I've been reading the newspapers, magazines first, and I get so behind with the papers I had to read pretty much to keep up. Now lonely. How gloomy and dismal this drizzly night appears without my husband's bright eye and gay romp to enhance the scene.

Mr. **[Reuben]** Moores and Sister Jane had just left, although late and dark and cold, and at once the night comes on.[2] "My God, protect thou and I while apart." Dearest Husband.[3]

[February 22, 1858] "Alone! Alone, how dreary it is to be alone." How hopefully and ardently I look for my husband tonight, and yet all in vain. He comes not. I have had his chair waiting before the fire from sundown until now and his supper on the table and by the fire, and me sitting by and sewing to while away "dull care"—something rare for me as I seldom sew at night. This morning I finished my preserves and then lay before the fireside resting **[page torn]** before dinner.

Mr. Griffin Sr. came in and surely frightened me. I had just rose from my pallet with my hair disheveled and was splitting some biscuit to have toast with preserves when he slipped in, finding fruit, biscuit, sugar bowl, and all in a pile before the fire.[4]

Goodnight Sweet Husband. "May angels guard and bless thy slumber light."

[February 23, 1858] Last night was a most wretched one to me. I was ill, very ill, and no one that I could depend on here near. I thought of Sister Jane, but her health is rather delicate,[5] and Mrs. Connally is too old to ride out in the night air, and I at last felt resigned to my fate and knew if I was going to die no earthly help could avail me anything, and if I was going to get over the spell it was best not to disturb any one on so cold a night.[6]

Today I have felt extremely weak, have lay on my palate and sewed most of the day. My husband came home this evening, bringing with him some shrubbery from Mr. Whitaker. I have it all planted out this evening, only what I sent Sister Jane.[7]

[February 24, 1858] Today was spent in sewing and working some clothing, attending my soap making. Mister Griffin called again today and makes application for an overseer's berth. David teased me no little, trying to make me say whether to employ him or not. Of course, I did not tell him what to do as that is out of the line of business; I do not think, however, that David will be pleased with him.

[February 25, 1858] *Was sick most of the morning though sewed some. Had a severe sick nervous headache just after and before dinner. Husband drove me down to the river, which helped very much. Riding out does me so much good, I could ride every day but for troubling David so much. I feel so weak now as to be hardly able to walk.*

[February 26, 1858] *I went over to Mr. Reuben Moores' with David and remained until about one of the clock and got Charlie to bring me home as David was gone on collecting.[8] After my return home I had a portion of my yard swept and leaved and mended some rents which had been made in my freshly ironed clothes and put them away. I feel weary and sick. My head has ached almost all day. David is just come in and we eat an early supper as he did not get any dinner today.*

[February 27, 1858] *I have sit down too much since the men have come in. I believe that is why I'm reducing so fast. I have fallen off considerably for the last week [illegible] though I have sewed almost without ceasing.*

[February 28, 1858] *Another dismal Sabbath—mist and wind but little rain. This evening I prevailed on David take a horseback ride as the buggy was broken. We only went as far as Mister R. Moores, and David went rather reluctantly that far as the evening was so inclement.*

[March 1, 1858] *I finished my seventh chemise today—commenced since the first of January—and this evening I altered the shape of a new bonnet, which I will be trimming tomorrow to travel to New Orleans. The overseer David employed the other day came in a few moments this evening with his son and says he will set in tomorrow.*

[March 2, 1858] *I trimmed my bonnet this morning but have been confined to my pallet all evening. It has been quite cold and windy since yesterday.*

David has his blacksmith shop completed today, or rather had his forge up and there was a blacksmith at work on it, and our overseer came in this morning, so our family is enlarged and I do not like that so well. Home is so much nicer when David and I are the only occupants unless a visitor comes who is pleasant.

[March 3, 1858] *I have been pretty much confined to my bed today. I have walked to my fowl yard once. Considered making a new pink watered silk as I shall need such a dress if I am able to attend the theater or opera whilst I am in New Orleans.*

[March 4, 1858] *I received two letters from home yesterday but little news. My Dear Pa seems anxious I should write often and keep him advised of my health. David also got a business letter which called him to Linden, and just after he left Mrs. Connally came and spent the day with me. I was so glad to see her, being so low and dull spirited. I did but little but talk, and she is a good listener and talks too. Sewed a little on my dress. Husband came while we were at the table. How good of him to ride so late to be at home to cheer his poor sick wife.*

[March 5, 1858] *I finish my waists today, cleaned my front porch, made* **[illegible]** *dust* **[illegible]** *up in the house, not feeling well enough to go to the kitchen, and whilst I was immersed in the pantry we cooked cakes—eggs, sugar, butter, flour, then Mrs.* **[Agnes]** *Johns walked in my room. So much for being a housekeeper.[9]*

I took another horseback ride this evening, alone though, but what a lovely evening.

[March 6, 1858] *Today I have remained all alone, David having to attend a lawsuit at Forest Home. I commenced and half-finished a superb transfer collar, but when David came home in the evening, hungry, weary, and dispirited, the suit having unjustly gone against him, I put my collar away and tried to soothe his perplexed mind.*

To think a woman should refuse to pay a just debt.

[March 7, 1858] *Another rainy Sabbath morn. Read, wrote, and rode in the evening. David would stop at Mr. Moores. Thinks this ride on horseback gentle though long enough for me, the buggy being broken.*

[March 8, 1858] *I worked on my collar today and after dinner David drove me down to see the Bluffs where he was to meet the men who were to haul cotton to Jefferson. In his haste to get* there, he drove more rapidly than usual and broke the buggy, which had just been mended, so I'm afoot again.[10]

[March 9, 1858] Was sick all day and worked not much on my collar. Commenced packing my truck as we expect to start to New Orleans in [illegible] days.

[March 10, 1858] Was very ill last night—indeed, one time in the midhour of night I thought I should never arise anymore from my bed of affliction! I'd never so suffered in my life. My husband was so unconscious by my side. He was so weary with a long day's collecting he did not waken to a sense of the situation.

[March 11, 1858] Another miserable night was last night to me. I must omit my suppers or I shan't stand it much longer. I made me a very pretty transfer collar today, though was sick most of the time.

[March 12, 1858] My husband has not dined but once this week with me. Oh, how dear his presence is after an absence of one day. He left me early as usual this morning, but just after he left Mrs. [Nancy] Baker, one of my neighbors who has never visited me before, came in company with one of her daughters and spent the day.[11] I replied to a letter I received by last mail from Mrs. Jane Moore.[12]

[March 13, 1858] David went over in Bowie today and will not return before tomorrow. I do miss him so much. I have been so sick most of the day, but I rode over to Mr. Moores' late this evening. Cut new cloak out but did not feel well enough to sew any of it.

Goodnight. Sweet Husband.

[March 14, 1858] This morning was spent in reading, writing, in the solitude of my own chamber. Just after dinner Sister J[ane] and Mr. Moores and children came over, and my husband came some two hours before night. He brought me some cedars from his Sister Jane's, which I'm *very proud of. Mr. Hooper, blacksmith, and Griffin, overseer, make our family larger than I can conveniently get used to.*

[March 15, 1858] *Have been busy today on my own wardrobe and sewing injures, so I must quit it. I have sleepless, restless nights. Oh, how long will this affliction continue. I feel I can not last long in this way.*

[March 16, 1858] *Sewed industriously this morning. Doctor Salmon and Mr. Peters came in on business and remained until after dinner. The constable came in just as we were leaving the table and just as he was through the blacksmith came too, and so I was detained an inordinate length of time at the table and this evening I was compelled to retire to my pallet with more than usual distress, and after this rains set in and two Negros came in and annoyed me no little with their noise.*[13]

[March 17, 1858] *Had a terrible night. Did not sleep any until after midnight. Felt every moment as if in nervous spasm. Sister Jane sent after Charlotte and Dr. Salmon, both, and I sent for Lizzie, but* **[illegible]** *says for herself.*

Charlotte brought good news from Sister Jane. Says she had a fine girl, which I found on going this morning to be the case. She calls her Ruth.[14]

Good Mrs. Connally was there and tried to cheer me. I was sick and low spirited when I went over and felt more than ever how vain and worthless are earth's joys. Oh! Will I, can I, ever have my health? I can't have hope for any. I came home early and repacked my truck.

[March 18, 1858] *Today was spent pretty much in confusion. Had Mr. Henshaw doing a little work on my room and dining room, and not being at all well it was unpleasant, and David left to spend the night, but, as kind fate works, he came just before ten and tells me I do have visitors tomorrow—how ill-timed when it is the last day at home.*

[March 19, 1858] *How busy all day, how weary tonight. Just as I was bundling up the last pair of Negro pants—cut, to be made up during my absence—our guests arrived and the hall was full to overflowing as the floor was being scrubbed, which I'd hoped to have had finished by their arrival.*

I must say this day was not very pleasantly spent as one of the good dames wanted provisions brought in for her children all day, and the other only asked me for twelve articles. Knowing her predilection in that way, I absolutely refused every request but one, and forgetting myself when she picked up a lemon and asked what it was, and give it to her if she "please ma'med"—all in the same breath—I consented. She had biscuit and preserves for a desert and called for a piece of paper to wrap up my real desert in. They left soon as dinner was over, much to my relief, as time was an item to me.

[March 20, 1858] *After arranging all the preliminaries as usual attending preparation for a trip, we set out about eleven of the clock and reached Mr.* [Archer H.] *Chappell's about an hour to sunset—calling en route to see Sister Jane and Mrs. Connally—where we were most hospitably entertained for the night.*

I have not been more pleased with a family among my whole Texas acquaintance. Mr. Chappell returned from New Orleans after we had retired for the night and on leaving next morning he and Mrs. Chappell solicited us much to visit them. I rarely ever had anyone to press me more.

[March 21, 1858] *We left quite early, hoping to get on board the boat Mr. Chappell had just come up on. Did not, as we designed yesterday, make any stops in Linden, but eat a cold meal we brought from home. Came by Mr. Whitaker's, but remained only a few moments and, much to our disappointment, when we reached Jefferson, the Caddo Bell had just gone and so we had to get aboard the Bloom, altogether a shady looking concern.*

No lady passengers, but the barman's wife and first engineer's wife were aboard. However, I'm not much predisposed in their favor. More particularly, I am displeased with Mrs. Bartender, as vanity seems the ruling passion.

[March 22, 1858] *Slept tolerably last night considering the boat lay ashore and made all the noise possible for it to make, unloading in such a place as Jefferson. We had a cold drizzle all* night and awoke still regretting our missing the Caddo Bell as it was still raining and the boat engaged in protecting what goods were out instead of unloading. My bath was not a pleasant one, having to take it in a blue bucket in muddy water, and then the room is barely large enough to turn around in when one has a hoop on. After an impossibly poor breakfast. I sat up to the stove to warm my feet and was unwilling audience to a most wordy conversation between the bar keeper's and engineer's wife. Their entire familiarity with the stewards was shocking beyond measure to me. The discussion unfit for a blacksmith, much less for a dyspeptic like poor me.

No friend, no respectables, and a long dreary evening. No books, no papers, and the weather too damp to walk on the guards if there were any to walk on.

[March 23, 1858] I awoke this morning much provoked to ourselves to be at Jefferson and only left there eight of the clock this evening. I was never more impatient to leave a place and felt immeasurably more pleasure as I saw the last plank drawn in and felt the motion of steam up!

[March 24, 1858] When my toilet was completed and I entered the cabin, I found a lady passenger had just come aboard at Swanson's Landing.[15] I was gratified as she appeared a nice lady, and as yet I have [illegible] to [illegible] the ladies before [illegible].

We reached Rives Landing just after breakfast where I expected to remain until the boat returned from Jefferson, but not feeling well at the time the boat started, concluded not.[16] Jimmie came aboard in the cabin to see me, but on reaching Monterey [?] at two in the afternoon, Jimmie insisted we should drive about three miles from Monterey [?] and see his sister, Mrs. Browning.[17] He accordingly produced a horse and buggy from his cousin, Mr. Myers, and we drove out and spent the night. I was much pleased with Mr. and Mrs. Browning, and then my old friend Sam, or Cousin Sam. I did not enjoy my visit though, as I had a most miserable headache.

[March 25, 1858] Soon as we breakfasted we left for the boat which we feared might leave us, but much to our surprise she had not unloaded and had between four and five hundred bales to come aboard, so we did not leave until some time in the night.

[**March 26, 1858**] *This morning just after breakfast we got to Rives' Landing and Mrs.* [illegible] *and Betty came aboard to see us and remained until the boat discharged a small freight. I then saw Mr.* [illegible] *for the first time was very much pleased with him. Whilst I am now writing, the boat is entering the* [Caddo] *lake again, which looks beautiful as warm sunshine. The trees in the distance are just putting forth their tender leaves and look refreshing. All things indicate an early summer. How balmy and soft the air is.*

The passengers who came aboard at Swanson's left us tonight at Shreveport to get aboard a better boat, which we had some thought of doing, but were fearful we would not make the trip any sooner but lose time.

[**March 27, 1858**] *The boat has plied most industriously today and yet we are only seventy-five miles from Shreveport and a most monotonous trip it is. I went on the hurricane deck with my husband this evening just before sundown, the heat being intolerable in the cabin. We sat for an hour or so in front, which was exceedingly pleasant, it being a bright moonlight night. Whoever can become so unromantic as not to admire moonlight on "The Waters"?*

I met and made the acquaintance of Dr. H____, a cousin of David's. I was most pleased with him, found him social, though timid. He seemed concerned about my cough and told husband he thought me consumptive.

[**March 28, 1858**] *What a lovely, charming, bright, pleasant Sabbath we have, and how the passengers seem to enjoy it. It is pleasant to watch them running up the hillsides as the boat is loading. What a beautiful floral bouquet David has just brought me, and such bright, clear water he has brought me to drink.*

Just after dinner I went forward again and set a few moments, but disliking the companion's position, I returned back to our narrow cabin and continued the vapor bath.

[**March 29, 1858**] *Have been unable to leave my bed today. I could not even sit to eat; yet have lost but little of the scenery to the south side of the "Father of Waters" on whose bosom we are gliding. I have gazed out until my eyes have become weary. When husband comes in, he laughs at me for telling him not to get between me and the coast.*

I can't raise my head for vomiting, and could not set, only in one position. This, [if nothing comes to prevent] is our last day as the Captain says we will be at New Orleans by midnight. I hope to feel better by that time, though it may take me nearly a week to recover from this spell.

[March 30, 1858] This morning, amid storm and tempest, we landed in the Crescent City. The rain fell in torrents and the winds dashed the boat hither and thither, so it was difficult to affect a landing. Soon as the hardest rain was over, David went out to secure room at a hotel and was detained in consequence of the storm some time, and whilst he was away I had a violent nervous attack and vomiting. I thought I was going to be thrown into convulsions for some time. I shall ever remember the kind attention of Mr. Marshall, the clerk.

When David returned, he took me to the City Hotel, and so crowded was the hotel it was with difficulty he could obtain a room. I thought he never could come and take me to a room, and believe I should have fainted had it not been for a kind lady near who raised a sash and gave me her seat near the window, and when we did get a room it was in the fourth or fifth story, and walking to it, I thought, would cost me my life.[18]

As soon as it was reached, I threw myself on a bed and told David to go out and find a private boarding house where I could have less walking to do. He looked in at Mrs. Kent's, a place that had been highly recommended as pleasant, and took a room. Soon as I had sufficiently rested, we moved. Soon as we came here, I lay down a while and then went into the parlor where I made the acquaintance of a nice old lady who had just arrived and was going to live here the same length of time that we were. She promised to go shopping whenever time we engaged. I've fallen quite in love with her. Soon as dinner was over, she called in my room and we sallied forth in our traveling dresses, gumshoes, and a headgear. I felt as if I were doing a great wrong to myself to go out at all; however, we did not go a great ways out and did not make any purchases of consequence. I feel so thankful to the Great Giver of All that I feel even so well as what I do at this time.

[March 31, 1858] Out shopping early. Bought and carried to the dressmaker a plain black silk. Shopped until dinner and from dinner until night. I came home weary and sleepy and, notwithstanding the fatigue, I feel better.

[April 1, 1858] *Out with husband looking at furniture. I have walked myself down and yet my bill remains unfilled. Goods of every description are exceedingly high. Clerks are extremely impudent, and both together vex me a little.*

Went to the theater tonight and saw "Son of Tai"[?] performed. The assembly was light. The [illegible] *much admired and the performers much applauded, yet I did not feel much interested, was somewhat disappointed.*

[April 2, 1858] *Today we nearly completed our shopping. Had my husband's ambrotype put in a pin, and when we had it taken, I saw a cameo artist at work for the first time. Had I not purchased a set of jets yesterday, I would have had me a full set made.*

Just after leaving the artist's hall, we went to the museum, which for a city like this I think a pretty poor affair, though I saw many curious things. One thing made an impression never to be erased. There was a calanli [?] taken from the human body. It was large as a hickory nut. Went out to the Vanities Theatre tonight and was most is bitterly disappointed. We saw only the "Innocents" performed, and that so disgusted me I did not remain long. Miserable, contemptible sight, to see females degrade themselves for "filthy lucre" and the coarse laughter of the men.

[April 3, 1858] *Out early in company with Mrs. Bush, our old friend. Came home soon, as Mr. Burns [?] was to go with me to the dentist. As he had not returned, I accepted Mr. Glaxen's presence, as he was going my way down on Canal. As Burns [?] deceived me, I did not get my work done. Commenced the job and before it was halfway complete, told me he had other engagements, and by the time I was ten steps from his office my tongue was so sore I could not think of submitting to another operation.*

After making a few more purchases we returned to our boarding house to dinner and then hastened to the "Joe Baldwin," [?] which boat we took passage on for Jefferson, and so we had just left the Crescent City after a stay of only five days. I feel weary, happy, and hungry, for our supper was a miserable affair.

[April 4, 1858] *Made but poor headway, so we had full time to examine the coast. The boat stopped near a large Catholic Church once, which was crowded and the adjacent grounds. The men mostly were in uniform. I suppose because it was Easter Sunday.*

There is a Dutchman aboard with his Yankee wife.[19] They amuse me with their ideas about Negros. They're much prejudiced against the institution of slavery, and yet they will own them in two months if they can. The woman really dislikes me because she sees two Negroes we have aboard working for me.

[April 5, 1858] *Today has past, as such days will, when the passengers are not remarkable for their wit.*

[April 6, 1858] *We have had to lay by the better part of the last two nights in consequence of the dense fog, and we travel slow at best. A few of our weary hours beguiled this evening by the appearance of a sprightly young widow who was going as far as Alexandria. The creature [illegible] and one ardent youth says he is literally bereft of his heart (brains, too, I think). I cannot see anything extraordinary about her, nothing beyond a sprightly conversation.*

[April 7, 1858] *Quite a gloom has pervaded the ladies' cabin all day, but more particularly this evening. It has been with much difficulty the boat could stem the currents and near crashed the rapids,[20] and this evening, while taking my siesta, the boat was thrown with much violence against the shore as to throw me off my berth, and at the same time a poor boatman was walking on deck and it threw him into the river where he immediately sank and was never seen more except one hand, and just after that I thought David was going to be whipped by our Dutchman's wife, and so it seemed catastrophes would never end for one day.*

An itinerant jeweler came in the ladies' cabin before noon and asked if the ladies had any jewelry to mend. I gave him my necklace, the catch of which was a little injured, and on his bringing it to me in the evening I discovered he had taken it entirely off and put a brass one on, and I told him so. He seemed to hate what he had done and left the cabin immediately. David came in as he walked out, and I handed the necklace to him, telling him what had been done.

"Oh, I'm glad he served you so." said he. "You had no business to let that Dutchman mend it. I have no use for Dutchmen anyway."

Upon which the Dutchman's partner flew into a most violent rage and said "You are no gentleman. You know Dutch people are aboard. and your wife is no lady. You are small potatoes anyway. fit subjects for the lunatic asylum.""Just so," David said. "Don't reply," said I.

"I think such conversation beneath you."And after grumbling for a few moments alone she hushed up. still looking the very personification of anger.

[April 8, 1858] I'm so weary of this slow traveling. I am sick of the [illegible] and do not feel safe on this boat or any other stern wheel boat. Many of the passengers set up all night.

[April 9, 1858] Reached Shreveport at noon today when two more lady passengers came aboard. One of them had [illegible] our friends on board. She came from New Orleans. but [illegible] relieved instead of much grieved. I never saw more indifference manifested about the death of a human being. It was the first-born and she was carrying it to its father who had never seen it. We reach the [Caddo] lake early this evening and a party of us went up on deck to enjoy the scenery. which was beautiful.

[April 10, 1858] We had a perilous night. Got lost in the lake in a considerable storm and lay tied to a sapling till near daybreak and have moved at a snail's pace all day. though the Captain said he would reach Jefferson at half past noon, it was near dark. His wife came on board at Benton. [Louisiana,] quite a nice lady.It seems we will never get a conveyance to leave here. My husband went up town three times to get horses to carry us to a hotel but did not succeed. and so I shall remain on board all night as I am not well enough to walk to a hotel.

[April 11, 1858] Got some ponies this morning. which we attached to our buggy and came out to Mr. Whitaker's this morning. Francy and Hugh had to walk. as we could get no conveyance for them. I found Mrs. Whitaker in the blues about her husband who started the week before to Alabama. I've been quite sick and am still so. My dyspepsia grows worse.

[April 12, 1858] *was very sick all last night. Had a cold, unpleasant drive to Linden where we spent the night with Cousin Elizabeth. I found her looking badly. We went out shopping in the evening and called to see my old friend, Mrs. Sutton.*

[April 13, 1858] *Had another cold, dismal ride to get home today. Shopped and dined with Sister Jane. Four of us will be at home, except one of the Negros.*

[April 14, 1858] *Have been busy looking after my home and poultry. A considerable frost last night, but had my vegetables all protected. Feel languid and dull spirited. Gabe, our buggy horse, was taken with blind staggers and I am uneasy about him.*

[April 15, 1858] *Sent for Sister Jane and Mrs. Connally to dine with me today and we had a pleasant day but for my stupidities. Poor Gabe grows worse and I fear we shall lose him. Sent for Miss* [Hila] *Baker to help make my carpet.[21]*

[April 16, 1858] *We made my carpet and put it down today. Though my wrist is fearfully swollen, yet I sewed half the day.*

[April 17, 1858] *My wrist is too sore to work much though I have cut and tried to make me a larger waist collar.*

Our good faithful Gabe died this evening. Never shall I appreciate another horse like him. As a harness horse, he was without fault, the most noble animal I ever owned.

[April 18, 1858] *We had to content ourselves without a ride today. No buggy horse and no mules at home that is safe. The clouds are black and threaten a storm.*

[April 19, 1858] *I have been a little provoked today. Our wagon got back from Jefferson with but little of our freight, and all Mr. Moores' things I most need is left behind. Miss Hila came to help me make a carpet for the parlor. Went to see Mrs.* [Martha] *Blain this evening. Her life's sands are nearly run out. How distressing to leave children for anyone else to raise.[22]*

I attribute my own present infirmities partly to not having an own mother to watch over my childhood—not that my stepmother was not kind and affectionate, but she did not use her authority as she should.[23]

[April 20, 1858] *Sewed on my dress when my hand would permit. David and I walked over to Mr. Moores' this evening. The walk was rather too much for me.*

[April 21, 1858] *Read, wrote a little, feel sad and stupid.*

[April 22, 1858] *Oh, how I miss poor Gabe. I haven't had a carriage ride since I came home. I feel it will make me sick as I am so accustomed to it.*

[April 23, 1858] *Heard this morning of poor Mrs. Blain's death and feel the probability of my being the next. I felt so sad that I could not stay home this evening and walked over to sit with Sister Jane. However, I should do so often, much as it hurts me.*

[April 24, 1858] *All alone. David had to go after Francy, who was sick at Mr. Whitaker's and I could not attend Mrs. Blain's funeral. I sewed all day to drive away my melancholy thoughts. Oh, how sad and oppressed I feel.*

[April 25, 1858] *Read and wrote this morning. Sister Jane and Mr. Moores came and spent the evening. Husband came a little before night. I've been quite ill all evening but kept my feelings to myself.*

[April 26, 1858] *I got cut and set Francy to making her some dresses today though I have not set up ten minutes. Was sick all day.*

[April 27, 1858] *Set Francy cooking today. She is the fourth cook I have tried to train, or commenced with, rather.*

[April 28, 1858] *Am very well pleased with Francy's performance, though she knows little or nothing about cooking. But seems attentive to what I say.*

[April 29, 1858] *Done little else today but look after my new cook.*

[April 30, 1858] *I went over the same routine today as yesterday.*

[May 1, 1858] *Little frightened this evening by three men coming up armed, looking for runaway Negros. Had a severe spell of my old complaint just after.*

[May 2, 1858] *Though it was Sabbath, I got husband to drive me over to see Mrs. Connally, having had no desire to go for the last two weeks, and this evening we took* [illegible] *by Mr. Griffin's. Made Mrs. Davis' acquaintance. Came back and I devoted some time to the study of my Bible, which I have neglected very much of late.*

[May 3, 1858] *Sewed and cried a little, which I seldom do. Set in the kitchen to learn Francy how to cook.*

[May 4, 1858] *Spent the morning in my poultry yard, garden, kitchen. Sister Jane and children came over this evening. Little Ruth grows very sweet. I haven't been well this evening.*

[May 5, 1858] *David stays more with me than ever before since our marriage. We have done little else today but lounge. However, I have been teaching Francy to iron starched clothes, something I know but little about myself.*

[May 6, 1858] *Have wrote most of today and had my house and things aired and have been unusually domestic about dairy.*

[May 7, 1858] *Wrote Virginia, my youngest sister, a long letter this morning in reply to her first attempt to me. Indeed, I believe she said it was her first attempt to anyone. I read Shakespeare's "Tempest" again. I was so much pleased with that I shall read it again soon.*[24]

[May 8, 1858] *Spent this morning in darning and fitting up heels and toes to my husband's socks. Made some new dish towels, crocheted a little, and read "Richard III," or nearly so. Was very sick just before and after supper. Oh, this horrid dyspepsia.*

[May 9, 1858] *Have been most bitterly disappointed today by the rain—prevented my attending church. Ill-health and other inconveniences have kept me at home, kept me from church, for the last seven months. Nearly all our Sabbaths of late have been inclement.*
Drove out as far as Mr. Baker's late this evening, though the clouds looked dark.

[May 10, 1858] *After my household duties were performed this morning, knit then till noon, a little before which time Mr. Johns came to make a settlement with husband. After dinner, which made me very sick, we drove over to Mr. Connally's. I was somewhat improved by the ride.*[25]

[May 11, 1858] *Went to Dr. Salmon and spent the day. Returned with a dreadful headache and feeling very ill otherwise. Oh, God, prepare my heart to meet Thee. I feel as if I can't stand my sufferings much longer.*

[May 12, 1858] *Felt stupid most of the day, though, as I always do, busied myself in the forenoon about my household affairs. Finished "Richard III," added to my **[illegible]** book, knit a little, read.*

[May 13, 1858] *Spent today with Sister Jane. Came home suffering much with sick headache. I heard news which preyed so much upon my mind I attributed my headache partly to that.*

[May 14, 1858] *Had my floors scrubbed this morning and, on going out to have my dinner put on, I became so indignant as to wish myself in a "free state!" Negroes are the bane of my life. I asked Francy, my new cook, for one of the kitchen knives.*

"Don't know where they are!" "When did you have them? You ha potatoes to slice this morning and bread to toast." "Don't know—Aunt Nancy took one and said it belonged to her." "When did she take it?" said I. "Don't know."

When the meat had to be cut, the meat axe was nowhere to be found. The butter made yesterday, because of my absence, was thrown into pan without being worked, and yet all yesterday she sat and done nothing, I suppose, but sleep. Though sick when I came home, I had to walk around and have feed put in the chicken trough—the milk vessels prepared, ready for the night's milk, etc.

Oh, I shall never speak again of cruelty to disobedient servants. They know I can't and won't whip them, and thus they treat me, and I dislike telling David. I wish the set of slaves I have belonged to some abolitionist.

Had my lunch basket filled this evening, ready to go fishing tomorrow in the lake near Mr. Connally's.

[May 15, 1858] Went as far as Mr. Connally's and heard the river overflowed so bad it was impossible to get to the lake, and so David and I spent the day. As everyone else had heard of the overflow, no one else came. I was not much disappointed, not being fond of fishing no way. The party was all I cared for.

This evening, after we came home, I saw the first fox chase I ever saw. Mr. Moores' dogs started one up near here and chased it all around on the lawn before the house and finally treed it and then he shot it just before dark.

[May 16, 1858] Having no church to attend that was convenient here, spent the day at home, taking a short ride in the evening and called at Mr. Moores' a little while.

[May 17, 1858] Spent the forenoon working in my shrubbery, looking after my garden, cuttings and fixing work for Harrit, etc. Cut and fit me a [illegible] this evening. Read [illegible] and took a severe headache and retired quite early.

[May 18, 1858] *Have wearied myself down trying to learn numbskull Negros to sew, cook, etc. I've had Harrit sewing two years and now she can't make a hem with bought thread without my basting it or spanking her every minute. What a martyr one is to household duties when one hasn't trained servants.*

Oh, such a headache this evening.

[May 19, 1858] *I can't tell whenever I was so busy as today. Set out in the kitchen to mend and have soap tended to. Made Francy the waists and sleeves of a dress. Sewed on my spencer.[26]*

*Sister Jane came over and spent this evening. My headache returned violently this evening. Mr. Baker came from Jefferson with some **[illegible]**, which I had to get up and put away.*

[May 20, 1858] *Mr. and Mrs. Connally, Sister Jane and children spent today with us, and Miss Hila Baker came to make up my parlor carpet, and just before they all came Mr. Henshaw commenced his noise upon the house again.*

We've been here three and a half years and yet are annoyed by hammer and nails, etc. I did not enjoy myself and know my visitors could rave for the noise and confusion. The furniture hither and thither all over the house, the turkey not well roasted for dinner.

Apologies are disgusting noise generally to me, but my nice dinners are always when I have no company, though for fear of not being believed, I don't often say so. My head ached as violently as it could for a while this evening.

[May 23, 1858] *Was poorly all the morning. I did not feel better until after my evening's ride. Surely, I will fail soon from my present feeling. Sometimes I feel it pleasant—Oh, so pleasant to die! To lay down all pain and care. Oh, what is an invalid's life? Why is it even prized by him? If we hope for a home in Heaven—which we all do who strive for the Crown—what want we a home in this "Vale of Tears" for?*

I feel it is my husband that ties me here. Everyone else is just so well off without me, and I often think he would be the same. But I have the infinite pleasure—thank God—of feeling that my little stay with him has been and will be productive of good results. Who is there that lives who doesn't exert a good influence on someone?

[May 24, 1858] *Did not sit up an hour today and been ill all day. Oh, is there no release from pain for me in this world.*

[May 25, 1858] *Have been confined to my bed all day. Only for a few moments to relieve my head, mind, and poor heart. I'm afraid I'm not sufficiently prepared for the great change which must soon convey my spirit to worlds unknown! The Bible, I love, but then it is most, I might say all, a mystery to me.*

I believe my greatest sin consists in taxing my mind too much with the cares of this world. I do not think it is in loving this world too much. I do not estimate an existence here as highly as many persons do. My husband I love almost to idolatry, and I am afraid that tie will be hard to lose, though I have tried to prepare him as well as myself for it.

He left me this morning to be absent until tomorrow and, oh, how long the time seems. If I could but be up, going about, half this gloom would leave me, but then I have a hot fever over my left lower ribs.

I think I know the worst. Oh God, most Glorious Heavenly Parent, have mercy on me, only give me a preparation of heart and Thy will be done.

[May 26, 1858] *Have been unable to set up at all today, only to rest myself. My strength seems fast declining. I wonder at my indifference. I must soon appear before the Majesty of Heaven. I can't shake the cares and perplexities of this world off as I wish. My husband will soon be home, and then I will throw off this care for his sake.*

[May 27, 1858] *Felt better this morning and sit up some, but, oh, this evening what a dreadful headache. It almost killed me. Shall I stand another such?*

[May 28, 1858] *Tried to make, or commenced making rather, some plum preserves, but my strength is not adequate to the task and they have been but poorly attended to. Husband drove me over to see Sister this evening.*

[May 29, 1858] *I finished one jar of my preserves and began the second and read a little, etc. Feel very weak and poorly this evening from over exertion—trying to will myself to do too many things. I have felt for this week past that exercise, both the body and mind, was killing me.*

[May 30, 1858] *A most beautiful bright Sabbath we've had today and no church near enough for me to attend, and I regret it more because I felt so much stronger since morning. We took a horse ride this evening after Sister Jane and Mr. Moores left.*

[May 31, 1858] *The Merrie Month of May has bade us adieu, and I can't say when I've been worse in health, spirits, etc. I can but feel and see this multiplicity of trials I have with disobedience makes me the creature of affliction I am.*

For the last month I have been indefatigable in my endeavors to learn to a cook—the fifth one, too, since my marriage—and now, unless I sit by and show her, she can't make a biscuit fit to be seen, much less eaten, and will salt nothing unless expressly told, and then she throws in a handful. Never again in life shall I wonder at a woman's health declining without any apparent cause if she has an African on the premises, unless they are made to fear and respect her.

David and I went over to Mr. Connally's this evening to see Mrs. Watson but did not get out the buggy as she was out visiting and turned back and went to see poor desolate looking Lucy Morgan and her poor little orphan nieces. Poor little motherless ones. No one can fill a mother's place. Being an orphan from the hour of my birth, most truly can I feel for this motherless brood.[27]

[June 1, 1858] *"Bright leafy June" again here. What old as well as pleasant recollections does this day bring. Just two years ago today I left my husband and home for Brandon, Mississippi, to be placed in the skillful (expected to be, that is) hands of Dr. Holmes to have my health restored. But, oh! Had I then known what I now know, I should* **[illegible]** *the first. Did as well as usual and doctor did all he could, but, poor man, it was but the small effort. I should never have seen Brandon or known Dr. Holmes.*

[June 2, 1858] *Sat before the sitting room window this morning and had my front walks cleaned off. Finished my spencer, made light bread and rolls, and completed the day eating rolls enough to make me rather uneasy after going to bed.*

[June 3, 1858] *Had just taken Harrit around and adjusted all the apartments down stairs, filled the vases with fresh flowers, when Mrs. Connally and Mrs. Watson sent me word they were going to spend the day with me, so I demanded a fresh dress, not yet having taken off my morning wrapper, assisted a little about dinner, setting the table, etc., and, feeling weary, lay down and napped a little before they came. They came at eleven and we had rather a pleasant day. Dr. Salmon came in just before they left and brought me mail matter from Sister Margaret and Mrs. Hobson.*[28]

I felt this evening after our company left how much my husband and myself would enjoy ourselves were I only permitted to enjoy health, but that darkens all my, would be, happiest hours. Oh, who can tell the bitter anguish that fills the heart of the hopelessly afflicted one. I think I can say most truly, too. God above—alone. Was so taken with household work I haven't sewed a stich or read a dozen pages. Cooked preserves, made some nice fruit cakes, and now I feel weary. One of my fingers pains me—is considerably swollen. Whilst gathering some plums to send to Mrs. Connally a wasp stung me. She didn't send for the plumbs, so my pain was all for nothing.

[June 4, 1858] *Was engaged throughout this day cutting out Negro clothing for the ensuing winter (including household duties, of course). Not finished, my finger paining me so much from the wasp sting.*

[June 5, 1858] *Had a drizzly morning and was busy fixing work for the Negro women—as soon as fixed, however, the rain ceased, and all my trouble was for nothing. David and I rode over to Mr. Connally's, called this evening on Mrs. Watson. Came by Mr. Moores and spent a few moments.*

[June 6, 1858] *Went ten miles from home to church and was then disappointed as the preacher did not come. It was a sore disappointment to me, not being able to attend church often. Heard but two sermons in a year. We came by Mr. Moores' and spent a few hours. I had a spell of vomiting, which made me feel badly all evening.*

[June 7, 1858] *Can't tell whenever I felt so languid as I did this morning. Did not rise until after husband and workmen breakfasted, and then lay down before taking half an hour of exercise after bathing. Merely sat until shortly before dinner, and after dinner had a violent headache, which I increased by riding, being all alone and feeling a little lonely. We had a nice little shower, though not near so much as my garden needs.*

[June 8, 1858] *Have had a most disagreeable shocking sensation, as if a large ball was rising in my throat. Nothing apparently, at times, would keep me from choking except spitting out my food, and that was in such small quantities as to afford only temporary relief. Though not well, I have made two little Negro dresses and read, etc.*

[June 9, 1858] *Had a considerable fever last night and have had every night for some time. Cut husband two nightshirts—nearly completed one and began making blackberry preserves. It rains, rains, rains.*

[June 10, 1858] *Sewed on my shirts, attended to my preserves, did various little household duties as today had to be washday—that nuisance of housekeepers. I always dread it.*

[June 12, 1858] *I finished my shirts, cut out some Negro clothing, and other things—finished my preserves and put them away. I have read less than usual today.*

[June 13, 1858] *Went to church at* **[illegible]** *and heard two Masonic rituals and saw the first Masonic procession I've ever seen in Texas. I did not think Rev. Grigsby, who preached the first, did as well as usual.* **[Illegible]** *did all he could, but poor* **[illegible]** *it was but a poor effort. Altogether, I* *did not enjoy the sermons or the procession as well as I anticipated but felt proud the ride did not fatigue me much as it usually does.*[29]

[June 14, 1858] *I felt very cold until near noon and then took a nervous attack which has lasted me ever since. though I have nearly made husband a pair of pants and read some of Shakespeare's plays. Too nervous to work.*

[June 15, 1858] *Last night, just before supper, I took a sick stomach and chillingness and went to bed from the table without eating anything and feeling that I should not reach the bed room—if ever.*

[June 16, 1858] *Felt better than I expected, however, this morning though weak and feeble. Sister Jane sent me our mail matter just before noon, and my three letters from home cheered me much and, withal, brought feelings almost inexpressibly dear as Mat is soon to take on herself the responsibilities of a wife, no trifling one* **[illegible]** *in my imagination. I think the match in every way suitable and can but pray she will be happier.*[30] *Sister J. Mrs.* **[illegible]***, and Mrs. Bacon* **[?]** *came over this evening and spend an hour so. They must have found me unusually dull, for their visit now appears as a dream. I had begun the reply to Mat's letter when they came.*

[June 17, 1858] *I have felt better today and been unusually smart. Cut out the Negro men's winter clothing, finished Mat's letter, read, sewed, and even spent an hour or so in the kitchen and dairy.*

[June 18, 1858] *Was feeble and nervous all morning. Did little but read* Harper's Magazine. *Sewed on husband's shirts this evening, attended to the cleaning of my pantry* **[illegible]***, practiced a little piano, I suppose.*

[June 19, 1858] *Not able to sit up much this morning. I lounged and read and sewed a little before dinner, and after dinner nursed husband and read a letter and then we had a pleasant ride to Mrs. Blevis's, and so we* **[torn]** *came by and wrote a letter to send Sister Jane* **[torn]** *as*

I always do from my ride, but when we **[torn]** *to retire, husband complained so much from a headache I was uneasy, and long after he went to sleep I lay thinking perhaps it was the prelude to a long spell.*

[June 20, 1858] *Dear husband is well this morning and is taking a ride, for which I'm so thankful, though from some circumstances I am gloomy. Though this is a bright, beautiful Sabbath, yet there is something in it of melancholy acuteness. Something that accords with my sadness, sadness of feelings. The very hum of the insect and song of the birds is now soft and soothing to my ear. It seems to be in accordance with my mood.*

[June 21, 1858] *Arose and dressed for breakfast this morning but went back to bed and remained there most of the day. Got up only to dinner and supper.*

[June 22, 1858] *Have felt considerably worse today than yesterday, though I have made a* **[illegible]** *even though lying in bed and yet I can't see why I did it. "Hope," though, 'ere not often die, I feel to be nearer hopelessly diseased than ever before at this time.*

[June 23, 1858] *With the excessive heat of this day and writing some letters* **[illegible]** *and my* **[illegible]** *now I am weary and sore and too nervous to write, though otherwise feel better.*

NOTES

[1]   "Editor's Table," *Harper's New Monthly Magazine*, 16 (December 1857–May 1858), 120–25.

[2]   Reuben Henry Harrison Moores was born on November 19, 1819, near Longtown, Fairfield County, South Carolina. In 1841, he was appointed as the first postmaster of Mooresville, Texas. He married Rachel Perry Godbold's half-sister, Jane M. Godbold, on November 10, 1847, in Columbia, Arkansas. He died on June 30, 1871, and is buried beside his wife in the Harrison Chapel Cemetery at Redwater.

[3]   Jane Godbold Moores, Rachel's half-sister, was the daughter of Ananias and Elizabeth Johnson Godbold. She was born on September 13, 1828, at Blackstock, Chester County, South Carolina, and on November 10, 1847, married Reuben Henry Harrison Moores in Columbia County, Arkansas. The couple's Cass County plantation abutted that of David and Rachel Moores. They were the parents of nine children: Charles Harrison, Rachel Perry, Mary Harrison, Jane Eva Godbold, Ruth Wooten, Reuben Henry Harrison Jr., Ananias Godbold, Judson, and Stanley. Jane Moores died on July 11, 1877, and is buried in the Harrison Chapel Cemetery at Redwater.

   Rachel's prayer for her husband's safety quotes Genesis 31:48.

[4] The federal census of 1860 shows L. Griffin, age sixty-five and a native of South Carolina, and B. M. Griffin, age twenty-six and a native of Georgia, to have been Moores' overseers.

[5] Jane Moores was, in fact, more than eight months pregnant at the time.

[6] Dempsey J. Connally, the Moores' nearest neighbor, was born in 1796 and was married to Lucinda McConnell Montgomery on December 13, 1821, in Jackson County, Georgia. They had nine children.

[7] Willis Loundes "Willie" Whitaker Jr., David H. Moores' brother-in-law, was born in Kershaw County, South Carolina, on September 28, 1798. In 1833, he married Sarah Harrison Ross Moores, the daughter of Mary Harrison and Charles Moores, and they became the parents of six children. He arrived in Texas in May 1840 and on November 1, 1840, received a grant of 640 acres from the Republic of Texas. In 1860, he was enumerated in the Federal census as a farmer residing at Linden, Cass County, Texas, and as the owner of $65,000 in personal property and $100,400 in real estate. Willis Whitaker Jr. died on March 19, 1867, and is buried in the Harrison Chapel Cemetery.

Sarah Harrison Moores Whitaker was born on November 10, 1810, in Fairfield County, South Carolina. She was first married to Dr. James Thomas Rosborough, and, following his death in 1842, on July 27, 1844, married William "Willis" Loundes Whitaker Jr. (after the death of his first wife, Sarah's sister Elizabeth Harrison Moores). Sarah Whitaker died on September 19, 1843, at age thirty-two at Cedar Grove Plantation, Cass County [or perhaps Bowie County] and is buried in the Harrison Chapel Cemetery. They were the parents of six children, all of whom are buried in the Harrison Chapel Cemetery. Ann Mimms Wright, *Descendants of Isaac Ross and Jean Brown* (Jackson, MS: 1911), 85.

Elizabeth Harrison Moores was born on September 3, 1814, in Longtown, Fairfield County, South Carolina. In a letter to her brother Reuben, then in Texas, Jane Ross wrote from South Carolina on December 16, 1838, that "Sister Elizabeth H. Moores was married to Dr. James T. Rosborough on the 22nd of November. Doctor Rosborough and his lady have been staying with us since they were married. I do not expect that the doctor will go to Texas as his practice is very extensive in his neighborhood, and he has a good practice in Longtown." Following Rosborough's death on August 15, 1842, Elizabeth joined her family in Texas where she married William "Willie" Whitaker Sr. They were the parents of two children. Elizabeth Harrison Whitaker died on May 30, 1877, and is buried in the Oakwood Cemetery, Jefferson, Texas.

[8] Rachel's nephew, Charles Harrison "Charlie" Moores, the son of Jane M. Godbold and Reuben Henry Harrison Moores, was born in Atlanta, Texas, on June 8, 1849. He was married to Martha Susan "Mattie" Odell on December 14, 1871. They were the parents of four children. Charles Harrison Moores died on February 21, 1922, and is buried in the Pine Crest Cemetery, Atlanta, Cass County, Texas.

His cousin, also named Charles Harrison Moores, was the son of Eli and Minerva Janes Moores. He was born in Bowie County on December 17, 1848, and on December 23, 1880, married Mary Tamar Hargrove of Brandon, Mississippi. By 1880, he was the owner of 320 acres of land on both sides of what is now Moores Lane in Texarkana, on which he built a colonial-style house. He also owned 1,200 acres of land on the Red River, which he farmed. He served as sheriff of Bowie County from 1892 until 1894 and from 1896 until 1898. This Charles Moores died in Texarkana on June 12, 1906, and is buried in the Moores Chapel Cemetery. "Direct Descendants of Charles Moores and Allied Families to Have Gay Reunion Sunday." *Texarkana Daily News*, January 26, 1958, reprinted in Nancy Moores Watts Jennings, comp., "Charles Moores and Allied Families," *Texarkana Pioneer Family Histories*, 129.

[9] Agnes Johns was born in 1846 in Alabama. She married William H. Johns on January 25, 1888, in Cass County. She died on May 30, 1913. She was the sister of Elijah Johns.

[10] The Bluffs was a landing place on the Sulfur River near the Moores' plantation, now inundated by Lake Wright Patman.

[11] Nancy Baker was the wife of John Baker and the mother of daughters Hila and Elizabeth Baker and of the notorious gunman Cullen Montgomery Baker.

12 Jane Ross Moores, Rachel's sister-in-law and the daughter of Mary and Charles Moores, was born on September 7, 1818, in Columbia, South Carolina.

She was first married to Harrison Ross Whitaker, but following his death in 1845 she was married to James C. Moore. They were the parents of six children. Jane Ross Moore died on January 19, 1877, at the age of fifty-nine and is buried in the Evergreen Cemetery, Paris, Texas.

13 The Moores' friend and neighbor, Dr. George Hansel Salmon, was born in South Carolina in May 1827, the son of Eliza Bird Salmon. He was married to Martha E. Rush on August 19, 1851, and was the father of six children. On May 10, 1882, he married M. L. McNight in Cass County. Dr. George Hansel Salmon died in 1889 and is buried in the Courtland Cemetery, Queen City, Texas.

14 Rachel's niece, Ruth Moores, was the daughter of Jane M. Godbold and Reuben Henry Harrison Moores. She was born on March 16, 1858. In 1879, she married Francis G. Wooten of Texarkana and became the mother of four children. She died in November 1935 and is buried in Texarkana's Rose Hill Cemetery.

15 Swanson's Landing, one of the first inland ports in Texas, was on the south shore of Caddo Lake in Harrison County. The harbor was of a comfortable depth for large riverboats. Peter Swanson, the earliest settler in the area, constructed a dock and warehouses for the transshipment of cotton, hides, and corn to New Orleans.

In 1857, Swanson's Landing was the starting point for the Southern Pacific Railroad, one of the earliest Texas railroads, but with the removal of the track in 1863, the shifting of riverboat traffic to Jefferson, and the clearing of the great raft from the Red River in 1873, the demise of Swanson's Landing as a port followed rapidly. Randolph B. Campbell, *A Southern Community in Crisis. Harrison County, Texas, 1850–1880* (Austin: Texas State Historical Association. 1983).

16 Rives Landing was located on Caddo Lake at the Texas–Louisiana state line, about twenty miles east of Jefferson. John G. Rives, an early settler, owned land in Caddo Parish, Louisiana, and in Marion County, Texas. Rives Landing was renamed Bonham Landing in honor of Rives's son-in-law.

17 Rebecca Ann Rives Browning was the wife of William Daniel Browning of Caddo Parish. Louisiana. Jimmie was her brother, James Jackson Rives.

18 The City Hotel, which stood on the corner of Camp and Common streets, was one of the great hotels of antebellum New Orleans. In 1865, with the collapse of the Confederacy, the city was full of returning Confederate soldiers, most of them penniless. The City Hotel provided $30,000 in food and shelter to "these brave but impecunious guests." John Kendall, *History of New Orleans* (Chicago: Lewis Publishing Company, 1922), 685.

19 "Dutchman" was standard American usage for any German-speaking individual from the word "Deutsch," for the German language. The term denoted Germans rather than, as today, Hollanders.

20 Alexandria is the seat of Rapides Parish, so named because of the rapids above the city. The Red River was generally not navigable above Alexandria from July until January each year due to the rapids, making the city essentially its head of navigation. When possible, cargoes were portaged around this impediment, but Alexandria also became the cite of numerous warehouses for goods moving up the river to Texas.

21 Hila Baker was the daughter of John and Nancy Baker and the sister of Cullen Montgomery Baker.

22 Martha McRoberts Blain was born in 1800, the daughter of Agnes Woodson Morton and T. B. McRoberts Sr. She was the wife of John Stephen Blain and the mother of Mary and Francis Blain. She died in Cass County, Texas, on April 22, 1858, and is buried in the Rocky Springs Presbyterian Church Cemetery, Deerfield, Virginia.

23 Rachel's stepmother, Elizabeth Dismukes Johnson, was born in North Carolina in 1810. On January 19, 1831, she married Samuel Ananias Godbold in Monroe County, Alabama. She became the mother of William Johnson, Martha A., Benjamin Franklin, Mary A., Harriet A., Virginia, and Samuel Ananias Godbold Jr. She died on February 15, 1870, in Pulaski County, Arkansas.

odbold, the youngest of Rachel's siblings, was born in Arkansas in 1847 or 1848, the daughter ...s and Elizabeth Johnson Godbold. In 1870, she was living in the home of her sister Martha and her brother-in-law Thomas Pleasant Mask. She died in Pulaski County on October 15, 1873.

[25] William L. Johns was born in Amherst County, Virginia. The name of his wife or the date of his marriage is not known, but his daughter Agnes T. Johns, born in Amherst County in about 1845, was by 1862 an orphan.

[26] A spencer was a short, close-fitting woolen jacket or vest, worn for extra warmth by women and children in the early nineteenth century.

[27] Lucinda Clementine "Clemmie" Watson, the daughter of Lucinda McConnell Montgomery and Dempsey J. Connally, was born on February 19, 1833, and was married to John R. Watson, a near neighbor of the Moores', on December 10, 1854. They were the parents of Robert J. Connally Watson. Following her husband's death at the Battle of Jenkins Ferry, Arkansas, on April 30, 1864, she married James M. Cauthen. She died on March 16, 1896, and is buried in Queen City, Texas.

[28] Rachel's sister, Margaret Perry Godbold, was born on April 9, 1823, in Monroeville, Monroe County, Alabama, the daughter of Rachel Perry and Samuel A. Godbold. In Arkansas in 1846 she was married to Samuel M. Johnson who served as her parents' overseer. Their children were Francis P., Lucretia, Samuel J., Allie, Elizabeth B., William Dickey Johnson, and Ella Johnson Godbold. After the death of Samuel Johnson in 1853, she married Joseph T. Powell on March 9, 1867. Margaret Perry Godbold died on February 22, 1901, at Prescott, Nevada County, Arkansas, and is buried in the Watts Cemetery in Willisville.

Sarah A. Hobson was born in Cumberland, Virginia, on September 30, 1829. She was married to John Samuel Hobson. She and Rachel had become friends in 1856 while Rachel was a patient at the clinic of Dr. Henry J. Holmes Sr. in Brandon, Mississippi. She died on September 25, 1896, and is buried in the Brandon Cemetery. (New Orleans) *Times–Picayune*, September 26, 1896, page 2.

[29] Justin M. Grigsby married Nancy A. Brantly in Cass County on September 24, 1857.

[30] Martha A. "Mat" Godbold, Rachel's younger half-sister, was born in Monroeville, Alabama, in 1837. In 1850, she was living with her family in Harrison, Ouachita County, Arkansas. She served as an attendant at David and Rachel's wedding. In June 1858, she married Dr. Thomas Pleasant Mask. The couple had one son, Charles, who was born and died in 1859 and one daughter, Octavio, who was born in or about 1866.

chapter two

WHAT A HEROINE I AM GETTING TO BE

The Hydropathic and Physiological School in New York City
July 1858–November 1858

F ollowing Rachel's extended illness from June 1858 through February 1859, she sought treatment at the Hydropathic and Physiological School in New York City. This hospital emphasized hydropathy—known as the "water cure"—dietary therapies, sanitation, hygiene, exercise, and abandonment of most of the materia medica used by allopathic physicians.

Rachel spent the three weeks following her sister Martha's marriage on July 13, 1858, at her father's home in Arkansas before setting off on her harrowing journey North. There she encountered such, to her, "new fangled" and shocking movements as spiritualism, Universalism, and bloomerism. Bloomers were divided women's skirts or short skirts worn over trousers, developed as a healthful and comfortable alternative to the corsets and long skirts then worn by American women. The garment achieved popularity in the early 1850s as a more healthful replacement for the corset, and soon became a symbol of women's rights and feminist reform. Although she met many accomplished and congenial people in New York and visited such cultural meccas as the city's Academy of Music, the Sultan Room, and the Saint Nicholas Hotel, Rachel returned to Texas in no better health than when she left home.

Drawing of the St. Nicholas Hotel, New York City, c. 1855.

XXX

[February 11, 1859 [1]] *Ah, me! How changes affect one when they begin to retrospect. I little thought when I laid my pen aside on the evening of the 23rd of June [1858] that the 11th of February [1859] would have whirled around on time's rapid wheel ere again those pages were pressed by my hand. But well do I remember how David insisted I should accept an invitation to take a seat with Sister Jane in her carriage on the morning of the 24th of June to attend the Masonic celebration at Mr. Cole's. He insisted I would feel better for the ride, and he had some workman [torn] he could not well leave.*

I went and enjoyed myself [ink splash] better than I thought I could without him, and felt very well in the evening, though much fatigued and went to bed immediately on [illegible] from which I did not rise under near three weeks except on Tuesday following. I had grown too ill and the fever seemed more violent each day until the night of the 10th.

On the 9th of July I was enabled for the first time to ride out, and David carried me to Mr. Connally's. I wanted to do some shopping as I had received a letter from Mat saying she would write soon for me to attend her wedding. On our way to Mr. Connally's we got the letter. The marriage was to take place on the 13th, and we had only four days to get ready and to get there in, and I was expected to spend the remainder of the summer. I found myself busy putting away and locking up, but—as I did not get a worthy [illegible] from Mr. Connally, I had no sewing which I wasn't able to do—so on the 11th of July, just seven months ago today, Husband and I started to Mat's wedding and on a health trip.

We were caught in a hard rain on the bank of the Sulfur, and David was scarcely able to reach Eli's, where we stopped for the night. He took something like a chill then and was quite sick all night.[2] We traveled forty-five miles the next day for want of a suitable place to stop at, and when we reached Dr. Bayless's in Falcon **[Nevada County, Arkansas,]** we were both so exhausted as not to be able to sit up a moment after reaching the house, and I have never lived through a night of more excruciating pain and torture. I eat largely of fruitcake and ham, both of which was poisonous to my dyspeptic stomach.[3]

The next morning, I nearly made **[page torn]** or more attempts before I could dress myself, and then with the assistance of a servant I was only able to get a morning dress on and started for Pa's, a distance of **[illegible]** miles and reached there about noon **[illegible]** rather merry than depressed **[illegible]** quietly four hours **[ink stain]** I stimulated myself enough to dress for the wedding, but the whole evening appears as a dream long past and the remaining three weeks spent at Pa's I only know I'd never felt well a moment, and after David left me to come home to make some preparation for us to start to New York, I felt I should never see him again.

I lived through it, however, and on the 13th day of August we started en route for New York and I consider it a miracle that we both didn't die that day. David had a dreadful cough and had trouble breathing, and the dust for twenty miles was almost insufferable. At times you could not see ten steps for the dust. I know I'll remember how I fretted and fumed at it and how Brother William and David laughed and coughed.

We took the stage on the fourth for Gaines Landing, had a more comfortable time as the rain had laid the dust somewhat on the east side of the Ouachita, and we had two or three very pleasant traveling companions and nice peach orchards occasionally for the first fifty miles—of which we availed of towards night. The passengers all got out, except two gentlemen, and they kindly took one seat between them, giving David and I one apiece.

I slept pretty soundly, only waking when a stop was made, but by next morning I felt somewhat weary, as with disarranged hair and dress damped from precipitation and rumpled from sleeping in it. I awoke **[torn]** when we stopped to change horses, drivers, and take on more passengers, of which there were four, and as we already had three besides husband and self, altogether making nine in a small "carry-all" comfortable for six, and two of the newcomers were invalids, one with consumption and one leg, the other with sore eyes and just convalescing from typhoid fever. The one with the crutches sat opposite me, and with him in constant motion I had but little room for movement myself, though I managed to keep my head to the window or leaning on my husband's shoulder.

Near noon of the clock, too, we were served at the breakfast house, and I felt so nearly famished I eat a huge meal of chicken [illegible] from being soaked in wine to keep it from spoiling and fish in the same dilemma, though the light bread was nice and coffee hot. The less [illegible] however, I only spent partly sleeping after leaving the breakfast house, for very soon we were in the bottom and there was a farmer driving a baggage wagon. The driver declared that he had instructions not to take the coach in the bottom as the roads were impassable for a heavy coach and this wagon had not [illegible] nor springs and plank seats, and my much afflicted husband had hot evening fever and cold, a miserable cough, and was aching in every limb, and I was hardly able to stand up though I had begun a sweat already from difficult breathing. David declared he would leave the coach [and walk with] his baggage provided the other passengers would do the same. Told them there were eight men of them and only two drivers and they could manage them, but they cannily submitted, and David cursed and raved at the drivers, took my linen duster off and made me an umbrella, they not having one on board. This scene [illegible] driver like a red hot oven lid and [torn] damp horses, Missouri [illegible] from [illegible] bottom of the "Father of Waters," and on we traveled, moving at a snail's pace, but presently the driver orders all out except this lady, myself, and says that the mules can't pull this load through the next two miles, and here I pouted and became furious for I certainly thought the hot sun would kill David. His fever had rose from the excessive heat and crowd, all four of us being on one seat, and, positively, it was not large enough for two small ladies with modern hoops, and I got up and looked at my small space and I could find when I sat there was no seat—so I suppose I sat on David and on the wall of the wagon, but when they got out it was worse, for the driver took through the woods and it was over logs and stumps and it threw me over [illegible] and satchels and bumped my head and beat my limbs.

At last came to a long, hot lane, which was to last for miles, and here our crowd got back, but this time I sat under their feet and parched for water. But, thought I, my parched lips will be cooler as we approached a large house I had spent a night at a few years before—but the driver had had some altercation with the agent who was staying there and, lo! he refused us a drink! But *our handlers were oh so importunate, after a while one of them obtained a bucket of "shriff" [?] they called "cistern" water, but great grief! It was the meanest kind of slop water, and I turned in disgust from it and for the next few miles I thought I would surely die of thirst, but after so long a time we came to a well by the roadside and here was pure, fresh water, and never was fountain more welcomed by a desert caravan. We drank—lay down on the grass—drank and sit down and then we drank and started and after this [illegible] my [illegible] bruised and when I reached the [illegible] Hotel at Gaines Landing it was a difficult matter for me to get in the house. I was sickened as soon as I did get me in and preceded to bathe and change my dress, lest a boat should pass by.*

The overflow here just dried off and our room was the repository for the icebox and the decayed, damp, diseased sawdust combined with effluvia that came from underneath. The lot rendered the room unendurable and fate damned us there two nights and days with nothing but ham to eat, and it being a [illegible] I had not tasted above three times in a year.

Then, next evening, after our having reached there, a crowd came who, like ourselves, was wanting a boat for Memphis, and as husband saw the steward advancing to summon us to supper, he told one of the gentleman to ask him what he had to eat.

"Oh," said he, "we have ham, hash, broil, boiled meats—He, he!"

But David said, "Ask him whether his hash is made of ham; his broil ham; his boil, ham."[4]

But that was the last ham supper, for next morning, as kind providence would have it, the Daniel Boone, a mail boat, came puffing up, and when she was yet ten miles off I had equipped myself of bonnet and duster and David had the baggage on the wharf.

We found pleasant traveling companions and were fortunate enough to find some who were to take the same route to New York and back on home. We made the trip from Memphis to New York in sixty hours—arriving a little past midnight. But most dearly did we paid for such folly, for neither of us recovered from this fatigue in a whole week, though we did manage to get out to a ten o'clock breakfast, which was no dispraiser to the Saint Nicholas Hotel, and after breakfast went down to Germaine's Baque [?] where I had to order Sorrxxx Moraxxx Dunlebt [?], and where I was provided with a Northern C. L. [?][5]

[the remainder of this page is torn away]

Hydropathic and Physiological School[6]

"At this institution diseases are treated on strictly hygienic principles. Especial attention is given to the management of female diseases. Stammerers are permanently cured by mechanical instruments with vocal exercises. Cancers are treated successfully on a new plan, continuing cauterization and congelation. The Electric Chemical Baths are applied for the eradication of mineral drugs and infectious viruses, and various Rheumatic, Neuralgic, Paralytic, and Nervous Afflictions. Boarders are accommodated with a physiological diet. Students are educated for Hydropathetic practitioners and Health-Reform Lecturers.

Prices—Patients $5.00 entrance fee and $7.00 to $10.50, or upwards, per week, according to rooms, of which we have a great variety. Borders, $5.00 to $7.00 per week. Transient Persons, $1.00 to $1.50 per day. Students, $50.00 tuition for the Summer Term, and $75.00 for the Winter Term. Students can get board in the institution at reasonable rates. Prescriptions for home treatment, verbal or by letter, $5.00. Each subsequent letter or advice, $1.00.

Dr. T[rall] has competent male and female associate positions for general practice in city and country."

"Water cure is, more properly speaking, a natural cure, and does not consist as many suppose in the mere application of water; but the same natural agents which are required in health are employed in the curing the disease, such as air, warmth, food, water, exercise and rest. By using the proper quantities and degrees, these simple means nicely graduated to the conditions and wants of the system, we do all that can be done to preserve health and cure disease.

Hydropathic and Hygienic Institute, 217

15 LAIGHT STREET, NEW YORK,

R. T. TRALL, M. D., - - - Proprietor.

THIS establishment, which is pleasantly and quietly located near St. John's Park, can now accommodate over *one hundred* patients. Office consultations are attended to by Dr. Trall personally; and out-door practice by himself and assistants. Competent female physicians are also provided; and particular attention is given to that class of diseases which require surgical or mechanical treatment. Patients who prefer to be in the country will be provided for at the Highland House Water-Cure, at Fishkill, N. Y., under the personal direction of Dr. O. W. May. Patients at either establishment can have the occasional advice of both physicians.

SCHOOL DEPARTMENT.

The New York Hydropathic and Physiological School, having become a permanent institution, the regular Lecture term will hereafter commence on November 1st of each year, and continue six months.

Additional Chemical, Anatomical, Surgical and Obstetrical Apparatus has been provided; the Library has been increased; the Philosophical rearranged and enlarged. Particular attention will be paid to Practical Anatomy, Dissections, and Obstetrical Demonstrations.

FACULTY:

R. T. TRALL, M. D., Institutes of Medicine, Materia Medica and Female Diseases.
G. H. TAYLOR, M. D., Chemistry, Surgery, and Obstetrics.
JAMES HAMBLETON, M. D., Anatomy, Physiology and Hygiene.
J. E. SNODGRASS, M. D., Medical Jurisprudence.
H. F. BRIGGS, M. D., Philosophy of Voice and Speech.
L. N. FOWLER, A. M., Phrenology and Mental Science.
MRS. L. F. FOWLER, M. D., Female Diseases and Obstetrics.

The design of this School is not only to qualify male and female practitioners of the Healing Art, but also to educate and send into the field of human progress, competent Health-reform Teachers and Lecturers. Ample facilities are provided for a complete and thorough medical education, and for practical instruction in all the details of Hydropathic home-practice, as well as the management of Water-Cure Establishments.

Students will have the opportunity of witnessing the treatment of almost all forms of chronic diseases in the Institution, and by visiting the cliniques and hospitals of the other Schools in the city, they will become proficient in diagnosis—the most important element in a physician's education, as far as success in securing public confidence is concerned—but also enabled to see the different medical systems practically contrasted; in other words, to witness the effects of water-treatment in contrast with the various modifications of drug treatment.

PROGRAMME OF EDUCATIONAL EXERCISES.—Usually there will be four Lectures daily, of one hour each. Half of each, morning and evening, will be devoted to gymnastic and elocutionary exercises; and specified portions of each day will be allotted to private study, and to conversation in the class. A clinique will be held every Friday afternoon; and on Saturdays the students will visit the hospitals and public institutions, where a great variety of surgical operations are performed, and where almost every phase of diseased and deformed humanity can be seen.

There will be a Lyceum debate on general subjects each Wednesday evening, open to the public, and a discussion every Saturday evening on professional questions, by members of the class exclusively.

SUMMER TERM.—There will be a Summer Term of six months, from May 1st to Nov. 1st, with occasional lectures and cliniques for such students as choose to remain the year round. Tuition $50; Do. with board, $100.

R. T TRALL, M. D., Principal.

15 LAIGHT STREET, NEW YORK.

Flyer for the New York Hydropathic and Hygiene Institute, c. 1855.

By the intelligent Water-Cure method of treatment, the patient is taught a lesson; a discipline is enforced, and conditions established which will ever after be of value; whereas, in the giving of drug medicines, the intellect is left blank, and the body too often, alas! a scene of devastation.

Cicero said, 'by no other way can men approach nearer to the gods than by conferring health on men'; whenever the people become thoroughly indoctrinated in the principle of Hydrotherapy, and make themselves acquainted with the laws of life and health, they will have little need of physicians.

What will it profit a man if he gain the whole world and lose his health? The only condition upon which health can be maintained until the gradual and painless wearing out of the vital machinery in old age is the right or proper employment of all the organs and faculties of our being. How important then becomes a knowledge of the laws and conditions so intimately connected with our existence, usefulness and happiness."[7]

XXX

[David H. Moores to Rachel Moores at the Hydropathic College, New York]

No pen that will make a mark
Longtown, South Carolina[8]
Monday, September 20/[18]58

My Dearest Wife,
I received yours of the 11th instant day before yesterday, which give me much pleasure to hear that you were improving that you had a pleasant roommate. Oh, Darling, I was so much disappointed that you did not give me any encouragement to go to New York to see you once more before I left for home. You

don't know how anxious I am to see your sweet face and get some sweet kisses from you. Oh, Darling, nothing ever shall part us again until death. Oh, how pleasant it would be to have you sitting on my lap kissing me today.

I shall leave today for Texas, and I will drop this at Columbia to be mailed and you will get it in three days.

The relations are all well, and Aunt Lucy Harrison sends her love to you and they all say they would be happy to see you. I showed them your daguerreotype and they sayed that they were so much pleased with it.[9]

I offered Uncle John two thousand dollars for a blacksmith. I don't know whether he will take it or not. He will let me know in a few hours what he will do. He is a number one smith, about thirty years old. I've tried to buy you a cook, but I could not find one that I was pleased with. Negroes are very high. I never want to see Carolina anymore after I leave it this time.

Darling, you must get you everything that you need. All I make is for you. If it was not for you, I would not try to make anything. It gives me so much pleasure to do for you and see you dress nice.

You said in your letter that I must mail your daguerreotype to Mrs. Hobson. I will do so when I get to Memphis. I will look for a letter at Memphis from you. That will be about the time this reaches you. I am well and have not been sick the least since I left you. You must not make yourself uneasy about me. I'll try and take care of myself. You must try and mend fast, and I am in hopes, when the few lines reach you, you will be greatly benefited.

So, farewell, Darling, until the next, which will be when I get to your father's.

Your own David

XXX

[David H. Moores to Rachel Moores from Vicksburg, Mississippi]

Vicksburg, July 7th, 1858

Wednesday Morning

Dearest Darling,

I am here yet waiting for a boat. They all tell me here that I will be sure to get a boat this evening. Oh, my Darling, how much more pleasant it would of been to remain with you until this morning. I could of had so many sweet kisses.

I was at the Presbyterian Church last evening. Very few was out.

If I should have been going down the river, I could have got twenty boats. I was on board of the Eclipse yesterday. She was on her trip to New Orleans.[10]

We had a fine rain yesterday and it is raining here now. I am in hopes that we're getting some of it over in Texas.

Oh, my Darling, what a pleasure it would be to hear from you every morning. You must write at the least twice a week to me.

I am very well with the exception of being worn threadbare waiting for a boat. I'm in hopes when I hear from you that you will be improving fast, Darling. I will write you again when I get to Gaines Landing.

Your affectionate

Husband, D. H. Moores

XXX

Hydropathic College

New York

September 20, 1860

Dear Husband,

Though I know you get only one mail a week and that **[illegible]***, yet I get so impatient to write you I find myself wishing you had daily mails. I directed two letters week before last to Carolina and last week one home and this is the* fourth and no word from you yet. I know not whither you are or now you are. I hope and pray well. Do, Dearest, write every mail. Oh, if I could see you just one moment, one hour, I would talk you to death.

I always hated abolitionists, but now "Oh, 'tis delicious, the scorn I feel for them."[11]

Won't I be beside myself when the time of [illegible] comes.

My roommate left me last Saturday and I much regret to see her leave. She was so warmhearted and kind. She says she is coming often to see me.

Mrs. Campbell leaves next week, as she will then graduate. The more I see of her the more I like her. She is much more reserved than when you left. We have attended church together both Sabbaths since you left. I shall have to go alone when she leaves as these Saints here are too Spiritualized and Negroealized to go to church.

We have a gentleman and lady here now from Key West, Florida. They will remain until sometime in October. Have been here before.

I haven't been in the Sultan Room only to hear Dr. Trall lecture. I don't know whether they Gymnase now or not. There was a grand dance in there last night. I was a looker-on from my back window. New fangled dancers, those!

Mr. King is here. Gets [illegible] the Spiritualists and complains to me of his not receiving the proper attention, of bad food, etc.

Oh, my dear, you ought to see a poor creature who came yesterday from Wisconsin with cancer of the breasts. Each breast has knots in it as large as three or four [illegible] looking Irish potatoes and much the same shape. Poor woman. Her suffering can only [end] with life. She is in my room and I am so sorry every time I look at her. Her husband left yesterday, and she is almost heartbroken.

Good night, Dearest. Angels guard and bless thee. It is so cold I must go down in the parlour to warm.

Oh, Heaven be praised! I have at last received a letter [from] you, my own Dear David. Oh, I was feeling most miserable at times because I could not hear from you, and what a burden is now lifted from my mind now I know that you are well and [illegible]. But I fear, Dearest, you are going to run some risks of yellow fever by leaving so soon. It is dreadful now in New Orleans.

You did not say anything of your trip to Georgia, whether it was pleasant or not. You must in your next tell me something of your travels and how you enjoyed yourself.

You say you are sorry I did not give you any encouragement to come back to New York to see me. Parting hurts my feelings, so I never again want it to occur. My very soul is hurt when you have to part, and I do hope it will never be again in this life and in the life to come that we may meet is my fondest prayer.

Finding my room uncomfortably cold for the last few days, I asked for and obtained one with pipes through it. I saw they did not want to make fires so soon and now they want to charge extra when they did, so I have moved down in the one opposite Mrs. Gordon's and joining the dining room, but is even from being a register in it and is just over the furnace. I know if I had to wait for the chamber maid to make a fire every morning it would be made after I was dressed and could do without it. But this room is not so nice, comfortable, and nothing but a fear of suffering from cold would have made me make the exchange.

I shall start home on the first steamer that comes here for New Orleans before the fifteenth of November and that will be about the twelfth of November. Oh, my husband, can I stay away so long from thy kind care and protection? No caress do I get, nobody's lap to sir on, and no kisses I like.

Speaking of the pleasures deriving from a husband's society reminds me of Mrs. Campbell's happy looking face today. Her husband [came] about noon and she really look of it she was proud to see him. He looks quite nice and is much more genteel in dress than she is.

You bid me get all I want, My Dear. I fear I shall not have more than enough money to carry me home. Instead of fasting[?] this extravagant spirit you will have to chide me. It looks like your money goes here like an [illegible] and you can't tell what goes with it though I keep an account of all I get. I got fifty of Dr. Gordon a week ago. I suppose if I should want to get one or two pieces of furniture in New Orleans, I could get a little money without any difficulty. I don't know but I'll have plenty, but I thought you could write to them if you thought proper.

I will send you something to read soon. Maybe some of Fanny Fern's tales. I used to like when her stories. Don't know whether she has improved or not.[12]

My Dear Husband, do take the best care you can of your dear self. Pray, eat no non-[illegible] meat, bathe often, write me every week is the wish of you own affectionate wife,

Rahci

XXX

[Mailed from Leake's Store, Arkansas, September 29, 1858, to Rachel Moores at the Hydropathic College, New York.[13] Her letters from there are missing until the one of October 8, 1858.]

Columbia County, Arkansas
September 27, 1858

My Dearest Wife,
I arrived here yesterday, finding all well, and I shall start home in the morning and your pa is going with me, and I will carry my trunk with me.

They received a letter here last week from Jane stating that there had been some sickness among the Negroes, but all was well then.

Cotton crops are very sorry. They have not had any rain since you left to do any good. The smith that I written to you about, I did not get, and I think it very well that I did not get him as cotton crops are so short. But, Darling, that need not make you want for anything. Just buy what you want, and I will send or bring you more money if you may need it.

Darling, I'm fearful that the Red River will not be up so you can come that way. If you think it best for me to come for you, I will do so. Nothing would afford me more pleasure. You must write immediately so I will know what to do. You know that it takes three weeks for a letter to come from there. If you come by New Orleans, and Red River is down, the way you will have to come will be up to Gaines Landing and stage it, and you know that will be so bad, no one with you. If you conclude to come that way, why, you must ship everything to Jefferson but one trunk. That is, if the river is down you will ascertain that before you leave.

I did not get any letter from you at Memphis. I had a very pleasant trip home, but how much more I would have enjoyed it if I would've had your sweet face with me so I could have had so many sweet kisses. Oh, Darling, Dearest, if any one mistreats you, let me know and I will be there in a short time and face them.

Goodnight, Sweet Darling. I will write as soon as I get home.

Your Husband

XXX

[Leake's Store, Arkansas]

Saturday, October 2, 1858

My Darling,

I reached home last Wednesday, finding all well, which was more than I expected. Dr. Salmon was called in once to see Francy. She was sick nearly all the time I was gone. She is one of the triflingest Negroes on the place. When you come home you may try Sally for a cook, and I will try and whip the stealing propensities out of her as I'm such a good hand to whip.

Murphy has a girl and it is doing finely and she is out at work.

I have got out twenty-five bales of cotton and ten or twelve more to pick, which will make thirty-five or -seven bales. I found the cotton much better than I anticipated, finding the crops so short in Arkansas. Your father, Mister [Thomas Jefferson] Watts, and Daniel [Godbold] will make between twenty and twenty-five bales.[14]

Dr. Fort of Bowie is dead. No other deaths that I have heard of. The health of the country is very good at present.

Mr. Blain and all his friends that come out with him from Virginia started back last Thursday, and he carried the remains of his wife with him.[15] He gave a tinner fifty dollars to come up from Jefferson and put a tin case over the coffin. He taken it in his wagon.

Darling, I am fearful that you won't be able to get up Red River. There has not been any rain here since I left, and no prospect for any. The garden is gone. Not a vegetable to be had but potatoes, and they are sorry. What will you do if Red River is down when you get to New Orleans, which I know will be the case? Dear, I fear you will not wait for me to come for you.

Mrs. Connally has not been home from Linden but once since you left. Clemmie [Watson] has an heir, and I heard that she was stone blind.

I'm going over into Bowie tomorrow. Your father will start back home in the morning, and I will send this letter by him as you will receive it some sooner.

Dearest, if your watch does not run, you must make them take it back and you go to Tiffany's and get you another.

Remember me to some of the Spiritualists[16] of the college, and tell Dr. Trall that he must write how you are getting on, and you must write how they are treating you now, and if they use any caustic on you.[17]

I am in fine health at present and hoping when these few lines reach you, you will be fit and perfectly well. So, farewell until next week, when I will write you again.

Your David

XXX

Hydropathic College
New York, October 8th, 1858

If I am to be denied the pleasure of your dear presence and communication, my own Dear Husband, I will most faithfully make use of the only substitution. I can't wait until Saturday, my usual mail day, but must tell you this moment how I long to "see thee," "hear thee," and "feel thou near."

There are times when I feel as if I can't contain myself longer without you, and then I can stand it fully well. Is it not so at times with you, Dearest? Don't think, my Darling, I am complaining and fretting because of our separation. I am trying to content myself, though I know that I am not getting well. My strength is improving and general health. I suppose I would weigh ten pounds more than when I came, yet the irritation and discharge keep up, quite bad at times. The caustic which Mrs. Smalley has used from time to time does nothing as yet to heal the inflammation.

Dr. Gordon asked me many questions about myself last week and tells me this evening that he has been studying my case ever since he investigated, and says the disease is chronic inflammation of the uterus, urethra. In short, childhood chronic inflammation of the generative organs, and that is what I've long believed it to be, though no one has ever mentioned it to me before. Mrs. Smalley had examined me two or three times without ever finding out what was the matter.

I suppose I offended her and Dr. Trall both by complaining to Doctor and Mrs. Gordon, but I do not care as the latter—both—have been more attentive to me than anyone here. I shall ever remember them kindly.

There is one way only, My Dear, to be cured, and that will take time and patience—more, I fear, of both than I shall have.

I regret to tell you, Dear, of the burning of the Chrystal [sic] Palace. Yes, it is too true, and nothing now remains but ashes and ruins of what was seemingly to me the perfection of art this time last week. I thought I should never get to see it. I could get no one to go with me for the first two weeks after the opening, and at last a Mrs. Hindman (who resides in the northern part of the state and who had been home for the week) and I concluded we would go in the afternoon and spend the evening, which we did Saturday last, taking our supper with us, and a most pleasant time we had and now how glad I am that I accepted her invitation to go with her as it was on the 5th—yesterday—entirely destroyed. Just think of all the beautiful statuary, furniture, jewelry, embroidery, etc., being consumed. It is thought to be the work of an incendiary.[18]

October 7—Doctor and Mrs. Gordon and myself went last evening to the Academy of Music. Mrs. Gordon concluded as she did not get to the Crystal Palace at all, and that perhaps the opera might be burned up, too, before she could see, and so she told the doctor that night she would, whether he would or not accompany us, and we had a most pleasant time though the opera was in Italian. Yet the music was good, as was the performance, and the building was the nicest of the kind I ever saw and by far the largest.

We had a rainy, gloomy day after a few of the most pleasant I have seen in New York. Yesterday was particularly brilliant, warm, and pleasant. If the sky remains this way long, I shall count the days until I reach my dear Southern home and all that is dearest, warmest, and most genial to the poor wanderer.

Five weeks from this day I trust will be "taking sail" and then "for a soft and gentle breeze" to bear me "speedily on."[19] I hope to meet with acquaintances

New York's Crystal Palace, Library of Congress Prints and Photographs Division, Washington, DC.

in New Orleans going up Red River, which I probably shall. There is some of my Arkansas acquaintances in the city now, at least I notice the name of Arrington in the list of arrivals at the Astor. I used to trade some with him in Camden.[20]

Mrs. Hettrick was here to see me this evening. Though it was storming without, we had sunshine within whilst she was in. She brought it.

You don't know, Dear, what a heroine I am getting to be—that is, to what I've ever been before. The strong-minded ones think me quite cowardly, yet I go out once or twice every day and have most accomplished my shopping. That is my money.

I shall be afraid to sail home with less than one-hundred and perhaps fifteen or twenty over. I'm going next week to have my teeth fixed. Have been waiting for someone to go up to Tenth Street but shall wait no longer.

Mrs. Farnham left this evening, and I afraid the house will lose its dignity. I don't see how it will stand the removal of so gigantic a pillar. I did not know when she left. We have authors and authoresses, the [illegible] Philosophes. In short, they include the bone and sinew of the new school that must so "congregate here."[21]

Do not let this frost kill my flowers and write me a word about the corn crop. I feel uneasy about it. My poor pen won't write without my using all strength.

Take good care of my Husband. Write often. Give my love to all friends, and kiss little Ruth for me. Farewell for the present, Dearest and Best of Husbands,

Most truly and devotedly,

Your Rachi

XXX

Forest Home, Texas, October 9th, 1858

My Darling Wife,

It has been one month since I heard from you. I am so uneasy, fearful that you are sick and not able to write, but if you was sick I know that you would get someone to write for you. I shall go to the office in the morning and I hope that I will get a letter from you. Oh, I am so anxious to hear from you.

Oh Dear, you may look for me by the 15th of next month if I can arrange my matters so I can come. If I come, I will return through South Carolina. The heirs wants me to come that way and buy Nancy Bell's lifetime interest in those Harrison Negroes, and then you can see the Old South State, which you have been so anxious to see.[22] But when you see it, I do not think that you will ever want to see it again. I think it is one of the last states in the Union.

I was over in Bowie this week and found all well. James Moore gained the will case in the District Court. The heirs is taking it up to the Supreme Court. I do not know how it will terminate there, but I am in hopes that the court may confirm it.[23]

I will make forty bales of cotton, and I won't have more than two-hundred bushels of corn to buy, and I can buy that for $100, so I think that I will be able to buy a cook for you or buy a boy and put in Eli's place and you can make him a cook. I can't stand Francy any longer. I shall send her Monday morning in the field to picking cotton and take Nancy in and try her till you get home. I've not had anything fit for a dog to eat since I came home, and do not expect to have anything fit to eat until you get home.

None of the Negroes' clothing has been made.

There has not been any rain here since you left. I have got out more cotton that I made last year. I went up to the mill yesterday at put in a bill for the battening ram and yard, but I am fearful that I won't be able to hire any workman to do the work. I'm going on Monday and try to hire someone to do the job.[24]

Betty Fore is married at last, and Sam Elliott and Mrs. Holloway has been gone to Georgia about six weeks. Your particular old friend, Jerrod, wants you to bring him a spiritual book from New York.

I will let you know by the next letter whether I will come or not.

So, goodnight, Darling, with pleasant dreams, and rise and eat your pears and brown bread for breakfast and no meat.

Your David H. Moores

XXX

Hydropathic College, New York
October 14, 1858

Dearest Husband,
Your letter of the 27th September written from Arkansas has just been perused and impressed[?].

Your letters are the greatest solace I have. What would I, could I, do without them? Nothing short of your dear presence would compensate for them.

I am so happy to hear of your good health and safe trip to near our own home! I trust you had a combination of such blessings and are now enjoying of all the comforts a home affords (save the company of a wife).

I regret to think of Red River being down so low and no prospect of a rise. I watch the papers constantly in regard to the rise and fall of water and cotton. I have only four weeks longer to stay, so I hope by that the fall's rain may be abundant. I will not, however, put you to the trouble of coming if after me, even if the rivers are down and I have to go by way of Gaines Landing. You have been put to more trouble already for me than half dozen such as I am worth.

Sometimes I almost feel contempt for myself and wonder why I cumber the ground. I thought that when I married you, my Dear, I would prove a blessing—felt great confidence I should contribute to your pleasures. But, oh, me, what pain, what anguish, it has been mine to know that I must necessarily be a hindering [illegible] a [illegible] to your enjoyment, yet I crave your heart's purest and undivided devotion. I cannot live without your love. One frown from you and I am undone. Some approbation is the only [illegible] that elicits in me a love of life.

I am, in health, as usual. I do not feel any change since last week. Have been having some work done on my teeth. That makes me a little nervous. My front under-teeth, the ones I was so solicitous about, the dentist thinks can't be filled. Says they are so sensitive and so decayed that filling would destroy the tooth quite as soon as it is going anyway. I'm very sorry they can't be filled as I hate the idea of losing them so much. I had one back tooth filled and am going tomorrow to have another.

I am glad you did not get the smith you spoke of, as I think him dear, or any Negro, at that price. I wish we could get a girl, though, a sprightly young girl. However, we can get on quite so well without.

Since I wrote you last, one of the Misses Ewerts called, which was Saturday, and on Sunday I attended Dr. Alexander's church with them and called again this week. They are so kind and warm hearted. Insisted so much on my spending the day, afternoon, or evening with them. I intend taking tea with them soon. They say they like the Southern people so much better than Northerners. Their father is a gentle and nice old man. Says he will call on me often. The young ladies teach school, and consequently haven't much time, but say they will go with me to the blind asylum and various other places I haven't been to. I am glad they found out where I am.

Mr. King left here Saturday last. Is boarding at the Clarendon House. He came to my door to bid me goodbye and said he would be most happy to serve me if I should need a favor. He said he did not improve much, though he gets his board from here, yet, I think.

You would be amused at Mrs. Gordon, here from Toledo, Ohio. She has taken a great fancy to me. Says she would go home with me if she could arrange her business to suit her. Says she would enjoy being lazy and waited upon like the Southern ladies. Says she would like a little darkey to trot after her.

We have considerable sport together. I tease her about "Yankee notions" and she me about indolent Southern ladies. I tell the reason we are so indolent: the men are good. They won't let us work. Mrs. Gordon says she will have no one but a Southerner, if she can rid of Dr. Gordon. She is kind and accommodating to me, but, oh, what a willful wife she makes. It makes me feel dreadful to see the little respect she has for him, and he is no better, and I tell her they won't let her [illegible] them. I know that is what she wanted.

Mary Ann left this morning. I suppose they were putting more on her than she could well do, and this morning Mrs. Porter and I bathed and dressed without a fire. Lizzie said she knows nothing of her, and at breakfast Mrs. Gordon asked if she were in my room. I said no one had had no fire, so they went to look her up but could not find her, so she was out probably looking for a situation. Her things were all packed up, and I suppose she is gone. I am sorry. She was a faithful, good creature and had a great deal to do, which she did faithfully.

You ought to be here at the grand dances they have in the Sultan Room. Mrs. Harrison, Mrs. Morrison, and I attend as spectators. I never saw such ungainly creatures as most of them are. The Bloomer cuts a high dashes[?].[25]

It is growing so dark I can't see, so I will have to bid my Darling Husband a pleasant evening. If I could see, I would write for hours, but supper is near ready and I want to get this off before. I know it is not worthwhile to ask you to write to your ever faithful,

Rachi

XXX

Home, October 17th, 1858

My Darling,

I have not received any letter from you since I got home. I know you write, but it takes a letter a ways to come. I was over the river the other day and Jane had received one from you and I was sorry to see that you was so despondent. Darling, you must cheer up or you never can get well. Oh, Darling, cheer up. I will be there by the 15th of November to bring you home, and I will take you through old South Carolina and Alabama. Oh, what a pleasant time we will have, traveling together through our home states. So, mend fast by that time so you can be stout and enjoy the trek.

Darling, I finished gathering my corn last evening. It turned out far beyond my expectations. I made two or three hundred bushels more than I've ever made before, and between forty and forty-five bales of cotton. If I could get it to market now, it would get me over $2000. So, Darling, don't you want for anything that you can buy. Get it. I will bring more money with me and we will take the shine off of the Carolinas when we get there.

Mrs. Gordon has just come in, bringing with her the sad intelligence of Dr. Read's death. He died of yellow fever in New Orleans where he was preaching most successfully. I am pained to hear it. Dr. Read was a fine specimen of a man, and you remember how kind and charming he was to me.

I suppose the Creoles, those who have never feared it before, are dying, and it is thought to be the real coolie fever—Chinese Coolie fever.

I shall not start home until I hear it is entirely abated. Mr. King was telling me a week or two since that it was different from anything that he's ever visited— New Orleans and that fever.[28]

I have quite a pleasant neighbor now in Mr. King's room—a Mrs. Frost. Mr. Frost is an American and she's a French woman. She is beautiful and quite accomplished. She amuses me sometimes with her descriptions of Africa. She spent some time there with her father in the French provinces.

Bathing hour is here, my paper is out, and I'm not half-done writing, though must quit. My ardent desire to see my Dear Husband will be granted soon, I trust. Until then, farewell.

Your own,

Rachi

XXX

Hydropathic College

New York

Sabbath Morning, October 24

Dear Husband,

I have just received a letter from you answering yours of [illegible] *home. The state of health of the Negroes etc. for which blessing I thank my Most Gracious and Heavenly Parent.*

Your plan to come for me now, my dearest and best of husbands, I am not willing you should take that trouble, fatigue, and expense. There is no [two words illegible] I have before [illegible]. I can go alone, I'm sure. Everyone tells me how I will have no trouble in going by steamboat. Place myself under the care of the Captain and all will be right. I feel that you are needed at home just now to have comforts made, etc. for your wife.

I received a letter from Sister Margaret at the time I answered yours. Sister is thinking of coming with you. Write when you are thinking of coming for me, but much as I would like to have her come, yet I do not want you to come for me. I feel that I would save you of any trouble I could [illegible] I am willing to suffer for your sake if [illegible]ing alone produces it.

Mr. King is going in three weeks and I probably [illegible] may go on the same steamer. I should like to meet with acquaintances and think I shall.

I long to see Mrs. Hettrick [illegible] her gentle—a pleasant time. Her adopted daughter gave me some nice music. I spend as much time as possible outdoors. Poor Mrs. Parker[?] is having such a dreadful time with her [illegible]. They are applying things now to [illegible] the [illegible] parts and she is in great agony. Oh, women, what a suffering lot is thine? [Two words illegible] this [illegible] reminds me of the torture Dr. Hobson inflicted on me. But what was pain for? For the sake of the money he was getting. God forgive him, I pray.

I went to hear Chapin today. He was sick, and Gilmore [?] of Boston occupied the stand. I suppose he is considered quite a talented man, but I was sorry Chapin was sick as it was the first time I ever went to hear a Universalist, and Chapin stands out as the head of the Universalist Church. The text was "Our Father who art in Heaven," of course. Such a text as that afforded a rich field for the Universalist.[29]

I am grieved to hear of Clemmie Watson's very great misfortune. Dear me, what is she to do with a growing family, poor woman. I so pity her and her mother. But one blessing . . . Mrs. Connally bears afflictions with so much Christian

Aunt Lucy said that she was anxious to see you. I told her that you was a great talker, so you must keep up and be ready for her when you get there. I know you will be perfectly disgusted with old South Carolina and never will want to see it again.

I think of starting this day two weeks and it will take ten or twelve days to make the trek. I'm going to the office in the morning and meet the mail, so I know that I will hear from my Sweet Darling once more.

I've nothing new to write, so give my respects to all abolitionists and spiritualists of the college. So, all well and I and in hopes that these few lines may find you so. So, goodbye Darling, until you see me, and in hopes that will be shortly.[26]

Your most affectionate

Husband,

D. H. Moores

XXX

Hydropathic College, New York

Thursday morning, October 21, 1858

Dearest Husband,

The most pleasant task is before me. Yes, My Love, if all the duties which devolve on me were as cheerfully performed as this one, what a world of bliss could be mine. My nights here would then be as radiant as this blessed bright morning. But instead of feeling so exuberant in spirits as I would like, am a little gloomy in consequence of not getting a letter from you for a little more than a week. I have only received three since you left and have written eight to you.

I will not keep you in suspense longer, as I know what you most eagerly look for in my letters. I feel just as usual, but look a little better, so the bo[a]rders *fortitude I often think what a brighter crown will be hers. Remember me most affectionately to her and all the family.*[30]

Dear, had you not better have our chimney lengthened somewhat to keep it from smoking? It won't hurt the looks, I think, and will be much more comfortable in the dining room, etc. I hope you will not forget to have the house well aired.

If Red River is down, I will go up the Mississippi and get Pa to send me home and do as you said in regard to shipping my things to Jefferson, but I do hope the river will be up though we don't have any rain here. I never saw such a fall. I know this will be about the last letter you will get, though I will write whilst I travel. Oh, what a joyous thrill I feel at the thoughts of leaving.

Always, your affectionate
Rachi

XXX

NATIONAL TELEGRAPH

PITTSBURGH, CINCINATTI, LOUISVILLE, ST. LOUIS, MEMPHIS, NEW ORLEANS

WEST AND SOUTH

OFFICE, TELEGRAPH BUILDING, 21 WALL-STREET

NEW YORK

Dated Huntsville, Nov 8, 1858

Received 8

To Mrs. D. H. Moores

15 Laight St.

I will be there on thirteenth.

DHM

XXX

Act of Sale

State of Louisiana

Justice, Union and Confidence

Be it known, that on this, the fourth day of December, Eighteen Hundred and Fifty-Eight, we, Owings and Charles of Hamburg and Greenville District, State of South Carolina, for and in consideration of the sum and price of nine-hundred and twenty-five dollars, cash in hand, to us well and truly paid, the receipt whereof we hereby acknowledge and grant acquittance in full therefore, do, by these presents grant, bargain, sell, convey, transfer, assign, and let over, with a full guarantee against all troubles, debts, mortgages, claims, evictions, donations, alienations, or other encumbrances whatsoever, unto

D. H. Moores

of Cass County, State of Texas

A certain Negro girl named Elizabeth, about twelve years of age, whom we hereby fully guarantee in title, and against the prohibitory vices and maladies prescribed by law, as also a slave for life.

Owings and Charles

Attest: I. I. Poindexter

Attest: Hugh O'Neill

NOTES

[1] Although this entry is dated February 11, 1859, it retrospectively describes the events of June 1858 through February 1859 and so is placed in that sequence.

[2] Rachel's brother-in-law, Eli Harrison Moores, was born on April 2, 1815, at Thorn Creek, Fairfield District, South Carolina. In 1841, Eli Moores saw military service for the Republic of Texas, for which on October 7 of that year he received an additional 320 acres in Bowie County. When, on November 7, 1847, Eli Moores married Minerva Ann Janes at the Harrison Chapel, "in consideration of natural love and affection," as a

wedding gift Charles Moores deeded to the couple a 188-acre tract located on the western outskirts of the present city of Texarkana with the plantation home, known as the Moores–Watts–Pryor House, at what is now 1609 New Boston Road. The couple became the parents of four sons and four daughters: Mary Harrison "Nannie" (Mrs. John C. Watts), Charles Harrison, William "Buck" Massack, Eli Harrison Moores Jr., Thomas B., Sarah B. "Sallie" Moores Clements, and Minerva Ann Moores Collum. Moores served as postmaster at Mooresville and, during the Civil War, as a private in Capt. James M. Nelson's company of the Seventh Battalion, Texas State Troops. According to family lore, Eli Moores traded a yoke of oxen and a wagon for a claim to 160 acres of land on which much of the west side of Texarkana now lies. According to his grandson, David Moores Watts, Eli Moores owned as many as 1,500 head of cattle, 1,500 range horses, 2,000 hogs, and a large number of sheep.

When the Texas and Pacific Railroad projected its line to Texarkana, Moores deeded to the railway not only the land for trackage and right-of-way, but ground for a new city as well. He also donated sites for the First Baptist Church, to the Sacred Heart Catholic Church, and the First Presbyterian Church. The couple is also said to have donated lots for two African American churches. Eli Moores died on March 10, 1885, at the age of sixty-nine and is buried in the Harrison Chapel Cemetery at Redwater, Texas.

Minerva Ann Janes, born on January 13, 1829, at Fisher's Prairie, Arkansas, was the daughter of Massack and Nancy Stephenson Janes. Minerva's father, Massack Janes, emigrated to Texas from Missouri in 1811 and was the second citizen in Wavell's Colony of the State of Coahuila y Texas. When his daughter Elizabeth married Charles Moores Rochelle, a grandson of Charles and Mary Moores, Janes gave them the land on which Charles built their home. Minerva Ann Janes died on June 8, 1868, and is buried in Harrison Chapel Cemetery. Walter W. Thornton, *History of The First Baptist Church, Texarkana, Texas, Commemorating its Semi-Sesquicentennial* (Texarkana, TX: 1952), 75; "Eli Moores, Bowie County Pioneer, Owner [*sic*] Land Where City of Texarkana Now Stands." Unidentified newspaper clipping in Moores papers, Museum of Regional History, Texarkana, Texas; "Direct Descendants of Charles Moores and Allied Families to Have Gay Reunion Sunday," *Texarkana Daily News*, January 26, 1958; Texas, Muster Roll Index Cards, 1838–1900; *Official Register of the United States, Containing a List of the Officers and Employees in the Civil, Military, and Naval Service Together with a List of Vessels Belonging to the United States*, vol. 2 (1905), 303.

[3] Dr. Samuel H. Bayless was born in Tennessee in 1823. In 1832, he married Eugenie E. Brown and following her death in 1880 he married Dezzina Brown. Doctor Bayless died in 1888 and is buried in the Rose Hill Cemetery, Hope, Arkansas.

[4] Until the rise of the cattle industry after the Civil War, pork was the meat of choice of most Americans. The British social commentator Harriet Martineau, traveling across the United States in 1834, found hog meat ubiquitous and inescapable. In Boston, she "never once saw an ounce of meat except ham," and in the South, she wrote, "the traveler meets little else than pork, under all manner of disguises." Harriet Martineau, *Society in America*, vol. 2 (London: Saunders and Otley, 1837), 203.

[5] The St. Nicholas Hotel at 507–527 Broadway in Manhattan's SoHo district opened on January 6, 1853, and immediately became New York's preeminent luxury hotel. By the later part of the nineteenth century, with most tourists preferring to stay farther uptown, the hotel had declined in popularity, and by the mid-1870s parts of the building were converted to other uses.

[6] The New York Water Cure Hydropathic and Physiological School was founded by Russell Thacher Trall, M.D., on October 1, 1853, at 15 Laight Street, in New York City, one of the first medical schools in the United States to admit women candidates for the Doctor of Medicine degree. In or about 1869 the school was moved to Florence, New Jersey, and continued in operation until 1875 when it was offered for sale.

[7] Advertising material printed on envelope from the Water Cure and Hydropathic Medical College. Moores papers, Museum of Regional History, Texarkana, Texas.

For another woman's experience with the water cure, see Catherine E. Beecher, *Letters to the People on Health and Happiness* (New York, NY: Harper and Brothers, 1855), 112–20.

8   Longtown, a small community in Fairfield County, South Carolina, was David Moores' birthplace and the home of the Moores family prior to its relocation to Texas.

9   David H. Moores' aunt, Lucy W. Harrison of Fairfield, South Carolina, was born in or about 1795. She was the wife of John Harrison.

10   Several steamboats named *Eclipse* plied the waters of the Mississippi River, but this seems to have been the one constructed in 1852 at New Albany, Indiana. A sidewheel, wooden hull packet, 350-feet in length and weighing 1,117 tons, she was constructed at a cost of $375,000. Documents claimed the *Eclipse* was "the fastest steamboat in the world," having made the run from New Orleans to Louisville in four days, nine hours, and thirty minutes. In May 1853, the *A. L. Shotwell*, in her great race with the *Eclipse*, made the run from New Orleans to Cairo in three days, three hours and forty minutes, whereas the *Eclipse*'s time was three days, four hours and four minutes. She was damaged beyond repair at New Orleans in 1860 when she was blown from the levee into the path of another boat. *New Orleans Picayune*, July 7, 1838.

11   Rachel here paraphrases a line from Thomas Moore's poem, "When I Love You."

12   Fanny Fern, the pen name of Sara Willis (July 9, 1811–October 10, 1872), was an American novelist, children's writer, humorist, and newspaper columnist in the 1850s to 1870s, writing for a mostly middle-class female readership. By 1855, Fern was the highest-paid columnist in the United States, commanding $100 per week for her *New York Ledger* column. *Fern Leaves from Fanny's Portfolio*, a collection of her columns published in 1853, sold 70,000 copies in its first year. Her best-known work, the fictional autobiography *Ruth Hall* (1854), has become a popular subject among feminist literary scholars.

13   Leake's Store was in Columbia County, Arkansas. Its post office opened in 1848 and closed in 1867.

14   Rachel's brother, Daniel Perry Godbold, was born on May 1, 1826, in Monroe County, Alabama. In 1850 he was living with his father's family in Harrison, Ouachita County, Arkansas. He was married to Lucretia Collins Johnson at Woodlawn, Ouachita County. Their children were Alice ("Allie"); William Nathan, born in Harrison, Arkansas, in or about 1852; Mary A. ("Mollie"), born in Harrison in or about 1855; May Hardin, born in or about 1857 in Harrison; and Margaret (or Margrett) Johnston, born in Harrison on April 9, 1860. Daniel Perry Godbold died on April 13, 1873, in Columbia, Arkansas, and is buried in the Watts Cemetery, Willisville, Nevada County, Arkansas.

15   For John Stephen Blain see Chapter 1, note 22.

16   Spiritualism was based on the belief that departed souls, having ascended into a spirit existence, could interact with the living. Such communion was thought to be both possible and desirable, with "spirit healing" as the result of spirit influence, and spiritualists sought to make contact with the dead. The beginnings of modern spiritualism may be traced to a series of apparently supernatural events at a farmhouse in Hydesville, New York, in 1848. Kate and Maggie Fox claimed to have established a code through which they could communicate with the spirit of a man who had been murdered in the house. News of the Fox sisters' "discovery" led to an explosion in spiritualist activity. Although church leaders associated spiritualism with witchcraft, séances became a popular pastime for both men and women in Victorian drawing rooms.

In 1851, researchers determined that the Fox sisters were producing the spirit's raping noises themselves and in 1888 they admitted that they had fabricated the entire experience, but this revelation in no way slowed the growth of the movement.

Rachel Moores seems to have been, at least to some degree, a believer in spiritualism. Shortly after she received the news of the death of her father, she wrote in her journal, "Oh, my father and mother, are you united in that world of spirits? Do you watch over the destiny of your erring children? Spirit of my departed parents, are you near me?" John Corrigan, *Business of the Heart: Religion and Emotion in the Nineteenth Century* (Berkeley: University of California Press, 2002); Robert C. Fuller, *Spiritual, but Not Religious: Understanding Unchurched America* (New York: Oxford University Press, 2002); Joseph F. Rinn, *Searchlight on Psychical Research* (London: Rider and Company, 1954); Robert Ellwood, "How New is the New Age," in *Perspectives on the New Age*, ed. James R. Lewis and J. Gordon Melton, (Albany, NY: SUNY Press, 1992).

17   Russell Thacher Trall, founder of the New York Hydropathic and Physiological School, was one of the first medical advocates of vegan nutrition. He died in 1877 and is buried in Florence, New Jersey.

18   Constructed in 1853 for the Exhibition of the Industry of All Nations, the Crystal Palace was designed in the shape of a Greek cross with arms measuring 365 feet in length and capped with a 100-foot diameter dome at its center. Walt Whitman judged it to be "unsurpassed anywhere for beauty and all other requisites of a perfect edifice." Although a replica of the building of the same name featured in London's Hyde Park during the Great Exhibition of 1851, it was, to the poet, "an original, esthetic, perfectly proportioned, American edifice." Located on 42nd Street between Fifth and Sixth Avenues, it was, at the time, the tallest building in the city.

The Palace was destroyed on October 5, 1858. Although constructed, as was its London prototype, primarily of iron and glass, the pitch pine that was used as flooring and in much of the framework "afforded a most inflammable pabulum for the conflagration to feed upon." The fire began in a lumber room on the side. Within fifteen minutes its dome collapsed, and in twenty-five minutes the entire structure had burned to the ground. No lives were lost, but the loss of property—which included the building, valued at $125,000, and statuary and other exhibits remaining from the World's Fair—amounted to more than $350,000. Walt Whitman, "Grand Buildings in New York," Brooklyn *Daily Times*, June 5, 1857; *New York Herald*, October 6, 1858.

19   *'Oh! For a soft and gentle breeze.'*
      I heard a fair maid cry –
      'But give to me the snorting breeze.
      And the wild wave hurling high!
      The wild wave curling high.
      The ship like an eagle free.'

20   A Robert Edgar Arrington is listed in the 1850 and 1860 US census as having been born in Nash County, North Carolina, on August 20, 1820, but was in 1858, employed as a merchant in Camden, Arkansas. The Astor, built in 1852 at the famed corner of Canal and Bourbon streets, is one of New Orleans' oldest hotels.

21   Eliza Farnham, an American novelist, feminist, abolitionist, and activist for prison reform, was born in Rensselaerville, New York, on November 17, 1815. She moved to Illinois in 1835, where she married Thomas Jefferson Farnham, an explorer and author of the American West, but returned to New York in 1841 following her husband's death. In 1844, through the influence of Horace Greeley, she was appointed matron of the women's ward at Sing Sing Prison. She advocated the use of music and kindness in the rehabilitation of female prisoners, was a strong advocate of the use of phrenology to treat prisoners and was influential in changing the types of reading materials available to female prisoners as a means of improving their character. Her methods were highly controversial, and in 1848, Farnham resigned as matron and moved to Boston where she was for a while connected with the Institution for the Blind.

She resided in California from 1849 until 1856, when she returned to New York. For the two years following, she devoted herself to the study of medicine, and in 1859 organized a society to assist destitute women in finding homes in the West. She died from consumption in New York City on December 15, 1859. Among her writings are *Life in the Prairie Land* (1846), *California, In-doors and Out* (1856), *My Early Days* (1859), an autobiographical novel *Woman and Her Era* (1864), which she identified as an "organic, religious, esthetic, and historical" argument for the inherent superiority of women, and *The Ideal Attained* (1865), a novel in which the heroine "molds the hero into a worthy mate." Jo Ann Levy,

Unsettling the West: Eliza Farnham and Georgiana Bruce Kirby in Frontier California (Berkeley, CA: Heyday Books; 2004.)

[22] According to the 1850 United States census, Nancy Bell, who was born in or around 1810, was the widow of J. H. Bell, a planter in Fairfield County, South Carolina.

[23] James C. Moore was born on May 4, 1814, in Charleston, South Carolina. By September 6, 1841 he had emigrated to Bowie County, and on November 20, 1849, received a grant of 640 acres. On February 24, 1840, he married Rachel's sister-in-law Jane Ross Moores. The couple became the parents of six children.

Moore served as sheriff of Bowie County from 1854 until 1856. According to family lore, Moore "always managed to get the family land." He is said to have instructed the slave he took with him when he asked Charles Moores for the hand of his daughter to say, when asked how many slaves he owned, "'Me and 40 more.' Thereafter, the slave was called 'Forty.'" James C. Moore died on August 8, 1893, in Paris, Texas.

[24] A battening ram is the heavy swinging bar on a loom that holds the reed and is pulled forward to pack down the weft.

[25] In October 1849, the *Water-Cure Journal*, a popular health periodical, began urging women to develop a style of dress that was not so harmful to their health. The garment takes its name from its best-known advocate, the women's rights activist Amelia Bloomer. By the summer of 1850 bloomers were being worn by readers of the *Water-Cure Journal* as well as women patients at the nation's health resorts. During the summer of 1851, the nation was seized by a "bloomer craze." The April 15, 1859, issue of *The Sibyl Magazine* extoled the virtues of the new fashion:

And now I'm dressed like a little girl, in a dress both loose and short,
Oh, with what freedom I can sing, and walk all 'round about!
And when I get a little strength,
some work I think I can do.
'Twill give me health and comfort,
and make me useful too.

Conservative authorities, of course, denounced the wearing of pants by women as a usurpation of male authority, citing Deuteronomy 22:5: "The woman shall not wear that which pertaineth unto a man, neither shall a man put on a woman's garment: for all that do so are abomination unto the Lord thy God." On November 3, 1860, an editorial in the *New Orleans Daily Delta* declared that the much-despised Republican Party was composed of "infidels and freelovers, interspersed by Bloomer women, fugitive slaves, and amalgamationists." Catherine Smith and Cynthia Greig, *Women in Pants: Manly Maidens, Cowgirls, and Other Renegades* (New York: Harry N. Abrams, 2003); Gayle V. Fischer, *Pantaloons and Power: Nineteenth-Century Dress Reform in the United States* (Kent, OH: Kent State University Press, 2001).

[26] This letter, posted on October 29, 1858, was mailed postage free the with the notation D. H. M. P[ost] M[aster]

[27] "Vain and Fleeting All Things Here Below" is the title of a hymn by Isaac Watts. Its first verse is:

How vain are all things here below!
How false, and yet how fair!
Each pleasure hath its poison too,
And every sweet a snare.

[28] Yellow fever is a viral infection transmitted by the *Aedes aegypti* mosquito. The first yellow fever epidemic in New Orleans occurred in 1796 when 638 people (out of a population of 8,756) died from the disease. In the 100-year period between 1800 and 1900, yellow fever struck New Orleans for sixty-

seven summers. Its main victims were immigrants and newcomers to the city, and for this reason it was also referred to as the "stranger's disease." The worst epidemic years were 1847, 1853, 1854, 1855, and 1858. In 1858, 4,845 deaths occurred, the second highest on record between 1817, when reliable records were first kept, and the last epidemic in 1905. In the summer of 1853, generally considered the worst year of the epidemic, 29,120 people contracted the disease and 8,647 died. By the end of the epidemic, approximately one out of every twelve people had died from yellow fever in New Orleans alone.

During the Spanish–American War, the US army sent Dr. Walter Reed to Cuba to study the cause and effects of yellow fever on American troops. In 1900, Doctor Reed verified that the disease was transmitted by the common mosquito, which bred in any open water container. George Augustin, *History of Yellow Fever* (New Orleans, LA: Searcy and Pfaff, 1909); Jo Ann Carrigan, "Impact of Epidemic Yellow Fever on Life in Louisiana," *Louisiana History* 5, no. 2 (Spring 1964): 5–34; Jo Ann Carrigan, "Privilege, Prejudice, and the Stranger's Disease in Nineteenth-Century New Orleans," *The Journal of Southern History* 36, no. 4 (Summer 1962): 568–78; Edward Jenner Coxe, *Practical Remarks on Yellow Fever, Having Special Reference to the Treatment* (New Orleans, LA: J. C. Morgan, 1859); John Duffy, *Sword of Pestilence: The New Orleans Yellow Fever Epidemic of 1853* (Baton Rouge: Louisiana State University Press, 1966); Donald E. Everett, "The New Orleans Yellow Fever Epidemic of 1853," *Louisiana Historical Quarterly* 33, no. 4 (October 1950): 380–405.

[29] Edwin Hubbell Chapin (December 29, 1814–1880) was a preacher and editor of the *Christian Leader*. After graduating from a seminary at Bennington, Vermont, he was ordained in 1838 and in 1848 became pastor of the Church of the Divine Paternity, later the Fourth Universalist Society in the City of New York. There he served for more than thirty years, drawing crowds of almost 2,000 each Sunday.

Chapin became widely known as an orator and author of works including *Duties of Young Women, Discourses on the Lord's Prayer, Moral Aspects of City Life*, and *Humanity in the City*. He was also the author of the poem "Ocean Burial," which was published in September 1839 in Edgar Allan Poe's *Southern Literary Messenger*. It became the basis for the popular cowboy ballad, "Bury Me Not on the Lone Prairie." Summer Ellis, *Life of Edwin H. Chapin, D.D.* (Boston, MA: Universalist Publishing House, 1882).

[30] This "affliction" was the death of the Watson's newborn daughter.

chapter three

TIME WAS SPENT MOST DELIGHTFULLY

April–July 1859

Despite her ardent desire to return home, once Rachel left the Hydropathic and Physiological School in November 1858, she remained in Cass County for only four months before she was off again, first visiting her family in Columbia County, Arkansas, in April 1859. Her letters to David from Arkansas contain, for the most part, news of her father's chronic ill health and her own, asking her husband rhetorically, "who knows better what a living death is?"

Then, in May, she and David embarked on an extended holiday, lasting until July 1859. Sailing from New Orleans, the couple first returned to New York and Rachel's "old recruiting establishment—the water cure college," by way of Cuba, that "Gem of the Sea."

Her journal entries detailing her journey North, written retrospectively in December 1859, are largely a travelogue. Having visited Central Park, which was then only beginning to be laid out, they left New York for a tour through New England and on to Canada. "Stopping as we did only at first class hotels," they visited Saratoga Springs, New York, where she and David "both benefited and delighted with the water and people"; New Haven, Connecticut, which did not much impress her although she found Yale College "inviting"; Newport, Rhode Island, which she found to be "a place of transcendental beauty"; and was "much disappointed in Boston," seeing "nothing but what I would call a mud puddle." At Bunker Hill, however, she experienced "soul thrilling emotions," and found Harvard to be "the most attractive seat of learning I've ever seen." She was delighted by Long Island Sound, with its "picturesque hills and luxurious valleys." They journeyed on to Portland, Maine, by way of Lynn, Salem, Beverly, Newburyport, and Portsmouth, Massachusetts. From Maine they journeyed on to the White Mountains of New Hampshire, where Rachel was thrilled by the scenery, and then on to Quebec, where her journal abruptly ended.

Although she did become acquainted with "a party of Boston ladies" who "proved themselves most agreeable companions," in general Rachel was not impressed by the New England character, being put off by "the presumptuous Yankee" who "tries to laugh and make sport of our rough backwardness when they have so much verdancy at home."

XXX

[Rachel P. Moores to David H. Moores]

Western Retreat, Columbia County, Arkansas
Tuesday morning, April 3, 1859

I made a little visit last evening which prevented my beginning the week's Journal, and as I think of doing the same this afternoon, I will seize the present moment. Sunday morning after concluding and sending your letter to the office, Pa grew rather worse and Dr. Hobson was sent for. He pronounced it a case of chills and fever, but said it was dangerous for him to have another and, of course, gave him quinine.

But Pa became extremely ill yesterday morning and would get out. Soon turned very sick, went to bed, and remained there all day, but was soon better. When I started to Brother Thomas's in the evening, was considerably better, but this morning is having a little trouble just now with his head.[1]

How perfectly delighted I was to hear in Jane's letter of the 24th all that you had moved near home and was in "such fine spirits." I'm sorry to say, though, all her news was not so pleasant. The murder she writes of is one of the most shocking the mind can conceive of.

Wednesday morning,

I did not make my visit to Brother Daniel's as I anticipated last evening, Dear. Pa grew so much worse I would not go. Dr. Hobson was sent for, and he remained with him until nine of the clock. He stimulated him very freely, and mother said he rested well until daylight when he had another spell. He is now very weak and feeble. Poor Dear Pa, who knows better how he feels than I do; who knows better what a living death is?

You ought, My Love, to have heard Dr. Hobson talking to me about my health last night. He says if I will go to a Scientific man, for instance Dr. Meigs or Hodge of Philadelphia, they will cure me at once, or tell me what is the matter with me.[2] He laughs at the idea of the doctors I've been to, and says they are hooted at by sensible doctors, and I laughed him and he at me, and he thinks me a fool and ditto, I think, and so the world goes.

A Mrs. Watts spent the day with me yesterday and Mrs. Pipkin is coming to Sister's and has sent for me to be there. If Pa gets no worse, I will go.

Are you still needing rain? Of what infinite advantage it would be here, just now. We haven't had a drop since you left, and a perfect hurricane we had last night. For a while, I thought the top would be blown off the house.

Our Dear Pa is much better tonight though. The house has been crowded with visitors all day. Two very nice young ladies spent the day and some [illegible] ladies. What a bustle they live in here, My Dear. How unlike our little quiet home.

Pa was well enough to set up some tonight. How very amusing it was to hear him telling the family how deeply in love he discovered me to be with you *when we met in New Orleans in Fifty-three. Said I [illegible] as to lose all control, and he ever after that period thought we might marry.*

Many, many dear kisses and a good night from
Your own
Rachi

Thursday morning.

A few moments ago, Frank drove in out here at Brother Dan's. Pa has been considerably better all day, and I thought best to make my stay here whilst he was on his feet; and, really, there is so much company at Pa's I get weary. Dr. Hobson, Dr. Barnes, and several others spent the day at Pa's. Sister's Negro was punished with her last old [illegible] and was gone [illegible] happy. It is dark, and I will close.[3]

Allie and myself have just retired to our room for the night, and while she is preparing for bed, I will tell you how well I've been all day. Why, My Love, I walked outside of the gate a few yards and eat cornbread and a little butter twice today but am amply repaid, however, in getting a little headache.

Allie sleeps with me and is so accommodating, and the children are untiring in their devotion and attention. May clings so and kisses me incessantly. Mollie sits near and often says tell Uncle David he must come back soon, and what do you suppose is my heart's response?[4]

I want to see you more as each moment flies, but then, my better judgment suggests the propriety of your remaining at home until we part no more soon. Oh, this severing of our very hearts' strings causeth the bitterest anguish! Who can tell? Only those who have felt it.

It grows cold, I must forbear; for your dear sake, I will. You always chide me for writing by lamplight. May the dearest of blessings rest on you, my own Dear, Dear Husband. May angels look down this night in tender mercy on us, separated in body but united in spirit.

Saturday evening,

"The day is passed and gone."[5] The sunset hour is here, holy, calm, and serene. Now, Dear, is such an hour for contemplation, sweet, but yet sad, and my thoughts of my Darling Husband.

When, Dearest, shall we meet? The middle or last of May was the time we set upon for you to come. Can I look for you then? Please do not delay your coming any longer than the middle of May, if convenient. If I am ever ready to travel, it will be then. I've been very well all day. Mollie came down this morning to see how I was getting on. She only stayed an hour or so. Mollie sends her best wishes and says she will hold you to your promise.

Tell Sister Jane I will write to her soon. Do, dearest, write me every week and come at the appointed time. Tell all the Negros howdy and be sure to tell them I'm mending.

With all the love a fond wife can bestow, I will ever remain, Your Rachi Pa is much better

XXX

Leake's Store, Arkansas
April 9th [1859]

Please, Dear, charge Nancy to be very particular about the yard, to keep it clean and nice. Mary Jane and Hank can't keep it so very clean. Hank has kept the grown turkeys in the garden as we did last year. He's not to suffer any chickens to come in the yard.

Be sure to bring all the things I wrote for. Give the Negros the clothes as I wrote and keep an account of all you give.

Bring my linen jaques.[6] It is in the bathroom wardrobe.

Tell Nancy to plant some squash seed the last of May without fail and attend to them carefully as I hope to be there the first of September to eat them. Also, plant corn and cucumbers.

Dear, please bring me some four of those Negro handkerchiefs. Where I have stayed the Negros and [illegible] have waited or rather cooked, etc. much [illegible]. I wish so to compensate them in a small way.

If I would think of your uncomfortable situation, I would be most miserable. All alone, no one near to comfort or administer the least kindness. No nice dinner or supper. You could make Nancy have you some nice dinners if you would. Do not forget your health, my love. Do not eat too much supper.

Good night for the present.

XXX

[from the Journal of Rachel P. Moores]

Yes. I have been upon "the ocean foam" for a week, have seen that "Gem of the Sea," Cuba, have traversed the streets of Havana and gazed upon its gray. time [illegible]. The Morro with its batteries and lighthouse; the Cabanas; the Casa Blanca! The "Castle of Atares"! and the "Castle of Principe," and the "Passo del Cason" surpasses any avenue I have seen in the United States, and I must think, any on the American continent.[7] It is embellished on either side with fountains, statuary, public gardens of the most exquisite flowers, shrubs, and ornamental trees the Passo is [illegible] miles in length, and very wide, with two carriageways and two footways, with rows of trees between [torn] object presented in our drive on the Paseo was [torn] with the garden of the richest and most beautiful of [torn] flowers, just in front of the Captain Yews.[8] But I must [torn] as I have neither time nor strength to describe half the impressions there were made in my mind in that curious city. As we only reached Havana just in time to be admitted into the harbor, just a few seconds before the sunset gun was fired, and only remained until noon the next day. We could see nothing of the country.

We reached New York in four days after leaving Havana and in eight days after leaving New Orleans, and long will it be remembered, for I suffered all the horrors of seasickness and it, added to my other infirmities, made me worse **[illegible]**, but immediately on arrival we made our way to our old recruiting establishment—the water cure college. We found, however, that it had changed hands, somewhat for the worse, but yet the fare was better, far better, than we could obtain at any hotel in New York.

Dr. Trall soon found out that we were there and called, and our good friends that Misses Ewerts called in a day or two as did Mr. and Mrs. Hettrick, Mrs. Gordon who had removed to an **[illegible]** on the Hudson called today whilst on a visit to the City. New York was but little changed since our last visit. The Central Park is rapidly improving. We rolled out in time to see the swans before they were poisoned, or supposed to be.[9]

New York's Central Park by George Hayward,
Manual of the Corporation of the City of New York, 1861.

As the Japanese arrived in New York whilst we were sitting at Goldwicks [Goldrick's?] for photographs, we were kindly offered a window and at this gallery, opposite the Metropolitan, and a full view of the reception. I scarcely know which was the more shocking sight—the lean, starving looking Japanese or the police beating back the eager street spectators.[10]

[torn] left New York on the 21st of December for Saratoga.

[December 25, 1859] [torn] we were both benefited and delighted with the water and people. I could not decide which charmed us more. The world-renowned Congress Spring deserves all that has been said in its favor, but still I gave my preference for the White.[11]

Leaving Saratoga on the 25th, we reached New York, for on that same day put up at [illegible] at the Griffin. Lived there until Wednesday noon, and then took the cars for New Haven. We only remained in this "City of Elms" one day and night. I was somewhat disappointed in the look of [illegible]—really saw nothing to admire except the broad, nice avenues and stately elms. The New Haven Hotel badly kept. The exterior of Yale College, I thought inviting. I really felt all the time I was in my uncomfortable quarters at the hotel that I would have liked to have exchanged for ramble through the college grounds but walked myself down in the public s quare. As New Haven is only a semi-capital, I must think the State House a semi-State House.

Leaving New Haven at ten A.M. we take charming route along the margin of Long Island Sound—the "Shore Line." The scenery of Connecticut is delightful, beautifully diversified with picturesque hills and luxurious valleys.

We reached Newport just at four P.M., but as my traveling dress (a grey poplin) was almost ruined from the boat's machinery oil, I did not feel equal to the task of dressing—I did not leave my room until just before tea, but donned my dressing gown and sent my traveling dress to the laundry, but the cabin maid soon returned, saying it could not be cleaned, which perplexed me so much that I did not give her any pay or sent any to the laundry, which rude act I regret to this moment.

The "Ocean House," at which we stopped, was most delightfully situated on Bluff Street and is the most fashionable hotel in Newport. I felt this place all that it was represented to be, elegant and fashionable as a watering place, beautifully located. I might say, a place of transcendental beauty and many great, charming, attractive people. Though scarcely able to set up, yet I enjoyed a four hours' drive around the city, reviewing its picturesque attractions with the greatest zest.[12]

On the third day we left for Boston, reached there the same evening, Saturday the 30th of June. Was much disappointed in Boston. The city itself, that is, but was perfectly delighted with its suburban villages, residences, and cemetery, etc. One of the most interesting features was, to me, its numerous and lengthy bridges.

I saw absolutely nothing to admire in what is its citizens call their "Charming Public Parks and Boston Common." From the inviting pictures of children playing around the Common in Parley's History, I had thought how charming and delightful it must have been to set or run about under these grand old elms and be the sharer of such sports; but, dear me! surely "tis distance lends enchantment to the reader."[13] I saw nothing but what I would call a mud puddle. Why, near my own home are a number of lay [?] acres which far transcended this in every respect.

The old Cambridge Road [illegible] was over a grand old bridge, by Longfellow's evidence near the headquarters of General Washington by Cambridge college. We got out of the cars

Sketch of a May Pole found in the *Peter Parley's Common School History*, c. 1857.

here and walked over this college ground—of Harvard College. There are some twelve or fifteen buildings, buildings connected with or composing the university. One of them, Gore Hall, is the most imposing edifice, contains the college library in the form of a Latin cross. I cannot say with which I was most delighted, the appearances of Harvard as a college or Mount Auburn Cemetery, which I [torn] as a burial place. Altogether [torn] the most attractive seat of learning I've ever seen. The grounds are as beautiful, pleasant, inviting, and the buildings are "venerable" grand, and imposing, and when I have ever spent an hour of more melancholy sweetness than that in which we rambled over Mount Auburn Cemetery.

We next visited Bunker Hill Monument, which, of all places around Boston I considered the most worthy of a visit. Indescribable were the soul thrilling emotions experienced as I fell on my knees over the rock inscribed as the place where the heroic Warren fell.[14]

I could not for want of strength ascend the monument with my husband and so rambled over the enclosed hill after resting from the ascent up the "hill," as it is marked by nearly 300 steps. The first day after our arrival in the "City of Notions" we went to the First Baptist Church and heard Rev. Neal made quite an [two words eradicated].

[5 July 1859] *We bade adieu to the "Athens of America" and took the cars for Portland, Maine, via Lynn, Salem, Beverly, Newbury Port, Portsmouth, and reached Portland just at dark. Spent the "Fourth of July" very pleasantly at the Peeble House.*

I was considerably amused at the country crowd that gathered on the piazza to witness the military display and celebration generally. I really feel mortified for the presumptuous Yankee who tries to laugh and make sport of our rough backwardness when they have so much verdancy at home. I never saw such rude behavior anywhere through life as on the Portland cars, and very little refinement I saw in Portland. I mean as a general thing.

We took that Grand Trunk Railway ninety-one miles [to] Gorham, New Hampshire, to visit the White Mountains the evening of the fourth and reach there just in time to take a stroll to the beautiful, limpid, pebble-bottomed Androscoggin River. So transparent and refreshing did it look that I could hardly repress an inordinate desire, after this dusty days' travel, to play and take a primitive bath. I did go so far as I could find a rock [torn] my feet from the bottom and gather pebbles a number of times to take home.

We returned to our hotel (the Alpine House), where a super awaited that a king might court—fresh, hot light bread, all kinds of tea cakes, biscuits, strawberries, butter, etc.

The next morning, we took stage for the Glass House, seven miles distant in the valley of the Peabody River, immediately at the foot of Mount Washington. For a base view of the mountains, it is said that no location could be so desirable. From the front plaza, there is nothing to obscure the grandeur presented by the three noble, majestic looking, rock crowned summits of Washington, Jefferson, and Adams, and though it was the fifth of July, the summits were snow clad.

My infirmities kept me from joining the group as did my husband, that ascended Mount Washington on the morning of the sixth, though I regretted it much, yet I enjoyed myself exceedingly with a party of Boston ladies who, after finding out that I was from Texas, sought my acquaintance and proved themselves most agreeable companions during my husband's temporary absence. At the hotel did I ever reserve the kind attention of a host as I met with at the Glass House? In my rambling about at the house on the mountains I met up with a lady leading a child. She asked just after our meeting if I were not an invalid and on answering in the affirmative she set down on a log and asked me all the particulars about my disease and telling me of her own afflictions. In the course of the conversation I told her one of my maladies was dyspepsia and, of course, in traveling as extensively as I had since the first of May, it was impossible to meet with the proper regimen for that disease, stopping as we did only at first class hotels (she emphasized) where cream was only nominal and that was the only seasoning my mouth could digest.

"Oh," said she, "I think you might obtain cream pastries anywhere by calling for them."

I told her my calls had been all in vain, and so we parted feeling a mutual interest. But just as dinner was announced, she came to the parlor door and said, "Mrs. Moores would find some cream pastry when the desert course was served." Now wasn't it fortunate that I had told her. Mr. Thompson (her father) and the king of hotel keepers, not knowing at the time Mr. Thompson was her father but because the fare was the best I almost ever set down to in a private house or fashionable hotel, and sure enough I found my strawberry tart all that my "fancy had painted it." If not "lovely and divine," it was most palatable, and it was a sweet not without its bitter, for no sooner had my husband cut and helped my plate than I was asking to please extend it as it looked more inviting than the rest, but the waiter kindly presented me with another of the same make.

We took stage in the afternoon for the Alpine House and thence by cars to _____ and thence by stage to Lancaster where we spent the night at the magnificent Lancaster Hotel and got accommodations at a farmhouse two miles distant from Lancaster. The proprietor had his stage drive us before the door, and after our baggage and selves were seated, mounted the box and acted as postillion himself, soon arriving at the farmhouse of Mr. Spaulding, where we were attended for one week, which time was spent most delightfully.

Being so weary of tiresome, tedious hotel life, David and I had meals in a cozy little dining room alone and with the elder Mrs. Spaulding near and sometimes the old man, feasting on creamed biscuit, potato cakes, delicious strawberries, butter, etc.

David began to look doleful as the day of our departure approached, thinking I would insist on remaining longer, being so pleased, and he was half famished, he claimed, having only beefsteak, roast turkey, vegetables, etc. Employed one of Mr. Spaulding's sons to convey us to the depot, and in the afternoon of the 14th of July we started for Quebec.[15]

NOTES

[1] Rachel's father, Samuel Ananias Godbold, was an invalid, confined to his room from 1845 until his death in 1863.

[2] Charles Delucena Meigs, an American obstetrician, was born on February 19, 1792, in St. George, Bermuda, and was graduated in medicine at the University of Pennsylvania in 1817. He became professor of obstetrics and diseases of women at the Jefferson Medical College, Philadelphia, Pennsylvania, in 1841, serving until his retirement in 1861.

Meigs was an opponent of obstetric anesthesia, warning against the morally "doubtful nature of any process that the physicians set up to contravene the operations of those natural and physiological forces that the Divinity has ordained us to enjoy or to suffer."

He was, on the other hand, a staunch believer in the dangers of contagion that could be passed from physician to patient. "Then, for heaven's sweet sake," he wrote, "I implore you not to lay your impoisoned hands upon her who is committed to your science and skill and charitable goodness, only for her safety and comfort, and not that you should, after collecting fees, soon return her to her friends a putrid corpse." Meigs died in Philadelphia on June 22, 1869. He was the author of *Obstetrics: The Science and the Art* (Philadelphia, PA: Blanchard and Lea, 1856) and was the father of Montgomery C. Meigs (1816–1892), quartermaster general of the US Army during the American Civil War. Howard A. Kelly and Walter L. Burrage, eds., "Charles Delucena Meigs" in *American Medical Biographies* (Baltimore, MD: Norman, Remington Company, 1920).

Hugh Lenox Hodge was born in Philadelphia and attended Princeton College and the University of Pennsylvania School of Medicine. In 1823, he began teaching at the Medical Institute in Philadelphia, and in 1835 became Professor of Obstetrics and the Diseases of Women and Children at the University of Pennsylvania, where he remained until his retirement in 1863. He died in 1873. Hodge was the author of *The Principals and Practice of Obstetrics* (Philadelphia, PA: Blanchard and Lea, 1864). Thomas Herbert, "Hugh Lenox Hodge: A Master Mind in Obstetrical Science," *American Journal of Obstetrics and Gynecology*, 33:5 (May 1937), 886–92; William Goodell, *Biographical Memoir of Hugh L. Hodge* (Philadelphia, PA: Philadelphia County Medical Society Collins, 1874).

[3] Rachel's half-brother, Benjamin Franklin Godbold, was born in Columbia County, Alabama, in 1840.

[4] Allie (Alice), Mollie, and May were Rachel's nieces, the daughters of Lucretia Collins and Daniel Perry Godbold.

[5] Rachel here quotes from a poem, later to become a popular hymn, published in 1792 by John Leland.

The day is past and gone,
The evening shades appear;
O may we all remember well
The night of death draws near.

We lay our garments by,
Upon our beds to rest;
So death shall soon disrobe us all
Of what is here possessed.

Lord, keep us safe this night,
Secure from all our fears;
May angels guard us while we sleep,
Till morning light appears.</poem>

[6] Jaques, or, more properly jacquard is a fabric with a floral, geometric, or other pattern woven rather than dyed into the cloth.

[7] Morro Castle, built in 1589, guards the entrance to Havana Bay. The Fortaleza de San Carlos de la Cabaña, colloquially known as La Cabaña, is an eighteenth-century fortress complex, the third-largest in the Americas, located on the elevated eastern side of the harbor entrance in Havana. Casablanca is a suburb of Havana, situated to the east of the entrance to Havana Harbor. The castle of Atarés defended the shipyard in the inner bay, while the castle of El Príncipe guarded the city from the west.

[8] The captain yew is a species of hedge or topiary evergreen.

[9] New York's Central Park was begun in 1858 to fill the need for a recreational facility for the rapidly growing city and to offer urban dwellers an experience of the countryside, a place to escape from the stresses of urban life. Located in what is now central Manhattan, the site was far from the built-up areas of the city. Sparsely populated, it was home to small farms, industrial uses, and dwellings scattered between areas of marshland and rocky hills.

According to designer Frederick Law Olmstead, the beauty of the park "should be the beauty of the fields, the meadow, the prairie, of the green pastures, and the still waters. What we want to gain is tranquility and rest to the mind." Its 843 acres included lawns, woodlands, streams, and lakes, all experienced by moving through the Park along winding paths, a carriage drive, and a bridle path. Sara Cedar Miller, *Before Central Park* (New York: Columbia University Press, 2022); Cynthia S. Brenwall, *The Central Park: Original Designs for New York's Greatest Treasure* (New York: Abrams, 2019).

[10] Townsend Harris, the first Consul General to Japan, negotiated the Treaty of Amity and Commerce, or the "Harris Treaty of 1858," securing trade between the US and Japan and paving the way for greater Western influence in Japan's economy and politics. The seventy-two members of the first

Japanese ambassadorial delegation to the United States arrived in Washington on May 10, 1860. Masao Miyoshim, *As We Saw Them: The First Japanese Embassy to the United States (1860)* (Berkeley: University of California Press: 1979); Chitoshi Yanaga, "The First Japanese Embassy to the United States," *Pacific Historical Review* 9:2 (June 1940), 113–38.

[11] Saratoga Springs on the Hudson River in the state of New York, with its wealth of mineral waters, was developed as a spa early in the nineteenth century. The arrival of the railroad in 1832 brought thousands of travelers to the springs, and a number of large hotels, including the Grand Union Hotel, in its day the largest hotel in the world, were constructed to accommodate them. Congress Spring was the source of the most famous of the Saratoga mineral waters, which were said to treat "lung, female and various chronic diseases" and to "aid dyspepsia, gout, and skin ailments." White Sulphur Spring was advertised as "an hepatic water of an excellent character," possessing "every essential element to render it equal for internal use to the best White Sulphur waters in this State, and far superior to most of them." R. F. Dearborn, *Saratoga and How to See It: Giving Information Concerning the Attractions and Objects of Interest of the Fashionable Watering Place with the History Analysis and Properties of the Mineral Springs* (Saratoga, NY: C. D. Slocum, 1872).

[12] Ocean House was a large, Victorian-style waterfront hotel constructed on Bluff Avenue in the Watch Hill historic district of Westerly, Rhode Island. It was demolished in 2005.

[13] Rachel refers to an illustration from *Peter Parley's Common School History: A Pictorial History of the World, Ancient and Modern, for the Use of Schools*, by Samuel G. Goodrich (Philadelphia, PA: E. H. Butler, 1851).

[14] Joseph Warren was a Boston physician who played a leading role in Patriot organizations during the early days of the American Revolution, serving as president of the Massachusetts Provincial Congress. Warren participated in the battles of Lexington and Concord and, although commissioned a major general in the Massachusetts militia, served as a private in the Battle of Bunker Hill, June 17, 1775. He was killed in action, defending the redoubt atop Breed's Hill. His death was immortalized by John Trumbull's 1786 painting, *The Death of General Warren at the Battle of Bunker's Hill, June 17, 1775*. Nathaniel Philbrick, *Bunker Hill: A City, A Siege, A Revolution* (New York: Viking, 2013).

[15] Although Rachel's journal makes no further mention of her northern journey, she and David apparently stayed at Quebec's Clarendon Hotel, Lewis Street, Upper Town, H. O'Neill, Proprietor, as one of her later letters was written on letterhead from that establishment.

chapter four

THE LONELY INHABITANT OF DESOLATE PLACES

Saint Joseph's Infirmary, Louisville, Kentucky
April–December 1860

B y April 1860, Rachel was again away from home. This time after a visit with her family in Arkansas, in August, still suffering from her many disorders, she became an in-patient at Saint Joseph's Infirmary in Louisville, Kentucky, where, although the sisters were "uncommonly kind," she was treated with the most barbarous medical procedures imaginable, and, as she wrote to her husband, "most cruelly did I suffer from it."

Although no longer hopeful of full recovery, Rachel was guardedly optimistic for her future. "I can live," she wrote to David, "and certainly I can forgo the pleasure of doing all I wish to. I must retrench my desires to accomplish so much. I know that society must have but few claims on me for the future." But, her course of treatments done, she took consolation in never again having "to resort to a northern climate or physicians for health," and in having, "in my quest of health," seen "much of the world that would have remained unknown to me."

Rachel's letters from the Infirmary reveal much about the state of medical care in the mid-nineteenth century. Although in considerable discomfort and often writing by candlelight, Rachel is at pains to instruct David as to how the household was to be run in her absence, sending him detailed instructions for the care of house and yard and of the enslaved persons on the plantation—especially for the training and supervision of the young enslaved women who worked in the kitchen—taking special care in assuring that they were properly dressed and that a newborn baby received a present—"if Murphy's baby is born, you will have to give it something."

"The Negro men," she instructed her husband, were to have "two shirts and two denim pantaloons. You can find out, and those that are to get coats and more of the children are to get clothes." In response, David replied, "you must write to me how to have the Negro clothes made. You know that I don't know anything about it." Further, he admitted, "I'm sorry to say that I can't train a servant. I am a poor manager among Negroes, and I see it plainer every day."

They also open a window on the great love that David and Rachel felt for one another. Like Rachel's letters to her husband, David's letters are steeped in affection. "Oh, my Darling, how could I live without you," was typical of his expressions of devotion. "I see more pleasure in one hour in your company than I expect to see until you come home. What is a home without a sweet Wife? Oh, it is misery." But his letters are characteristically matter-of-fact and business-like, revealing the severity of economic decline of the summer of 1860. "Times are very hard," David wrote. "There it is no money in the country and there is no sale for Negroes," a circumstance that no doubt exacerbated the already volatile political tensions in the state. Reporting a general crop failure throughout Texas in consequence of "the hottest summer that ever was known," David admitted that he "won't make more than ten bales of cotton and my corn crop is very sorry." Moreover, "we have no vegetables. There is nothing in the garden." Moores was "compelled to sell a Negro" in addition to having to liquidate land and his beloved carriage horses. "I don't know what the poor people will do that has no crops nor no credit," he reported sadly. "There will be a many hungry babies this season."

XXX

Elizabeth's[1]

Center Ridge, Arkansas

April 14, 1860

Saturday morning,

You see, my Dearest Husband, I have now changed my "local habitation." When my last was written, I was, at Bro. Dan's **[Daniel Perry Godbold]** *but left there some three days sooner than I expected in consequence of Lucretia's confinement.*[2]

When I went over to spend a week, I told them I wanted to be sent to Pa's when the acchouher was sent for, so on Monday evening last, before I was made aware of any unpleasant sensations on Lucretia's part, Brother Dan had the carriage brought round and immediately I started, and by ten o'clock a little girl was born to lighten or embitter the parents' fond hearts. I would enormously regret the latter.[3]

Things otherwise than I have just related have gone on pretty much after the usual course. Dear Pa is still improving. All the kinfolks keep well. The weather continues unpleasantly—only one wee bit of a shower.

Daniel Perry Godbold, brother to Rachel Perry Moores.

I wonder if it would be news to tell you how much one poor little invalid misses and longs for a reunion with the best of husbands, and wonder if that dearest of husbands would be flattered to know that he was the ever present theme with that invalid wife?

May I tell you, my Dear Husband, that so much have I improved since your last that if a public conveyance were near I would go and spend a few days at my dear little home with my Dear Husband. Oh, how dreary home must be without the one who makes it comfortable, and how we miss those who we are accustomed to find there, though they may be to us a care and anxiety.

As I before remarked, I came up to Pa's Monday, and Thursday evening I came over here and have been staying with Brother Thomas and Sister Elizabeth, but will return to Pa's this evening or tomorrow morning.

Brother Thomas started to Gaines Landing, but did not go farther than Camden. There was some disappointed about the sale of the lots.[4]

I rode around the church grounds the other evening in coming over here, and how many associations, some pleasant and some sad, clustered around each familiar spot. But, dear me, what changes hast time conveyed! Can I have changed as much? Not one time, though, my Love, did I wish myself "a girl again."[5]

No. No. Though afflictions have come upon me and some the bitterest trials ever known to a wife have been mine, yet I say in the presence of my God that the purest happiness I've ever experienced has been during my wedded life. I have found in you, my Husband, what my heart has ever craved, and, without your love, what would I ever be but the most wretched of beings, and before high heaven I can truly say that for no other purpose do I want health as much for as to repay your, or rather, to live the personification of gratitude. The Father of Lights, though, my Dear Husband, will reward you for all you have done that is laudable. What a pleasing thought and should be on "the great day of retribution."[6]

I hope you are getting on smoothly with your business and all have kept well and hope you will find it quite convenient to come the second week in May. Sister speaks of giving a party about the time you leave and would like to know when you will be here. I told her I hope not later than the middle of May, anyhow. I would be afraid to pass through New Orleans later than that.

Sister says tell you she wants very much to see you. Dear little Liz is just as darling as she can be. I now have held one of Sister's children so much, I am getting anxious to see Lucretia's baby. Must go soon down soon as I can. I've made no visits, only in the family and do not feel much like going round.

My tongue is very sore and throat also. The ulcers are right bad again. I eat some butter a few days ago, which I think caused them. Otherwise, I have mended beyond my expectations. Indeed, I do not remember ever to have grown strong so fast, but I must eat crackers again while my tongue gets well.

I do hope, Dear, to get a letter from you tomorrow. I have felt so disappointed every mail. It is not worthwhile now to say write, as you will be coming soon after this reaches you. At least this is the hope of your ever affectionate

Rachi

[P.S.] You had best bring the things I wrote for in the little black trunk as I will want to send some of my winter things home. I will not need them, as I think. If we go North, we will return by the very first of September.

I told Dr. Mask what you said about Betsy. He said he knows he could sell her anywhere about Falcon for twelve-hundred dollars, but I can't give you any more satisfaction than that. Sometimes I think best to keep and then I think best to sell her. She is unusually lazy.

Make Nancy scour the dining room and bathroom before you lock them up and wipe up everything nice. I dislike to find things so amiss. Bring your latch key with you. It is in my jewel case in the bureau drawer. Tell Nancy to attend

carefully to the strawberries. There will be quantities of them. Tell her also I shall

look for a nice yard when I get home.

Tell Louisa and Charles that Hannah had a baby on Wednesday. She calls

him Sandy. Poor thing. She has two who can't walk.

Pa rode over for me this evening and I came home with him, so I am "home

again."

Lucretia calls her girl May-something, after Leslie May-something. Give

Sister Jane my love and Mrs. Connally also. Remember me to inquiring friends.[7]

Saturday night

XXX

Saint Joseph's Infirmary, Louisville, Kentucky

August–November 1860

Early in the nineteenth century, Mother Catherine Spalding founded a school in Louisville, but a cholera epidemic left a number of her students as orphans, so Mother Catherine founded a children's home. As the facility had a few extra rooms she used them as a hospital.

In 1836, the Sisters of Charity of Nazareth opened the St. Joseph's Infirmary, a "spacious and accommodating" building for the purpose of treating the infirm with kindness, as the sisters had long done throughout Europe and the United States. Additionally, the sisters noted that patrons undergoing treatment at St. Vincent's would "contribute to the maintenance of the female orphans under the care of the same Sisters of Charity." The infirmary was headed by Mother Catherine Spalding, with her fellow sisters acting as associate nurses, and two physicians attended the infirmary on a full-time basis.

By 1853, St. Vincent's Infirmary had grown large enough that it needed to expand and so moved to Fourth Street and was renamed as St. Joseph's

Sketch of St. Joseph's Infirmary, Louisville, Kentucky.

Infirmary. Between 1856 and 1926, St. Joseph's served as a hospital and as a charitable organization.

The infirmary charged $7.00 per week for boarding and nursing with an additional $3.00 weekly fee for medicines and "the attendance of the physicians of the house."[8]

XXX

Saint Joseph's Infirmary, Louisville, Ky.

August 5th, 1860

My Dear Husband,

Both day and night I have I have passed longing and bereft of thy dear presence, and as I have no one to praise me, I will risk being scandalized and tell you what a heroine I have been. I slept soundly and woke near five, even though my dreams were of a most doleful character, making me the lonely inhabitant of desolate places. Though I didn't "dream that I woke in marble halls," yet I have been almost as cheerful as usual today.[9]

The Sisters here have been very kind, indeed. All them that visit this floor have made me repeated visits during the afternoon yesterday and today, and Sister Matilda insisted on sleeping in my room and says she would rather do so for a few nights.

I suppose my Dear Husband would like to know how I spent today. As I have to live alone here all the time, of course, I can do but little except read. Sitting is so disagreeably wearing, I could do but little of that—no dressing, no walks, and, you know, no going out to meals. I can do my dreaming Dearest, at the window where we sat each day in this much-loved twilight hour and you and I: "When, love, I hope, art gliding sweetly on the beautiful Ohio, and methinks I can see what thy thoughts are." In imagination, I am clasping thy dear neck and asking, "Am I right?"

Tuesday, [August] 7th: Turning to the treatment, Dr. Miller operated on me yesterday morning. I was kept from adding anything to my Journal last evening, much as I wanted to pour out my thoughts to my beloved husband.[10]

Dr. Miller operated on the uterus yesterday, by making deep incisions, and tomorrow morning he is going to insert a silver ring (I believe it is) to keep the incision from growing up in order to enlarge the mouth of the uterus. He says it is so contracted it must be enlarged by artificial means. The treatment is not so excruciating as was Dr. Holmes', but, really, if I had known it to be as arduous as it is, I doubt very much if I would have submitted to it.

Yesterday, while pushing down too cruelly, I forced his hands away and plead for mercy, and what reply do you think he made? "Why, Mrs. Moores, why don't you be quiet. You must be. You are the most nervous, hysterical woman I ever saw." I was in too much pain then to say anything, but this morning I told him how unkindly he talked to me. He laughed and said, "Oh, I only wanted to raise your Irish, to draw your mind from your pain." I told him I was going to tell you how he treated me. He said I must forgive him, and he would forgive me for all I said to him! As if I said anything he didn't deserve.

Mrs. Farris,[?] the lady who roomed opposite me, left this morning and Miss Ogle from opposite me has moved up, and I find her very pleasant. She was brought in and introduced to me this afternoon and sat with me two or three hours. Mrs. Harris of the Planters Hotel also called on me this evening.

I have not seen any of Mr. Hoyt's family since you left. Aunt Harriet sent a message yesterday morning to inquire after my health and said they would have come but for indisposition on Cousin Mary's part. She and Margaret are both abed ailing.[11]

Sister Mary Bernard and two other sisters went to the Mathias House at Nazareth this morning. They are going on retreat for a week or two—that is, they will isolate themselves for so long a time, fast and pray all the time and speak to no one to atone for any sin they may have committed. I came since last retreat, which takes place once a year. Then new Sisters come up to take their place.

Sister Matilda still sleeps in my room here and Sister Mary Agnes. Each are remarkably kind and attentive, express much regret at not being able to bid you goodbye, and many wishes for your good health and safe journey home.

As the doctor will treat me rather roughly tomorrow, of course I won't be able to write any, and just as well that I didn't. I haven't sat up, only to my meals, write this lying down, and my writing is dreadful. The doctor has had it [illegible]. Fortunately, it does not hurt to write. It rather rests it as it my holds my arm up.

My nurse comes up with supper, and so goodbye, Dearest. I must leave my blessings with thee for the present. God keep you, My Darling Husband, is the fervent prayer of your absent wife.

Thursday[, **August**] 9th[:] *Dr. Miller treated me yesterday morning and most cruelly did I suffer from it. Surely if this pain he inflicted had of lasted minutes instead of seconds I could not have lived through it. Oh, my dear Husband, is my life worth the pain of this separation and cruel treatment? Why, it is dreadful, and then God only knows whether it will avail me anything or not. Is it not hard to bear so much as we can* [illegible]*?*

I did not leave my bed all day yesterday and can't tonight—just pure suffering. I seldom ever saw a worse rising than I have in the left breast, which extends round my arm. It hurt me so excruciatingly all last night, I tried to persuade the doctor to lance it this morning, but he said he couldn't until tomorrow morning, and I have just had a real child's cry because I've no one to nurse it as I always nurse you, Love.

Dear, how often you would have me look at yours and gently rub it, and now I pass hours without seeing anyone and, of course, such [illegible] *delicate attentions are only expected from the nearest friends, husband, wife, or child. Home is the best place for us, if there we have a kind companion to see that all is made comfortable for us. One can't feel the freedom to call upon others that we do upon home friends.*

Won't you forgive me Dearest; I didn't mean to make such a complaint as I have, really, and I assure it is the first time since you left I have indulged to such excess in melancholy. I will have to [illegible] *that. Can't get finished.*

Thursday evening after I finished writing to you, Cousin Mary sent all the children to see me. Eli's baby looks so sweet and reminded me of Dear Darling Alice's [?] *orphaned Lizzie, sweet, innocent. I wonder if I shall ever see her angle* [sic] *face again.*

Aunt Harriet and Cousin Mary came yesterday morning. They were here when the doctor came. Sent again this morning to know how I was. I never leave my room (only to cross the hall whilst my room is being renovated) and seldom leave my couch. I am now leaning from it against the table to write.

The doctor is again trying the pills or half-pills. He has me to cut them in two and yet says they are what he gives infants—but I am fearful they won't do. My head is as crazy as my body is full of the pills. [two lines illegible]

I like the fare somewhat better than when you were here. They won't put any grease in the [illegible] *and serve up fowl every day for dinner, and the Sisters continue uncommonly kind. But* [illegible] *is quick as can be, so even, and when the Sisters are at Mass or prayers she seldom answers to our bells. I've had to report her on several occasions—but as yet there is little improvement though they have punished her.*

We had a delightful shower two days ago, but the weather quite warm again. I haven't suffered as much in years with heat, and I have been as anxious about you on that account and will be until I hear, which I hope won't be long as you will write from Gaines Landing.

Friday evening, 10th:

Having been kept in bed all day from one half of one of these execrable pills and my [illegible]*, I will not be able to finish my letter as I expected this evening as it is six of the clock. Dr. Miller has just bound my breast, and as he was doing so, Aunt Harriet, Cousin Mary, and a Miss Anderson were announced, and when they left a few minutes ago I determined I would get up and try to write, but have to hold my arm with one hand and write with the other. The lancing was very painful; made me sick for a few moments, but then it discharged quantities of blood and pus and I think when the draining is over it will be surely well.*

The doctor says he will hurt me again tomorrow morning. Heaven only knows what he is going to do. I will try and not fear it so much. Aunt Harriet told me this evening that he told her he was almost sure of a cure. God only grant that he may not be mistaken.

But what do you think the old Bugger said to me when I told him how that half the pill served me? "Why," he said, "Here, if that half a baby's dose serves you so, you ought to be killed. It ought to have killed you!"

Well, will take [illegible] tomorrow if there is life enough left in me. Will finish this letter, but I know you would want to wait a few days to hear how I stood the treatment.

And now, a kiss and all my love.

Saturday[, August] 11th. The doctor came this morning cauterized the uterus and vagina. The pain less than any, but he's [illegible], though have not left my bed a moment.

But, oh, Dear, how better was I prepared for any bodily sufferings. He brought with him a letter from Brother [illegible]. It was post marked at Niagara Falls and its contents—oh! how sad, how agonizing, how full of bitterness. Poor, poor sister and dear little children. Poor John. How much he needs that earthly parent's care. Best of fathers, for there was never a better man and a truly affectionate one.[12]

But we must bow us in submission. It must be the hand of God Who hath dealt this blow. Does he not say he will take the good man from the evil to come? I feel that my dear brother has been taken to Him, and, oh, Heavenly Father, I feel that thou wilt bind up the bleeding and contrite spirits of the poor bereaved ones.[13]

Think not, my love, I am giving way to great despondency. He has given me more composure and beauty than I ever hoped to see.

> *What though in lonely grief I sigh*
> *For friends beloved, no longer nigh.*
> *Submissive still would I reply,*
> *"Thy will, be done!"[14]*

How much, my dear, I have to be thankful for. Doctor Miller said today, just after treating me, that he did not fear at all his ability of returning me to good health, but then, if he does not do that, say he only puts down this deep-seated inflammation circulation, and if he succeeds in properly replacing that[?] uterus, why, I can live, and certainly I can forgo the pleasure of doing all I wish to. I must retrench my desires to accomplish so much. I know that society must have but few claims on me for the future.

Mrs. Ogle has just been in, and so sad and poor and frail. She is so patient, so enduring, and so resigned. I shall miss her so much when she leaves. The doctor thinks she will be able to go home in two or three weeks. I hope, yet I fear for her.

Now, Dearest, are you taking all the care you promised of your dear self? I would hope and pray so. I would be so proud to have you read the Good Book much. I'm sure you would profit by it.

Dr. Miller is considerably inclined to cleanliness. Makes his patients bathe daily and even more than that.[15]

Tell the Negros all howdy and try to have me some baking hens by the time I return. Negro cloth [illegible]. Now I know you feel like boxing my ears, don't you? But, really, you will have to have employment for your new maids. Give Lizzie much love and kiss the little ones. [illegible].

I must now say farewell as it grows too dark to write. Praying my God may bless and keep you, my Dearest Husband, is the faithful prayer of your own

Rachi

XXX

Saturday evening, 7:00
[David H. Moores to Rachel P. Moores]

Gaines Landing
Aug 14/[18]60

My Darling,
I arrived here this morning at two o'clock and had quite a pleasant trip with the exception of being on a sand bar sixty hours. The weather is cool and pleasant,

and I am feeling very well. The carriage has not arrived, and I have buggy and a wagon to carry me as far as Monticello and then I will have to hire from there on. I written to P[ayne] and H[arrison] to send the carriage to Jefferson. The Negroes are well and seem to be very well satisfied.

Your Darling,

D. H. Moores

XXX

Saint Joseph Infirmary, Tuesday

Louisville, Kentucky, August 18, 1860

Dear Husband,

I have written to you since Saturday evening—Sunday being taken in writing to Sister and reading—and yesterday, though it was another rest day, I felt in no frame of mind to write. I don't know when I ever have been so unhappy. All because I don't think I am mending fast enough, and that is simply because I'm trying to bathe and wait on myself more than I'm able under treatment.

Why did I break the vow I made whilst at Dr. Holmes' never to be left without a servant when a patient under anyone? It seems to me, knowing my own infirmities as I alone can know them, I must have been demented to have let you carry off the girl you got for this very purpose I most need her for.

Don't be alarmed, Dear Husband, and think I am suffering for any of the real necessities, for I am not. But Dr. Miller wants me to bathe frequently in morning till near breakfast. The Sisters are at Mass. They leave that worthless girl to go to the water well. Sometimes I get it in good time and sometimes the breakfast is carried in the other rooms first and then into my room and I've got to get out with a back weakened and suffering from treatment and get towels, blankets, then bathe, rub myself, and by the time I'm through I'm worn down, and then I begin to cry and in comes a Sister. I tell her about the girl's neglect, and she says it shan't be so again, but it is so again, and every time she reproves her, she commits the same offense again. It is the worst I suffer, for my fare is just as good as I deserve. They always have plenty of fruits.

I had my warnings when you left me here after treatments was begun I would need more attention, but I had decided not to involve a heavier expense by having a servant, feeling in hopes I may grow stronger. But never, no, never, will I ever be placed in this situation again. If I'm not to keep a servant, I will stay at home. Somehow, my husband, you seem to think I was troubling about what would become of this servant at home, when all the time it was what would become of poor me. I had endured it once.

I do hope you found all well at home and crops not so bad as you anticipated. We're needing a rain very much here at present. At least they say so. I never leave my room, though, as you know, I have a few visitors in. Aunt Harriet and Cousin Mary miss but few days they don't come to see me, and you know that is very pleasant. They sit much more in the afternoon than they did at first. It seems to hurt them very much whenever I look low spirited. Sister Nickolova has just this minute gone out. When she came in, she said I looked too down in the mouth to write and begged me not to write. I told her what was troubling me, and she promised to have Aunt Gilda come in and bathe me every morning. I don't know how it will be.

Wednesday evening, August 15. My Darling Husband, though the doctor treated me this morning, I've had a comparatively comfortable day. It was quite amusing when he came this morning. Aunt Harriet and Cousin Mary and two very interesting young ladies and the mother of one of them were in to see me. The doctor stayed longer than usual in Mrs. Ogle's room. At last he sent Sister Matilda in to tell me he too would like to come in. It was amusing to see them bustle, and the room was empty in a moment.

Mrs. Tyler said if it would be agreeable, she would come often. I told her not only agreeable would it be, but perfectly delightful. I'm so fortunate in that one respect.

I asked the doctor how he thought I was doing. "Why," says he, "faster than I ever hoped for. I never saw inflammation yield more readily." But, My Dear, he can't do anything with the ulcers. They're very bad on my tongue and in my throat! As I am in bed, I can't well write longer, and, oh, I'm looking so anxiously for that letter you promised. I do hope it will come tonight and that you are well and [illegible] on your journey safely and pleasurably—is that faithful Wifey.

Wifey

*Thursday[, **August**] 16. Not having to undergo any treatment today, I feel better, though quite down in my back, and I believe this cool spell has made it worse. The weather has been so cold since Sunday that every patient except myself has a fire in the stove—but it heats the room so I will put it off as long as possible, and then it is growing much warmer today. The citizens, however, say we won't have many more very warm nights.*

Mrs. Ogle had the pleasure of receiving a visit today from Mr. Hobbes's family. They brought her [illegible] and fruits, all of which she shared with me. Oh, she is so kind and good. I feel sorry as the time draws near for her to leave. The doctor thinks she can leave in another two weeks.

I hope you do not need rain, My Love, as we do here. It is so much more disagreeably dusty than when you were here. I don't think I should venture in the streets, even if I could, with all the rain.

Have you read any of the new books? I have just finished "Grace Woman-hood.[?]" Think it a well written book and worthy of being read, by Governor Winn.[16]

I find my Bible, though, more interesting than anything else. I hope you will find the large Bible more companionable whilst you are in want of one that you think more agreeable.

It grows late. The people are coming out on the opposite porches. The clock has, I think, spoken, and so good night, My Love.

Friday 17th. Well, another day is passed, and evening finds me all alone as usual, but with the blessed privilege of communing with my dear husband, though it be not by word of mouth. I did not take any treatment today and feel somewhat improved except my mouth. I think it is not so well as usual.

Oh, My Husband, I do miss your dear person. If I but had you occasionally to draw your chair up, slip your arms around my neck, and use such sweet, endearing words of encouragement as only an affectionate husband can, I would appreciate it so much. No one to kiss. No lap to sit on. Yet I want to be thankful, for the Sisters are kind. Dr. Miller laughing and encouraging—though he scolds me sometimes.

Now love, you will never scold me again, will you, after all I am bearing? So many cruelties I have to undergo; so many pleasures forgo. But I pray it may be all for the best. That it may be that means of drawing me to the Kind Father who disposes all our afflictions, and that the years to come will be lighter.

Your ever-devoted wife,
Rachi

XXX

Sunday morning, August 20, 1860

Dearest Husband,
The sound of the church bell just dying away, and the street in front of me is all life and animation with the flock which is gathering there. What a bright

Heaven-lit day it is to go to the sanctuary to worship the True and Living God. I hope, My Love, you have the privilege of so doing this blessed day. Sometimes I wonder if I shall ever enjoy that comfort again?

Evening. I had another fever yesterday afternoon and night, but it was much lighter and I slept much more comfortably last night, and I very much wish it may be the case this evening and night.

I wonder, when I'm lying awake, my Dearest, at night, how you are faring in your desolate home with no one to meet you at your coming, but I do hope you will make the servants keep your house bright and pleasant. I would wish, dear, you would be a little fastidious, be not easily pleased, and then that would get them in a way of doing things right. They have a notion that I'm hard to please, and the blame all rests on me. They don't consider that the execrable cooking I complain of is not for me but for you, and I would have you, Dear, particularly in my absence, to let them know that there is a right way and they have got it to learn.

Doubtless, Dear, you think this a nice Sabbath lesson, but this evening, as I sat me down to write, it came to me what kind of a supper was spread for you, whether palatable or not.

Too dark to write more. A kiss and goodnight

Rachi

Monday p.m., 27 [August 1860].

I've been much better today, my Dearest. No fever as yet, and it is almost dark, and I sewed and read a long time. I know I'm reading too much, but I left allow [illegible]. Dr. Miller had another patient to take a room in the Infirmary today. A lady from Georgia. Dr. Bush's patient also arrived today. She occupies the room opposite mine. I have had only a glimpse of her yet.

Tuesday, 28 [August 1860]

I had no fever and all last night and feel much better today. Sister Matilda gives me two nice baths a day and rubs me well. She says now she understands, she can do it right. Sister Mary waits in my room now. She is more attentive than Sister Matilda was and has a sprightlier mind—yet I don't think her altogether so sociable. They're all remarkably kind me to, though.

We're having such heavy rains every day now and it is quite warm, too, in daylight. Our nights are pleasant. Cool enough generally for me to keep a hot brick. But I think there is some improvement in that region of my body, and Dr. Miller insists there is great improvement somewhere else, but if there is, it must show it, for certainly it don't feel much improved.

I had a visitor this morning, a Miss Shipp. She has called before, is a very kind old maid and a member of Mr. Hoyt's church.[17]

I have visitors plenty. You know I don't like much company. It is very irksome to me and talking much hurts my throat. The ulcers on my tongue and in my throat are now pretty bad. I'm eating too much, I expect, now eating a small portion of meat most every day, yet everybody thinks I'm eating too little, and it does look like a small amount.

Sister Matilda just stopped in to fill my sugar dish. She sends her respects to you and says tell you, "Your wife is improving admirably. You would be proud to see her."

Don't you think I'd improve faster, Love, if I had someone to pet me just a little now and then? But I won't repine, though I haven't my husband to see. I haven't the care of servants to fret me, rather a poor consolation, but I must find it, Love. I can.

This little [illegible], *Miss M*[illegible], *would vex me no little if I'd let her, but I tell on her often. She's gotten so dreadful impudent all the ladies tell on her.*

I haven't seen any of Mr. Hoyt's family since Saturday. The children were here to see me then. The baby grows very sweet, and Hallie is such a joyous sweet dear child. Mullin is so vain I don't like her near so well as Hallie.

Dear, do kiss Sister Jane's children for me and write me all the news from the servants—all about Murphy. I want to hear from them all—not particularly Louisa—and one or two of the neighbors.

I'm going to send this letter without waiting, as I am better than when I sent the last letter off. I have written these last two letters by candle, the first thing I've ever done by candlelight since I've been here.

Oh, Dear, how long the time seems, and it is so much worse for you home alone—but for the servants, who can afford you no companionship.

I pray Almighty God to keep thee, my Dear Husband.

Rachi

[Enclosed in same envelope. No date.]

Dear, please have the elm trees that are dead replaced when it is cold e nough to get some buddings from Mrs. Moores and plant out until I come. Don't forget to have those round tables made to go in the dining table room and made up the same color as the dining table is. The Negro children all need clothes except Mary Jane, Cora, Aylle, and Gennie. If Mary Jane can do without, I would rather have hers made when I get home as I think of taking her in the house. I hope the cloth can soon be woven so you can have it made up, as you will be afraid to get these new girls out and them not needed in the house. Mind that new girl and keep things locked. You don't know about her. She may be put up to. If she gets out of work, ask Sister Jane to set her some churning out and make her watch them.

I got a bolt of sea island [cotton] in New Orleans. The Negro men to have two shirts and two denim pantaloons. You can find out, and those that are to get coats and more of the children are to get clothes—only those I mentioned and Dan and [illegible], and if Murphy's baby is born, you will have to give it something. I had no cloth. Someday, when you are going to be at home, have all my things aired, but you must notice what is put out. Can't you have our chimney lengthened to keep it from smoking?

XXX

Cass County, Friday, August 24/[18]60

My Darling Wife,

I arrived home last Tuesday night about eight o'clock. Found all well and am well myself. I had to [torn] three but [torn] today from [illegible]. I sent the other girls on a mule wagon as far as Monticello and there I put them in the stage and sent them to Woodlawn and I and the boy rode the horses and then I borrowed a two-horse wagon from Mrs. Watts and hitched the horses to it and come home, which I made the trip in two days. I shall start Charles back with the wagon in the morning.

I would have written sooner, but it has been raining every day and was raining when I got home. I thought by writing by Charles and have it mailed in Arkansas that you would get it a week sooner than to have it mailed here.

The Negroes has had very good health and the doctor has been here twice since we left and that was to Louisa. She was so smart. Place of using the door, climbed out of the window and she miscarried. She was about six months gone.

I am going over to Mr. Moore's in a few days and carry Nathan and see if he will buy him. I will be compelled to sell a Negro. I won't make more than ten bales of cotton and my corn crop is very sorry, but I think that I can make another one. Crops are very sorry through this country [torn] there is no crops and will, further, [torn] the cotton has never come up. I don't know what the poor people will do that has no crops nor no credit. There will be a many hungry babies this season.

Cass County is better off that any county in Texas. A great many are going back that are able to get back. I understand that down in Harrison County that they offer the Negro women and children out for their food. Their cattle will all die. They offer them for two dollars a head. Our cattle is fat and fine and we get more milk than we ever did this season of the year. We milk twenty cows. I won't have as many peas as I planted, and I don't know what we will do for pea seed next year. This has been the hottest summer that ever was known. I know it must have been here. The sperm candles that you left in the parlor was melted.

Jane has a little boy. She named him for his father.[18]

I settled with Mr. Griffin and shipped him.

I written to you from Gaines Landing, which I hope you have got before this. I written to Payne and Harrison from the Landing. If they had not shipped the carriage not to ship it until they hear from me. If I thought the river would not be up when you come home, I would still write to them not to ship it to Gaines Landing. I don't think that the river will be up before the first of next year.

Reuben Harrison Moores, older brother of David H. Moores.

Darling, you must ask Dr. Miller when you can start home and write me and you can advise me about the carriage, where to have it shipped. If the river is not up, I think it would be best to ship it to Gaines Landing and you could let me know when to meet you there.

Darling, you must write to me how to have the Negro clothes made. You know that I don't know anything about it.

Mrs. Connally is at Linden and Mr. Connally is elected sheriff and he is going to Linden to live. They won't make more than three hundred bushels of corn and six bales of cotton.

Murphy has a boy. She says it is the finest and largest child she ever had.

We have no vegetables. There is nothing in the garden.

Jane and Reuben are going to start to Arkansas in a few days, and I will write by them again. You must give my respects to the Sisters and remember me to Aunt Harriet and Mr. Hoyt and family and kiss the children for me.

Darling, you must not think too much about home. I will try to get along as well as I can, and you must not write too many letters. You must write to me. [Torn] when you write to Arkansas you must write a general letter. I would not think of writing to them all or even answer all the letters that you may get. I don't think that you ought to write much. I think it will keep you from mending as fast as you might. I told them that they must all write to you and you could not answer all of their letters.

I will have to bid you good night, my dearest Darling.

Your affectionate Darling,

D. H. Moores

XXX

Cass County, Texas

Thursday night, August 30, 1860

My Darling Love,

I received yours of the 11th today, which give me much pleasure to hear that you was doing as well as I expect, and what give me more pleasure than anything else in this world, that is for you to be restored to health once more, which Dr. Miller told you at Aunt Harriet's that he thought that there was not a doubt but he could cure you. I'm in hopes that it may be true.

If so, it matters not what his charge may be, I never will regret it. It will be worth more to me than all the rest of the world. Oh, my Darling, how could I live without you. I see more pleasure in one hour in your company than I expect to see until you come home. What is a home without a sweet Wife? Oh, it is misery. No man can tell me that he has any happiness without a wife. If he tells me so, I can't believe him.

I was so sorry to hear that the treatment was so severe and that you suffered so with your rising. I hope before this time the treatment has ceased to hurt you so and that you are mending fast.

Darling you must not trouble and fret about me and home. I am very well at present, and I'll try and take your advice and take care of myself. We ought to take care and try to preserve our health for each other's happiness.

Reuben and Jane and all the children will start over to your father's in the morning, which I intend to send this letter by them to be mailed, which I think you will get it sooner than if it was mailed here.

It is been remarkable healthy this season through this country. There has been no sickness and there is none now.

I was over in Bowie a few days ago and found all well. I did not see Toad. She and Mrs. Hovey was in Boston. Mr. Moore is going to start in ten or twelve days to take Toad and Mrs. Hovey to Winchester, Tennessee, to school. Jane don't want Mr. Moore to go. She wants me to go with them. But I will not go.[19]

I did not sell Nathan. I shall go over tomorrow or the next day to sell my horses to the railroad contractor for $400.[20] I will have to let Mr. Whitaker have my land down by him at two dollars per acre to raise money to pay Reuben and to pay Payne and Harrison. I will not make more than ten bales of cotton.

Oh, Darling, what you think? The carriage got to Gaines Landing a day or two after I left. You must advise me what to do about it. I thought I would sell the horses and come after you and buy a pair of mules, or you could meet me at the landing if you could tell when you could start. I could meet you at the landing.

Times are very hard. There it is no money in the country and there is no sale for Negroes.

You said that you wanted me to have some well-trained house servants by the time you get home. Darling, I'm sorry to say that I can't train a servant. I am a poor manager among Negroes, and I see it plainer every day.

Mrs. Connally was down at a large meeting in the neighborhood of Reverend Cole, and Crawford Connally was elected sheriff and he is going to Linden to live. I think his wife is delighted with the idea of going.[21]

I've not been anywhere only to Mr. Johns. I was up there today to get him to send his children back to school. They had one-month vacation. Anderson [Moores] is sending Virginia to Mr. Moore's to school.

Mr. Alfred went on to Ohio and married Miss Belletter. Mary Lola and Nannie are over in Bowie. Crawford [Connally] and Cousin Sarah has been down and visited all of the relatives except Reuben's family. Mr. Moore paid him what I owed him, Charlie, and [illegible] for the sale of their Negroes that we brought from Carolina.

I got Jane to cut out Negro clothes.

It has been raining about one week.

You must remember me to the sisters and give my love to Aunt Harriet and Cousin Mary, Mr. Hoyt, and all of the children. I must now say farewell, my Darling Wife.

Your husband,
D. H. Moores

<h2 style="text-align:center">XXX</h2>

Saint Joseph's Infirmary, Louisville, Kentucky
Tuesday evening, September [5,] 1860

My Dear, Dear Husband,
How I long to whisper that dear epithet into your ears instead of committing it to paper. Oh, could I but seat myself on your knee, clasp your dear neck in my arms and give you as many kisses as I should want in return. God knows it would make me happier than anything else on earth, unless, indeed, it were to feel and know that I was well, and that is an event I most certainly never look for on earth.

When I lay the burden of life down, I expect to end my maladies, though Dr. Miller says I have every right to hope. Hope! It is that that sickens me. To see it flicker—occasionally flame up—and then die out. It is these horrible suspenses, my Own Love, that wear on my spirit.

One year ago last March, when I rose up from that long spell of illness without one ray of hope that I should ever again know the enjoyment, up to the last of July when Dr. Miller began to treat me, I was ever happy because when pain and low sinking spells came, I was prepared for them. I did not look for anything else. But now I'm in a physician's hands, I look for him to ward off those spells. He gave me hope, and each spell disappoints and embitters my life.

"There is a strength of self-possession which is the sign that the last hope has departed. Despair no more leans on others than perfect content-ment, and in despair pride ceased to be counteracted by the sense of dependence." That is a truth I've contended for for several months. I believe I am an example, but no one would ever agree with me until I met with the above quotation. Most assuredly George Eliot was one who subscribed to that one sentiment.[22]

It is too bad, My Dear, for me to sadden you with every ill I may be "heir to," but then, I've no one else. Dr. Miller never sits with me long enough to hear anything more than what I'm feeling just then. Like Dr. Trall, he is always in a hurry, though he creeps so.

You may rest assured, my Love, of nothing being kept back. I pour out my whole love to you—who else will give so much pity and so sympathizing an ear? No one! No one ever loved me as my Dearest Husband.

Now won't you forgive me for what I can't at times prevent—a saddened spirit. Think how lonely, Dear, to be shut up in a room for five long weeks and often for days not seeing any one but the Sisters, who are kind to be sure, but then they have only time to attend to your real wants and hardly that if they be many.

I made the acquaintance of a most pleasant lady today, a Mrs. Marsden from Georgia. She rooms opposite me, and I hope now to have Mrs. Ogle's place filled. She's been here over a week, but I took that violent attack I wrote you about and haven't been able to leave my room; but today I met her in the hall. She invited me to her room, and I sat some time with her and she came in and sat with me.

Wednesday, [September] 6th.

I have felt better today, Dearest, in body and mind. My head is troubling me a little, though, and my risings, too, and I have them running. One, in a very bad place, bursted and relieved itself is morning, and I was most thankful as

Dr. Miller was spared the job. He has not been to the Infirmary today from some cause.

I have sewed some today and written to Pa and entertained my new acquaintance who has paid me some half-day visits. She is a curiosity and I think her doctor will learn it to his sorrow. She doesn't obey him in anything, but is taking drugs and thinks he does not give her variety enough.

Thursday, [September] 7th

Last evening after I finished writing my friend, Miss Shipp's, letter and sat until near my bedtime. She is quite social and possesses such a kind warm heart—though an old maid three-score.

I felt stronger today than usual, but a bit troubled with that same disagreeable sensation you have heard me so often complain about my head. Two of my boils discharged their contents and I hope to get some relief now. I have dressed, read, and lay abed as usual today.

I read too much sometimes—but isn't it better than thinking too much, Love? I read Adam Bede last week and the week before and am now a reading a new book Mrs. Tyler brought me, The Queens of Society. It is quite interesting. I have also had Goldsmith's works loaned me, and occasionally I re-peruse one of his estimable poems.[23]

Do not get frightened, My Dear, and think I'm hurting myself. For some days I don't read anything but my Bible.

Mrs. Marsden continues extremely social. Calls quite as often as I would have her. She certainly amuses if not interests me. Dr. Miller has not called again today, and I can't imagine what "can the matter be." No visitors from the city today as it has rained, misted, or been cloudy all day.[24]

Friday, [September] 8th.

All at once I am immersed in a sea of news. Dr. Miller brought me three letters this morning. One from your dear self and one from sisters Margaret and Mary.

Yours, My Love, I read with mingled feelings of joy and regret. Joy that you are so well, found all so well at home, and regret the poor prospects for our crop and the prospect of so many suffering for the necessaries of life. It is truly distressing, and, added to that, Mary writes that the whole town of Marshall has been burned, and twenty Negros hanged and two clergymen. Do write me the particulars. Was it an insurrectionary movement or what?[25]

I'm pleased to hear of Murphy's fifth abortion being so vastly superior to the others. You may believe me, My Dear, that mishap of Louisa's was purposely done. She achieved what she wanted, and I expect that has ruined her constitution.

What a time you had getting home. Oh, how badly I felt ever since you wrote me about not meeting the carriage. I cannot say now about going home, as Dr. Miller left soon after handing me my letters, but I do not think I will be dismissed before midwinter, and, Mollie writes me, Pa says come by and he will send me home. So, had you not better have the carriage shipped to Jefferson? Won't it be cheaper for me to go by Gaines Landing in stage?

Saturday [September 9]: When Dr. Miller came this morning, I asked him how long I should have yet to be here and told him why I asked. "Oh," said he, "You will be up in time." But he shan't put me off. I will keep my letter until he does tell me.

He gave me the same treatment this morning, which kept me in bed until an hour since, and I went to bathe, and whilst in the bathtub, Aunt H[arriet] and Cousin M[ary] came, and soon as I could dress and receive them Miss Tyler came and they have all just left and now comes supper to the lonely room of your most true affectionate

Rachi

Monday morn [September 11]. Dr. Miller says he can't tell when, can't name any time. Says I will be well, but he can't say exactly when. When he can, he will let me know it.

XXX

Wednesday, September 9th, 1860

Darling Wife,

I received yours of the 17th of last month yesterday, which I was sorry to hear that you was so unhappy. You think that you do not mend fast enough. You know that the doctor told you it would take four or six months to relieve, so you must have faith and patience and I think that he will benefit you if he does not cure you entirely.

I am sorry that I did not leave Louisa with you, as that trifling thing that they have there will not wait on you. If she doesn't do better, I would report her to the Sisters every time she neglected her duty if that was twenty times a day. And if that did not do any good, I would tell them if they did not give me another servant that I would have to leave and get another boarding house.

I was over the river a few days ago and sold my matched horses to Mr. Ives, the Railroad Contractor, for four-hundred dollars, due the first of November, and I am going to Mr. W. Whitaker's in the morning to sell him my land that joins his plantation for what he offered me for it, which was two dollars per acre. If anyone else would give me the same, he should not have it. But times is very hard, and they will be harder. I can't collect one dollar, and I am bound to raise two thousand dollars. The land will bring one thousand, and I will try to sell a Negro for the other if I can.

Darling, don't buy anything that you can do without this season, as money is scarce. I am fearful that you won't have money enough to pay your board and your passage home. If I can sell a Negro, I can get along very well. I think when I get news from Mr. Whitaker's, I will go down and see old Mr. Larey and try to sell him a Negro boy or girl.[26]

If I don't meet you at Gaines Landing, you must come by your father's. He said that he would send you home.

Oh, I wish the time had arrived for you to start home. There is no charms for me at home unless you was there. I shall wait for answer to the letter that I wrote you last week before I determine about what to do about the rockaway that is at Gaines Landing for me. I written to the Landing to let me know what the charges would be on the rockaway.

James Moore has not started with Mary and Mrs. Hovey to Winchester, Tennessee. He says that he will start this date, week.

I was over at Mr. C[onnally]'s today and found Mrs. D. C. alone. She was well and inquired after you and she said that she would write to you soon. I was down at Courtland yesterday and called at Dr. Salmon's. Found all well, and the doctor inquired very particular after your health.

We have had a very wet spell for the last two weeks.

Tip Cole is to be married on the 13th to a Miss Locket.[27]

There is nothing new turned up since you left, so I will [sic] a kiss and bid you good night.

Your affectionate husband,

D. H. Moores

XXX

Cortland, Cass County, Texas

September 11th, 1860

Tuesday

My Darling,

I'm going to the office this morning and I thought I would write you a few lines it has not been quite a week since I written you. I hope that I will find a letter in the office from your sweet hands.

I written you in my last letter that I was going to Mister Whitaker's to sell my land. I give it to him at $2 per acre, which amounted to $10,177, which will about pay my debt in New Orleans. If I can sell Nathan, I will be flush in money once more, which I can send you some more if you should need it. Darling, don't you suffer for nothing that you may want. I can get money and send you or if I come for you, I can bring it. I feel like that I can't let you come home by yourself.

Oh, Darling, you don't know how much I miss your sweet face. Home—there is no home for me without you. Oh, how much I would give for one kiss this lovely morning. There is but one thing would give me more pleasure. That is to hear that you was sound well once more. Oh, how happy I would feel. I would not know what to do with myself if that was the case. Darling, I hope by this time the treatments has ceased to hurt you and that you are mending fast.

Oh, how happy I will be when I get you home once more. Nothing looks right about home unless you are here. Oh, Darling, if you was well and at home, I know I would be one of the happiest men in the world. What does men live without wives for? I know that I have seen more happiness since I have been married in one year than I seen in all the balance of my life since Mother's death. I have had no one to love me until I married.

Reuben got back from Arkansas last Friday. He left Jane and the children over there. He is going after them in about two weeks.

We are going to have three or four days meeting at Forest Home, which will commence on Saturday next. I would like to help support the meeting, but I have no one to attend to anything. It is about as much as I can do to get some food for myself to eat, but I think it is better for me. I won't eat too much as it is not before me to eat.

I commenced gathering my corn yesterday morning. I think that it will make a plenty to do me but is very sorry. It has the smut in it very bad. I never seen corn have the smut before. I am fearful that it will kill all of the mules. I guess we will have to do it like the wheat that has the smut, that is, to wash it. Flour is worth in Jefferson $18.00 per barrel. I don't think that there will be much eaten until the river rises, and then I think that it can be bought for $8.00 per barrel.

Ananias Godbold and young Mister Waskom came home with Reuben on their way home. Mister Waskom and Lizzy Lary is to be married on the 12th of December. He asked me to come down. She is nothing but a child and he is a little boy. That will be a nice match, won't it?[28]

James Moore is to start with Toad tomorrow to Tennessee to school.

My cotton is very sorry, and it will run me close to make ten bales. If we have fair weather, I will have it all gathered by the first of next month. Darling, I must conclude as I want to get back to dinner. One kiss and goodbye.

Your affectionate Husband,

D. H. Moores

XXX

Saint Joseph's Infirmary

Louisville, Kentucky

Friday night, September 14, 1860

My Dear Husband,

I have been so terribly afflicted with boils, risings, carbuncles, etc. I have not been able to write a line since Monday and I'm no better at present, but am propped up to write you a few lines that you may not be alarmed as I felt you would have been had you no news of the poor absent one there this week.

I have the sixth opening to the carbuncle under my right arm, and for the last four days I had one just below the thigh and can't set, walk, or lie with any comfort. Dr. Miller just came in and says it is the most painful place an abscess could be and says it will be days before I get any rest from it. But be patient, he always preaches. It matters not how much patience you have. I told him he didn't give me any credit. Oh yes, he says, he feels it if he doesn't say so.[29]

He brought me a letter from Grace[?], and I want you to scold her. She did not write a whole page. She said you carried Bob[?] home. Had sold your blacks—I suppose she meant the carriage horses—and said her pa was going to start the next week to Washington, Texas, with her to school, and that was all the letter.

I am sorry Betsy was not left with Dr. Mask, as he felt assured he could sell her, and I never will want to have her to deal with again.

My Dear, how hard it is for me to keep from mourning at your fate. You at home, with no one to share its joys or cares, and I, an invalid far away from all I hold most dear. But yet it could be worse. Dr. Thrall says I will be restored to my health.

One poor invalid was released here last eve at sunset of all her earthly woes, and is now, I trust, with the blest. She has been most anxious ever since she came for the final dissolution. Said the evening she got here two months ago she had come to die, was willing, ready, and waiting. Her disease was consumption. Oh, what sufferings. She gasped all the time for breath and couldn't, from the time she came here, bear for anyone to stoop over her lest she should smother.

Her husband left here a few days ago for Cincinnati and no one knows his whereabouts, and so she will be put in a vault until he returns. She is now in the church beyond the infirmary.

Two weeks ago a gentleman died here, but I did not know it until the other day, and Dr. Miller requested that I should not see this lady or know of her death, but, oh, when I know of one to whom death has no terrors and who suffered as this poor woman did, I rejoice with that friend.

I could hear her breathe in my room all day yesterday. The bishop and a priest were with her.

I have not seen more of Mr. H[oyt]'s family since I wrote last, and I think, Dear, they came more from duty than inclination. They do so worship fashionable people. Yes, they have been very kind to me, and I love them for it, but *you know we would not be human if we did not have our weaknesses and that is theirs.*

I know, Dearest, you can't read this. I'm flat of my back with the limber sheet before me in my hands, and I have to write without looking at it. But, oh, don't I feel assured that what can be read will be welcome?

Love to friends, and, oh, do write by every mail that you are well and may remain so is the prayer of your own wife,

Rachel P. Moores

XXX

Cass County, Texas
Monday, September 17, 1860

My Darling Wife,
I received a letter from you by the last mail, which I was very sorry to hear that you had a bad rising and in such a bad place, and that you were having some fever at the time you wrote. I hope long before this time it has disappeared and that you are mending fast.

Darling, you don't know how much I miss you when I go to Preaching. I don't enjoy myself without your sweet presence, and there is no enjoyment for me without you there. I can see more happiness in your company in one day than I can in one year without it.

There is a protracted meeting going on at Forest Home, which commenced last Friday, and I do not know when it will break up. I met with Mr. Chappell and the Rev. Mr. Jones from Douglassville. They inquired very particular after your health and how you enjoyed your trip.[30]

I sold today one hundred fifty acres of land at two dollars per acre, which he will be here tonight to settle for. Now, if I can sell a Negro, I can get along very well. But I think it is very hard to sell a Negro for money. It is very scarce and times hard. Darling, you must not think too much about home. You won't mend as fast as you ought.

Mr. Connally is to pay the one hundred fifty dollars tomorrow at church, and I think that I will get another letter from you in the morning. He is to bring it, and I will send this to the office by him.

Darling, you must remember me to Aunt H[arriet] and Mr. Hoyt and family and also the Sisters and tell the old doctor that he must be in a hurry to cure you and send you home. It is very bad living without you. You must tell him how lonesome I am and that he must hurry up and cure you.

Rueben is going over to Arkansas in a few days and I'll write you again, so I will have to conclude. Mr. Kelly has come. One sweet kiss and goodnight, Darling.

D. H. Moores

XXX

Saint Joseph's Infirmary
Louisville, Kentucky
Sunday noon, September 23rd, 1860

Dearest,

How much I thank my Heavenly Father that He permits me once again the privilege of pouring out my soul to thee, the only sharer of all my joys and woes. This is the first time, Darling, since the 14th instant, the day on which I wrote you whilst lying on my back, that I've been able to write at all. A day or two after your letter was written I undertook to reply to Sister Margaret and then grew so bad I took something for a colic. I know it was not exactly that, but it was nearer that that anything else, and in two hours my bowels were in a flood and would not be contracted, only for a few hours at a time until day before yesterday. I don't know when I suffered such agony.

Dr. Miller just had my bowels leached for a pain in my left side, this and this leg abscess leached, as it would not collect sufficiently to be leached, and that, together with the soreness in the bowels from the frequent discharge and chills attendant upon each discharge, makes me almost wish for the "King of Terrors."

To see you, My Darling, was all I wanted. Dr. Miller was very kind, visited me twice every day and assured me there was no danger of a sudden dissolution. Said that if there should be any danger he would not wait for me to tell you but would send immediately for you. Now this disease has been arrested, my bowels present symptoms of having ulcers in them, which I know have injured the entire system.

Today, Love, is one of those rare pleasant beautiful days which must make every creature who is able to enjoy it thank the Hand that made it. Who could not praise the God of this holy Sabbath day. I think, I pray, my own Dear Husband, you are spending it as you ought.

I am happy to tell you, My Darling, how near and dear God has been to me during this last week of affliction. Oh, Father, I pray thee, be ever as near My Dear Husband. We cannot, My Dear, be independent of God. If we want health, we must ask it of Him. If we would enjoy, we must ask of him this right. Always remember we are helpless in His hands.

Dr. Miller had such a nice sweet loaf of light bread made at home and sent me, Dear, last week while I was so sick. I told Cousin Mary about it, and she sent me another quite as nice. I eat nothing last week but grapes and bread.

Aunt Harriet and Cousin Mary came to see me twice last week. They always inquire very particularly about you and Aunt Betsy. So, send some word about her. I think Aunt Harriet thinks I ought to go home. She don't know what to make of my not being well yet or at least not able to walk out yet.

I've never been off this floor since I came on it, and I am growing very weary of it. Dr. Miller said yesterday morning I could go home by the first of January a well woman, or maybe a little before. He knows a deal, and yet he's no prophet, though I could pray he might be one in this.

In your next letter, Dear, send me one and a half yards of the **[illegible]** *pink ribbon in the box. If there should be any passing, please send my brown merino dress. It would be so warm and nice for this climate.*

Oh, I must tell you how kind Mrs. Marsden was to me and still is. She can walk around and is so kind to sit with me so much . . . is in my room every few minutes.

Dear, I never felt that I ever wanted to see you half so much. Oh, how long will seem these months. Oh, how can you endure the dreary hours all alone, my Dearest, Kindest, and Best of Husbands? Oh, Dear, what could I ever do without you?

God bless you, my dear, dear husband, and repay you for all your devotion to me, who, though she may never be able to repay it, can much appreciate it. Be certain to write—I never received your letter this week, but I know you have written. Not one word yet have I ever received from Sister Jane.

What is **[illegible]** *news at present but the love of your ever devoted*

Rachi

XXX

Saint Joseph Infirmary
Louisville, Kentucky
Tuesday, September 25, 1860

Dear Husband,

I felt disappointed that I did not have more time to reply to some portions of your letter received yesterday morning. Dr. Miller came in and handed it to me, inquired after my health, and left the room, bidding me read my letter and prepare for treatment whilst he was looking around after the other patients, and as he left the instruments in my room I knew he had no other treatments to make, and consequently would be back in ten minutes, and I had not even the time to prepare my bed, change my clothes, or sit me down to write when he came, exclaiming, "How fast the patient mends."

Dearest, I have not interfered, yet it would relieve me to vent my feelings in this when I think of all your troubles and I the cause of nearly all of them. You bid me make my shopping expenses small as possible. I assure you, My Love, I never endeavored more to retrench than at present. I haven't spent two dollars of pin money since you left, and independent of my board and medical bills (including leaching) I spend nothing but for washing. My leaching has amounted to nine dollars, but I think I shan't need any more now. I haven't an article of winter underclothing here. I do not intend to get one cent's worth. I will put on more of the light clothing. You need not fear, My Dear, of my getting into any unnecessary expense. I don't think you have ever had any right to in such emergencies.

I regret so much to hear of your selling your land at such a sacrifice to Mr. Whitaker. I'm sorry you can't raise the money any other way. It seems strange you can't sell the Negroes for their value at home. They are selling at enormous prices here. I hear of persons constantly giving such very high prices here.

September 26. I'm proud to tell you, My Love, how very much better I'm feeling today, and Dr. Miller says I may take a short walk this afternoon. Won't I feel like a bird let loose? I really wonder how I shall feel. When I get back, I shall tell you. We have a glorious day—bright and bracing—a good shower last night to lay the dust.

And, indeed, I have been downstairs—out in the street and walked the length of two blocks, went one block the other side of Broadway. Why, what beautiful private residences they have here. I never saw any more beautiful anywhere, and the yards are so beautiful and grass and shrubbery so tastefully arranged and the selection so nice.

I can assure you, My Love, I did not bound up the stairs as when I first entered the Infirmary. I had to pause between every step, but then the walk was decidedly beneficial. I was so tired and felt as if I could [illegible]. I eat my supper, and now, as I came in, and now that my Bible has been read, my last duty been performed. I'm ready to say good night.[31]

Thursday 27th. Although we had a rainy morning and a murky, cloudy day, yet I have taken an evening walk, rather a short one though, as the mist began to fall, but then, it is most gratifying to me to be able to go out at all. Dr. Miller was here when I returned. He came into my room with me to find how I was getting on, and said he was in high spirits about me.

"Oh," said I, "Doctor, you say I'm getting well because I'm improving. I have mended quite as fast before and fell back again as rapidly."

"Oh," said I, "how can it be possible for one diseased so long and so much ever to regain health. I never saw anyone restored who had been so low."

"Oh," said he, "you lived always in a dark corner and never saw much."

"I put myself to no little trouble," I replied, "to see what could be done in the enlightened corners."

He says if I have no backset now, I can go home sometime in December. But you must not count on my being entirely restored. He will in a great measure relieve my female weaknesses, but my dyspepsia is quite as bad. I have to be very strict with my diet. I'm more convinced than ever that fresh beef or mutton is superior to anything I can eat. Nothing agrees with me so well. Oh, this miserable bakers' bread. I feel that every mouthful of it I eat is poisoning me in a small way.[32]

Have you read the new books, Dear? I have read them and found them very interesting release, but for the last week or two I've read nothing but my Bible and find nothing half so interesting.

Sisters Mary and Matilda send their kind regards to you. Mrs. Marsden says she made you an eggnog, but you wouldn't partake.

I must close, but I could say a thousand things and more, too, but, oh, I pray God we may not ever again have to part here below. Take the best of care of yourself, My Dearest, is the fondest wish of your own

Rachi

If you do not send to the care of Dr. H. Miller, my letters may get lost as there are many Millers in Louisville.

Dr. Miller has just brought me your letter of the 5th instant. Oh, My Husband, I'm so sorry you are compelled to sell lands and Negroes on my account. How can I ever repay you?

May God do so if I never can.

The doctor is going to hurt me this morning, and Mrs. Jackson came in.

Your wife

XXX

Home, Saturday night, September 30/[18]60

My Darling Wife,

I was so disappointed last mail not getting any letter from you. It is the first, and I am in hopes that it will be the last, time that I will fail to get one.

Reuben and family got back last evening from your father's, bringing V[irginia] Godbold and your uncle G[asaway] Godbold with them. Your uncle is on the way to Harrison County. Your sister V says that she is going to stay with Jane until you come home. Frank [Godbold] and his cousin A. Godbold are waiting on Miss A. Johnson, so there are two cousin rivals. Which one do you think will succeed, or either? I do not think that either will.[33]

Doctor Larey will be here tomorrow to buy a Negro. I have paid all of my debts in New Orleans that is due. The note that Mister Hoyt went on is $300 and is payable the first of January at the office of Payne and Harrison, which I will have the money there by that time, and that is all that I owe in New Orleans. I still owe Reuben one-hundred and fifty dollars, and them is all the debts that I owe, which makes $450.00.[34]

If I can sell a Negro, I will have money a plenty, and I think that I can. Darling, I written to you that money was scarce and that you must not buy anything that you could do without. Darling, I am sorry that I written to you anything about it, and I am fearful that you may suffer for the want of things and you won't buy them. You must buy anything that you may need. I have got and will have money enough to do us. I will make about fifteen bales of cotton, which will bring about seven-hundred dollars, and I will sell a Negro for twelve-hundred dollars, and I will get the four-hundred dollars the first of next month that I sold my horses for. I will then have twenty-three hundred dollars, and I will only owe four-hundred and fifty dollars out of that, which will leave me eighteen-hundred and fifty dollars which I will have to come after you with and pay Dr. Miller. If I do not pay him this year, I guess that it won't make any difference, which I told him that he would have to wait until I make a crop.

I have nothing new to write you, but the health of this country is better this summer than it has been for ten years. There has been less sickness amongst our Negroes this summer than we have had since we have been married. You must not trouble yourself about my health. I am living very well, indeed, getting plenty of vegetables: cabbages, squashes, beans, tomatoes, butter beans, okra, and peas, and sweet potatoes, and I have them cooked nice, and I have plenty of nice butter, but I have to see after it.

Reuben is going to send Charlie to Daniel Coats to school. They have a young lady there for a teacher.

The mail comes to Cortland tomorrow night, and I will send this down tomorrow evening by Eli and let him wait until the mail comes and bring my letter. I know that I will have at least two from your sweet hands, Darling.

Oh, me, how happy I would be tonight if I had you here, sitting on my lap with them sweet arms around my neck and what sweet kisses I would have. You must remember me to Aunt H. and Mister Hoyt, to family, and also to the Sisters. So, I must conclude as I have nothing of interest to write. So, one kiss and goodnight Darling.

Your affectionate husband,
David H. Moores

XXX

Saint Joseph's Infirmary
Louisville, Kentucky
Monday evening, October 1st, 1860

Dear Husband,
It has been now five days since I sent my last leaf and not one line have I written to add to this next, and I have not seen Dr. Miller since (yes, the next day) and this evening I dressed up for the first time since you left and visited a lady. The lady, not being at home, I turned back and headed out or up or down town. I haven't been a while yet, and just as I passed the infirmary gate I saw our jovial old doctor drawing up at a fast pace, and as I nodded, he beckoned to me to stop, and he drove up and after the usual enquiries he told me the causes of his detention. Said he had a son and family to come up from the interior of the state with a child for treatment, and that a series of misfortunes had befallen them this week and that he was coming on purpose to see me to tell me why he hadn't come to see me on Saturday; that he would be here as usual tomorrow morning, and said it is my wish now that you walk just as often as you may feel like it, and so he bade me good evening and turned his horses and was gone out of sight, and I went to a shoe shop and ordered a pair of stout walking boots. The streets are so muddy here.

I've been very fortunate in many respects. The day after your letter was sent, little Maddy Tyler brought me a jar of such nice brandy peaches, and the next day Aunt Harriet and Cousin Louise walked with me. The next morning, Mrs. Hoyt and Cousin Mary came and set a few minutes, and when they went home they sent me a book and a number of newspapers, and Mr. Hoyt said he would send me his daily papers after they were through with them, to which I objected. And this same evening Mrs. Tyler and Miss Anderson called, but I was out walking. But, as next day was Sunday and very inclement, I did not leave the house.[35]

October 2. Dr. Miller gave me a treatment this morning, but I was up to service and walked out this evening. But, oh dear, how tired I am. I haven't sat through many services. I returned and now, though only eight o'clock, I'm going to bed. One lady called on me while I was in my bath, and, as she was in a hurry, left before I got out.

Too sleepy to write now. Good night, Love.

Wednesday 3—I walked this morning as far as Mr. Hoyt's church, but was so weak and tired, did not sit up one second after until dinner and Dr. Miller came just as I was finishing and replied to my telling him how weak and badly I felt.

"Oh," said he, "you walk too much."

"I have caught the contagion. I'm sick, too."

After dinner I took my lounge, got up to the bath at four, took quite a short walk but a few steps from the gate. Of course, I was unable to go farther. I know what it is that makes me so weak and nervous. I've never had my period since the first week I came here. All the hot baths the doctor may prescribe will [illegible] *unavoidably while I get over what I've lost from being leached. Oh, My Love, don't flatter yourself and I shall ever be well. I may be improved very much, but never well.*

The diet here—the worst is the oven baked bread. Dr. Miller said he had some made for me yesterday, but said it was so sour he would not have it sent. I wrote to Dr. Thrall today to send me two dollars worth of Graham Crackers.[36] Dr. Miller says they will get here in three days by express.

I know you wonder, My Dear, how I'm spending my time—whether lonely, homesick, or low. I can assure you I'm not the least lonely. Mrs. Marsden is with me quite as much as I like to have company. It's not that she is one of the kindest and merriest of the sex—I could say more—but a more feeling, sympathetic creature I never saw—she always accompanies me on my walks—but I usually return alone. She's walking much farther than I can do.

Sister Mary still attends my room, and she keeps it so nice. There is such a nice fire for me to dress and bathe by every morning. She also slept in here when I had my last bad spell. I read a little, sew a little, longue little, walk a little, write a little, eat a little—or want to rather—a great deal. The Sisters serve more now since several patients here left.

I weighed this morning. My, how lovely, weighed 115 nearly. You never have thought that little? Why, I look as if I might weigh at least one and thirty. I never saw my face look fuller than at present.

Though not the least lonely hour, there is "an aching void." I long to be with you, to attend to your little wants. What a pleasure to sew on buttons for you—to do anything for you—except cut your hair. Sometimes I really get worried when Mrs. Marsden comes in. I want to indulge in thinking about you, but then I suppose it is better for me not to think too much, but, oh! how delicious to daydream of those we love best.

May God keep you and bless you, My Darling Husband, is the prayer of your own

Rachi

Thursday, [October] 4—At last a letter from the dearest "object of my affection." This morning Dr. Miller came smiling and pulling out the "dear token"!

"Oh," said he, "If I had not found one in the office for you, I had determined to write one for you."

"I don't think you could counterfeit this writing," I said.

I told him of your extreme nervousness—he said he had noticed you are a very delicate gentleman. I told him that you had as much need of doctors as myself, though you would not admit it. Was that true, Dearest?

I took quite a short walk this morning, and, for the first time since you left me, a ride this afternoon. Mrs. Marsden and I took the omnibus before the gates and went out to Cedar Hills as far as the line runs.

I never felt before that I was in Kentucky until I got out in the country. We saw one beautiful farmhouse and beautiful green lawns all around on which roamed splendid meat oxen, grazing. I wished for you to admire the aspect, remembering your proclivities. The ride refreshed me considerably, and I think I shall take another soon.

Dearest, I could not get through reading your kind letter until I thanked my Heavenly Father for such a noble husband. I do not suffer for anything, My Love, but I get nothing but what I am compelled to here. You shall not make all the sacrifices alone. I will enclose a copy of my expenses that you may judge for yourself.

[October] 5th. I was too weak and nervous this morning to walk. My sewing had to be laid aside. Then I finished the last book Mr. Hoyt sent me, the "Mill on the Floss."[37]

Dr. Miller did not make a visit morning, and this afternoon I walked as far as Green Street and had to take an omnibus to get back. Am having such weak nervous spells now and dyspepsia is rather bad just now. I will finish on the enclosed sheet.

Graham crackers	2
Leaching	6
Medicine	8
Flannel to sew with	.40
Board besides your deposit	39.00
Washing	4.50
Fruit and candy	.75
Omnibus rides and gloves	1.00
Envelopes	.50
Dimity edging	.70
Boots	4.00

October, Friday 5th. My shoes have not yet come in, but I have money enough to pay for them. I have over forty of the money you left with Dr. Miller. The fruit and candy, My Love, I bought for Cousin Mary's children and to give to the Sisters. They were always giving me every nice apple and peach that was sent them, and I would have [illegible], and my washing will not be so much now that the leaching is over with. My rides now, however, will be a trifle if I continue them. My board, I suppose, will continue the same.

My Love, don't you find my letters too dull to read with any interest? Not going out mixing with the world and only receiving fashionable calls from strangers who can only ask if I am improving, when I expect to leave, and do visit them without fail, and so forth. Now all this serves only to while away time that might otherwise drag heavily on me, but how much more would I appreciate the visit of one dear warmhearted, kindhearted, and sympathetic friend; one who was not afraid of forfeiting their fashionable dignity, for instance, such friends as Miss Ewerts.

Cousin Mary has been kind to call often, but never sits much longer when alone. Miss Shipp and Mrs. Tyler make me the most sociable visits I have yet received. You know, My Love, I disapprove of an undue vulgar familiarity much as anyone and have as keen an appreciation of dignity as far as it is necessary—but so much snobism I think perfectly disgusting.

October 8: I was quite smart this morning, My Love. Took a walk before breakfast—a short one though. After breakfast I asked Mrs. Down [?] to darn my stockings, and before I got through the old doctor brought me a letter from Sister Margaret and Dicky, and before I perused them one was brought in from Mrs. Ogle. Now you can judge of my delight, and yet yours always gives me infinite more delight than one apiece from every other friend I have and the world.[38]

Sister M. wrote but little news. Sister Jane makes a long visit home, and Sister M. says they're all enjoying themselves exceedingly. I do not think it would mar Sister J.'s enjoyment much to write me one letter at least. Not one line have I ever received, not one letter from her yet.

I finished my stockings, worked a little on my embroidery, read a little, nursed my heartburn with medicated napkins, received two visitors, took a walk to the shoe shop after my boots, got home just at tea time, which I enjoyed immensely though it consisted of bread, butter, and peach sauce. But the bread was some of the nicest light bread Dr. Miller sent me, and now My Love, a pleasant Saturday night.

When I awoke this morning, Dearest, the rain was falling hard and fast. After breakfast, the rain only fell in light mists. The clouds began to chase each other away. By ten there was no rain or mist, nothing but a few shadowy clouds. By eleven I saw the church goers pass, and so, I thought, I, too, felt well enough to take a walk, and by half after I was dressed and on my way to Church. Would you believe it? Yes, I went to Mr. Hoyt's church.

At the Church gate I asked a carriage driver how long till services began.

"Oh," said he, "just now," and at the door the sexton asked if I wanted a seat, and after answering him in the affirmative, seated me, but Mr. Hoyt did not occupy the desk but another minister I did not know. After being seated some

time, my eyes wandered over the congregation, and whom should I see but Dr. Miller, and him only did I know until near the close I saw Mr. Hoyt's back and in the same pew, Aunt Harriet.

At the church porch I met Dr. Miller who extended his hand and said, "I did not expect to see you here."

"I did not ask your permission," I replied, "but nevertheless I came."

I was afraid when I saw him, I should get a scolding, but he smiled, and I know now he wasn't vexed.

I will now close this and beg you, Darling, to write me longer letters. They are so short, I read them over and again, which is the greatest pleasure I have.

My earnest prayer, dearest, is that we may meet soon.

R. P. Moores

<h1 style="text-align:center">XXX</h1>

Tuesday morning, October 2nd, 1860

I could not send to the office last evening on the account of the rain. It commenced Sunday night and never has ceased. It is misting now, but I shall send to the office. I can't wait any longer for it to cease. I am anxious to hear from you, but I am in hope that you are mending fast and nearly well.

Oh, Darling, you do not know how happy it would make me to hear that glorious news. I am so anxious to hear when you can start for home. If this year or next I want to know what to do about the rockaway. It arrived at Gaines Landing a few days after I left there. Wasn't that too bad?

One of the girls that I bought (Mary) came in a few minutes ago and sayed that she was sick. I guess she is going to have a child. So, I will conclude as I have nothing more to write. So, one kiss and good morning, my Darling Wife.

Your affectionate husband,

D. H. Moores

XXX

Lonely Home, Texas

Monday afternoon

October 8/[18]60

My Darling Wife,

I received yours of the 11th of last month last Tuesday, which I was so very sorry to hear you thought you was not mending, though you stated Dr. Miller said that you would be well, which that gives me pleasure to hear, which I hope and think will be so. So, Darling, you must not be so despondent. You know that makes very much against your health and, Dear, you ought to know that if you would be cheerful that you would improve much faster.

Oh, Darling, you have no idea how much pleasure it would give me this afternoon to have you home and well and sitting on my lap, and so many sweet kisses I would get, which I miss so much, having no one to kiss and no one to kiss me. What a pleasure we are deprived of, though I hope that it will be no longer than the first of next year, which is only two and three quarters month off.

Do you want me to write you all the particulars about the burning of Marshall and hanging Negros and clergymen? It was all false reports. There was no houses burnt in Marshall nor no one hung. The town of Dallas and Henderson was some burning in, and they hung a few Negros and some white men, but I can't say how many.[39]

I'm going to build your dairy and washhouse. I have a part of the logs. They will be twelve feet square, the same size as the bathroom, and I shall build one Negro cabin. I commenced Charles this morning to paint the yard palings. I will get Mr. Henshaw to build the half-round tables that you wanted for your dining room.

I have had a very bad rising on my arm. It is much better. It's been running some. You must not say it was meat that made the risings, it was not. I have not had any meat cooked for two weeks, and we live on a vegetable diet.

Do tell Dr. Miller that he must tell you when you will be well enough for him to discharge you over to me so I can come for you. Tell him that I'm getting very tired living without you at home.

Darling, I got Jane to cut out the Negro clothes, and I have had all of them made up but a few shirts.

It rained all of last week and it is very warm now.

Darling, I bought you a fine riding pony. I paid two-hundred-and-seventy-five dollars ($275.00). That was not in money. It was in ponies, and I do hope the next letter I may get I shall hear of your mending fast and hear when I can come for you.

So, I will have to kiss and bid you good evening until next week.

Your affectionate Husband, D. H. Moores

XXX

St. Joseph's Infirmary, Louisville, Kentucky

Wednesday evening, October 10th/[18]60

I don't have the heart, Dearest, to write when I reflect how long, how very long, it takes my thoughts to reach you. Oh, Husband! Dear Husband, I want so much to see you this moment. Daylight is fast disappearing and twilight is gathering—"The hour for you and me." Methinks I can now see you riding up, dismounting, and entering all alone a cold dreary house. No one to keep a warm bright hearth. No one to have a clean nice washcloth, and lastly but not least, no one to have a nice palatable supper spread and no one to sit by and tell you [illegible] the [illegible] and [illegible] and scold you for eating too much, too little.

I have just returned from my evening's walk, Love. Called on Miss Shipps, who is living with her great nephews in a beautiful home only two doors from here. I walked down Broadway a piece after leaving them.

The doctor gave me a treatment Monday morning and a severe one it was, though late in the afternoon I walked down to Main Street. Returned with half a pound of cheese and some fruit. So much for my going past a longer [illegible] that time.

I promised Aunt Harriet, if I was well enough, to spend the day there yesterday, but [illegible] the doctor the morning but went after my four o'clock bath. I found Aunt H. at home. Mrs. Hoyt and Cousin Mary were out looking at a house. I enjoyed my visit marvelously though and felt all the time as if you were there, it being the first time since you left that I've been there. Aunt Harriet set out a nice apple tart (cream pastry) and certainly I never enjoyed anything more. It was so nice, and the remains I brought home. I carried Lillie a pair of [illegible] I embroidered for her and my fruit to the bellman[?].[40]

Friday. [October] 12th

What a change we had in the weather last evening. I arose with the sun this morning and walked out before the earth was dismantled of her beautiful robe of frostwork. How Louisville has been transmogrified! The shrubbery all, or nearly so, has been removed to the cellars since my morning walk I noticed on my return a few minutes ago.

I have to walk alone now, Love. Mrs. Marsden is quite ill today and has suffered considerably for several days. I walked yesterday morning before breakfast but was sick the remainder of the day until evening when I walked out shopping for some cotton flannel to make me some drawers. I am but poorly prepared for cold weather in the way of underclothes. I shall do better now that I have made me a pair of drawers today.

I had to write to Dr. Bush for Mrs. Marsden. He was absent in the country. Then I wrote to Dr. Miller. He came but refused to prescribe as her doctor would be back soon. I also went out to an apothecary shop and got a box of pills the doctor prescribed for me. Have I not been smart, my Dear? Had not Sister Mary Agnes been so pertinacious, I might write you another page tonight. She made the gas man come and put on another burner. [illegible] and it is so dark I can scarcely write one line. How [illegible] that means when writing was all the solace one poor absent [illegible] could have. My own husband, God bless you this night, my Darling husband, is the prayer of your ever [illegible] wife.

Saturday, [October] 13th

A cold rain, windy, dusty disagreeable day, and yet I've taken two walks, then sick a long time today. Met Aunt Harriet and Cousin Mary on my return and promised them to attend church tomorrow if able. [illegible] synod has been in session for several days, and I haven't been able to attend at all.

Mrs. Marsden is quite sick and sent for Dr. Bush twice today. She wants him now and I want my bed and so must answer her call [illegible]. Dr. Miller has not been to see me today.

Sunday, [October] 14th

While as usual I felt quite [illegible] on awaking this morning. Took my seven o'clock walk, [illegible] my own room up after breakfast whilst Sister Mary Bernard was at eight o'clock mass. Lay down to rest at ten, intending to get up and be dressed by eleven and go to church. I arose in time but was so slow at dressing (never feeling strong after breakfast). The clock chimed out twelve by one. I got more than halfway and so I came home and by the time I got [illegible] and was on [illegible] trays was brought up and you ought to have been with me, Dearest. I had apple pie and cream sauce. I got them to send to the mill after some Graham flour and yesterday I sent a [illegible] to the Sister who attends the culinary department to make me an apple pie. I got up from my evening lounge at four, put on my travelling costume, and walked down to Mr. Hoyt's. They being absent at church, I sat with the children an hour and *just in the act of starting when Aunt H. and Cousin Mary came. They sent their buggy back after Mrs. Hoyt [illegible] me though expecting the Right Reverend Robert Breckinridge to tea.*

I reluctantly consented and [illegible] for the honor of taking tea and spending a portion of an evening with so distinguished an individual. You know his celebrity far exceeds that of his nephew who is nominated for the presidency. Though a D.D. of the Old Presbyterian church, he is nevertheless a [illegible] politician, a man of a fiery [illegible] will, exceedingly [illegible], and I think him an extraordinarily talented man.[41]

In answer to a question of Mr. Hoyt's: Did he think Lincoln would be elected? And if so what the results would be? "Why," said he, "I have not a doubt of his election! [illegible] in case he is we are bound to have trouble [illegible] it will eventually come." Oh, My Love, it made me tremble to hear such an opinion from such a man.

Cousin Mary brought me home as she went to night preaching. Mr. Breckinridge preaches at Mr. Hoyt's church tonight and I am sorry I am not able to attend.

I can't say [illegible] that I find any improvement [illegible] I can't [illegible]. I suppose the doctor will treat me again tomorrow morning. [illegible] light and no newspaper, but, Love, thoughts and kisses without number from your wife,

Rachel P. Moores

XXX

Sunday night, October 14, 1860

My Darling Wife,

I received yours of the 14th of last month Tuesday last, which I was sorry to hear that you had so many risings and carbuncles. But, Darling, I hope you have been relieved of them all long before this time. Oh, Darling, I know that you must look very thin and bad and feel worse than you look. I know how annoying risings are. I had one last week, but it is now well. You must be cheerful. The time will soon roll around for you to come home. It can't be more of than two and a half months, and I hope not more than two, so you can eat Christmas dinner at home.

Oh, how happy I will feel and how proud to see you at home once more and well. There is no home for me without your sweet presence. If I could only lay my arms around your sweet neck tonight and the sweet kisses that I would get, I know you would have to say what you did on the night of the 6th of February 1855. That was, "I am not fond of kissing." Don't you think so, Darling?

Dr. Miles's son-in-law, Mr. Hill, was married this week. He married old man Dobbs's daughter. His wife died last May. She had been dead about five months when he married.[42]

I'm going to have the road cut out in the morning that leads from here to Linden, so I will have to get up as soon as light and try and finish it tomorrow. We had a frost last night and I think that we will have another tonight.

I guess you have frost in the last month.

Darling, you said that I must write you every week. I have written you every week, and I would write oftener if there was more than one mail a week. You may look for a few lines every week, Darling, so you may know that I am well and the Negroes. Nothing new to write but what I have written, so, one sweet kiss and good night.

Your affectionate husband,
D. H. Moores

XXX

Saint Joseph's Infirmary, Louisville, Kentucky
Wednesday morning, October 17, 1860

Dear Husband,

Dr. Miller has just left my room. Says I may go home by the middle of November. I told him if I went alone what I thought of doing. I could not settle with him, but that as soon as I went home you would make arrangements with your commission merchants in New Orleans. I did not ask what his bill would be, knowing he never bills until he dismisses his patients.

Now, my Love, I think I had best go alone if the expenses will be less, which looks reasonable. They would be even if the carriage is at Gaines Landing as it can be shipped home with less expense than your buying horses here at the risk of selling again. If the river is not up, I could stage to Pa's. He sent me word he would send me home and Mollie with me.

Now, I write lest you should be angry, Love, if I went alone, but indeed you must let me if it will cost less, and then I could hire a [illegible] to go to [illegible] and will and [illegible]. I will wait until the [illegible] of November for you, and if you are not here and I do not get a reply to this letter I will start then (provided I continue to improve) for home.

When the doctor told me I could go, said I, "Doctor, are you sure?"

"Oh, you are well, but you won't believe it," said he.

"[Illegible] but," I said, "I [illegible] with so many pains and aches.

"Oh," said he, "they will disappear, for there is not a particle of inflammation visible about your womb now."

I know I feel much improved, but I know I am not well. I don't deny I am well as ever men can make me, but the [illegible] is gone or never was there. Dr. Miller thinks I grunt[?] from habit, but you know me better. [Illegible]. I know a good many patients who do so, but I know I conceal or hear too many things for my good.

I hope I have been explicit in saying I would wait for you until the 20th of November, but I think it would mean [illegible] than hard times to go alone. I want to some teeth problem. I can scarcely eat, but as Dr. Miller says I had better *wait until they are all out and have an **[illegible]**. If I find I have money enough I will have some filled.*

Sister Mary Bernard has just brought in the largest paleula [?] taken from the bladder of a poor little child here today by a private physician.

I am in no great haste to add another word, my Dearest.

Your Rachi

XXX

Saint Joseph's Infirmary
Louisville, Kentucky
Thursday, October 18th, 1860

Upon further reflection, My Dear, I thought perhaps I had better give you until the 26th of November. I wrote yesterday to you saying Dr. Miller said I could be well enough to start home by the middle of November. I did not know but you might want to come after me. Yet I know I can go alone unless you want to come and settle with him, and I know arrangements with him through Agent Harrison.

If it will save any expense, My Love, you had best let me go alone. I have no fears. If the Ouachita is up, I will go that way, and if not, I will go from Gaines Landing. If you do not come, write immediately, but if I am well enough, I will not wait longer than the 28th.

I shall be very happy when the time comes to meet you, my love, but, oh, how infinitely more so would I be if I were going home perfectly sound and well, but that I never can be. However, My Own Dear Husband will think none the less of me—respect me none the less—love me none the less.

I long to get some clear water to wash in, some good bread to eat, clean towels when needed, and a dear darling husband on whose knee to sit—around whose neck to put my arms and whose dear lips I can kiss ever and again.

Cass County, Texas

Saturday Night, October 21st, 1860

My Darling Wife,

I received yours of the 23rd of last month Thursday last, which I was so sorry to hear of your having colic and suffering so much agony. But I was happy, too, to hear that Dr. Miller says that you will be a well woman by the first of January or maybe before.

Oh, Darling, it is bad to be separated so long as we are, but we ought to stand and be contented. To have you restored once more to good health gives me more pleasure that anything else could in this world so you could enjoy yourself a little while you live as you never have been able to do so since we have been married. But I hope the latter part of our married life will be more pleasant than the first. But I never would want to be more happy than I have been if it had not been for your suffering so much. Oh, Darling, you do not know how much I want to see you and have you to sit in my lap and put them sweet arms around my neck and the sweet kisses that I would get.

Two months more before we meet, but that will soon pass off and we will be together again, I hope, and enjoying our little home to ourselves. Won't that be pleasant, Darling?

I was over at Mr. Connally's today and Mrs. C. had just come from Linden. She said all was well, but the old lady was looking very bad and failing very fast. She had a very severe spell this summer and they said that she was willing to die and you know that she has been always very scary for fear that she would die. So, you can tell Aunt Harriet all about her. She never has heard of her sister's death, as yet. Cousin Lizabeth knows of it and won't tell the old lady. She thinks that it will make her worse.

Mrs. Connally sends her love to you. John Connally's wife has a baby and Mrs. Watson will soon have another. I also seen the old man Connally today. He come up from Courtland. He has not been home but three or four times since you left here. He always inquires very particular after your health and he was after his wife today to write to you. She said that she had written and he said that she ought to write oftener.

Darling, there is no pink ribbon in the box. You must buy it and anything else that you may need. You must not think of the advice that I give you some time ago that was not to buy anything that you could do without. Buy anything that you may need, Darling. We can't live always and no one won't thank us for anything that we may leave.

I was so happy to hear that Dr. Miller sent you such a nice loaf of bread and then Cousin Mary sent you one. I think that she might send you one before the doctor did as she was a cousin and he nothing but a physician.

Darling, if they did not have anything at the Infirmary that I could eat, I would send out and buy something that was nice and that what suited me. You must eat plenty of apples. You know that you won't get any when you get home and you won't get any biscuits either until we get some flour from New Orleans. There is no wheat in the country for sale, but I shall write to New Orleans and have some by the time you get home. I guess 200 lbs. will do us until wheat comes in.

All is well but Murphy. She has a diarrhea but is about well. Virginia and Charley was over this evening and brought me some grapes and cakes. Jane sends me something nice to eat very often. I have killed three beeves and want to kill two or three more. The beeves are very fat.

I have nothing new to write, but I remain your affectionate Husband,

D. H. Moores

XXX

Cass County, Texas

Sunday night

October 28, 1860

My Darling Wife,

I'm so uneasy not getting any letter the last mail. I fear that you was sick and unable to write. The date of the last letter that I received from you was 23 September, five days over a month. The mail comes tomorrow evening to Courtland, and I shall go down sometime tomorrow and wait until the mail comes in. It is nearly night when it gets there. If I don't hear from you by this mail, I will start to Louisville to see about you and what is the matter.

I hope that it is in fault of the mail, not you, Darling. Surely if you could not write, Dr. Miller would, and let me know how you was. Darling, tell Dr. Miller that I would be happy to get a letter from him how you was improving and what time you could start home.

Darling, I know it would be best for me to come or meet you at Gaines Landing as the rockaway is there, and I will have to go for it. I need more time than I have got. One of my mules has been sick ever since last spring, and I know that he never will be worth anything. So, I think it will be best for me to come for you, and I can buy me a pair of mules. Don't you think that will be best?

I will make twenty bales of cotton. When I wrote you last, I thought I would not make more than fifteen bales.

I tried the sausages that you put up in lard and found them very nice. But I like beef better than pork, and I'm having some very nice beefs killed this fall. I wish, Darling, you was here to help me eat some of the nice fat beef that I have to eat alone. Beefs are fatter this fall than they have been since we was married.

I have gathered my peas and got my killing hogs in the field. I have forty head and three or four sheep for mutton for you and one beef so you can have some fresh meat when you get home.

I'm going over into Bowie next week and try and get me an overseer, if I can find one. Old Griffin is not worth one shilling. I'm going to get one for next year so I can go about with you when you come home. I don't want you to stay at home all summer. We will travel over Texas some.

I've not heard from Bowie in sometime. I do not know whether Mr. Moore has got back from Tennessee. Reuben and family went today to Cole's to preaching. I did not go. I have been home reading all day.

I've not gathered potatoes yet. The frost has not killed the vines as yet. I expect to sow wheat in the potato patch. I shall enlarge it some little to make about five acres at ten bushels per acre. That will be fifty bushels, and that will be aplenty for us. I'm going to plant next year for seventy-five bales of cotton. I hope that it won't turn out like it did this year when I planted for sixty and made twenty.

Cousin Betty Vining and her husband has parted again. I have nothing more that is new to write you. You know that never go anywhere to hear any news unless I have business.[43]

So, I'll bid you after a kiss goodnight until next Sunday night and I will write you again. So, good night again, Darling, and pleasant dreams from your affectionate husband,

D. H. Moores

XXX

Cass County, Texas
Sunday Night, November 4th, 1860

My Darling Wife,
I received yours of the 6 of October Monday last, which I was so happy to hear that you was able to dress up and go out calling, riding, and to attend church. I hope that you will still continue to mend fast so you can soon start for home.

Darling, I don't think now that I will ever leave you again. If it is so that you have to stay from home, I shall stay with you.

Darling, my hair wants cutting very bad. I am sorry that you are not here to cut it as you want to do something for me so much.

You said that I must not flatter myself that you never will be well, but I think that you will, and I shall be very much disappointed if you are not well. Dr. Miller says that you will, and I shall still think that you will or he would not of said so.

Day after tomorrow is the Presidential election. I shall go to Courtland and cast my suffrage for Bell, but the state will go for Breckinridge and Lane. I hope that Bell may be elected, but I do not think there is much chance for him. I think Lincoln will be our next President and, if he is, Negroes won't be worth much.[44]

I am going to gather my potatoes in the morning. I think they will turn out very sorry. I have finished gathering cotton. I have twenty-three bales. I want to put up the well house and washroom this week and then will put all hands to clearing land.

William Henry Harrison
Moores, older brother of
David H. Moores.

I went up to Havana yesterday to hear Parson Clark preach, but he failed as usual and also today.

Reuben's family stayed all night at Old Man Waddle's. They returned home this evening. They made up a subscription to get Mr. Clark to preach for them next year. They made up three hundred dollars which I foolishly promised to pay him ten dollars which I do not expect to hear him preach, for every time that I go to hear him he is certain not to come.[45]

I think Virginia is getting homesick and she came to stay until you come home.

I shall go the last of this week to Bowie to get the money for my black horses that I sold to Mr. Ives and the same time try and get me an overseer for the next year. I think of getting one of the Elliott's but not Sam. Darling, what do you think of that?

XXX

Cass County Texas
Monday noon, November 12/[18]60

My Darling Wife,
I've not heard from you since the sixth of last month. I'm so anxious to know how you are getting and if you are not nearly ready to come home. I went over to Bowie last Saturday and just returned and set down to write you a few lines. I found all well in Bowie. I stayed all night at William's. Matilda has another boy, but I forgot his name.[46]

This and last week was court week in Boston. Mr. Moore's and the heirs' suit is not been tried and decided. The jury hung and it was put off until next court.[47]

John R. Rochelle is married. He married some six weeks ago, and he has taken his bridal trip to South Carolina, and Mary Ann Rosborough went with them. John is going to be gone some two months and Mary will remain in

Carolina until next spring before she returns home. I neglected to say who John married. It was Miss McCutcheon of Myrtle Springs.[48]

R. M. Lindsay of Boston on yesterday taken a razor and cut his throat. He bled to death in a few minutes and he will be buried today.[49]

I told you that my trip to Bowie was to hire an overseer, which I did for next year, but he won't set in until the first of next January. I promise to give him three hundred dollars. The gentleman is Mr. David Elliott, a brother to Sam Elliott, the one that you are so partial to. But, Darling, if you don't want me to hire him, I will turn him off.[50]

I had my rising that was coming when I written to you last lanced last evening and it relieved me so much and I had such a good night's rest.

I built one Negro house and got your well and washhouse raised and will finish them soon so you can have a nice place for your butter and milk next summer.

I will commence sowing wheat this afternoon. I have made twenty-three bales of cotton. I've nothing more to write that would be interesting, so a sweet kiss and a pleasant afternoon.

Your most affectionate husband,

D. H. Moores

XXX

Saint Joseph's Infirmary

Wednesday, November 21st, 1860

My Dearest,

For fear that you did not receive my two last letters in which I said (in one that I would remain until the 25th or there about, [illegible] the last day of this month). You know in the first of the three that I wrote you about coming I said I would only wait until the 20th and then because [illegible] the letter might have become lost. It might have reached you and the next day I sent one saying I would wait until the 25th again. I still was afraid I had not given you long enough and in a day or two more gave you until the 30th.

Then when you did not reach here yesterday as I was suffering very much with a cold and torpid liver and somewhat otherwise.

Dr. Miller is giving me blue mass every night and a tonic for my stomach. I think my dyspepsia case puzzles him no little and I think he will agree with Dr. Gordon in thinking me incurable.

If I did not have one of the best husbands in all the world and did not think it my duty as a professing Christian to submit cheerfully to my fate, I would be a lunatic in two weeks.

You cannot imagine, my Darling Husband, the feelings of a confirmed sufferer, the bitter feelings of desperation that will sometimes seize them and sicken them with moments of pain and phrenzy for death. But God helping me I will be reconciled. I will bear it all and more, too, if must be.

Now, Love, I write this in order that you may know when I will start if you are not here on the last day of this month. If you are not here, I will leave on the first day of December for home.

God bless you my husband is the prayer of your wife, Rachi

XXX

[From the Journal of Rachel P. Moores]

[December 25, 1860] [Torn] *Today has been quiet, as have all the Christmases I've spent in my own home. David had our new carriage horses harnessed up and gave us—Mollie, Virginia, and myself—a nice ride. The horses are noble looking steeds, matched well, and carry the carriage almost at lightning speed.*

One year ago, today, I was not able to set up three hours at one time, and how much better I am now. I feel weak and nervous, but the doctor said I would feel so for some weeks from treatment and fatigue.

I almost wonder that I can breathe after one of these Gaines Landing trips, and I never was this more true than at this time. Oh, I do pray my Father in Heaven that all Dr. Miller's predictions may be true in regard to my health and that I may never have to resort to a northern climate or physicians for health, for I have suffered, Heaven only knows how much, to be relieved, and yet I can't believe it a permanent cure. But some consolation is yet mine. Some have lived years and endured more suffering, and then in my quest of health I've seen much of the world that would have remained unknown to me.

NOTES

[1] Rachel's sister, Elizabeth Evans (Godbold) Watts, was born on July 9, 1820, in Fairfield County, South Carolina. She was married to Thomas Jefferson Watts, Sr. (born on March 14, 1810) on March 21, 1843, in Selma, Alabama, and in 1847 the couple moved to Harrison, Arkansas. She was the mother of John Comer Watts, Sr.; Mary P. Watts; and Elizabeth Eva "Lizzie" Watts. Elizabeth Eva Watts died April 18, 1886, and is buried in the Watts Cemetery, Columbia County, Arkansas.

[2] Lucretia Collins Johnson Godbold, Rachel's sister-in-law and the wife of Daniel Perry Godbold, was born in Tennessee on August 10, 1834. She and her husband resided at Harrison, Columbia County, Arkansas. They were the parents of May (Godbold) Hartin; Margaret Johnson Godbold; and William Nathan Godbold. Lucretia Godbold died on February 2, 1890, and is buried in the Watts Cemetery, Willisville, Nevada County, Arkansas.

[3] An accchouher is a physician or midwife who assists at the delivery of a baby. Margaret Johnson Godbold was born on April 9, 1860.

[4] Gaines' (or Gaines) Landing was known as the gateway to Southeast Arkansas. Located in Chicot County on Maj. William Gaines's plantation on the west bank of the Mississippi River, it quickly became a vital shipping point between Helena and Vicksburg. A road west from the landing through Drew County was one of few in the area leading inland away from the river, making it highly important to settlers and merchants.

[5] This phrase seems to be an allusion to a passage from Emily Brontë's 1847 novel, *Wuthering Heights*. "I wish I were a girl again, half savage and hardy, and free. . . . Why am I so changed? I'm sure I should be myself were I once among the heather on those hills."

[6] The earliest use of his often-quoted phrase seems to be from William Melmoth, *The Great Importance of a Religious Life Considered: To which are Added Some Morning and Evening Prayers* (London: W. Ginger, 1774), 109. "When the great Day of Retribution shall come, I may look up to my most merciful Judge with Joy and Comfort, and may hear those ravishing Words pronounced unto me, Well done, thou good and faithful Servant."

[7] May Godbold, the daughter of Lucretia Collins and David Perry Godbold, was born in Hempstead, Arkansas, on January 8, 1857.

8   *The [Louisville] Courier Journal*, January 9, 1979; *The* [Louisville] *Courier Journal*, January 21, 1837; Mary Ellen Doyle, SCN, *Pioneer Spirit: Catherine Spalding, Sister of Charity of Nazareth* (Lexington: University Press of Kentucky, 2006); Mary Ellen Doyle, *Catherine Spalding, SCN: A Life in Letters* (Lexington: University Press of Kentucky, 2016).

9   Rachel alludes here to "I Dreamt I Dwelt in Marble Halls," (also known as "The Gipsy Girl's Dream,") a popular aria from *The Bohemian Girl*, an 1843 opera by Michael William Balfe, with lyrics by Alfred Bunn. The aria begins with the lines:

> *I dreamt I dwelt in marble halls*
> *With vassals and serfs at my side,*
> *And of all who assembled within those walls*
> *That I was the hope and the pride.*
> *I had riches all too great to count*
> *And a high ancestral name.*

10 Dr. H. Miller was a consulting physician at Saint Joseph's Infirmary, Louisville, Kentucky.

11 Mary Jane "Harriett" Harrison, who was born in Georgia in 1834, was the daughter of Kirkland Harrison, a brother of David Harrison Moores' mother, Mary Harrison. On May 7, 1850, she married Thomas Alexander Hoyt, the minister of Louisville's First Presbyterian Church, located at the corner of Sixth and Green streets. "Cousin Mary," the couple's eldest daughter, Mary Harrison Hoyt, was born in South Carolina on August 29, 1851, and died in Louisville, Kentucky, on May 27, 1862. Her sister Harriet Margaret was born on November 2, 1854, and died in Nashville, Tennessee, on August 5, 1931.

12 Rachel's brother-in-law, Thomas Jefferson Watts, Sr., died on June 20, 1860. He was the husband of Elizabeth Evans (Godbold) and the father of John Comer Watts, Sr., and Elizabeth Eva "Lizzie" Watts.

13 Rachel is here paraphrasing 1 Corinthians 15:50–58: "The righteous perisheth, and no man layeth it to heart: and merciful men are taken away, none considering that the righteous is taken away from the evil to come."

14 This is a verse from "My God and Father! While I Stray," a poem by Charlotte Elliott published in 1834 in *The Invalid's Hymn Book*. It was set to music in 1874 by Arthur S. Sullivan. Of her own physical condition, Elliott wrote: "My Heavenly Father knows, and He alone, what it is, day after day, and hour after hour, to fight against bodily feelings of almost overpowering weakness and languor and exhaustion, to resolve, as He enables me to do, not to yield to the slothfulness, the depression, the irritability, such as a body causes me to long to indulge, but to rise every morning determined on taking this for my motto, If any man will come after me, let him deny himself, take up his cross daily, and follow me." "Thy will be done," is from Matthew 6:10.

15 Florence Hartley, a mid-nineteenth century authority on women's proper behavior, opined that "in nervous complaints, which are more or less the besetting evil of womankind, the bath, in its various forms, becomes an invaluable aid." Florence Hartley, *The Ladies' Book of Etiquette, and Manual of Politeness: A Complete Hand Book for the Use of the Lady in Polite Society* (Boston, MA: G. W. Cottrell, 1860), 273.

16 Robert Nicholas Winn, a banker, was a partner in the Deposit Bank of Winn, Simpson & Co. in Winchester, Kentucky. In 1860, he enslaved three people in Clark County, where, on February 5, 1861, he was confirmed as a notary public. He served as the wartime governor of Kentucky, but no evidence seems to exist of his having written a book.

17 Helen Elizabeth "Betsey" Shipp was born in 1775 and died on April 21, 1861. She is buried in the Cave Hill Cemetery, Louisville, Kentucky.

18 Reuben Harrison Moores, Jr., was born in August 1860. He died in Fresno, California, on August 27, 1924.

19 "Toad" was the pet name of Mary Elizabeth Moore, who was born on June 5, 1844, in Bowie County, Texas, the daughter of Jane Ross (Moores) and James C. Moore. She was married to John Frank Hooks

(April 14, 1837–October 18, 1895) and was the mother of one child, Robert W. Hooks. She died on July 10, 1925, and is buried in the Evergreen Cemetery, Paris, Texas. A Daniel Hovey is listed on the Bowie County tax rolls from 1859 through 1863.

When Bowie County was organized in 1841 the centrally located community of Boston was selected as the county seat. A post office was established there in 1846. The town served farmers throughout the central part of the county, and during the 1860s the community's population reached 300 to 400. When the Texas and Pacific Railway built through the county in 1876 it bypassed Boston to the north by four miles. The town of New Boston was laid out on the railroad and most of the merchants from Boston moved to the new town. By the early 1880s, the population of the original Boston had declined to seventy-five. *Dallas Morning News*, March 6, 1938; *Texas Observer*, December 23, 1988.

[20] Construction of the El Paso and Pacific railroad began in Bowie County in 1857 but was discontinued due to the outbreak of the Civil War. Work was not resumed until 1869. The Texas & Pacific railroad was not constructed through eastern Cass County to Texarkana until about 1872, but by 1876 the narrow-gauge East Line & Red River was built from Jefferson through the southwest corner of Cass County and in 1884 was acquired by the Missouri, Kansas & Texas and was converted to a standard gauge road.

[21] John M. Crawford Connally, the son of Lucinda McConnell Montgomery and Dempsey J. Connally, was born in Georgia in or about 1825. Connally was named postmaster of Forest Home (also known as Springdale) on May 5, 1859, and in 1860 he was elected sheriff of Cass County.

[22] Here Rachel is quoting from George Eliot's (the pen name of Mary Ann Evans) 1859 novel *Adam Bede*.

[23] *The Queens of Society* is a collection of short biographies of notable European women published in 1860 by Grace and Philip Wharton, pseudonyms for Katherine Byerley Thomson (1797–1862) and her son, John Cockburn Thomson (1834–1860).

Oliver Goldsmith (November 10, 1728–April 4, 1774) was an Irish novelist, playwright, and poet, best known for his novel *The Vicar of Wakefield* (1766), his poem "The Deserted Village" (1770), and his play *She Stoops to Conquer*, first performed in 1773. He is also thought to have written the classic children's tale *The History of Little Goody Two-Shoes* (1765).

[24] "What Can the Matter Be?" (also known as "Johnny's So Long at the Fair") is a traditional English nursery rhyme, dating to the 1770s.

[25] This report was false, but several such incidents, fed by an hysteria over supposed abolitionist saboteurs having infiltrated Southern communities and incited slaves to acts of violent rebellion, did occur in North Texas in the years immediately preceding the Civil War. Richard B. McCaslin, *Tainted Breeze: The Great Hanging at Gainesville, Texas, 1862* (Baton Rouge: Louisiana State University Press, 1994).

[26] Henry Michael Larey was born in South Carolina in or about 1802. By 1860, he was a planter near Sulfur Fork, Lafayette County, Arkansas. He was the father of Dr. John Michael Larey.

[27] Pulaski DuBose "Tip" Cole was born on February 1, 1838, at Union Springs, Bullock County, Alabama, the son of Nancy Wood and Daniel M. Cole. At some time prior to 1855 the family moved to the Mooresville area in Cass County, Texas. In 1860, he married Martha Rebecca Lockett, the daughter of Louisiana "Lou" Sanders and Reubin Winfrey Lockett, Sr. Martha Rebecca Lockett was born on April 12, 1846, in Marion County, Georgia, and died on July 17, 1866, in Cass County, Texas.

[28] Rachel's nephew, Ananias R. Godbold, was born in Conecuh, Alabama, in about 1835, the son of Nathaniel and Harriet Godbold. He enlisted in Company A of Col. Elkhana Greer's Third Texas Cavalry. Private Godbold was wounded in the Battle of Pea Ridge, Arkansas, on March 8, 1862, but saw further action at the battles of Iuka and Corinth, only to die of "dropsy of the heart and chest" on September 24, 1863, in Kemper County, Mississippi. *The* (Shreveport) *South-Western*, January 13, 1864.

Sanctus Emmett Waskom, born in Mississippi on October 16, 1837, married Mary Elizabeth Lary, born in Alabama in 1845, in Harrison, Texas, on December 12, 1860.

29 A carbuncle is a swollen cluster of boils that are connected to each other under the skin. A boil (or furuncle) is an infection of a hair follicle that has a small collection of pus (called an abscess) under the skin.

Most carbuncles are caused by *Staphylococcus aureus* bacteria. These bacteria can cause infection by entering the skin through a hair follicle, small scrape, or puncture. Filled with pus—a mixture of old and white blood cells, bacteria, and dead skin cells—carbuncles must drain before they can heal.

30 A. H. Chappell was born in Georgia in or about 1799 but by 1860 was living in Douglassville, Texas. James T. Jones was born in Jefferson County, Arkansas, on June 28, 1827, but by 1850 had moved to Cass County, Texas. He died in 1886 and is buried in the Powell/Jones Cemetery at Douglassville, a small community in northern Cass County. The site was settled in the early 1850s and named for John Douglass, an early resident. Most of the early settlers came from Georgia and Alabama, and many established plantations along the Red River. A Douglassville post office was established in 1854. The town was a supply point and market for area farmers. In 1884 it had two churches, a school, two gristmills, two cotton gins, and a population estimated at 150.

31 In her great enjoyment of walks, for both health and pleasure, Rachel was perhaps an anomaly. In 1857, the editor of the *Harper's New Monthly Magazine* offered the opinion that "upon the whole our city people take as much exercise—certainly as much out-door exercise—as is habitual with a large class of county girls." He claims to have known farm women to "look upon a walk of a mile to church as an intolerable grievance," and to "have been amazed to find the idea current in some county families that walking is hardly a desirable process, and that a stroll through the pleasant green lanes to as great a distance as a city belle often condescends to sweep with her dainty crinoline in Broadway or the Avenue, is a thing not to be thought of." "Our Daughters," *Harper's New Monthly Magazine* 16:91 (1857), 73.

32 Sylvester Graham's 1837 "A Treatise on Bread and Bread-Making" called for the use of coarser, unsifted whole wheat flour, because mass-produced bread removed the nutrient-rich layer of bran. The process of refining and whitening flour added such unhealthy additives as copper, alum, clay, and chalk. This new white flour, he wrote, led to a "lazy colon." In the face of the era's rapid industrialization, Graham believed that all bread should be homemade, and he laid out a process for making whole wheat flour and turning it into "Graham bread." Graham was physically attacked in Boston by a mob of bakers and butchers who blamed him for declining sales.

33 Gasaway Godbold, Rachel's uncle, was born at Prince George, Georgetown County, South Carolina, in about 1790. In 1815, he married Elizabeth Hinds. In 1820, he was a resident of Fairfield, South Carolina, and in 1840 was farming in Conecuh, Alabama. He died in Texas in 1868.

Benjamin Franklin Godbold, Rachel's half-brother, was born in Alabama in 1839. He served as the captain of Company B in Col. Thomas P. Dockery's Nineteenth Arkansas Infantry. He was killed in action at the Battle of Big Black River on May 17, 1863.

34 John Michael Larey, a Cass County physician, was born in Autauga County, Alabama, in 1826. By 1850, he was living in Sulfur Fork, Lafayette County, Arkansas, but by 1860 he was a resident of Cass County. He was first married to Mary M. Kelly, but after her death in July 1862 he married Ann T. Roach in October 1863. Doctor Larey died in Bright Star, Alabama, on November 7, 1883.

35 Alice Louise Hoyt, the daughter of Mary Harrison and Thomas A. Hoyt, was born in September 1856 in South Carolina. She died on May 26, 1945, in Philadelphia, Pennsylvania.

36 Sylvester Graham (1794–1851), a Presbyterian minister who became a leading figure in the temperance movement, was deeply interested in human physiology and nutrition and ideas of vegetarianism and abstinence. He believed that human lust caused physical maladies, ranging from minor inflictions like headaches and indigestion all the way to grave conditions like cholera, epilepsy, and pulmonary consumption. To Graham, the more immoral the sexual thought or act, the more harm inflicted upon the body. To Graham, masturbation "inflame[ed] the brain more than natural arousal," and could result in insanity.

The only way to tamp these depraved carnal urges, he believed, was to adhere to a strict diet that eliminated meat, fat, spices or condiments, coffee, and tea. He also advocated a regular exercise regimen, wearing only loose-fitting, utilitarian clothing, taking cold baths, sleeping on hard mattresses with the windows open regardless of the weather, and abstaining from alcohol and tobacco.

Some of Graham's lectures were published under titles such as "The Young Man's Guide to Chastity" and "Discourses on a Sober and Temperate Life." Adherents of his lifestyle became known as "Grahamites" and opened male-only "Graham boarding house" facilities in New York and Boston. Stephen Nissenbaum, *Sex, Diet, and Debility in Jacksonian America: Sylvester Graham and Health Reform*, (Westport, CT: Greenwood Press, 1980); Kyla Wazana Tompkins, "Sylvester Graham's Imperial Dietetics," *Gastronomica: The Journal for Food Studies* (Winter 2009), 9:1, 50–60.

[37] *The Mill on the Floss* is a novel by George Eliot, the pen name of Mary Ann Evans, published in London in 1860. The first American edition was published by Harper & Brothers later that same year.

[38] William Dickey Johnson was Rachel's nephew, the son of Margaret Perry Godbold and Samuel M. Johnson.

[39] For a discussion of such false rumors, a product of the hysteria created by rumors of Abolitionist incendiary plots, see McCaslin, *Tainted Breeze*.

[40] Lillie was the Hoyts' fourth daughter, Lillian Tyler Hoyt, born on April 17, 1860.

[41] Robert Jefferson Breckinridge (March 8, 1800–December 27, 1871), the son of Kentucky senator John Breckinridge, was a politician and Presbyterian minister. As a youth, Breckinridge had been suspended from Princeton University for fighting, and following his graduation from Union College in 1819, engaged in a life of partying and revelry. Nevertheless, he was admitted to the bar in 1824 and elected to the Kentucky General Assembly in 1825. A serious illness and the death of a child in 1829 prompted him to turn to religion, and he became an ordained minister in 1832.

As a theologian, he was extremely conservative and a stalwart for the Old Church faction of Presbyterianism, a stance for which he was rewarded by being elected moderator of the Presbyterian Church's General Assembly in 1841.

After a brief tenure as president of Jefferson College in Pennsylvania, Breckinridge returned to Kentucky, where he became pastor of the First Presbyterian Church of Lexington and was appointed superintendent of public education. After six years he was appointed a professor at the Danville Theological Seminary in Danville, Kentucky.

A staunch Whig, Breckinridge was a slaveholder who opposed slavery and a conservative Southerner who opposed secession. An ardent Unionist, he supported Abraham Lincoln and the gradual emancipation of the slaves and their colonization in Africa and opposed his nephew, Vice President John Charles Breckinridge, who ran against Lincoln in 1860. James C. Klotter, *The Breckinridges of Kentucky, 1760–1981* (Lexington: University Press of Kentucky, 1986).

[42] David seems to have been mistaken. Holden Lafayette Hill married Martha Elizabeth Dobbs, the daughter of Rachel R. King and Cyrus Dobbs, in Cass County on January 23, 1856.

[43] Elizabeth Perry Harrison, a daughter of Anne Perry and William Henry Harrison, married Wade H. Vinning in Cass County on May 25, 1862. It was her second marriage, her first husband, John Green Rives, having died in 1846. She died on June 24, 1870, at Myrtle Springs, Bowie County, Texas, and is buried in the Rives Family Cemetery, Vivian, Caddo Parish, Louisiana.

[44] The 1860 United States presidential election in Texas was held on November 6, 1860. Texas voters chose four electors to represent the state in the Electoral College. As David predicted, Texas voted for the Southern Democratic nominee John C. Breckinridge of Kentucky, who received more than 75 percent of the vote, his largest majority in any of the states. Moderate Constitutional Union candidate John Bell of Tennessee won slightly less than 25 percent of the state's vote, carrying only three counties. Neither Republican Party candidate Abraham Lincoln nor the "Northern Democrat," Stephen

A. Douglas, appeared on the ballot in Texas although Douglas did gain eighteen votes as a write-in candidate.

[45] William Henry Waddle was born in Virginia in or about 1802. He died at Douglassville, Cass County, in 1868.

[46] Rachel's sister-in-law, Matilda Walker Cooper, was born in Alabama in 1830. On December 23, 1852, she married David's brother, William Henry Harrison Moores. Rachel Moores described Matilda as "a good woman, and most affectionate and amiable wife, and, oh, what a kind sister she has been to me." She was the mother of three children: Elizabeth, who died at about three years of age and is buried in the Harrison Chapel Cemetery; Richard Harrison, who was born in Bowie County in or about 1856 and died sometime before 1870; and Jane "Janie" Ross Moores. No record of a child born to this couple in 1860 can be found. Matilda Moores died on October 24, 1862, and is buried in the Harrison Chapel Cemetery, Redwater, Texas.

[47] Internal evidence in Rachel's journal suggests that her brother-in-law, Thomas Briggs Moores, upon his death in 1852 bequeathed his entire estate to his sister Jane Ross (Moores) Moore. His other siblings, David excepted, sought to break the will and have his property divided among themselves.

[48] Mary Ann Rosborough, the daughter of Elizabeth Harrison Moores and Dr. James Thomas Rosborough, Sr., was born on September 10, 1839, in Fairfield County, South Carolina. In Bowie County, she married James B. Hooks. She died on August 15, 1899, and is buried in Texarkana's Rose Hill Cemetery. "Direct Descendants of Charles Moores and Allied Families to Have Gay Reunion Sunday," *Texarkana Daily News*, January 26, 1958.

Nancy E. Moores, the eldest daughter of Charles and Mary Moores, married James Fay Rochelle, Jr. Following the couple's death in a South Carolina smallpox epidemic in 1843, Charles Moores brought their four sons—John Ross Rochelle, Charles Moores Rochelle, Henry Pinkney Rochelle, and Eugene Rochelle—to Bowie County. John Ross Rochelle was born on October 17, 1827, in Jefferson County, South Carolina. On October 5, 1855, he was appointed postmaster of the Myrtle Springs post office. On October 3, 1860, he married Sarah Ann Priscilla McCutcheon of Hooks, Texas. He died in Hooks on March 13, 1881. "Direct Descendants of Charles Moores and Allied Families to Have Gay Reunion Sunday," *Texarkana Daily News*, January 26, 1958.

[49] Robert M. Lindsay was born in York, South Carolina, in about 1830. He had been appointed postmaster of Boston, Texas, on February 25, 1850, and was elected justice of the peace for Beat 2, Bowie County, on August 2, 1852.

[50] A David E. Elliott, born in Tennessee in about 1829, died of tuberculosis in Bowie County in April 1870.

chapter five

OH, THE HARDSHIPS THIS WAR HAS BROUGHT US

1861–1862

A lthough Rachel Moores did not, the overwhelming majority of the white population of northeast Texas supported the secession movement during the winter of 1860–1861—so much so that in December 1860, when Secretary of State Lewis Cass resigned his post when President James Buchanan declined to defend the federal forts in Charleston, South Carolina, Cass County changed its name to Davis in honor of the Confederate president, and so it remained until May 1871 when the Republican-controlled state legislature returned the name to Cass. When the Ordinance of Secession was ratified in February 1861, Bowie County residents approved it by a vote of 208 to fifteen, and Cass County voters approved the ordinance by a vote of 423 to thirty-two. They also wholeheartedly supported the war effort of the Confederacy, sending thousands of men into the Confederate army.

Although the Victorian lady did not properly evince any interest in politics or any other issue not pertaining to home and family, Rachel held quite definite views, boldly supporting Millard Fillmore over James Buchanan in 1856, deploring the possibility of Abraham Lincoln's election in 1860, and declaring in her journal that "I am no monarchist, but assuredly not a black republican! Demands of too much democracy is not a good thing. It breeds too many demagogues!"

Although she admitted in 1860 that she had "always hated abolitionists," during the secession crisis of 1861, in common with a great many of the South's plantation elite, she remained at least a "conditional Unionists," and although she later became a wholehearted advocate of the Confederate cause, confessed that when the war began she "made up [her] mind to subjugation." Although she had met and enjoyed the company of many Northerners while a patient in a New York hospital and on a vacation trip to New York and New England in 1860, by the spring of 1862 she was writing, "I cannot think that a Merciful God will give us over into the hands of such a merciless, relentless, foe."

In her home, "the War was discussed as usual" by ladies and gentlemen, and during the first year of the conflict political and military activities were frequently detailed in her journal entries. In December 1861, she commented on the *Trent Affair*, predicting that Great Britain would enter the war on the part of the Confederacy or at least raise the hated Union naval blockade. This, of course, was not to be. Early in March 1862, she reported "hearing that Price and McCulloch had defeated Frémont in North Arkansas." This rumor was also false. The Battle of Pea Ridge resulted in a stinging Confederate defeat and the death of Brig. Gen. Ben McCulloch, a former Texas Ranger captain and a hero of the Texas Revolution.

With the storms of spring in the Gulf of Mexico, Rachel predicted that "Lincoln will groan for his fleets now in the 'Perils of the Sea.'" While she denied actually praying for their destruction, she did hope that "the will of God be ours, and if it results in their destruction, why, I say, Amen." Instead, by April 1862, that fleet was in possession of New Orleans and northeast Texas cotton exports were interdicted for the war's duration.

After the spring of 1862 and the deaths of two of her brothers, Rachel ceased to write of the war except in so far as to record how it affected her daily life and security.

The war greatly increased her household duties, and Rachel presumed that "if the war continues, I shall sink into a domestic drudge." By 1862, she could not imagine "what I will next use for dresses—dyed towel, may be," and early in 1863 she complained of bathing "for the first time, with homemade soap. My stock of Castile and perfumed soaps are too much diminished" by the Union naval blockade.

But these minor deprivations were the least of the troubles that the war laid at her door. Rachel Moores was forced by circumstances into situations beyond her traditional circumference, and she worried about "having to exercise my own judgment in matters wherein I am no judge, and have no expertise."

Rachel almost daily knitted socks, made shirts, and rolled hundreds of yards of bandages for "the poor soldiers"—an activity well within the confines of what a woman might do and remain a genteel lady. But in addition to fulfilling the traditional women's roles in time of war, she seemed astonished to note in her journal in February 1863 that "for the first time in my life I went to the crib and measured corn" and found herself "transacting business from which my natural inclination shrinks as well as my capacity."

Although Texas remained relatively unscathed by the war—"We have felt nothing yet to what a majority of the Confederacy have felt," Rachel admitted—war-time depredations, runaway slaves, scarcity, and constant anxiety concerning loved ones in military service rendered the conflict a nightmare for Texas women.

As historian Drew Gilpin Faust has written, the white women of the South had been "socialized from an early age in the doctrines of paternalism with their implicit promises of reciprocal obligation," and Rachel took great comfort in her husband's "kind care and protection."

The war violated the norms of femininity, however, allowing many women to take advantage of the way that "previously fixed boundaries—between states, genders, and races—suddenly seemed mutable."[1]

In May 1861, the feminist writer and editor Elizabeth R. Burnell wrote that "we would not say . . . home is not the center of the true woman's sphere . . . but we do say that it is not necessarily it's circumference." The home, she contended, may define nineteenth century women, but it need no longer confine them.[2]

When Southern women confronted the new social order created by the war, they struggled to cope with the destruction of a culture that had "privileged them as white yet subordinated them as female," and many sought a new definition and role for themselves, outside of the traditional Victorian ideals of gentility and dependence. Rather than embracing the opportunity to expand beyond the restrictive bounds of the cult of true womanhood and take joy and pride in the ownership of her own destiny, however, Rachel Moores, a thorough-going cultural conservative, clung tenaciously to the mores of the Old South and continued to yearn for the traditional role of the submissive, dependent Southern lady.

Rachel's fear of the depredations not only of runaways and local renegades was well founded. One such bushwhacker was Cullen Montgomery Baker, the brother of her friends Hila and Eliza Baker. This desperado had been born in Weakley County, Tennessee, probably on June 22, 1835. The family moved to Texas in 1839, eventually settling in Cass County where Baker established a reputation as a hard drinker, quarrelsome, and mean-spirited. With the outbreak of the Civil War, Baker enlisted in Company G, "Morgan's Cavalry Regiment," at Jefferson, but by February 1862 he was reported as a deserter. With the end of the war and the beginning of Reconstruction, Baker returned to Cass County where he attempted to earn a living as a ferryman on the Sulfur River, possibly at Moores Landing. His principal enterprise, however, was—as the leader of a gang of outlaws—the harassment and murder of Union soldiers, Freedmen's Bureau agents, and freedmen. According to an undocumented statement by one Baker biographer, "Dave Moore, [sic] an early settler and large plantation owner and also founder of old 'Forest Home' was said to have built a huge tunnel leading from his home . . . to the Sulfur River. Baker was known to hideout [sic] somewhere the vicinity."

As Baker and his gang largely restricted their killing to federal soldiers and freedmen, he gained the sympathy of many whites in Cass County. Although few in the county would have ridden with Baker, many were willing to help him elude capture.

His reign of terror was brought to an end on January 6, 1869, when he was killed by a group of his neighbors. He is buried in Oakwood Cemetery, Jefferson, Texas. Decades later, a local writer stated that Cullen Baker was "hailed as a hero, and by many, even as a Moses who had appeared, to lead them out of the wilderness of Northern Political Tyranny and oppression."[3]

XXX

[from the Journal of Rachel P. Moores]

[December 6, 1861] *Had company all day. Miss Dee Rush and Miss Sarah Salmon having kindly accepted the invitation I sent by Eli yesterday. I was not very well able to entertain, having a most acute misery at intervals throughout the entire day. Wrote to Mat, though, since supper.*[4]

[December 25, 1861] *This morning I was much engaged* [torn] *my sausages hurry up and attending to the bones, spareribs, etc., giving the Negros something for Christmas* [torn]. *Sent Dr. Nelson's parents some fresh bones, etc., which gave me much pleasure, knowing these hard times such things are hard to procure.*

Sister Jane spent the afternoon with me, or a portion of it, and then David drove us out until dark, and then we were alone but happy.

[December 27, 1861] *Was in bed almost all this morning but rode over to see Sister Jane and Mrs. Connally this afternoon. Sister Jane had company; Mrs. Connally was not at home. Read until bedtime as usual when David is in. Read when he is out.*

[December 28, 1861] *Wrote and read this afternoon and went to see poor Dr. Salmon this afternoon who is suffering most excruciatingly with bone felon. I never saw so bad a finger. Our visit seemed to cheer him so much I was so happy that we went.*[5] *Made the acquaintance of his sister, Miss Orpha Salmon, whom I think a sweet interesting young lady.*[6]

[December 29, 1861] *James and Mollie Hooks called at the gate on their return from her Christmas visit to her parents. They only talked a few moments at the gate. I sent Miss Morrison some shrubbery and jam. Mollie, I gave a quart of jelly for* **[illegible]**. *Just after they left, William came in on his way to Mr. Kennel* **[?]** *for his mother-in-law and visited with us, then rode over to see Mrs. Connally after* **[torn]** *I did not find her at home. I spent* **[illegible]** *two with Mrs. Brown while David went to see John. Returned by Reuben's.*[7]

[December 30, 1861] *Have been unusually busy today, sewing and making Negroes' winter clothes, renovating my house, washday, and I am head chambermaid today. My dear David has gone to drive surrey in good earnest. I have seen him only at dinner and now darkness covers the earth and yet he lingers. If I thought so, wouldn't I have a lonesome time?*

[December 31, 1861] *"Alone! Alone! How drear it is always to be alone." So says Mr. Willis, and sometimes I feel it a little dreary myself, though I rarely, if ever feel lonely. If I am only usually well, I do not feel so, for a housekeeper's task I think pleasant at most times, and pleasant work is better than stupid company at any time. But I'm reading too much for my health. My head is not right tonight.*[8]

I mended up a winter calico this evening, read, and put up the fresh ironed clothes and, as usual on washing and ironing days, washed the dishes. Nancy just presented herself at the window to tell me she is in misery—for the twentieth or thirtieth time this year—and she only lays in from one to six weeks at a time!

I hear the gate. My husband's come. No more working after he's in!

[January 2, 1862] *Arose early, eat by candle as husband wished to go and return from Courtland before dinner, but noon came and I ate dinner and still he tarried, and not until supper was begun did he come. Sister Jane and children spent this forenoon with me. So it was New Year's Day.*

I mended up David's clothes, or one pair of pants as that was all I **[torn]**. *I then tried to make all the Negro pants that was necessary to be made in my house, insofar as lay in my power. Oh! There remains much to be done yet. I spent an hour or two late in the afternoon working among my flowers. Most of my cuttings—and I brought a number of them from Arkansas—are living and doing well.*

Husband brings some cheering news. Old England has demanded Mason and Slidell, our ministers who were seized on the _ _ _ _ _ [Trent] English steamer bound for Liverpool to represent us at Saint James court.[9]

When is this cruel and unnatural war to end? Heaven forbid, I pray, that more blood be spilled by those who waged it.

I finished my book that I was reading and picked up To Cuba and Back *again today.[10]*

Spent today entirely alone. Wished very much to go to Mrs. Connally's, but had no one to harness the horse. My husband has been in the field all day, from early dawn until dark. I have been very busy trying to finish a set of chemise begun before I had the fever last August. Have worked myself down twice in my yard and once in my garden. Am easily overcome today. It has been very warm for the season. Having trouble to deal with smoke-making in the smokehouse. Have read but little and that that whilst lounging after dinner.

[January 3, 1862] *Went to work early this morning in my garden and whilst there Mrs. Connally came, but as it was the last day Henry was to remain at home for some months, she did not remain until dinner.[11]*

Miss Paralee Rush and Miss Orpah Salomon came before Mrs. Connally left and are still with me. We have spent a most delightful day. Miss Salmon, I think most interesting in conversation and, from what little I've seen of her, a charming girl. I have and **[torn]** *her acquaintance and friendship.[12]*

I played and sang so long tonight for the young ladies my throat hurts me much and I am not a little weary. Can't set up another moment.

[January 4, 1862] *Miss Paralee insisted so much that I should accompany her and Miss Orpha to Mr. Reuben's that although it was misting a little when we started, I went with them and returned in the rain, the young ladies accompanying me back, it raining too much for them to go home. I committed the same error tonight, sitting up and singing too late, although I slept but little last night and was sick well past midnight. I find Miss Salmon so pleasant I shall regret to give her up.*

[January 5, 1862] *The young ladies, Mr. Moores, and myself went up to Havana to hear Reverend Porterfield preach, and was most disappointed when Reverend Sheffield took his place. The sermon was very good.*[13]

[January 6, 1862] *Sent for reel today. Reeled two and a half hanks, spinning for the Negroes. The first attempt we have yet made to get anything like a task out of them, and the one had this task—Charlotte. I feel really much fatigued from close confinement to the reel and doing chamber work. My chamber maid* **[Lizzie]** *is getting such an invalid she is more waited on than to wait on.*

[January 9, 1862] *Spent today, as usual, all alone—sewed, cleaned out my pantries as I always do or have to do when Lizzie's sick. She keeps them in such confusion.*

I must think this winter unprecedented in its heat, for certainly I never experienced anything like it. There has not been one suitable day for killing or curing meat all this week, and today has been worse. I have been no little wearied trying to keep the flies from getting to the meats. It is "make a smoke" one minute and in five there is a blaze and it is "put it out." Then build another and so on throughout the entire day, and unless there is much smoke, the swarms will not disburse. So wearied had I become of it that for a few hours this afternoon I fled from it and spent the time with Sister Jane but found my smoke better on my return than when I left.

[January 10, 1862] *Another spring day. The heat is almost insupportable. The buds are swelling. The grass springing up, the bluebirds singing, and all things betoken spring although it is now midwinter. I find outdoors much more pleasant than in. I sat for an hour or more in our place this afternoon, really wondering if I should not send in and get my work and spend the remainder of* the afternoon out, but then little remained unfinished, and house servants idling away their time, and, last but not least, I was not quite through with the life of Bascom, that great and good man, enriched by [illegible] not of his own seeking and admired by the rest of the world.[14]

I was interrupted a while by the entrance of the woman, a newcomer who is gadding whilst her husband is making rails at fifty cents a hundred for the necessaries of life. So goes the world.

[January 11, 1862] I was disappointed today and [torn]. Rose early and dressed myself for a visit to Dr. Salmon, but my husband is afraid to have me go alone, as he calls it, when I only take a servant. The horses are perfectly safe, but I went hurriedly to work and footed some socks the men had out, helped to sweep my yards, and wrote some letters home, read a hundred or two pages, and so the day has passed very pleasantly; yet I do not think I ought to sit here, day after day, with no one to change a word with, no human face but the Negros. I have been told by physicians that I ought never to be left alone—that it was detrimental to my health—but at times I enjoy it very much. Oh! I love solitude. It has many charms for me.

It has been a little cloudy today, but cooler and more pleasant than any former day this week, yet the warbling songsters remind one of spring. Once more has "night come o'er the plain" and yet my husband tarries. I see I must eat alone or eat my supper too late.

This morning threatened rain, but this afternoon has been clear and still warm. I thought for some time in the forenoon we would have some sleet or snow with rain, but all appearance has vanished. I covered my jasmines for night and then uncovered them for the night. My orange trees haven't been covered this winter, only from the trees under which they are placed.

[January 12, 1862] Sunday. No church within reach. Mr. Moores took me out for a long drive. Thought I would see Mrs. Connally but was disappointed for the fourth time. We turned our horses toward the river bottoms, called before this hut of willful filth and poverty, for certainly I never saw [torn] happier face than this man possessed [torn] at the gate, though his skin looked as if it had been guiltless of soap or water for weeks, and the partner of his joys looked as if she was encrusted in sediment that would surpass the bottom in which she dwelt in growing vegetables, but there she stood, gazing at me from the door of her smoked hut at which loathsome little children played until driven from her sight. Poor untended little ones.

After dinner Elijah, John, and Agnes [Johns] rode over, the former making his last visit before returning to the army, his furlough being near out.[15]

It has turned very cold, so much so I have had all the tender flowers and fig trees covered.

[January 13, 1862] *Quite cold this morning. David has his last hogs killed today and tomorrow. I shall be busy in the kitchen as I have been in my room today, trying to learn Lizzie to spin wool, and I never spun a thread of it before in my life, but I surrendered finally and twisted a reel of knitting thread for David's socks.*

[January 14, 1862] *I feel weary, worn and nervous tonight; have spent a most unpleasant day. The Negros were not disposed to get at work in the proper manner this morning; did not get the lard on until very late.*

I went over to Mr. Reuben's to get a lard barrel at David's request and whilst there a servant came from the field for a buggy to bring Charlie to the house who, he said, had broke his leg. Poor Sister was so distressed, and Mr. Moores seemed much worried about [torn] making him very nervous. But, oh, it is the mother generally who suffers in such cases.

[January 15, 1862] *David drove me over quite early to see Charlie this morning. He was looking much better than I anticipated. Found Sister Jane administering to his many wants with untiring zeal.*

I have written too much today, read too much, and, oh, what a terrible headache I have coming on. I shall have to abandon my way of living again. I have used a little fresh hog meat for the first time in five years and it is producing such headaches, sour stomach, and a number of ills and aches.

[January 16, 1862] *Was disappointed today again as I thought of visiting the Salmons, but my husband is unwilling to have me go alone and he thinks himself too busy to accompany me. I resorted to that means always convenient to cure a disappointment—active exercise. I cooked most of my dinner, all of my supper with Mary Jane's assistance, and, as it was washday, did most*

of Lizzie's chamber work, read books, knit a little, and almost finished a dress for Betsy. What well woman would do as much as that, more than that I mean?

[January 17, 1862] *Knit, read, and, as it was a rainy ironing day, received, folded, and put away the clothes. Spent a large portion of this day making smoke. The weather is unpleasantly warm. The atmosphere damp and excessively disagreeable.*

[January 18, 1862] *Surely was there ever such weather? The meat house floor like a marsh and the meat dripping like a heavy shower of rain. I never was so tormented with anything as with this meat to keep the flies away.*

[January 19, 1862] **[torn]** *never been called a fine morning* **[torn]** *all is just as balmy and just as clear and warm. A more lovely day I never experienced, and sad to think that such a Sabbath had to be spent away from the Sanctuary of God—no church, no minister to even visit us. The only chance to hear a sermon on Sunday is to ride ten miles and then listen to one of the weakest men I ever saw make an attempt to edify a congregation. A good man, though, I think Parson Porterfield is.*

We have a weekly appointment at Forest Home when the M. E. circuit riders preach, and for the last two years we have had most excellent itinerants and have this year again. But though we go when the weather will permit [the old church is only a fit den for rats—no fireplace, no comfortable seats [)]—and treat them with the utmost respect, yet they feel under no obligation to visit us. My husband not a professed Christian, and I belonging to a different church.

Rode over to see Charlie this morning and to see poor old Mr. Baker this afternoon. Poor old man, he seems near the confines of another world and yet I am afraid he is neglecting to make the necessary preparations.[16]

[January 20, 1862] *Put my cook in the garden today and went in the kitchen and made Lizzie get dinner, made the pastry myself in my room. Knit, sewed, and read my Bible. Have committed to read it through this year.*

[January 21, 1862] *David carried me to Dr. Salmon's today and I spent the afternoon at Dr. Salmon's and I did not enjoy myself in consequence of David's unwillingness to go. Though I did not ask him to carry me, yet he felt it his duty to go, knowing that I needed more recreation that I was getting. This close confinement I feel to be pernicious and detrimental to my health. I try to labor more but find the old adage true that "all work and no play makes Jack a dull boy" if not "a dull me"! Poor old Dr. Salmon is one of the most distressing objects I ever beheld. They seem quite comfortably fixed in their new home, however.*

We returned home by the **[illegible]** *with this delay and then the increasing cold we had a most uncomfortable time getting home.*

[January 22, 1862] *Another cold day. It seems as if winter just set in. Captain Connally spent a part of the afternoon with us. He seems delighted with camp life and is most sanguine about the final success of the Confederate Army.*[17]

Grit **[illegible]** *fed and nursed my pet lamb, which was brought in Monday in wagon, its maternal parent refusing to acknowledge it.*

[January 23, 1862] *Was sick all night, and then we set up two hours today. David found another mother for my lamb today.*

[January 24, 1862] *Went to church today, though unusually small. Felt the disappointment keenly by Mr. Porterfield not being there. I presume he is sick as he is so faithful.*

[January 25, 1862] *A day of all work this has been, and yet not much done. I undertook to make my pastries as I usually do on Saturday and it proved too much for me, and Mr. Grissel came in with my reel just as was going to lie down and rest and so I foolishly began to reel and so tired myself out into spasms and had to go to bed.*

[January 26, 1862] *Have felt poorly today—capricious appetite—something unusual for me as is this nausea I've felt all day. I finished Genesis and began Exodus, which I nearly finished. Rode over to Mr. Moores' this afternoon and felt the better for a few hours chat with the folks over there.*

[Torn] *shrubbery and garden seeds and today but* [torn] *the weather last night being so warm I feel* [torn] *from it. Could scarcely hold my knitting in my hand since supper, and my eyes are so heavy I could not read a dozen chapters in my Bible.*

[January 28, 1862] *Sent Louisa to the field, who has been filling Nancy's place for three months, and went into my kitchen and made Lizzie get dinner, cleaned the kitchen as it is only cleaned when I sit in there. Took up the butter and worked it and made, my husband says, the best biscuit for dinner he has eat this year!*

[January 29, 1862] *A rainy day, left all alone as usual, heeled and laced*[?] *some stockings, mended husband a pair of pantaloons, which took me three hours by the watch, read over a hundred pages in* Commodore Perry's Expedition to Japan, *reeled two hanks.*[18]

I find myself compelled to keep my hands employed to keep from thinking myself to death. Since the first day of this month I never see my husband, only at meals, except for Saturdays, and often I am done eating both dinner and supper when he comes in. How am I to spend this year? I have lived several quite as much alone but did not mind it so much as now.

It has been dark over an hour, the rain is slowly dripping from the eaves. The Negroes sit around knitting, all in state, tea is waiting, and yet he tarries.

[January 30, 1862] *Was reeling this morning just as I got up from my breakfast and in comes a Sister Jane at my back. I was so shocked for a few moments I could not even say "be seated." I can't account for this nervousness I feel on anyone entering the house. It makes me feel as much so at times when my husband comes in as any other person, and yet I know his step.*

Sister Jane staid but a short time, only coming to change some sewing thread. I reeled until my reel broke and then attended to my soap making and darning my stockings. Read but little today.

[January 31, 1862] *Another cloudy gloomy* [torn] *I went into the kitchen and helped Lizzie to get dinner and put away the fresh ironed clothes. Knit and kept my soap pot boiling this evening* as I sent Lizzie to Mr. Moores to finish reeling Manny's **[?]** breaches. I do not find much time for anything when meat is to smoke and soap to make.

[February 1, 1862] Donned my shade bonnet and comfort and took a chair to the soap pot, and a most uncomfortable day I've had. The wind blew from every quarter and kept me chasing around the pot, the smoke nearly putting my eyes out and the day cuttingly colder, but I succeeded in making a nice pot of soap, though my hands are miserably chapped from having them so constantly in the lye.

I feel sufficiently tired to sleep tonight as I only took Lizzie and Mary Jane to boil ashes to make lye to make soap and to get dinner, too. Oh, for a cook that would never get sick!

[February 2, 1862] It has rained without ceasing since nightfall yesterday, a slow pelting. It being Sunday, I read my Bible until my eyes ached, then rested and read "Memoirs of the Bourbons in Spain" until my husband came, then drove out in the afternoon in the drizzle and read my Bible until dark.

[February 3, 1862] Rained all night and has been cloudy all day. I went into the kitchen and superintended the making of another pot of soap. Spent the afternoon with Sister Jane and her bad news from the state of war. Can it be that my poor brother is among the prisoners that been recently captured in Kentucky? Great God forbid, is my prayer. Oh, that this unhallowed warfare would cease. I sometimes have but little hope, but, oh, I can but trust that this is the will of my Heavenly Father.

[February 4, 1862] [torn] felt gloomy all day. I suppose in consequence of the melancholy news heard last evening. Dreamed last night of going home to my father's house—thoughts **[illegible]** became so exceedingly anxious about Dear Frank that I prevailed on my husband to carry me home and thought, just as I sprang from the carriage, I heard mother called Frank to attend her, and of course my joy was great, unspeakably so. I thought it prayers.

Spent the forenoon in the kitchen with my young cooks. Drove over to Mr. Connally's and spent most of the afternoon, and as I had no one here who knew how to unharness the *horse, tried to do it myself, but my husband came up much displeased at the disorder I put the harness in.*

I left Lizzie to twist me some thread—found only one slip twisted and that **[illegible]**. *If this war should result only in the emancipation of the Negros, I should take delight at the trophy, provided they were to be sent off for colonization. They are little else than a nuisance.*

[February 5, 1862] *Knit a sock this morning, having a desert already made. Cooked our dinner in my own room and twisted thread enough to make a pair of socks. Read the book of Mark in the Testament and planted some beet and mustard seed.*

I would have proved a valuable acquisition to my husband had I always accomplished as much, every day, instead of the heavy drag I have been compelled to be from Fate. I am far from well and have not had an easy moment all day, only whilst I was in action and motion, and then I could not feel the spasms that are so distressing to me.

I presume if the war continues I shall sink into a domestic drudge, tho, not that I feel it all servitude, but I am compelled to take much exercise, and my husband thinks every expedient should be employed in order to ensure the success of the Confederate Army, and by attending **[torn]** *leave some man out of business who will have no excuse for not joining enlisted, though he has commissioned him a crop* **[illegible]** *made himself, yet he is constantly expecting to be called into the army. Now my poor heart throbs when I dare think of it.*

Husband not having any time to drive me out as has been his habit, being left so much alone leaves my mind free to indulge in these gloomy anticipations, and but for keeping my hands employed, I do not know but I should become fond of the life of a recluse. I've always loved solitude and yet I think it's as detrimental to my health as a continued round of gaiety.

Hark, does not that sound precede from a galloping horse? If so, I shall soon be the recipient of a score of kisses and a hearty squeeze.

[February 6, 1862] *Rained all day. Had to dry yesterday's washing before the fire, which kept me pretty busy turning clothes. Knit a sock foot and read most of the gospel by Luke.*

This day I have been married seven years! and it is with mingled feelings that I retrospect those years of deep afflictions that they have been; yet they have brought me many joys. In my husband I have ever found an ardent sympathizer and such devotion as is not often met by one who has been such a constant ailer as I have been. Yet God only knows how hard I have tried to recompense him and feel that he appreciates my efforts, for he is ever reproving me for enslaving myself for his comfort.

[February 7, 1862] *Another rainy day. Had severe neurotic sick headache and vomiting this afternoon.*

[February 8, 1862] *Saturday. Knit a sock foot, darned husband's pantaloons he has been wearing in the* [illegible] *this week. Spent two hours in kitchen and visited two of the Negros who are invalid.*

[Torn] *Have been all alone since breakfast. David went to Bowie this morning. I passed a most unpleasant night, restless and sleepless.*

Just as I was getting a little warm and composed, Harry[?] *came and said Nancy was sick, and as I knew an accoucheur was needed, I told him to hurry for Dr. Salmon, and just as I was getting quieted from the excitement, "bang" went the front door and Dr. Salmon had come. It was five of the clock, and soon as a fire was made and my bath was ready I sprang from the bed which had proved so uncomfortable for the last twelve hours.*

Passed all the day reading and writing as Dr. Salmon left just after breakfast, or rather just after David. I shall read my Bible until I hear the well-remembered sound.

[February 10, 1862] *David came last evening with a pocket full papers and today I had a feast. My mind is much relieved at present about Frank as the battle the Confederate army lost in Kentucky was under Zollicoffer's command—who was himself killed—but our loss, though considerable, was not one fourth what we heard it was. This the first defeat we have suffered, and I must think there was treason somewhere.*[19]

I see the Ohio and Indiana papers are turning with abuse on the administration (Federal). They seem just now to have awakened to the fact of their president being a fractive, a nuisance, despot, tyrant, plunderer, etc.!

Dear Me! Who should have thought anything else of such a physiognomy whose only sense, wisdom, and talents consist in foolhardiness. Northern fanatics sowed the wind, and now both sections reap the whirlwind.

[February 11, 1862] *David went to Courtland to give in his taxes and remained until late in the afternoon. Sister Jane and children spent the day with me, and so it is the first day I've had company all day in some time, and when David came he brought me three letters from the Dear Ones at home "with the glad tidings of 'all well,'" and when I had read and reread the home news, I began on a pile of papers that he also brought.*

[February 12, 1862] *Read the papers, knit, and* **[torn]** *after making the pastry. Planted some garden seed.*

[February 13, 1862] *Read until time to get dinner as it was* **[torn]** *was chief cook. Knit this afternoon. Mrs. Cooper and two servants came this evening on their way from William Moores to Mr. Kincaid's, another son-in-law of hers.*

[February 14, 1862] *Mrs. Cooper left quite early this morning though the weather was unpleasantly cold. Went through with the usual routine in my domestic affairs as heretofore since Nancy's indisposition.*

[February 15, 1862] *Read, knit, attended my yards, cleaned, and to dinner. Little Tily Brown bringing me a dozen partridges, and since dark I have amused myself with picking them, having Lizzie and Mary Jane assist me.*

[February 16, 1862] *A beautiful, bright though very cold Sabbath. Read in the forenoon and rode to Courtland in the afternoon to get some news, and, oh, what sad news we found in store: the loss of Fort Henry.[20]*

Oh! Father, Almighty in Heaven, save us, we do pray Thee, from another such disaster. We beg Thee, afflict us as Thou will, but save us from these, our inhuman enemies.

[February 17, 1862] *Read and spent the day superintending my domestic concerns intermingled with many petitions for our country's safety. Wrote to Sam, who I was gratified to receive a letter from last evening. Poor boy, now undergoing the perils of a camp life. May God be with him.*

[February 18, 1862] *Tried in vain to make soap today, my lye being too weak. Went over to see Sister Jane this evening. Her husband is gone to court and Ruth sick.*

[February 19, 1862] *Have been confined to bed all day.*

[February 20, 1862] *Have set up but little today. Had some soap* [torn] *Mr. Harrell's appointment but* [torn] *and no one there, as it was eleven of the clock, misting rain, we did not go in the church, supposing by the lateness of the hour no one would be there, and got home in time to miss a pretty good wetting in our faces at least, for it has rained unceasingly ever since we got in the house.*

I've had a severe headache all evening and, indeed, since I woke this morning, but was almost blind with it for a few hours after dinner. Rained all evening.

[February 23, 1862] *Do not feel well. Have set too much, exercised too little, indeed, none except a little cooking for tomorrow. Have been so absorbed in Poets and Poetry of Europe as to have almost forgotten everything else.[21]*

Mrs. Connally came early after dinner and glad as I ever am to see her, yet it was with regret that I had to resign my book. Sister Jane and her little one came over too. Poor little Ruth looks badly. I fear she has scrofula, though her parents think differently, and I hope as they think.[22]

[February 24, 1862] *Read this morning and went to the office this afternoon. Called on our return at Dr. Salmon's. Spent an hour or two very agreeably. Poor man, he looks so much the object of commiseration. Reached home at dark and read our latest paper, and, oh, how my poor heart bleeds as I read our reverses. Three of our forts have been successfully attacked and taken.[23]*

But I cannot think that a Merciful God will give us over into the hands of such a merciless, relentless, foe. Oh, no! Let us trust in Him. He is able, and if we ask, He is willing. He has promised, if we ask in faith, to grant us our desires.

[February 25, 1862] *A bright pleasant day this has been. My mind has been ill at ease. My dear husband seems already in* [illegible] *although the day has been only pleasantly warm. I rode on horseback with him nearly to* [torn] *lines this afternoon. I feel as if I want to be with him all the time.*

[February 26, 1862] *Sat all morning with my knitting in the kitchen. Read* European Poets *this evening and am delighted with Goethe. In Dante, I find many ennobling sentiments. In Wordsworth's best verses, indeed, I find so many beautiful things, and a greater number of them, I scarce know to which is my preference given.*

Why is it that I can enter into, appreciate, enjoy, the beautiful lines I read and yet I am not able to compose one line of decent poetry? I cannot even express intelligibly at all times my thoughts. Sometimes burning, bright thoughts crowd through my head to my very soul. All my family suffers from this a malady. There is not a good conversationalist in the family.

[February 27, 1862] *Worked in my yard today. Had fig trees set in the fowl yard. Knit, read poetry— Heaven inspired poetry. Read* Acts of the Apostles. *Feel a growing interest in the Bible, which I* [illegible] *the Creator.*

[February 28, 1862] *Washday. Got dinner with my own hands. I would be extremely anxious Nancy should be able to cook again but for the improvement in my health since I superintend the culinary department, but then, when I'm so infatuated as I was with Tasso this morning, I should never enter a kitchen but for reasons above named, and my husband's tight pinch just at this time and so many of the Negros ailing—all the women.*

Well might Byron exclaim ("Childe Harold's Pilgrimage") his description of Ferrara, Italy. "Tasso is their glory and their shame."

"Peace to Torquato's inspired shade. 'Twas his in life and death to be the mark where Wrong aimed her poisoned arrows, but to miss. Oh, victor unsurpassed in modern song!"

How true when Byron says of the Duke of Ferrara, "Alfonso, how thy ducal pageants shrink from thee! If in another station born, scarce fit to be the slave of him thou mad'st to mourn."[24]

[March 1, 1862] *Have reproached myself taking up the European Poets when Josephus remains unfinished, which I began on the* **[illegible]** *of last of October and which I was so much more interested—intensely—than ever in anything before read, until I came to the "Jewish Wars," and it being in part a reiteration of what it contained in the first volume, I grew tired and laid it aside. But after perusing a few pages, became as much interested as ever, but, oh, horror! That siege by Vespasian, that terrible, awful, appalling siege, being almost in a state of siege ourselves, rendered it the more forcible, and I could the better realize its horrors.*[25]

"O Jerusalem, Jerusalem, thou that killest the prophets, and stonest them which are sent unto thee, how often would I have gathered thy children together, even as a hen gathereth her chickens under her wings, and ye would not!"[26]

Behold, your house is left unto you desolate: and verily I say unto you, Ye shall not see me, until the time come when ye shall say, Blessed is he that cometh in the name of the Lord."[27]

Saturday [March 1, 1862] *Made soap today, read Josephus, exercised much in the kitchen.*

Sunday [March 2, 1862] *Brown, our last year's overseer, came in whilst I was reading my Bible, which I much hated to lay aside to listen to his gossip. Oh, these tattlers, these scandalmongers. He had heard, he said, enough about Mr. Moores Friday at Courtland to make him mad and almost get him into a fuss. It does seem to me the girth of a turnip seed would hold the soul of that man whose only delight is in breeding disturbances.*[28]

[Torn] to every man whom he hears evil spoken of and [torn] dissention, he succeeded in what he wanted to do, in making my husband angry, for which I have hardly forgiven him yet. However, the anger was much more against his officiousness than lies [torn] or any other such holes or sights[?] as he had [torn] scandalizing the reputation of a man whose character is

above reproach because he will not, as they do, take up other people's business, concerns, and character at the neglect of his own.

His home is his Empire, the governments of its affairs his chief delight, and, Heaven be praised, his wife, his Queen on whom he lavishes all his leisure moments, leaving the offices of the National Government to those whose thirst seems insatiable for it; which the Athens Post *says, and very truly says, too, "A thirst which nothing short of death or the Judge can quench," and, in nine cases out of ten, for their own self-aggrandizement.*

Well, I have digressed, and yet I intended writing no homily at first on news carriers, but only intended commenting to thee, my faithful Journal, my thoughts of this most disgusting carrier of news, for I verily loathe the presence of such a mass of corruptions, and yet, for the sake of his poor and downtrodden wife, I tolerate his business visits here.

[Monday, March 3, 1862] *Was sick all last night, very sick after midnight, when I generally succeed in getting a nap. Charlotte came to the window and announced Eliza's approaching accouchment, and so I was nervous and restless until day, and then felt sick all day.*

Old Mrs. Grissel called and wanted meat, soap grease, and potatoes. Poor old creature, it is most pitiable to witness such a wreck as hers on life's great ocean. When everyone casts nets, many find fish, and yet she, with a large family, lives in want of most of the comforts of life.

I have been stupid all day now, suffering with sick headaches. Must not eat any more cabbage. I thought as I tried them last week without harm, I could do the same now. Have tried reading, sewing, and knitting, all in vain. Did work among my flowers an hour so and found some relief, but soon as I sat down my head grew worse.

[Wednesday, March 5, 1862] *Pursued the same routine as has been my wont for the last month or two. As my husband started for the Harper field this afternoon, I set up on his horse behind him and we returned by Reuben's and spent an hour. A novel way for me to ride, but I was more than paid for my jolt on Fanny Gray in hearing that Price and McCulloch had defeated Frémont in North Arkansas. I pray it may be true.*[29]

[Thursday, March 6, 1862] *One of the most disagreeable days we have had this winter (spring now). High, dry winds—perfect gales. I presume Lincoln will groan for his fleets now in the "Perils of the Sea." I do not pray for them to be wrecked, but the will of God be ours, and if it results in their destruction, why, I say, Amen.*

In perusing European Poets today, I read a portion of Lessing's drama, Nathan the Wise, and think it the most beautiful drama I ever read. Wish I could get it all.[30]

[Friday, March 7, 1862] *Suffered dreadfully last night and today with cholera morbus. I am better tonight.*[31]

[Saturday, March 8, 1862] *Husband went to Courtland today to attend a matter—the making of a military company—and so I eat dinner alone and await him to supper.*

[Sunday, March 9, 1862] *These dark, gloomy clouds, heavy peals of thunder, lurid flashes of lightning, are all, all, in accordance with enemy spirits and disturbed, tortured senses. David, my darling husband, has agreed to enlist next Saturday, provided the company is made up and what he thinks properly officered. When he told me last night, half in jest, I did not believe it, and only when Dr. Larey looked gravely* **[illegible]** *on being called on for his testimony it seemed* **[torn]** *spasms. I grew cold, then hot. I was hard pressed to gain the mastery over my feelings in my husband's presence. But, oh, who can tell the bitter anguish that seized upon me. Selfishness does not allow me to say it, but my husband is one of the last men who ought to go—no constitution, no* **[illegible]***, over thirty Negros to watch over, and in a neighborhood where there are people who are more to the dreaded than Lincolnites in the absence of protectors, as black hearted and evil as ever disgraced the revolutionary pages of Seventy-Six.*

God be with us, I pray. Oh, do not, most merciful Father, forsaken us and give us over to our implacable enemies. Rather, Father, cut us off with disease. But, oh, Most Gracious and ever to be adored Maker and Ruler of all, save our souls. Let death come as it may, that we all without the loss of one may inherit Thy kingdom is my fervent ardent prayer. Amen. Amen.

[Monday, March 10, 1862] *Thanks to my Heavenly Father, I do not feel so oppressed in spirits tonight. Was weak and nervous all the morning and went to bed from dinner table with nausea when, lol, visitors were announced, and on going to the parlor, who should I see but Mrs. Salmon, Senior and Junior, Mr. and Mrs. Peters and children. They came to spend the day, and as one dinner was over, had to have a supplement added. They all seemed a little mortified at first when dinner was announced, but I laughed and told them I often did the same thing, which seemed very gratifying to the older Mrs. Salmon. We spent a very pleasant afternoon which sped on "eagle's wings." Oh, I do wish I could have company often when I am gloomy; not that I crave it, but because it benefits me so much.*[32]

[Tuesday, March 11, 1862] *Felt gloomy all morning. Sister Jane and little girls spent the afternoon with me.*

[Wednesday, March 12, 1862] *Tried to make some hard soap, but made a failure. Can I ever get my full consent for my [torn] wars. What shall I do? God help me— us—all.*

[Thursday, March 13, 1862] *Busy in yard and kitchen all morning. Spent the afternoon with Sister Jane. Oh, that [torn].*

[Friday, March 14, 1862] *Last night was one of storm, thunder, lightning, hail, and rain, and it has rained incessantly all day, and yet my dear husband had to brave the wind and rain and go over to Courtland to give in taxes.*

Have been reading Goethe's Faust *today, which I must say I'm disappointed in, yet I like it well.*[33]

Haven't had my foot outdoors but once today.

[Saturday, March 15, 1862] *This day has been a prelude to what I will have to pass through for one week and maybe one year. God only knows. David went to Linden today and from* thence he will go to Shreveport. If the company is made, that is, completed, that he joined and he finds it to be officered credibly, he will remain and be sworn in. If not, he will withdraw, and in this moment "the die is cast."

[Sunday, March 16, 1862] *Sent Eli to the office for the mail and news from Linden. The company broke up, but David and others have formed themselves into an independent company and will go anyway. Oh, it grieves me to hear it. I don't approve such companies.*

Went late this afternoon to see poor old Mr. Baker. Sent over this morning to hear from him and send him some butter, and heard he was so bad, and when I went I was shocked. I know he is dying. Such is life. Mutability is written on all things.

[Monday, March 17, 1862] *Passed the morning out doors* [torn] *ill, confined to my bed since dinner.*

[Tuesday, March 18, 1862] *Was very sick all night and haven't left my bed all day. Mr. Powell came this morning for plank to make poor old Mr. Baker's coffin. Sister Jane and Ruth came over a short time this morning. Mrs. Connally, Mrs. Brown, and Samuel called on their way to the funeral and spent an hour or so. Mrs. C[onnally] said she was going to come back and spend the night with me, and as it is now night I am looking for her.*

[Wednesday, March 19, 1862] *Mrs. Connally came last night after supper. We set up late, I having been in bed all morning, so we talked until after midnight. A storm came and went, and yet we talked. But this morning I feel better and remained up several hours today.*

[Thursday, March 20, 1862] *Read, knit, and could not rest. Thought of that cruel separation which takes my husband away. God only knows when.*

[Friday, March 21, 1862] *Exercised in the garden today. Tried to work a little in it as Nancy is sick and I sent Lizzie and Mary to wash for Miss Hila Baker yesterday. Consequently, there has been no work done in it for a week as my own washing and ironing was to do the first of the week.*

[Saturday, March 22, 1862] *Dear husband, how long and hard I miss thee this Saturday night. I feel lorn and sad without thee. The winds keep up a low moaning wail, methinks a dirge for the mighty, the dead who are so constantly falling in our ranks.*

Can it be true. This news of just heard that General McCulloh has fallen? And that the **[illegible]** *was not yet in when the news left, but in now. The scales are turned, and when* **[illegible]** *our* **[illegible]** *stand? I dare not think or rather give expression to thought.*[34]

[Torn] *have been made at the tonight, too happy to* **[torn]**. *My darling husband is home, is with me. Can I* **[torn]** *for my week of loneliness already by his presence.*

[Monday, March 25, 1862] *Went with husband as far as Dr. Salmon's. Spent the day. Feel tired tonight and he is sick from not eating any dinner, and so I cannot feel well.*

[Tuesday, March 26, 1862] *Have sewed most industriously today. Cut me out a dress this morning and then almost made it. I sent the skirt for Sister Jane to sew up and hem on the machine, and so I shall have to go to work and pay her.*

[Thursday, March 27, 1862] *I finished my dress this morning and almost made myself sick sitting so much. Mrs. Grissel came over for more meat. Mr. Woodbury Salmon is come in to spend the night with Mr. Moores. Is going to accompany him to Bowie tomorrow.*

[Friday, March 28, 1862] *"All alone my watch I'm keeping" this night. Husband, Mr. Salmon, and Mr. Crawford started for Bowie a soon as dinner was over. Mrs. Crawford from home, and Sister Jane spent portion of the afternoon with me. All of which makes me feel my loneliness the more.*[35]

[Saturday, March 29, 1862] *Well, I've had a busy day and accomplished almost a New England housewife's work, and had but sit me down when, lo, that well-known voice calls out "Rach!" and in comes husband and three other gentleman and not even a spark of fire in the kitchen and my supper had been over three hours, but thanks to a good supper* **[illegible]**.

[Sunday, March 30, 1862] *David was sick all night and day. But a short ride. Sister Jane spent the afternoon. Mr. John Carr a few minutes.*[36]

[Monday, March 31, 1862] *A splendid day for gardening, which we took advantage of.*

[Tuesday, April 1, 1862] *A broken pen and nothing of note or interest to record this week only my* [torn] *poor, desolate Hila and Eliza Baker. I had not been to see them before since their father's death. They take it better than I felt they would.*

[Saturday, April 5, 1862] *David has been gone to Courtland all day and I've been alone and busy as a bee. David brought me a beautiful book to read from Mrs. Salmon and such a dear little note in reply to my own to her accompanying a bouquet to herself and napkin of sweet-meats to her husband. Such acknowledgements are gratifying when they come from the heart and by note.*

But I never liked to have one make such return to my favor before anyone. God only knows how much I strive to be charitable to the distressed and afflicted and what poor encouragement I have thus far received, the present instant excepted, and if the family do not repulse me it will be a heartfelt pleasure to administer comfort in any way most needed to poor old Dr. Salmon. Oh, who can know the pangs endured by the hopelessly afflicted. Oh, Father, help comfort and cheer the afflicted!

[Sunday, April 6, 1862] *Read until my eyes were weary then took a long ride—too long for my good.*

[Monday, April 7, 1862] *Planted me a strawberry bed in the garden today. Commenced reading the* Pillar of Fire, *the book Mrs. Salmon send me, and much pleased with it.*

[Tuesday, April 8, 1862] *Read all day and nearly over my book.*

[Wednesday, April 9, 1862] *Through the* Pillar of Fire *and feel much enlightened regarding the plagues sent on Pharaoh and Egypt in consequence of the detention of the Israelites. I thought, as did Sesa, King of Tyre, that they were only an arbitrary display of power of the Deity!*

Our gallant friend Scott Connally spent last night with us. He has been from the army on the Potomac **[torn]**. *Wrote to Sister E*[lizabeth]*, worked in my* **[illegible]** *some roses.*

[Thursday, April 10, 1862] **[Torn]** *a rainy day. I worked my ottoman until my eyes were worn, and then went out looking for turkey nests, the rain abating a little. Found our hen sitting. Brought her and the eggs to the house.*

[Saturday, April 12, 1862] *A most trying, busy, and perplexing day this has been to me. Lizzie has stolen my keys again and refused to get them or the cowhide to be whipped with, and whilst out pretending to look for them she ran away and hasn't returned yet.*

[Sunday, April 13, 1862] *Read, took a ride to poor old Mr. Grissel's and carried him a bag of meat and potatoes.*

[Tuesday, April 15, 1862] *Sick all day and confined to my bed this afternoon.*

[Wednesday, April 16, 1862] *In bed all day. Read First and Second Chronicles and Ezra.*

[Thursday, April 17, 1862] *Have worked on my ottoman, though in bed nearly all day. Sister Jane came over a few minutes this evening.*

[Friday, April 18, 1862] *Wrote to Sisters Mat and Virginia and John Watts, and tonight to Sister Margaret.*

[Saturday, April 19, 1862] *Saturday night and what a week's work accomplished in three days! And since Thursday, ten of the clock, I have cut out and made twenty-two pairs of* pantaloons with the assistance of Mary Jane and Lizzie and Betsy today, but they only sewed the seams. All the rest devolved on me, but I'm feeling this effort of being so smart. My shoulder aches so awfully and feels much bruised.

[Sunday, April 20, 1862] *No church and a rainy day. Read my Bible and went over to Mr. Reuben Moores' this afternoon.*

[Monday, April 21, 1862] *Sewed on the Negro children's summer clothes. Poor old Mr. Grissel was here to fix the well but was not able. Through pity we gave him a pair of pantaloons, or rather cut them out and gave him. My husband gave him an old blanket coat, then I gave him a lecture about his inhuman, unnatural children who, in vigorous health, is letting their poor old father starve and freeze from lack of food and raiment, and bowed down to the earth, too, with deep affliction. Heaven help such unfeeling wretches. What* **[illegible]** *made for?*
    Read the **[illegible]** *again today.*

[Tuesday, April 22, 1862] *Made two Negro dresses. Commenced* **[torn]** *"deformed, transformed." Read my Bible a considerable time. I now study every day. One of Rhea's men have come* **[illegible]** *spend the night on business; he is a young thing and does have a look as if he were capable of enduring the hardships consequent upon a camp life.*

[Wednesday, April 23, 1862] *Read, sewed, worked my flower beds. I practiced a little.*

[Thursday, April 24, 1862] *Feel weary and stupid. My poultry is doing badly. Had ten little turkeys killed today, and yet I've been watching them.*
    Up all day and working my flowers, none of which are in full bloom and looking most beautiful, and the air is filled with the fragrance, or rather, my head, as I have decked it with buds of the attar roses for tea, or rather, clabber, as husband calls it, as he has exchanged tea for clabber for his evening meal.
    After supper I took a long walk (for air) with husband to look at his stock. I'm sorry, being a farmer's wife, that my taste is so limited for poultry, stock, etc. I love to ride in and around the

plantation and look at the green corn and wheat, etc., but then my tastes are sated. My ramble so helped my head that I came in through the parlor, and though it was almost dark when we returned, I played some organ tunes, which David seemed to think was sweet in the dark.

[Friday, April 25, 1862] A day of clouds, mists, rain, and gloom. A few rays of sunshine this afternoon, which time I spent in the kitchen preparing Sunday's pastry, and tomorrow I can spend all day in having my yard dressed.

[Saturday, April 26, 1862] Spent the forenoon with the house servants in working my yard. The afternoon, Misses Hila and Eliza Baker spent with me. David has been all day to Courtland.

[Sunday, April 27, 1862] The morning spent as my Sabbath mornings usually are, reading and walking. Went over to see Mrs. Harper's poor little afflicted babe this afternoon. Its liver is swollen until it protrudes out from beneath the ribs. Poor little sufferer. Were it mine, I would long to see its pulses stilled in death and know its poor spirit was [torn].[37]

[Illegible] morning in the kitchen as I worked the [torn] after last week's beating rain I sent [illegible].

[Monday, April 28, 1862] [Illegible] both in there. Went to see Hila and Eliza Baker this afternoon, and on our return followed up the branch into huckleberry country. I have been wishing for a tart some time, and now I have the berries gathered and picked, but just a little, as the buggy is broken and had to ride behind David.

[Tuesday, April 29, 1862] A rainy day from "Morn till dewy eve." Took advantage of my imprisonment to write to my Dear Pa, my only surviving parent; and yet I do not love so much better than my Stepmother. He was always the most thoughtful for me. She the most affectionate. Read, embroidered, rambled about among the flowers with my cloak and overshoes.[38]

[Wednesday, April 30, 1862] My reflections are not of the most pleasant nature this evening. Sister Jane has on several occasions deeply wounded my feelings, and the last time it occurred—

Saturday week—I promised myself that should it ever occur again, I would seek an explanation and we would have a better understanding such as sisters should have, and so I endeavored to do today, having had my feelings cruelly hurt for the three weeks, but I saw that she justified herself and put all the blame on me, and though she said she was not hurt when I left, yet I think I know better, if she made a true exhibition of her feelings.

She was evidently much excited, and I know that I was, though I did not mention them, yet a remembrance of past wrongs rose up and so overwhelmed me as to render me entirely unfit to make all the explanations I desired to.

[Friday, May 2, 1862] *Embroidered, read, wrote* [torn].

[Saturday, May 3, 1862] *Have passed today alone, David having gone to the blacksmith shop, etc. Embroidered, read, looked after my* [torn]. *The morning bright, balmy, and beautiful, and the afternoon cool.* [Torn] *clouds and rain—a real May day.*

Alas! Has the May of life deserted me? And is the summer here? So soon! Why, it seems but yesterday I was a little child, sporting amid the flowers, chasing the butterflies, and looking for birds' nests, my favorite sport.

Oh, yes! I well remember when the diminutive wren's nest with its three or four tiny eggs was worth infinitely more to me, or was more dearly prized or [torn] and sought for, than e'er was a casket of pearls by countess, dowager, or princess.

But now those blissful days are over, and my joys are subdued. Not so much, perhaps, as they would be at my age.

David has returned and brought the Negros home (twelve of the clock when came home and rested half an hour) from the field to wash their clothes, and most fortunate he did not remain any longer as he found two horses and their colts sick from the buffalo gnats, which had been two or three months later than they were ever known to make their appearance before and consequently no antidote had been used and the Negroes did not care if they all died in plow. Would not ever come home for [torn] and driving their horses when they knew they were sick.

[Sunday, May 4, 1862] *One mule dead this morning and another died at four of the clock. The horses are better, though sick.*

These making in all eight horses and mules David has lost since he commenced keeping horses, and but two of them cost him less than one hundred and fifty dollars, and his matched ones cost him two-fifty each, and the favorite one he lost.

We've had a day of alternate rain, clouds, and mist, and now at sunset pouring down thick and fast.

[Monday, May 5, 1862] *So much rain and damp atmosphere has almost made me sick, and the buffalo gnats has been the greatest nuisance today of any insect I ever saw owing to the humid atmosphere which has been so heavily laden with the perfume of flowers it has been with difficulty I have breathed for the last five hours. Indeed, I became apprehensive of fatal consequences and had all the fragrant flowers cut down and carried into the woods away from the windows. Just after sunset, David [torn] most as much as myself, and said he felt relief [torn] entered the room on their removal.*

Embroidered, read.

[Tuesday, May 6, 1862] *Today has been somewhat more agreeable than yesterday. More sunshine and fewer gnats. I have been endeavoring to have the yard cleaned of all the decaying vegetable matter, weeds, and grass that have been cut from the squares and left to dry to be swept, but the rain has caused them to mold and emit a bad odor, or I imagine so. The walks, I have swept every few days, but find the squares hard to rid of the weeds as they are but little used. Laid off and began to embroider me a gown yoke.*

Feel ill, and since I began to write am chilly. My knees ache and my head feels dizzy, brain confused. My liver is inactive, or, rather, it is so inflamed it is affecting my kidneys; yes, whole system.

My dear husband went to Bowie today. As the carriage is broken, he had to walk from the [illegible] to Mr. [illegible] and consequently cannot return tonight and I am alone. Alone! How drear it is to be alone at times. Nothing to beguile the weary hours when one cannot read.

It is seldom, but in moments like the present that I feel within me an inordinate desire for that greatest of blessings (or curses, whichever it proves to be), an affectionate child. But these moments of gloom and as a despondency do not last long.

[Wednesday, May 7, 1862] *Imposed a variety of employments on myself today. Succeeded in manufacturing my first hard soap. My husband with me tonight and all's well.*

[Saturday, May 10, 1862] *I have worked most industriously on my yoke and gown, and have the embroidery all done, sleeves and yoke, and it remains only to put together, which I should have done this afternoon but for an increasing indisposition. Though the sun has just set yet I must retire.*

[Sunday, May 11, 1862] *Have been confined to my bed all day and such a lovely day it is, rendering the affliction double in consideration of the pleasure one loses in not being able to get out.*

[Monday, May 12, 1862] *Have been up today, or part of it, and tried to work but am not able.*

[Tuesday, May 13, 1862] *Tried to sew, but such dizziness in my head.*

[Wednesday, May 14, 1862] *Suffered an arm hurt last night with headache. I have been ill all day. Too many peas for supper, the first peas and beets I have had this year.*

[Thursday, May 15, 1862] *As usual, some better, were the* [torn] *been well, though up all day.*

[Friday, May 16, 1862] *Sewed, read, and wrote. Dr. Salmon spent a* [torn] *of today with us and the War was discussed as usual, but little news besides the blockading of the mouth of Red River. The fall of New Orleans I had heard of, but was prepared for it, but, oh, God, deliver us from this worst fate, falling into our enemy's hands, an entire defeat.*[39]

[Saturday, May 17, 1862] *We have had clouds and sunshine alternately today. A clear sunset, however.*

[Sunday, May 18, 1862] *No church. Read, rode over to Mr. Reuben's this afternoon. David went to the office.*

[Saturday, May 24, 1862] *The monotony of the past week was broken by visit of business from Mr. Anderson Moores, who is the nearest crazy to marry of any widower of any one it has been my misfortune to see.*[40]

We had a most refreshing shower on Thursday, which we were needing much.

[Sunday, May 25, 1862] *Heard a very good sermon at Forest Home today by Rev. Sheffield. Rode out as far as Mr. Connally's this afternoon to see Mrs. Brown.*

[Monday, May 26, 1862] *On examination yesterday morning, found insects in some of our meat, and today have it all out—eighty-seven hams and one hundred and twenty-six shoulders. I'm very sorry David did not dispose of the joints instead of the sides, as I am fearful we're going to have trouble with it.*

[Tuesday, May 27, 1862] *Spent all the forenoon out having the meat attended to. Finished the pincushion I began last week to embroider for Mrs. Hooks.*

[Wednesday, May 28, 1862] *Spent more time than was pleasant at the meat house today and am fearful we will lose much of it.*

When my husband finished the book he was reading I went into the library to make a selection for him, but when I returned to the lounge with Alone he had turned over for a nap and I soon became interested myself and will finish it before I give it to him.

[Torn] portion of my morning in the garden among the vegetables, the remainder reading and sewing.

Finished *Alone* today and am more delighted, if possible, than with my first perusal. Also finished my sun bonnet began day before yesterday.

Sister Jane and Ruth rode over the middle of the afternoon and spent about thirty minutes. She brought news of our defeat at Corinth and loss of 30,000 men. But, oh! I do hope, do pray to my Merciful Father that the rumor is false. Oh, is there to be no end to bloodshed? God save my brother, cousins, and friends and all whom it will be Thy will to save is my prayer. [41]

[Saturday, May 31, 1862] *After my morning duties were over read Pollok until dinner, and this afternoon have been making my culinary preparation, and somewhat more extensive than has been my wont for the last year past in consideration of tomorrow being the Sabbath. I always have less for variety then than on other days, but still, by examining myself closely, I find that I can still render less onerous the duty of servants on that day, which we are commanded to keep holy.* [42]

But dear life! What a transgressor I am. How many new resolves made this last week, year, yes, years. I make promises but do not keep them binding enough, so I am fearful I shall not be able to keep them. But in the last week I have vowed to myself to serve my God more diligently than I ever have. But what temptations, besetments, embellishments! one finds themselves continually in. Truly, St. Paul says, "the flesh is weak," and again, "when I would do a good, evil is before me." Surely the way to heaven is "the narrow way," and, oh, the obstructions one finds therein. [43]

[June 1, 1862] *A bright, beautiful, soul inspiring Sabbath morn is this. We rode out and called a few minutes upon unhappy Grissel family. I carried them a shoulder of meat, which I think the old woman construed into an act of conciliation, as on presenting her husband some clothes not long since I reprimanded him severely about rearing a family of such ungrateful, indolent* **[torn]** *children and grieve about their welfare, when they allow him to suffer for all the comforts and most of the necessities of life.*

On our return, called on a poor, forlorn looking Eliza Baker. Found her alone with a little niece, poor child.

I rode over towards Courtland to see if we could get any mail matter or hear from the Erwins. Did not get farther than Dr. Salmon's. Dr. and Mrs. Salmon presumed the mail had not come, as it was four days late last week. Spent an hour quite pleasantly with herself and daughter. But. oh. the sympathy I feel for that afflicted old man.

[Monday, June 2, 1862] *Spent today with Sister Jane. Walked to and from there and have taken considerable exercise and hope I shall sleep well tonight as the weather favorable for sleep—cool. exceedingly cool—and a warm fire quite pleasant.*

[Tuesday, June 3, 1862] *Did not sleep much or well last night and have suffered extremely all day with headache. Think I stayed out in the hot sun too long this morning. It being ironing day I undertook to accomplish too much myself.*

As I cannot sew or read much with headache. I made cake this afternoon—beautiful nice cake.

I do wish the crops were laid by as I so much wish for a ride this evening. or either I wish the mules had not died and then I could ride every day as the buggy is mended. No other reason why I should not.

[Friday, June 6, 1862] *Have been confined to my bed since Wednesday. Not feeling well today. having read too much whilst lying down. I get so listless when I'm in bed and when doing nothing that I read and shell peas and snap beans. etc., etc., and consequently do not feel so well when I get up as I should. Sister was over Wednesday morning a few moments.*

[Saturday, June 7, 1862] *How much we're needing rain. The yard is like a clay bank and vegetables beginning to wilt. Busy at a little of everything. not able to do much of anything. Poor appetite and but little strength.*

[Sunday, June 8, 1862] [Torn] *pleasant. Sabbath. and as usual* [torn] *a living death. We do not even have a parson to visit us and converse with us about things. Most truly can I say the Bible is my only guide. and shame on me that I do not study it more, with more earnestness. I feel that I am but a stumbling block to my husband. Oh. that I could be that means of his conversion. but. alas for human frailty! We cannot do anything without God's help. and that we cannot obtain without earnest seeking for it.*

[Monday, June 9, 1862] *Though up and going, do not feel well; poor appetite and nausea of the stomach.*

[Tuesday, June 10, 1862] *Oh, I'm so wearied looking at and having the meat ashed and sunned, etc. One hundred and fifty pieces out now, and more than half as much in the meat house. Were fortunate enough to sell four hundred pounds today but had to let the best go.*

[Wednesday, June 11, 1862] *Was sick all last night with a headache though rode as far as Mr. Johns.' Stopped to leave some meat purchased of us for Mrs. Balty.[?] and what a den of filth I found her in. A pretty, interesting looking little woman she is, too. Why is it, when everybody that is well can live neat, why do they live otherwise?*

[Thursday, June 12, 1862] *Sister Jane spent today with me, and old Mrs. Gilssel was "to get a few things." I do not like to encourage, but what are we to do. I know I am censured for taking any notice of them, but they are miserably poor and afflicted, the most downtrodden of God's creatures I have ever seen. The poor old man, I believe, tries to do his duty and would, I think, to God and man, but for his beggar of a wife. But what shall I say when called to account for turning them away empty and naked? That the mother and wife was too coarse to feed the sick and hungry father and children? I do not bestow alms before other people, only when asked, and do try not to let my right hand know what the left is doing.*

Agnes Johns came this afternoon to spend the night with me. I'm glad to see she is somewhat [torn].

[Friday, June 13, 1862] *Have been sick all day, though cut and fitted a jaconet duster for Agnes and cut out some shirts for my husband.[44]*

[Saturday, June 14, 1862] *Turned pastry cook and chamber maid this morning, as the house servants are still working at the meat. Finished reading* Alone, *which I began to re-peruse a few days since as David had it out of the library reading it himself. Agnes left this evening.*

[Sunday, June 15, 1862] *Drove over to Mr. Reuben's this morning and brought Harry and Judson home with us. Mr. and Mrs. Brown spent the afternoon.*[45]

Out having my poor dried up and dying roses watered and dry leaves partly covered them to retain the moisture. Some of the prettiest ones have died from the drought. Oh, how much I do regret to see my vegetables dying for want of rain, and I almost fear our corn will be cut off. David says without more rain we would not make one grain. Should such a calamity befall us now, Heaven pity us. Oh, our Father in Heaven, avert such a disaster.

Sewed and wrote a letter home this morning.

[Tuesday, June 17, 1862] *Sewed this morning. David drove me out far as Dr. Salmon's on his way to Courtland, but Dr. George Salmon detained him on his way there and he did not go to his office so we got no mail matter but spent a most pleasant afternoon with Mrs. Salmon and Miss Sara and all Dr. George's family, the older Mrs. Salmon sending for them.*

Among other things, I learned that the reason of our (my husband and self) unpopularity among some of the good citizens was we put cup towels (table napkins) on the table and would only drink out of silver goblets and was generally too **[illegible]**. *Uncharitable people, I pity more than I condemn you. Surely you never look only into the "front wallet."*

[Wednesday, June 18, 1862] *Had a chill last night just as I was disrobing for bed and have been sick all day. Difficulty breathing. Palpitations since and nauseated stomach, yet I have been up most of the day* **[torn]** *after showers of rain, which I thank my* **[torn]** *for. It will prevent corn and other things from dying if we have another in a few days, though it was not enough to run.*

Sister Jane and Ruth rode over a few minutes this afternoon.

[Thursday, June 19, 1862] *Have been confined in bed until half the day and part of the other half. My good husband drove me out this afternoon.*

[Friday, June 20, 1862] *Had to forgo the pleasure of going to church this morning on account of indisposition. I really feel I shall take the fever. My skin and is cold and clammy, and then for a few* minutes too warm. My eyes are weak and pain me much, very much, and altogether I feel as if I had been sick a month. Had a cup of broth before breakfast and one before dinner.

I insisted, though, on my husband going to church, and he said he heard a good sermon and is pleased with the looks of the new minister, who, so he says, looks goodness.

Miss Dee Rush and Miss Sarah Salmon have come to spend tonight. I do not know how much longer.

[Saturday, June 21, 1862] *Do not feel better than three or four days ago. Do not think I'm going to have chills. Took a long ride this afternoon as far as Mrs. Baker's and back by Mr. Reuben's.*

[Sunday, June 22, 1862] *Feel better today. Went to church to Forest Home. As the minister, Mr. Sheffield, was to dine and spend the night at Mr. Reuben's, we drove over and spent the afternoon with them. I feel much better tonight. But, oh, horror! Another murder—cold blooded!*

[Monday, June 23, 1862] *Had most delightful drive this morning over to the river. I went to pick blackberries but found very few. Husband, Mary Jane, and myself did most picking-more than enough for two desserts and supper tonight. I went in hopes of getting enough to make cordial and feel disappointed that we got so few. I cannot give up the idea of cordial making yet and must put away one jar of jam.*

Read most industriously this afternoon as an antidote for fever. I fear I shall not succeed in keeping it off as I have every symptom.

[Tuesday, June 24, 1862] *Assisted Lizzie with her ironing* [torn] *wore dress and had a drive down to Mrs. Baker's and took her some sweet and Irish potatoes. The girls gave me eggs, which I much needed, my hens scarcely lying. Found Miss Hila quite sick and Eliza looking miserable.*

[Wednesday, June 25, 1862] *Mrs. Brown was over this morning and gave David most of the particulars of that horrible murder. Young Lindsey* [or Linsay[46]] *killing Mr. Harris, a most excellent and peace-loving man from all I've heard of him. They live at Forest Home, our nearest church—*

two brother-in-laws murdering in cold blood and both murdering young—not arrived at their majority when the deed was committed, and both of their victims elderly men with large families.

Cullen Baker, Mr. Bailey's murderer, I saw at his father's house last evening, and that I much respect his sisters. I have a loathing contempt for him. Gary **[or Torey?]** Lin**[d]**say is in custody awaiting his trial. Will be tried in a magistrate court.[47]

[Thursday, June 26, 1862] Spent the morning in making cake, but Lizzie spoiled several in baking them. Did a little house cleaning this afternoon, floors whisked up, beds aired and shifted, etc. I'm in preparation to entertain twelve or fifteen persons each night of the meeting commencing at Forest Home tomorrow morning and to be conducted by the Baptists. I would hope my trouble would not be in vain or pleasure, rather. It is so seldom I—we—are called on to assist in supporting a religious meeting that I find it a heartfelt pleasure.

[Friday, June 27, 1862] Owing to Linsay trial, there were few persons present at church today. We have no company tonight except the ministers, Reverend Sheffield and Porterfield.

Do not know when I, my, patience was ever so sorely tried as it was this morning. Yesterday I only made Nancy cook one meal—dinner—and milk morning and night and had her clean the kitchen things before noon and the kitchen on this afternoon so she might go to rest at dark. That she was **[illegible]** up early this morning and cook some meats to carry to church, as the weather is too excessively warm to prepare them in the oven at night. But instead of obeying me, she set up much longer **[torn]** one piece of meat, ham, on last night **[illegible]** all night and a mutton leg she put in the pot of hot boiling water which only served to **[illegible]** and blistering it over on the outside, and sent it to me in less than an hour from the time she carried it the kitchen. So, at breakfast time, only two hours from church time, I had to have a ham boiled, another mutton joint roasted.

Seeing that she was possessed with an evil spirit, I knew that she would do nothing well, so I superintend the cooking of the meats, and thought best to make the biscuit myself and warned her, as I generally have too, about scorching, and came and laid me down to rest a few minutes on the lounge.

I'd taken more exercise than I usually take so early, for in addition to doing her business, I had made a large jelly cake and sponge cake without any assistance whatever. But I did not remain on the lounge but a few minutes, remembering her humor, and when I went to the kitchen she had a red hot lid on the oven and the biscuits badly burned, and though on such occasion she always puts on a long face and same time a serious air, and assumes a pitiful accent—yet I could see from the workings of the corners of her mouth that she was trying to conceal the delight she experienced in trying to annoy me, and it was more than I could bear, or thought I ought to bear. So, I picked up the pot hooks and pelted her shoulders, and smart. She was so surprised, it being the first time I ever struck her or any other grown woman, that she performed all the feats, I think, the most skillful actress or tragedienne ever conceived of. I never saw "Rachael," the French tragedienne, but she lay Madame Gassier, Cortesi, and all the others I have seen vastly in the shade, and screamed so wildly that her Master came running, morning paper in hand, to learn the cause of the histrionics, and he gave her a real lashing with a halter he picked up en route for the kitchen.[48]

[**Saturday, June 28, 1862**] *More in attendance that I would have thought, and Mr. Sheffield gave us a very good sermon this morning. I did not feel like sitting up in* [**illegible**] *and went to the buggy and took a nap. Mr. and Mrs. Lockett* [**torn**] *child spent the night with us and also the minister took tea with us. I am much pleased with the Locketts.[49]*

A still larger audience today, but I do not think the sermon so good in the forenoon as yesterday in the forenoon. I heard neither afternoon sermons. I felt quite mortified, as I did not arrive in time to hear the text read. Having sent the house servants on ahead, I was delayed longer than I thought to have been, dressing and cleaning the house. After resting a while and eating supper, we rode over to Mr. Reuben's and remained a few minutes.

[**Monday, April 30, 1862**] *Spent the early morning in the garden, having vegetables gathered for dinner and the Negroes. A vegetable dinner I found a real luxury after eating meat and pastry dinners for three days.*

I fear unless we have rain in a few days, we have had almost the last beans and cucumbers that we will have this season.

I put my own breakfast in my basket and bonnet and mantle on my chair of clothes, as we design taking a daylight start for Bowie and only intend remaining two days—just long enough to gather and make some blackberry cordial—not to visit, as our friends from that side do not visit us.

[Tuesday, July 1, 1862] *We were threatened with rain and a storm this morning and did not leave for Bowie, though we had neither here. We drove over to see Mrs. Brown this evening, and to my utter delight and astonishment, dear Mrs. Connally met me at the gate, and with feelings of regret and sadness we embraced, and what a wreck she is to what I expected to find. Though I knew her grief would be timely for the dear ones laid in a distant land to "sleep the sleep that knows no waking"—one in the early bloom of boyhood, the other a new made husband and father.*

But what a consolation must be the thought of whose **[torn]** *and to the Kingdom of Glory. "For then shall be great tribulation, such as was not since the beginning of the world to this time, no, nor ever shall be."*[50]

Barring an unanticipated hindrance, I shall go to Bowie tomorrow.

[Wednesday, July 2, 1862] *Have been sick all day and consequently did not go to Bowie but insisted on my husband going as I knew he felt the disappointment more than myself. But what a long, long day to me. No one to exchange one word with and too sick to do more than wake Mary Jane up to her work.*

I have tried to read but it worries me to hold a book long at a time when they are compelled to lay on their back, and, when I'm sick enough to be confined to my bed my eyes are very weak.

[Thursday, July 3, 1862] *Slept well last night though all alone, except servants, but feel extremely weak and nervous this morning.*

Sister Jane and children and Mrs. Connally came at eleven of the clock to spend the day. David, too, came just before dinner, and so I unexpectedly had a table full when I expected none. After Mrs. Connally had her horse caught this evening to start, David prevailed on her to spend the night and went for Mr. Crawford Connally, whom she did not like to leave alone or with the overseer's family.

It was a real pleasure to me to have her with me, but, oh, at nightfall her sighs and moans were ever truly distressing. It seems to be strangely true that our minds are more accessible to grief, or tender remembrances, at the close of the day than any other season of it. If I am the least gloomy or given to contemplation, it increases as that period comes on. If anyone has hurt my feelings through the day, at twilight the vivid remembrance of "wrong inflicted" rushes in my mind. **[Illegible]** at the circumstances that occurred.

This afternoon I felt particularly sad, and dear Mrs. Connally's sighs but aggravated the feelings. Why, oh, why? do we despair at what is intended for our ultimate good. I thank my Heavenly Father for the crosses that drive me to the foot of Thy Cross.

[Friday, July 4, 1862] My heart is too much filled with **[illegible]** painful emotions to revert to the past as associated with "the Glorious Old Fourth," anniversary of our National Independence. My husband has given his Negros today, as has been his wont ever since he came to slavekeeping.

Mr. Connally and his mother left this morning. Mr. Moores went out hunting with Mr. Connally, and short time after Mrs. Connally went away, and whilst he was out, I fell into a melancholic strain from which I have not been able to extricate myself. Indeed, I have not felt otherwise since dinner yesterday.

We drove down to Bell's this afternoon as I wished to make some arrangement with Mrs. Bell about having some cloth woven. But, oh, what a hovel of filth and poverty and little dirty-faced, matted-haired ignorant children!

[Saturday, July 5, 1862] Rode over to see Sister Jane this morning to get some instructions relative to sending my thread to the loom. I remained so much longer than David thought that I should he became uneasy and came to see what was the matter, and as he rode over to Mr. Johns, I spent the day with Sister Jane. Came home sufficiently early to make pastries for tomorrow.

[Sunday, July 6, 1862] When I seated me here, at this cool, shady window, it was to pen a few thoughts about this beautiful, bright Sabbath morn and about Sabbaths generally in their influence on country homes and households, but just as I seated myself, my eye wandered out to the landscape, and such a scene of a rural enchantment was presented that all else was for the time forgotten in my admiration for nature, animate and inanimate. The gentle zephyr swaying the green oak boughs and apple limbs which almost breaking beneath their treasures, and the birds, blue, red, and mockingbird singing, chirping, twittering, and hopping from tree to tree and from branch to branch.

[Torn] I answered myself, watching the mockingbird whose nest I found a few evenings since who expressed the deepest concern lest I should find her little home, which contains her future hopes. She flickered from the garden palings to the apple tree where was the most perfect gem of a little nest I ever saw.

I wish this scene of domestic bliss and quiet would be emblematic of a National Peace. Oh, Father, from Thy Throne above, hear and grant the prayers of many who are supplicating Thee this morning for thy intercession in our behalf. Oh, does man ever pray Thee restore peace and quiet to our distracted land!

[Monday, July 7, 1862] I have passed a most pleasant, though somewhat melancholy day. Last evening, in searching the library in quest of something for my husband to read (he is more difficult to suit in a book—never as well pleased as I am) I selected Jane Eyre, and as he was complaining of a headache and did not wish to read, I devoured the first few chapters, and then we took a drive, which was prolonged 'till near dark, and this morning, after my early household duties were over, the time most opportune, my husband being called to Courtland to pay taxes, I took it up again and had almost completed the perusal when David came at five in the afternoon, and an hour after he had rested so as to read the papers, I finished it.

How that book fascinates me, the heroine just to my taste, and what an admirable character I think Rochester was. I never look into the book without being reminded of my husband's best qualities, at least the traits which first called forth my esteem, my earnest affection—his indefatigable energy and perseverance, his daring coolness and not-too-be out-done spirit in trying moments, in great perplexities, his independent, defiant spirit doing homage to nothing but true merit or genius regardless of what the world may say, and it is that which still keeps the flower alive. Not a [torn] what the world generally calls an amiable [illegible] me. I want to look up to my husband and admire as well as love him, and I want him to respect as well as pet me. I cannot be happy without either.

A tyrant, I heartily despise, have but little less fancy for an unctuous husband. I cannot subscribe to those lines of Moores which say, "I know not, I ask not, if guilt's in that heart, I but know that I love thee, whatever thou art."[51]

I can see my husband give way to violent fits of temper or impatience and love him just as well after, because I know he was never made to restrain or control his passions in boyhood. His parents, it seems, did not deem it at all essential or important or did not very well understand how to impart the lesson. I'm not prepared to say which, but suppose it, since of all I know he could do it now but for his health, but never, as long as it forms a part of his groundwork, of his fretfulness, can he gain the Mastery.[52]

But I have digressed. I'm not only melancholy, [illegible] is not the only ailment. "Night comes o'er the plain," and I must take a little moonlight ramble to get any sleep.

[Tuesday, July 8, 1862] For the first time since our marriage, Captain Whitaker, my husband's brother-in-law, came and spent a few minutes in our home, accompanied by his two youngest sons. His wife, Mrs. Whitaker, my husband's own sister, has never "darkened our door"! though lives only a little over half a day travel from us, and we have made three especial visits and called three or four times, besides.

But I'm not a favorite with my husband's sister because I am an invalid and my husband takes expensive journeys with me when all the other means fail to prolong life, or seem to. They are necessarily expensive because extensive, and they are equally beneficial to my husband who takes the greatest pleasure in affording his wife comforts, pleasures, etc. But Mrs. Whitaker contends his money (means) would be much better [torn] to his relatives, who are less [illegible].

[Torn] strikes me that I was remiss in what I was saying on the preceding page about what elicited love or admiration from me to my husband and what my disgust. I merely said I loved him nonetheless in consequence of his unrestrained temper because I did not hold him altogether responsible, and then it rendered him more enthusiastic, more affectionate, and less secretive if, on the other hand, he was a cold and impassive but difficult to be appeased when aroused.

This afternoon I sewed most industriously until near sunset when I heard my husband's voice in the forest adjoining the orchard, and seeing some bright blazes along the road, I hied thither and joined him where he was watching the Negros, or his trash gang as he styles them, clearing the road out by collecting the limbs and sticks that lay in it and making brush heaps and burning them, and two of the men were cutting down trees from the corners of the fence and cutting them to put fire in, and I amused myself running along with the little Negroes, throwing pine knots into the places to make them blaze.

At last I climbed up on the fence and sat down with my husband, and before we were aware the moon shone down on us, so delightfully had the time passed. Equally pleasant was the succeeding hour spent on the portico "in concourse sweet" in the bright moonlight.[53]

[Wednesday, July 9, 1862] Cloth making has added considerably to my labor of daily duties, as I have to spend a portion of each morning reeling the women's thread. Mary Jane is not getting through her morning's work early enough to do it all herself. But, thanks to my Heavenly Father, I am able to do much more than I ever have done since a housekeeper.

I do not know anything about cloth making, only to reel the thread and have it dyed with maple bark. That is, the cotton. I dyed eighty hanks of cottonade yesterday, and in a day or two I will have the worsted dyed, and dread it, as I know of it only what people tell me and everyone tells a different tale.

Sewed and took a ride behind my husband to the blackberry patch. Uncomfortable it was [torn] though I did not tell him, and the birds had eat all the berries, but then rode too late, if there had been any to pick. As has been our wont for the last three or four weeks (with one are two exceptions) we enjoyed a pleasant moonlight tete-a-tete on the portico.

[Thursday, July 10, 1862] Sister Jane sent for apples for pastry today and an invitation for me to dine as she has company, Dr. and Mrs. Salmon. But as David was away to the bottoms and I was having a very nice dinner for ourselves, I declined, and went over and spent the afternoon.

[Friday, July 11, 1862] What a day's work for me—have actually colored seventy-one woolen hanks. I will not say "dyed," for most of them are unevenly colored. I had only Lizzie and Betsy's assistance, not wanting to take Nancy in from her spinning, and they're poor dependence, and then it takes so long to get over with morning's work.

Apples to pick up and what few vegetables there are to gather, and reeling cotton, and since more than half of each day I never let the reel stand still. In the forenoon when Mary Jane is in the orchard or garden, I reel.

[Saturday, July 12, 1862] *Oh, dear! I feel really sick tonight, with a cold last night. My husband is so restless as to keep the cover one half the night, through I'm constantly fixing it on.*

Wishing to have my yards clean today, though it is like an ash bank. I went to the orchard to gather apples myself and got exceedingly warm, and on my return to the house set down to sew in the hall and, a swift current of air passing through, I took more cold and soon feeling so stiff I went to my room and lay down on the lounge when, presto, here came Hila and Eliza Baker to spend the day. I got up and have worried through the day somehow, trying to entertain them as best I could. They called for **[torn]** *instrumental, and I tortured my poor piano trying to play. How I pay for such folly now.*

[Monday, July 14, 1862] *Never suffered much more than yesterday. Nearly died from some symptoms of the throat. I fear the results, but feel better, much better, today. Set up this afternoon some.*

[Tuesday, July 15, 1862] *Have been most of the day knitting and reeling.*

[Wednesday, July 16, 1862] *I feel somewhat disappointed in not attending Miss Orpha Salmon's* **[illegible]** *and* **[illegible]**. *I really would have liked very much to have gone but was not well enough. Can scarce speak above a whisper, and the weather dry and very dusty. Oh, for one good refreshing shower. Yes, yonder is a little weak cloud. I should not wonder we did have a little shower.*

Well, the shower came, just as I was taking my afternoon siesta, and a hot sunshine succeeded it, but we discovered in our evening's drive that it did not reach to the lower farm, and the dust is not settled in the yard.

[Thursday, July 17, 1862] *David spent the morning at Cortland, taxpaying day. This afternoon we carried our first piece of cloth, thread, rather, to the loom, to Mrs. Thompson's to weave. Dark when we returned.*

[Friday, July 18, 1862] *Have had a hard day with starch making. I had Betsy and Lizzie squeezing out two barrels full yesterday, and as I did not return until dark last night, they idled their time away, and this morning I found nearly all the bran to squeeze out yet and strain and put away.*

*But I was repaid for my trouble, for on entering the house my good husband had a nice watermelon out for me and some nice peaches, the first of the season. We have had the most, most delicious peaches I never saw anywhere since our orchard began to bear four years ago. But owing to the drought this summer, there is not one apiece on the early trees, and I'm sure the late trees will do but little good, they're so stunted. And our apples are **[torn]** being summer apples, but are not good as if it **[torn]**.*

Made up my pastry and cake today, as I am somewhat hoping for company tomorrow, and I was nearly out of cake. Being a great convenience, I never wish to be without it. Took a nice short horseback ride with my husband to his new ground since supper.

[Saturday, July 19, 1862] *As the sun is generally so hot by the time I get bathed, combed, and dressed of the morning, I impose the more agreeable part of the chamber work on myself each morning that I'm too late to get out, which is nearly every day. But I was much earlier this morning and was necessarily confined indoors, but think I shall make a new commencement tomorrow morning, or rather Monday.*

Drove over to Reuben's since supper and have practiced since my return.

[Sunday, July 20, 1862] *I think this decidedly the hottest day I ever spent, or this year, at least. The chairs, the sofa, are too hot in the rooms. I stroll in the hall, then the wind is too hot. I flee back, and nowhere find an asylum from this oppressive heat.*

Spent the day in reading, eating fruit, and this evening my husband took me on a long drive down to the river by way of the new road he cut two weeks ago.

[Monday, July 21, 1862] *Today I have felt more melancholy than ever. Resolved before leaving my bed that I would bear the petty vexations of my life with more fortitude, be more resigned to that which I could not control, but, oh, this struggle is hard. "The spirit is willing, but the flesh is weak!" Hear me, oh, my Father in Heaven. How illy my spirit brooks the harsh censures I oft times have to bear, unmerited reproaches, how they chafe me, and they too often from those who have known the longest and ought to know me well. Yet, they I understand me not. Sometimes I wonder why my Heavenly Father has given me such a sensitive nature when it is so often futile to feel all the poignancy such a spirit must feel when wronged or insulted.*

Sister Jane came over after breakfast and set a few moments. Came on business for her husband who does not visit us from causes unknown to us. I do not know that we do right in going over there so often.

Heaven only knows how hard I have striven to maintain social intercourse with my husband's family, and yet, because they all with one exception, besides my husband, are at law with their younger sister (Mrs. Moore) and he does not join them, they dislike him, but yet spend their approbation on me, thinking perhaps I influence him. It is no influence of mine, God only knows. But if he was disposed to sue his sister at law because another brother left his estate to her, I should certainly endeavor to dissuade him from so rash an act. If his parents, one or both, should have left their estate entirely to another brother or sister, I should have been willing to go to the law with them. A parent has not the right to disinherit an offending child.[54]

I have done a good day's sewing today and feel none the worse as yet. Commenced to make me a dress, also cut it out.

[Tuesday, July 22, 1862] *Sewed on my dress. Prepared a nice dinner for my guests who did not arrive.*

[Wednesday, July 23, 1862] *Sewed, read, and cut melon rind to preserve. Mr. Peron came on business and remained until dark, and just as he left Mr. Graham, the land surveyor came.*[55]

[**Thursday, July 24, 1862**] *Finished my dress but* [**torn**] *alteration as it is too long. Graham and his assistant spent the night again; got here after our supper had been over an hour. I should dislike to live where company would be coming in often, at unreasonable hours. It is so fatiguing. As it is, it is generally a pleasure, on my husband's account, who feels the want of male society. I imagine so, at least. It is so scarce.*

[**Friday, July 25, 1862**] *Altered my dress and ironed it over this morning and wore it to church to Forest Home. Heard an excellent sermon from Mr. Palmer, the minister who succeeded Mr. Hammel. Sister Jane spent a portion of this afternoon with us. I packed my satchel, put my breakfast in my basket, and intended to go to Bowie should I feel well enough tomorrow morning.*

[**Saturday, July 26, 1862**] *Started a little before five this morning, breakfasted at the river, and reached Mr. Moores' at eight, and spent a pleasant day in conversation with Mrs. Moores and the new teacher, Mrs. Hathaway, and at dark my affectionate little niece Toadie* [**Mary Elizabeth Moore Hooks**] *came, bringing her husband. I was delighted to see her, dear child. May her passage to the tomb be strewn with flowers. She does not need affliction to give her a meek and humble spirit—a feeling heart. Yet, she is all sympathy for suffering humanity. Her heart is overflowing with affection for her friends and relatives. Not so do I find the majority of my relations, and consequently they are like unto icicles near the North Pole.*

[**Sunday, July 27, 1862**] *Returned home this afternoon, but was caught in a storm in fifteen minutes after leaving Mr. Moores.' We were in a dense pine forest and the limbs and trees were falling all around, our eyes almost put out with the small pieces of bark and pine straw that filled the air. David sprang out and kept moving the buggy when he thought danger eminent from a threat of falling timber and to keep the horse from running away* [**torn**] *step until we crossed the river.*

[**Torn**] came from there home in our wet garments, and on reaching home that the rain was most [illegible] on the other side of the river, there having been but little here, except wind. I was hungry this evening and eat too much supper. Have a colic.

[**Monday, July 28, 1862**] *Was quite sick all night and did not rise from my bed until dinner. Do not feel much better this evening. I have read too much. Commenced reading* Explorations to the Arctic Region *by Dr. Kane. Am much interested.*[56]

Many indications of rain, but none, as yet.

[**Tuesday, July 29, 1862**] *Made me two underwaists today, or rather, remodeled them. One I was married in, the other made some months before. How my form has changed so much, so much smaller across the shoulders and larger in the waist, the effects of my dressing more naturally now.*[57] *I have naturally broad shoulders, and when I used to compress my waist, my shoulders expanded. Oh, could I but recall that one error of my girlhood. How much suffering I would have been spared. But alas! for the follies of youth, which nothing less than a bitter experience can cure in the most of us.*

How often and how much I have wondered at one expression of Lord Byron, that was "he did not know that he should alter any course he took in youth, or make any change in his conduct, did he have his life to live over again." Oh, infatuated man! Thy life seems to me to have been almost a mistake. Such a misapplication of talents—talents the most brilliant the Creator ever endowed the created with.

[**Wednesday, July 30, 1862**] *I have done much today, but have but little time to record it. Spent several hours this afternoon with Sister Jane.*

[**Thursday, July 31, 1862**] *Today has been spent in* [torn] *drawers etc., mending and sewing buttons on shirts, dresses, etc., and I consider it most profitably spent, but regret that my darning is not quite complete.*

Did not read a hundred pages in my book today but am more pleased with it the farther I go. Poor Kane, how I pitied himself and men whilst in "search of the lost party," the last day of March, the thermometer seventy five degrees below the freezing point; fifteen men, and their "sole accommodation a tent barely able to contain half that number who were obliged to keep from freezing by walking outside whilst the others slept." Under those circumstances, their halt was short, allowing but two hours' sleep for each, when they found their almost frozen party and their halt was shorter on their return, and all sick, maimed, and frostbitten, and two dying from the effects.

[Friday, August 1, 1862] *Finished my yesterday's work, and it kept me so busy I have found but little time to read. I feel stupid. I think it the effect of eating fruit between meals, a habit I have long discarded for health's sake. But our fruit is so nice—that is peaches and figs. (I seldom eat a summer apple. I am not satisfied with them as a sauce for breakfast and dessert for dinner.) I never saw such peaches anywhere as we have. They are of a most delicious kind, and we let them get so ripe on the trees that you cannot possibly gather them without inflicting a bruise.*

How it thunders. Each succeeding day we are threatened with a storm. Have a deal of distant the thunder, have lightning every night, and yet not one shower sufficiently heavy to plant garden seed. Nor have had since the twenty-third of May. And we cannot any day get more than two kinds of vegetables. That is another reason why I eat so much fruit.

Mr. Johns dined with us today.

I went to Mr. Thompson's this forenoon after our [torn] pieces of homemade cloth. Mrs. Thompson complained that it was hard to weave, and said she must have more for weaving the next piece, and we're already paying fifteen cents—five cents more than one towel costs us per yard. Oh, the hardships this war has brought us, and we have felt nothing yet to what a majority of the Confederacy have felt.[58]

Mr. Whitaker's Henry came this evening to see his sister, or rather, his Master sent him to Mr. Reuben's on business and, as his relatives were here, he had permission to spend his time here. He said his Mistress sent for me and her brother to visit her. Absurd to the last degree!

[Sunday, August 3, 1862] *Heard by riding over to see Sister Jane after supper last night that a protracted meeting was going on at Havana and concluded to go, but misery! What a disappointment! Who should be heard in the pulpit but Mr. Burkhalter, looking as much like a comic picture in a comic almanac as possible, and his language and gestures not belying his looks. But, after all, I suppose he is fulfilling his mission, but I would like to have been at home resting instead of enduring so much heat, dust, and fatigue for nothing.*[59]

[Monday, August 4, 1862] *A run-about I am getting. Went to Courtland to see and spend the day with Mrs. Crawford for the first time since her removal there, but lo, I found the house empty, and, as David had to remain until the polls were opened to vote, it being election day, I contended myself until eleven o'clock, and then came to a shady nook by the road side and eat our dinner and then drove to Mrs. Salmon's and spent the remainder of the day. Mr. Connally brought me a letter and half a dozen papers whilst I was at his house. We'll have a treat tomorrow.*

[Tuesday, August 5, 1862] *Read our papers and knit this morning and went over to see the Miss Bakers this afternoon, and on our return set out a large box of rose slips* [illegible] *to take root. Sister Jane came whilst I was gone and followed me to Misses Baker's—a long, hot walk, I imagine, for one in her situation.*

[Wednesday, August 6, 1862] *Tried to make light bread, but failed. Finished my preserves and put them away. Knit and read. Put Mary Jane to spinning. Want to make her spin enough to make poor old Mr. Grissel a pair of pantaloons for winter. I cannot take any from the Negros to do it, but can do some of Mary Jane's housework and have her do it.*

[Thursday, August 7, 1862] *Wrote two long letters home today. Knit half a sock foot. Read on, but slow, in my Arctic Exploration.*

[Friday, August 8, 1862] *Knit. Carried Mr. Grissel some cakes and fruit. I heard he was all alone, his wife being sick at her daughter's.*

[Saturday, August 9, 1862] *Began to make peach preserves today, a job I dread, as I wish to make eight or ten gallons.*

[Sunday, August 10, 1862] *I have spent this day most unprofitably and feel most unhappy in consequence. This morning, as we were riding out, I thought I would call at her gate and tell Mrs. Thompson I could get a slay made, and if she could not weave on the one she had, to send the thread home.*[60]

But as we were passing Mr. Connally's, Brown, as usual, came running to the gate and said himself and family were coming over to spend the day, and so I awaited them until David returned and came home and had a Sunday dinner prepared, a thing I very much dislike, and Mrs. Brown and her daughter came and spent the remainder of the day, and, oh, my! What an affliction, to be compelled to listen to and entertain people who have neither cultivated heads nor hearts.

Just as they left—supper time—Sister Jane and her husband drove up. He did not, however, get out of the buggy. She set ten or fifteen minutes [torn] risen so early in months or ever [torn] heard yesterday he could get salt in Jefferson [torn] at four of the clock this morning and in [illegible] Courtland from Dr. Salmon, who was [illegible] from them, that it was all a mistake. They were only selling it, ten cents per pound, and, of course, he only wanted it by the sack and ten of them then.

Agnes Johns and her father came this afternoon. She wishes me to assist her in making a dress –a bad time for me to render any assistance to anyone, being so busy preserving and attempting this morning to dry fruit. Put up enough myself to fill half dozen dryers and filled one by dinner myself. David scolded and fumed not a little when he came and saw me peeling peaches. Said if he had went on to Jefferson, I would have killed myself.

Cut Agnes's waists and fit on her.

[Tuesday, August 12, 1862] *Have been overhead in work today, having dryers filled, going through all the preserving process, dress fitting and making, though was very sick all night. The way I've felt for a few hours was really frightful.*

Agnes left this evening late and I kept her waists and dress, poor ignorant child. She wants fine things but does not know how to make or keep them. But she is an orphan and I will never refuse assistance in anything reasonable, and yet it does not look reasonable to make a dress for her when I hire the most of mine made.

Sewed, read, preserved, et cetera, a pleasant evening on the portico with moonlight and my husband.

[Thursday, August 14, 1862] *Am afraid I shall not escape a spell of fever this summer. It is just one year since I was attended last with fever, and the only spell of fever I ever had alone, and I suppose that was connected some way with my* [illegible].

Still preserving and working on Agnes's waists and sleeves. Finished the first volume of Arctic Exploration *tonight.*

[Friday, August 15, 1862] *Felt miserably stiff and stupid this morning. Kept in the lounge and read. Sewed most industriously all afternoon, for me. David drove me over to Reuben's for tea (buttermilk and clabber). I had a mutton killed this evening and think some chops for my breakfast will improve my feelings.*

[Saturday, August 16, 1862] *Had regular housecleaning today. Something unusual for me, as I have each room fixed as it needs it. And I do not know that it particularly needs it now, but my preserving pans have attracted the bees, and they have stained the windows, bed drapery, etc.*

A few nights ago I gave away one of my housemaids in marriage to one of the men, and I have been busy collecting up a lot of household goods for her, that is, shifting them out from Lizzie, with whom they had been kept, and having a mattress and some bedclothes fixed up.

Though she thinks to the contrary, I'm really pleased to get rid of her. Would have sent her to the quarter long ago, but knew she would go to the dogs. But troubled me no little in trying to make her mind her clothes, which I could not do, after having been washed for her, and she is to punish every week or so to make her even wash her skin, and now, I know, when from under my protection, the vermin small will run riot over her filthy body. She will find a difference in washing for herself and being washed for, in cooking for herself and being cooked for, in patching for herself and being patched for. But fools will learn in no other school but the dear one of experience.

[Torn] *passed this afternoon by a visit from* [illegible] *who I had twice met at Mr. James Moore's as* [illegible] *acquaintances, however, of my husband. Mrs. McAdams* [illegible] *is staying at present down at the ferry whilst* [illegible] *with the intention of acting as accoucher to Mrs. Whitaker's approaching confinement.*[61]

How strange, how extraordinary, it seems to me that a woman should place herself in the hands of an almost blind and quite helpless imbecile old woman, upwards of eighty years old. Why, I had to lead her in and out doors and from room to room, and she had declared her intention of surveying the whole house, as she said, to see if the reports she heard of David's "fine house and fine things" were true. The furniture that was nearest the windows, she stooped down and eyed very closely. That in the shadow or recesses, she assessed by touch. She concluded she had not heard an exaggerated account.

I told her the house was quite ordinary, as neither workman nor lumber could be present to make a "fine house," but the furniture was as nice as we could get in New York. Not so expensive, as it was not carved, but vastly preferable to our tastes.

After spending a few hours and having us fill her satchels with wool and peaches, she left us, gladdened by an opportunity of contributing, as we had done this evening, to the gratifications and pleasures of Old Age. I wish I could have an elderly—I mean, a very old person—visit me often. It is so pleasant to do little acts of kindness to those whose pilgrimage is so nigh ended.

I thought whilst performing a few kind offices for this poor old woman that Dr. Kane was mistaken when he says, "I felt that with them (speaking of the Eskimos) as with the rest of the world, pity was a less active provocation to do good deeds than the deference which is exacted by power." I had read this part and given it many thoughts when this old lady came in.

[Sunday, August 17, 1862] *Have spent this Sabbath more profitably* [torn] *was spent. Pray, my Heavenly Father for a continued* [illegible] *divine blessing. Oh, why don't I live a more consecrated life? Why do I grieve and fret at any of life's vexations, at any obstacles I may meet to obstruct my way to a better world? If ever I put up a heartfelt petition for my husband's conversion, it was this day. Oh, if he could see as I do and feel as I do, could there be more congeniality in the most important matter that I should make more rapid progress. But, poor dear husband, he seems not to feel the interest he should or feel any necessity for it. I do fervently pray my Gracious God may turn him from the error of his way.*

He is too doubtful and thinks if he could not be the best Christian, he could not be one at all. More than all, he has never had any religious instruction whatever, a sad, fearful thought to me, that a parent should bring a child in this world of sin and pollution and not feel the deep responsibility resting on them of giving them the earliest possible religious instructions!

Help us, oh! help us all, great Redeemer, and receive us into Thy fold, where we shall worship Thee, world without end. Amen.

[Monday, August 18, 1862] *Assisted Lizzie until noon in drying fruit. Sister Jane spent this afternoon with me which I passed in knitting. I'm out of something new to read, having finished* Arctic Exploration *by Kane yesterday evening, after which David and I drove over to the Reubens.'*

I feel very anxious about my husband's health again. I began to think he was going to stand this summer pretty well, his health has been so much better up to this time than for the last few summers.

[Tuesday, August 19, 1862] *Have not been well today though I've kept on my feet and been unusually busy, picking out and leaving herbs to dry, sewing up my fruit that is dry enough to put away. Since dinner I have been threatened with erysipelas, have almost every symptom. My left eye and that side of my face is swollen and pains* [torn] *stomach and fever and am really afraid* [illegible] *for fear I shall have a spell.*[62]

[Wednesday, August 20, 1862] *Was most successful at dying today. Dyed over* [illegible] *and five white cotton hanks a beautiful dark purple and have many wool ones in cold walnut leaf dyes. Do not know how I shall succeed with them.*

The tide has turned this year. The Negroes are laboring for themselves, and nearly all my pursuits devoted to clothing them, something entirely new to me. I don't know what I should do if we had not towel enough on hand to last me one more year. I fear I should never get the towels and kerseys, too, but by having enough when the war began and by buying some at forty cents since we can get far enough ahead with the kerseys to get one year's supply of towels made before what we have now on hand is exhausted.[63]

David and I spent this afternoon and Mr. Reuben's. Saw Dr. Miles, the new groom.[64]

[Thursday, August 21, 1862] *My poor husband was ill, quite ill, all last night with headache. Groaned near all night. Better this morning. Took a quantity of blue mass, which has relieved his head and stomach so much that we took a horseback ride to Mrs. Baker's, the buggy being broken.*[65]

Superintended my dying operations this afternoon.

[Friday, August 22, 1862] *Had the dryers filled for the last time this season, there being but few peaches now on the trees. Made and filled some dozen cups of nice peach jelly, though have been in bed near all the time since ten of the clock this morning and suffered much, too.*

[Saturday, August 25, 1862] *Sewed most industriously today, though on my back most of the day. Put stripes down one pair of pantaloons that were too small for my husband and seamed them all over. Being rested up, patched another pair.*

For the last hour or so, have been watching the Negros' merriment at the well whilst washing their clothes. Poor ignorant creatures, little did they know how to appreciate their present happy state. I only mean our own, not knowing how all fare.

[Sunday, August 24, 1862] *Finished reading the Old Testament, which I began (the last time) in the latter part of [torn] I think, perhaps a little earlier and maybe later. The reminder of the day was spent in lounging and reading European Poets and Humboldt's Travels, etc. [torn].*

I have been unusually stupid and listless, have a strange unnatural feeling in my head as if it were enlarging, with a roaring and rumbling in it. The monotony of the day has been broken several times, however, by the neighbors' children coming in for fruit. Strange today should be selected for such errands.

A Negro woman came in today near noon accompanied by her Master's only daughter, a girl of some ten years, for peaches for dinner. What can that mother expect of her daughter, when she is constantly under such influence? Does she know who her servant may have encountered on a walk of two and a half miles? What intimacies her daughter may have been eye witness to, and no excuses, for the little maid has two brothers older and two younger than herself who might have come with propriety on a horse or walked instead of having his sister trudging along the highway on Sunday when everybody's Negros have free passes and no other protection than an ignorant Negro. She may be a well meaning Negro, but any male of her own color would be acceptable that might fall in with her for a short while, and on the way home would be still more agreeable.

I sometimes think these things prey too heavily on my mind, and it may be that the kind Ruler of the Universe has foreseen with what anxiety I would watch over a family, thusly rendering life burdensome, and has in mercy spared me the pangs. I know it is for some good, all of which is not known to me, poor frail mortal that I am. Well might Shakespeare say in more senses than one, "Woman, thy name is frailty," or at least it would be applicable to me in a different sense to what he applied to the Queen of Denmark—Hamlet's mother **[torn]** and read today.

Agnes Johns and her sister spent the day with us—came for her dress waists. Mr. Johns **[illegible]** Senior is spending the night with us.

[Tuesday, August 26, 1862] More thread dyed today. Sewed and read "Pygmalion."[66]

[Wednesday, August 27, 1862] Spent the forenoon with Sister Jane. The afternoon in basting the pleats in husband's shirt bosoms, ready for the sewing machine.

[Thursday, August 28, 1862] Assisted in filling all my fruit dryers again this morning. Sewed on my shirt bosoms again this afternoon. I stopped time enough to fix up three little bags of dried fruit for Sister Jane. I sent three kinds because I could not spare but half bushel of the nicest kind, and having three qualities, I sent an equal portion of each.

The Negroes are now picking cotton. Commenced last Monday, and now I make my daily record and then practice until he returns. There are so few events worthy of record in my outside life that a few lines is generally sufficient "for the day thereof."

[Friday, August 29, 1862] Sewed and ironed some for exercise in the forenoon. I felt unusually unwell sometime after dinner. Though went to the orchard with my husband and assisted him in gathering some peaches to carry tomorrow to his sister, Mrs. Moore, and think **[illegible]**. Then put up some dried fruit, fed turkeys, et cetera.

When I was married, she gave me fruit, turkeys, and other little et ceteras altogether important to young housekeepers who have no market in reach, and Sister Jane very kindly let us have our second year's fruit dried at her house and would have given me fruit the first year but for Mrs. Moore supplying me so profusely, and she gave me, too, quite a number of chickens, which favor I never shall be able to return as she so far outnumbers me every year and [illegible] in raising chickens.

I know that our relatives do not wish these favors returned, as there are other ways of remuneration, but David and I have no children and therefore it is not proper we should accept any favor we do not return, and more besides.

[Saturday, August 30, 1862] *This has been the most joyless day [illegible]. Not one thrill of happiness—not one ray of sunshine—one cheerful emotion has cheered my poor heart today. I have been sick. My diseased liver is affecting my spirits, my vision, and other diseased organs.*

My dear husband went to Buwie today in order to weigh his cotton. It was a relief to me as I felt so nervous and such a sense of suffocation I experienced that the house became intolerable. I felt the little ride would do me so much good that I only came in to shut the house and went to Reuben's, wishing to go, aside from the benefit I received from the ride.

But the mare (Fanny Gray) walked so intolerable slow that a storm was up betime I got there, though I saw no cloud when I started, and on my return I saw some very unfavorable symptoms in the poor little colt, which made me fear it won't live long, and I am afraid David will think it was following me, but I'm sure from the symptoms and the leisurely gait we traveled, that that is not the case, but it always distresses me to have my husband think me unwittingly wanting in prudence when I cannot see where I am to blame. I know if he had been here, he would have insisted on my riding over horseback, as the buggy is broken and no other way.

Never did I feel less like staying alone than tonight. May God protect you and I while apart this night, my dear, darling husband, is the prayer tonight.

[Sunday, August 31, 1862] *Have been much better today. Husband got home at ten of the clock, but much complaining himself. Poor little colt almost helpless and suffering much. We took a long* ride for invalids this evening after tea, although I am afraid to no purpose as I feel my supper a dead weight.

[Torn] sewed most perseveringly today and do not feel myself much the better for it. What a task I find. Half a dozen shirts, which I wish to last as long as these, and that is until the war is over, and I much fear it will be a long time. No prospect now whatever of the cessation of hostilities. On the contrary, it seems to be prosecuted by the Federals with more vengeance.

Intensely hot this afternoon.

[Tuesday, September 2, 1862] Sewed all day. My good old friend Mrs. Connally is at home again and sent me word before breakfast this morning to spend the day with her, but am not well enough to ride horseback and we could employ no smith to mend the buggy or anything else, and so I had to send my excuses and regret exceed exceedingly I cannot see her. Dear old lady, she has been a great comfort me in my "days of affliction."

[Wednesday, September 3, 1862] Could not forgo the pleasure of seeing my old friend and rode over this morning. Found her looking quite thin and desiccated, low in spirits, yet I spent a few hours with her most pleasantly and returned before dinner. Sewed all the afternoon.

[Thursday, September 4, 1862] Sewed. Took a long ramble over the orchard this morning and repeated the exercise this afternoon.

[Friday, September 5, 1862] My husband went off early this morning and I sat me down to do a large day's work, when, presto, here comes a wool buyer, and what must I do? He has refused every offer he came heretofore. But I think he will refuse no more as he says he cannot get thread for it at the factory and we have enough spun to last this winter, and so I let this boy have twenty pounds, and before he gets out of sight, here is another from Bowie County. It must be twelve noon, and I insist on his remaining until Mr. Moores comes, which is at two, and before he gets away, another comes for forty pounds. Poor people, it is hard to buy wool and then have it spun and make the clothes.

Mr. Moores is at the pen weighing **[torn]** *and I have just come in from a long reverie on the portico, thinking upon human mutability. Yes, mutation is written on all that is earthly and most of all, our pleasures, what we* **[torn]**.

[Torn] *with nervousness and other commutant* **[illegible]** *woman's device last night and this morning. My husband insisted on my taking a ride, which I did, over to Mr. Moores'. Have felt better since, but far from feeling well tonight, though I have done a large day's sewing for me. When the "heart feels most" if "the lips moan not" the fingers generally keep time to the emotion within.*

[Sunday, September 7, 1862] *How lazy I've been all day and what an enormous appetite I have had. Lounged, read, eat fruit has been the order of the day with me. I'm afraid I'm going to be bad sick.*

[Monday, September 8, 1862] *I'm real sick tonight, and what a day's work I've done, with what little assistance Lizzie could render me and Mary Jane. I put the finishing touch to six shirts, put in sleeves, worked buttonholes, and put buttons on. Too much for a nervous invalid like me to do in one day. But I wished to finish them e'er I leave home to go home to my dear Pa, which will be in a few days, and I have some work to do for Mary Jane who I shall take this time as maid.*

[Tuesday, September 9, 1862] *Feel worse than I did last evening. I believe if I were to sew as I have the last two weeks it will kill me in a month or so. Made Mary Jane a dress today and packed my trunk.*

[Wednesday, September 10, 1862] *Sewed in the forenoon. I have a fever this afternoon but bathed it away. As the time approaches, I grow more anxious to see my dear kindred and more loath to leave my dear husband. I'm sad at the thought.*

[Thursday, September 11, 1862] *Today I've been most busy putting my last things in the trunk and arranging all things for three weeks absence. Oh, I shall hate to say farewell to my husband and leave him without any companionship, but I pray the kind Ruler of Heaven to watch* **[torn]** *not* *enjoy the trip as much as if he were going with me. It is late. He is in bed, and though not tired I must to bed as I wish to take a daylight start.*

[Wednesday, October 1, 1862] *Reached my own dear home this afternoon. My good husband did but illy brook my absence and pretended to understand me to say I would be back in two weeks to keep the home folks from ridiculing him for getting anxious and coming for me. However, he only came to Falcon as I was making my last visit to Mat and on my way home.*

Dear, kind husband, will I ever forget all I owe thee, should I live a century the longest?

He told them he was most angry. I had disappointed him, and he was very angry with me. When we retired to our room, he threw his arms around me and kissing me most passionately said, "I could not stand it any longer, my darling wife. I grew perfectly wretched every time I came in your room. Oh, I am ruined, ruined, without you, dearest one on earth. Oh, you now can know how dear you are—how anxious I ever feel when absent from you. No one can ever know the agony endured by a man who has an invalid wife and that fearful, frightful heart condition which I fear will give no warning and take you when away from me."

I could not repeat in one hour all the anxiety he expressed to have felt during my seventeen days absence from him, the first **[illegible]** *we spent together at the Nash's.*

I'm too much fatigued to repeat all the emotions I experienced the first evening of my arrival at the old family mansion. All my sisters were present when I arrived except Sister Jane, whom I had left at home, and Mat, whom I saw when I passed Dr. Mask's. Many of my old friends and dear were present, all standing on the portico, wondering, they said whose carriage, so travel stained, could be approaching so rapidly **[torn]**.

[Torn] *last night with cholera morbus* **[illegible]** *walk today. Rode over to Mr. Reuben's a* **[illegible]** *to see my new kinfolks—little Ananias, Sister Jane's last addition.*[67]

Badly as I felt, I had to stay up and await Charles's return from Linden, whether we sent him in quest of opium and laudanum for poor William Hobson.

I feel mortified that I told Hobson anything about having opium or laudanum as we had so little of our own, but he insisted so much and said the least bit would be most acceptable. We sent three-quarters pound of opium and six ounces of laudanum.

[Friday, October 3, 1862] *Made an extensive effort today to have the yards cleaned, which Lizzie so miserably neglected during my absence.*

Finished the first perusal of Beulah today, and I don't know whenever a book fatigued me more. I kept my mind more on the [illegible] *I got. I was intently interested all the time. I commenced it at Pa's, but could not finish it as all my time was claimed.*[68]

Oh! When will I again meet all the dear friends I left at Pa's? Poor Mary Ann Daly. What a reminder she is of the past. Yet her face is just as fresh, bright, and beautiful, though as I told her, her frame looks like a something to dry clothes on, and she does manage her child with such remarkable tact and good sense.[69]

Before my husband left this morning for Courtland, I engaged the services of three of his field hands—women—and undertook the renovation of the house, which Lizzie neglected even more than she did the yards. The very walls of the library were to be scaled, and she had moved her bedding all over the room and carried the bed bugs everywhere she went. Had never cleaned the floor, hearth, or anything else. I never had my hands so full and never felt less like exertion of any kind, though put myself on a "forward march" all day and got through time enough to read several chapters of a book Mollie loaned me, Fallings by the Way, and put all the women borrowed and house hands to sweep the yards all over.

David did not bring the buggy, so I could not go over to see Sister Jane.

[Sunday, October 5, 1862] *Rode over horseback to see Sister Jane this morning quite early. Read until dinner. I read from dinner until five of the clock. Took a long stroll with husband, and on our return took a seat under a shady tree in the back where we took our supper. We read until bedtime.*

[Monday, October 6, 1862] *I never know what to do with myself when my husband left this morning to be gone all day. I have tried half dozen things and failed to interest myself in, or with, anything except my new book, and that has given me two or three headaches.*

Had four bolts of cloth and think to cut out some dresses, but cannot want to work though made two waists. I don't remember that I ever missed company so much before on returning from my old home. I miss my conversations with Pa whilst the rest was all at supper. Miss my walk into

Mother's machine factory and chat with her about the beautiful gray cloth being manufactured for the poor soldier boys. My poor brothers.

[Torn] Cut out only two more dresses. Oh, when shall I get the Negros' clothes cut and made up for winter?

Feel so sad tonight. Sister Jane sent for me to spend a few hours with her this afternoon. Is feeling badly about an enlargement she has under her throat. I am distressed about it, myself, fearing it may give her some pain and trouble and a great deal of inconvenience. Oh, I do so pity one when mind is depressed with cares about an invalid body—with apprehensions of any kind about the health. No one can pity more than I—yet I am not competent at all times to cheer and soothe one's feelings about such things.

[Wednesday, October 8, 1862] *Have done a deal of cutting today, yet been sick all day. Every bone and nerve in me aches, and I have some fever. I do hope I will not pass such another miserable night as last night was. I did not sleep until near day.*

Exercised on my feet all I was capable of to make me sleep well, but I fear all in vain. Will take a blue pill **[blue mass]** *as my liver is torpid.*

[Thursday, October 9, 1862] *Better today. I have done a deal of cutting and sewing and feel some the worse for it.*

[Friday, October 10, 1862] *Cut, sewed, and read* Ramblings by the Way. *Rained all day.*

[Saturday, October 11, 1862] *Just had got in a good way of cutting and having sewing done when Miss Lewis (teacher employed by Mr. Reuben Moores whilst I was absent in Arkansas)—Janie's and Ruth's—came to spend the day. I had a pleasant day with Miss Lewis, though my cutting was suspended, and, of course, all the figures under my charge were suspended.*[70]

A clear, cold, bright, frosty morning **[torn]** *frost myself, for by the time I emerged from my bath all the shrubs and flowers were dew spangled with bright, glittering* **[illegible]**. *My white tea roses looked like emeralds set with pearls and besprinkled with diamonds.*

But I must confess to the morning being a little too cold for my comfort. I love fall above all seasons, but I like the transition to be more gradual from summer to fall. On Monday last an organdy only was endurable, the lightest fabric one dons for summer. Yesterday and today I have not got sufficiently warm, and as in winter, a double Afghan, without hovering around the fire or with a winter shawl placed over my shoulders.

Been all alone all day, David having gone to Bowie. Went over to Sister Jane's a few moments this afternoon.

[Monday, October 13, 1862] *David came at dark last evening and brought news of the death of William Moores' oldest child, little Elizabeth, and also Matilda, her mother, lying quite low with flux and an abortion. Poor Matilda. I should feel distressed to hear of her death. She is a good woman, and most affectionate and amiable wife, and, oh, what a kind sister she has been to me. She is the one in my husband's family who is done naught but to make me love her. I earnestly pray for recovery. In bed today.*

[Tuesday, October 14, 1862] *Mr. Woodbury Salmon came last evening, and, thinking it was the doctor when his name was announced, I invited in my room and felt a little abashed when he entered, as I lay on the lounge en dishabille. However, I recovered and rattled on at a high rate until Mr. Moores came in.*

Though sick in bed, I cut out four pairs of pantaloons.

[Wednesday, October 15, 1862] *Sewed today and entertained Mr. Salmon, as David was compelled to go to the field most of the day. It is Mr. Salmon's last visit as he leaves for the army Tuesday next. Poor boy, I hope he may be spared to "meet his friends over there."*

[Thursday, October 16, 1862] *We felt so uneasy today. David went over to see how Matilda was. Found her better, thanks to a kind providence. Cut out and sewed twelve pairs of pants for husband today.*

Tried very hard to make a pair of pantaloons for David today, but did not succeed, and am fearful they won't fit as I have taken extra pains. I regretted it much, too. I sewed most industriously and did not make one pair of pantaloons. I am tired, too.

[Friday, October 17, 1862] *Took the rounds with my husband. He concluded I was sitting too much for my own comfort and health. Called on Mrs. Salmon, Senior, on our way to the office, and spent an hour so very pleasantly. Got no letters, but two papers. Called on Mrs. Webster on our way to the tan yard, whose acquaintance I had not made before. Found her pleasant and entertaining and, withal, a most sensible woman in the strict management of her children.*

[Saturday, October 18, 1862] *Cut all the women a woolen overcoat today and woolen suit for poor old Mr. Grissel, which I intend giving him, and yet do not wish to uphold his wife in her indolence. I believe, too, it is meanness. Believe she had rather see him toil in pain and suffer from cold than let him wear one hour's labor of her own. Old, obstinate, callous, heartless piece.*

Lizzie has gone to bed sick.

[Sunday, October 19, 1862] *As David starts to Jefferson tomorrow morning and I have not written "home" since leaving there, I wrote to Sister today, hoping it will reach them sooner from Jefferson than it is likely to from here. Husband drove me down to the river this evening—a most delightful evening this to drive out.*

[Monday, October 20, 1862] *Bed time and all alone. How many, many nights I have passed thus, with servants, alone. I always endeavor to keep my hands employed when in this situation, and that furnishes food for the mind. I do not often give up to reading when alone. It fascinates me, leads me beyond the bounds of prudence. I have sewed almost all day on my husband's pantaloons, and yet the finishing work has not been done. But then, I have done considerable other work, a little exercise. But yet I feel that sewing is hurting me.*

[Tuesday, October 21, 1862] *Finished pantaloons, mended another pair that were badly torn, and made an old waist over again: put new back and lined the front, put in buttons, etc. Practiced a* few minutes this evening and rambled as far as the quince orchard. Very few [torn]. The fruit is beautiful, of a bright, golden color. I shall soon have [illegible].

The hogs got in the yard last night and destroyed the [illegible] pomegranates in the yard. The prettiest ones I ever saw.

Well, I'm puzzled to know what to do with Lizzie. She has acute nervous affection—pompholyx, I think. The entire half of her neck—the right half—is covered with water blebs, varying in size from a mustard seed to a partridge egg. They began to break yesterday and the whole surface is now beginning to present an ulcerated surface. She has but little fever and does not seem to suffer much. I am treating her hydropathically.[71]

I know if I were to send for a[n] allopathic physician (and there is no other here) he would prescribe an ointment for the skin and an active purgative, neither of which would I give if she were my own child, and I shall treat her accordingly.

It is, perhaps, a pity I do not esteem medicine more highly, as I am so denounced for my skepticism on that point.

Another lonely night. May the Father of Mercies watch between me and my absent husband. I will close my Journal and read my precious Bible until bedtime—bedtime for me when alone. My usual bedtime is long since passed.

[Wednesday, October 22, 1862] My husband arrived today at noon, and what a gloom is over my soul. He brought the sad, sad intelligence of poor dear Matilda's death. Yes, she, the good, gentle, affectionate wife, mother, daughter, sister, and friend is, I trust, realizing the joys of that blessed abode where the souls of the just are made perfect. What a friend I have lost in dear Matilda.

She was ever kind, affectionate, amiable, and sincere in her intercourse with me, and no one save my husband knew the strength of my attachment for her. Once, when I was eulogizing her goodness and beauty to a much nearer, much less amiable relative, "Oh," said she, "you only praise her because she makes you think yourself faultless." I was stung to the soul at the injustice of the repartee. Unjust alike to both of us, for, in sincerity, I can say Matilda never flattered me during the whole course of our acquaintance. That she was a warm, attached friend, I very well knew, and that she was true, and such insults offended me.

[Torn] *her goodness, or amiability, **[illegible]** her kindness, her sincerity. The last time I saw her was the evening before Toad's**[?]** marriage, the **[illegible]** of December last. When we drove up, she came out greeting me with a smile, and her first exclamation was "how glad I am to see you, Rachel. I was so afraid you would not come."*

> *It came from the heart—it went to the heart.*
> *But what binds us, friend to friend,*
> *But that soul with soul can blend?*
> *Soul-like hours were those hours of yore;*
> *Let us walk in soul once more.*[72]

*I never have, and feel that I never can, love another sister-in-law as I loved Matilda. I loved her for her pure uprightness, her true womanly traits—she was a true woman in every sense of the word. William will never get another that will **[illegible]** to him, fill her place. More brilliant, more entertaining, and superior housekeepers he may frequently find, but never again another as pure minded, forbearing, and amiable as his much-cherished Matilda. He was, as well he might be, devoted to her.*

[Thursday, October 23, 1862] [Torn] *all day. Never had but one spell like **[illegible]** and Dr. Salmon called it uterine colic, but I think the bursting of an internal tumor or ulcer **[illegible]** has been so confused. I've tried sewing on my **[illegible]** to divert my mind.*

[Friday, October 24, 1862] *I have had uterine spasms and all its miserable symptoms. Surely a long spell of it will bring on insanity! Why, I can't tell how I feel at times, wild, wild, wild! Oh, Father, before that fearful moment comes, take my soul to Thine own Kingdom.*

Woman! Mine own sex! To say I imagine and I am sick—imagine I have diseases that do not exist! Just as I was busiest with my fall sewing, in the very middle of it all! Just made David one pair of pantaloons and three more pair to make and all my waists and sleeves to close at the wrist—here comes furious ulcers and spasms. But, oh, many have been worse afflicted. What one woman has borne, woman can bear. But I have borne what I cannot bear again.

Fixed over pair of sleeves today.

David tells me I can't go to Bowie tomorrow to see poor, poor Catherine. Says the wind is too high. But I won't be well enough.

[Saturday, October 25, 1862] *A bitter cold day and high winds, some sleet, and a few drops of rain. Doctor came in just before dinner and he, David, and myself had a long conversation on the war and our prospects for peace.*

Sewed this afternoon—made Henry a shirt. Yet have had some of the strangest spells since Wednesday—every few hours. Feel as if I had set up for nights without sleep or anything to eat. Such a feeling of emptiness and of goneness! A sick, faint feeling, a gnawing at my vitals.

[Sunday, October 26, 1862] *This morning the earth was covered with the whitest frost I ever saw. Myriads of rosebuds are dropping, and every vegetable "hath perished." Nothing left in garden except cabbage.*

David and I called at Mr. Temple's in taking our ride this afternoon, but could not, or did not, remain long, I having one of my sick spells whilst there—before I went and since I came home. What a strange affliction. I never felt anything like it before. I feel constantly as if I had set up many days and nights in succession as well as a loss of food and loss of sleep.

[Monday, October 27, 1862] *Cut out and commenced another pair of pantaloons for my husband. Poor old Mr. Grissel came just after dinner and left and commenced such a tirade against the secessionists that I was compelled to defend them, though was as much opposed to them at the beginning as anyone. Poor, poverty-stricken old man, he says to secession what an indolent and depressed family hand down for him.*

When I gave him the suit of clothes I cut out for him last week, he said he wished to pay me for them, but I did tell him he was now more indebted to us that he ever could pay, or would be if we had charged him for half the favors we had done for him. Nothing but a broken pin, and it just came from the jewelers in a worse fix than it went to them in.

Capt. William Johnson Godbold, brother of Rachel Moores, who died from his wounds received in the Battle of Corinth.

[**Tuesday, October 28, 1862**] *Sister Jane spent today with me. Her little baby grows very fast. Sewed this morning and tonight until bedtime.*

[**Wednesday, October 29, 1862**] *David came home today, cross with fever. Mr. Lindsay came for him to send hands and instruct him about getting Mr. Haygood's cattle on the river. He sent assistance and drove me down to the river. He returned with a fever. I feel alarmed about him.*

[**Thursday, October 30, 1862**] *Had a most miserable night. My poor husband was very ill. Had a very high fever all last night. Finished a pair of pantaloons last night and commenced another pair today.*

[**Friday, October 31, 1862**] *David had an exceedingly high fever last night again, though he was up all day yesterday, and today he still has fever, though rode out horseback and drove out this afternoon. Returned by Mr. Reuben's, yet I feel very uneasy about him. It has been three days now since he took fever.*

Finished my third pair of pantaloons tonight.

[Saturday, November 1, 1862] *Spent the day outdoors and feel sick tonight. Ache dreadfully. David still has fever and his whole surface is covered with red splotches with a transparent water bleb in the center, which becomes opaque in a day or so after* **[torn]**.

[Torn] *my husband is suffering dreadfully—almost every breath* **[torn]** *his head is aching, throat sore, and eruptions paining him most severely, and, oh, how uncomfortably do I feel. Yet I hope he will continue to grow better since he is bathed and been wrapped up with warm applications. Says he already feels better.*

Notwithstanding he has been so unwell all day, he has taken two rides. This afternoon we drove as far as Dr. Salmon's, and he says he is no worse from the drive. The doctor says he is at a loss to know what is the matter with him, but, agreeable to the Hydropathic Encyclopedia, it is herpes

My poor Sufferer has dropped off to sleep and is muttering and jumping in bed. Oh, could I but see him in the enjoyment of good health—perfect health—what would I give. I will creep to bed for fear of disturbing him with the noise of my—not pen—but scratching.

[November 19, 1862] *"A change has come o'er the spirit of my dream" —yes, and such a change How different this life seems to what it did that night I laid my pen down—a watcher at my husband's sick bed. I laid it down in anxiety for my sick husband. I resume at a mourner, for my dear, darling Brother William who fell at the late Battle of Corinth, fighting for his country, his liberties, his principle. Being taken a prisoner, wounded, from the battlefield by his enemies, he died in their hands receiving, in his last moments, the ministrations of his deadliest foe.[73]*

The only mitigation—consolation—I can find, is the thought that he was not afraid to die. He expressed his perfect resignation to divine will, and he fell in his country's service, and when I take in consideration the peril that it times seems imminent, I feel that the good are taken from the evil to come.[74]

But it is human nature to lament the circumstances, be what they may, that takes our friends from us forever.

Yes, though it has been near three weeks since the cruel tidings came, yet it seems hard for me to realize the truth—that I shall never again behold his dear face. Oh, it can't be so! Oh, my darling brother! My dear, affectionate brother, it is hard to give thee up.

Oh, that thy death may be a **[torn]** to all of the family to renew their vows **[torn]** God. May firm resolutions be made and carried **[illegible]** to reach that blissful land where war and **[illegible]** are unknown. What a contrast, even in imagination, to this now confused, distrustful, devastated land, which a few short months ago blossomed as a rose, a land on which Heaven had showered her richest, choices blessings.

[Torn] David left today at noon for the salt works. I will spend a lonely three weeks, perhaps a longer time, perhaps not so long.

Dr. Salmon brought Dee Rush today to spend a portion of the time during my husband's absence. As I have taken her into my room, I shall not journalize any during her stay.

I cut out a coat for David yesterday, and it will employ all my faculties—all my time—to make it as it should be made. I do not even know where to begin but will keep the old coat before me that I ripped up to cut it by and take the stitches where those were taken.

[Saturday, November 29, 1862] One week has elapsed since I laid my pen down. Yesterday at nightfall my husband drove up, most unexpectantly to me, but a most agreeable surprise it was. But I am doomed to a severe disappointment. The coat that I've been taking so much pleasure in making is much too large in the neck. The one I ripped up was made for a gentleman in New York and was, David says, much too large as this one is, and does not wish me to alter it in any way. But I cannot have it so. My first coat must be a perfect fit. It is really, my husband thinks, elegantly made, and I could cry if t'would do any good.

Dr. Salmon came after Dee this evening and brought little Mattie. She came for me to play for her on the piano and she was a little frightened bird when I began but was soon delighted.

[Sunday, November 30, 1862] We started to Courtland to church today, but on reaching Dr. Salmon's found there was no preaching. David went to the office and I remained at Dr. Salmon's in the forenoon and spent the afternoon with his mother. Miss Orpah was at home and I passed today most delightfully, considering I dined out on the Sabbath, which is never pleasant to me.

[Friday, December 5, 1862] *David drove me out today [torn] the first time my foot has been out the door since Sunday. I have been very unwell most of the week, though made a pair of pantaloons for my husband.*

Today, Mrs. H____ sent her son to ask Mr. Moores to build a house for her. Since her husband's death she has lived in the house with her sister-in-law—only one little cabin and two poor women and six children, and so Mr. Moores went down soon as he received the message to learn when she wishes it built, etc. I accompanied him. Called at Reuben's on our return. She also sent to him to assist, but he says he hasn't time.

Feel much better for my ride.

[Saturday, December 6, 1862] *Wrote to Mat today and knit most industriously, finishing another set of socks for the soldiers. Finished three pairs this week, with Mary Jane's assistance.*

[Sunday, December 7, 1862] *Went to Courtland to church today. I heard a good, though not very edifying discourse from Mr. Cole. He looks all goodness, and I think to know him must be to love him. I never saw a better countenance.*

We called at the post office after church and Mr. Connolly had given our letters and papers to Brown, his overseer, and we came by there for them and he had sent them home, and so I found a letter from dear Maw which I had read before warming my fingers. She wrote no news. All she said was about my darling Brother, whose spirit I would fain hope is worshiping around the Throne of Him who created it.

Dear precious Brother. Shall I, oh, shall I never again behold your dear darling face. Oh, could I but have known when I saw thee last it had been the last meeting, the last parting on earth. I knew I was parting from someone for the last time. I felt the presentiment when I bade adieu to each member of the family circle just one year prior to his decease. One year ago, now.

[Torn] David went to Forest Home to build, or commence building, Mrs. H____'s house, and since dinner I've been entertaining Mr. Eilbeck Mason of Virginia, brother to our minister plenipotentiary to the Court of Saint James. He rode up just after my dinner and sent me his name and the nature of his business, or rather that he was employed by the government and that he

had an engagement with some gentlemen who were to meet him here to examine the iron veins at Thomas's old place, and if he thought it advisable, an iron foundry would be erected there.[75]

is quite a dignified "Old School Virginian," and as uncompromising as a Virginian ever gets to be. Is "war to the hilt" on the Yankees, and who would blame him. He is an exiled from home, has not seen his wife and children since last May one year ago, nor has been permitted to see them. He had to leave home the day the Pawnee *arrived in Alexandria loaded with Federal troops, the eventful day when Jackson and Ellsworth were killed.*[76]

The same day the Federals took possession of all the property held by secession men in the vicinity of Alexandria, and consequently Mr. Mason's family and all his earthly possessions is in their hands. His wife and children were even tried in Washington City for corresponding with him a few days after he left, and that nothing else was proven against them is all he has heard from them since a separation from them.

This conversation is exceedingly interesting to me in as much as he has always resided near Mount Vernon and is intimate with the Washingtons, Lees, Forrest, etc., and a long list no less well known to fame and very dear to many Southern hearts.

[Tuesday, December 9, 1862] *The duty of entertaining our honored guest has again devolved on me as David's business for a few days is preemptory. I think he grew tired of my incessant tongue this afternoon as he retired to his room some hours to read and sleep. His friends still tarry. Yesterday was the day appointed.*

[Wednesday, December 10, 1862] *Our guest was not so well today* [torn] *as badly swollen, so much so as to close one eye. He has been confined to his bed all day. David is house building, etc., etc. Knitting and having Mr. Mason about has been my occupation today.*

[Thursday, December 11, 1862] *Mr. Mason's friends are delinquent, which I think deserves punishment though he doesn't seem at all disappointed. Has read* To Cuba and Back *and is now on* Beulah. *It is most fortunate for me that he is able to read and be up today as David is compelled to be absent all day at present and I have to be sole entertainer.*

Finished another pair of socks today.

I was made sad by the desponding tale of a Mrs. Sager who visited me for the first time this afternoon. She wanted sheep, wool, blankets, and corn, and no means to get either with. Says she has no wool to spin cloth for her children, and as I had no wool to sell, only enough for socks, I gave her cloth enough to make her two little boys a pair of pants apiece, but charged her not to say anything about it, even to her husband or children. If it is known, I shall have to listen to many such tales, and the Good Book says we must not let one hand knoweth what the other does. And poor Mrs. Sager has a female disease, and that always melts my heart, and then she says she works very hard. God help her, I pray.[77]

[Friday, December 12, 1862] *A rainy day. Knit and read my Bible. Went into the parlor to practice a little, but Mr. Mason came in and so I flew up. Rained some little today.*

[Saturday, December 13, 1862] *This has been a most eventful day to me. The morning filled with a number of cares and perplexities incident to housekeepers on rainy days with company in the house and no eggs. Muddy floors and a constant tracking in and out. I overlooked Lizzie and the rooms this morning and made quince preserves. This afternoon I did not feel like it, though entertained some company. Sister Jane's children, Miss Lewis, Mrs. Brown, and with the latter came Francine Henshaw Ironmonger to throw herself on our mercy.[78]*

Her tale is one calculated to excite one's sympathy, yet it is a most unpleasant task to me as I had much rather live without any other in reach of our little home, yet I could not turn an orphan away—one who had neither mother nor father (or what is worse than no father) and whose grandparents are so unfeeling as she represents hers to be.

I have frequently heard of her step-grandma's cruelty, but never heard anything of her grandpa's maltreating until she made her complaint to us last evening. I somewhat fear her own temper has something to do with her unfortunate situation. She tells me, in answer to my queries about her deportment to her grandparents, that she has never sauced them or acted insolently to them in any way but has always endeavored to please them. But says her grandma's temper is so irascible—so violent—that it is seldom that one can please her.

Says the old woman often wishes she was dead, curses her, jerks her hair out, strikes her with an axe, stick, or anything she can get hold of. Tells her she always hated her father, who from all accounts must be a fiend of the blackest dye, and says her grandpa and brother are but little better.

[Torn] Mr. Mason was reading when we arose this morning [illegible]. [Illegible] whenever David [torn] evening when we took [illegible] in short, we have had a rainy day throughout [illegible]. It has been in accordance with my troubled spirit, though. I'm anxious and perplexed.

[Monday, December 15, 1862] Rainy morning. Mr. Crawford Connally came to tell us if we will not keep Francine Henshaw, as demanded by her grandparents, he would. Said he learned I told Mrs. Brown I would keep her until she got another home. I told him I thought myself incompetent for the task, but told her—Franny—she could remain so long as she found our house agreeable and pleasant, mutually so—so long as she will be influenced by me—so long can she stay, and I think Mr. Connally's promises of a home under any and all circumstances will have a most deleterious effect.

She said soon as she left she would go there, but as we promised to send her to school next year, she would remain here. I think Mr. Connally decided hasty in the matter. He never saw the child before, does not know that she has a violent temper herself. She is bright, but I know self-willed. I do not blame her for rebelling against the tyranny of her grandmother.

The partiality the old woman exercised towards her brother was sufficient within itself to alienate her affections from her and cause her to feel the greatest aversion to them both. This is if she tells the truth, but I suspect her of embellishing much that she tells on the old lady. I was [illegible] to see she doesn't adhere to the truth. I fear I shall have trouble with her. I already see she is inclined to lounge about and skip over leaves instead of reading, yet she says she is fond of reading.

[Tuesday, December 16, 1862] A bright, clear, frosty morning [illegible] Mister Mason left to finish his government contract and then says he is going to erect an iron foundry in a mile or two from here where he and David examined last evening.

I insisted that Franny should spin her some thread to make her some stockings as she is miserably in need of them, but she piddled and dilly-dallied till noon, and then spun some twenty rounds and it is unfit even for strings.

Poor thoughtless child. I pity her.

David drove me over to see Mrs. Turner and Eliza Baker, both of whom I found much annoyed and perplexed about the conduct of their brother, who, having got his share of his father's estate long ago, is going to try now and take another share. Eliza seems almost frantic about it.[79]

[Wednesday, December 17, 1862] I see very plainly Francine is going to put me to a deal of trouble to get her to do anything for herself. She has not spun any better today and will not take any pains with what she did spin. I walked over to Reuben's to make some arrangement about sending her to school. Will start her the first of January if she remains here until then. I have done nothing but knit, knit for the last two weeks.

[Thursday, December 18, 1862] Have knit until my shoulders ache. Am trying to knit one sock today, but I could not make Franny spin. I gave it up and gave her enough for a pair of stockings, three cuts, and took her piece of a cut to give to the Negros to quilt us tie brooms with. She has been here four workdays and has not positively done one hour's good work, and not one good suit of clothes to her name and nothing else but the most voracious, inordinate appetite I never saw any one have, and I know she will be sick as she has always been allowanced to an insufficient quantity. Her grandfather told me her grandmother never gave her [torn] of milk and a piece of bread or a slice of [illegible] at one time, and now she's eating as much butter, milk, fruit, etc. as a laboring man ought to consume at one time.

I feel very great delicacy in correcting the child about, and know it is [illegible] will make her so stupid she can't learn, and I already see one of the reasons why she could not please her grandmother. She does not take the slightest pains with anything she does—is one of the most slovenly persons in all she does I ever saw. But I do pray she may be cured of all these faults and make a useful woman.

[Friday, December 19, 1862] *Spent most of today leveling the yard, filling up the washed places. I don't know, though, what is the matter with me. I grew so nervous twice I thought I should snap in the yard. I felt as I used to when dyspepsia was so bad on me. I am sure though, I have been sitting too closely for my good. I have been too busy knitting.*

[Saturday, December 20, 1862] *Though very cold, we took a drive this evening. When as far as Mr. Woods, as David's business led him thither.*

[Sunday, December 21, 1862] *I feel most uncomfortable this evening in consequence of Franny's going over to Mr. Reuben Moores' this morning to spend the day without my knowing where she was. She had been sitting so steadily for a day or two—I might say every day since she came here—that I proposed this morning she should take a little ramble as I have done, and she went off to Mr. Moores, and when dinner came on I started a Negro off to look her up, not to bring her home. But she came, and Miss Lewis with her, before they eat their dinner and sometime after we had eaten. When Miss Lewis started home, Franny went with her and came galloping up twice here after David and I had taken a ride of six miles in the buggy, and then she returned to Mr. Moores' a third time and came home at dark with a Negro boy! My poor husband has fever again, and many things conspire to make me uncomfortable.*

[Monday, December 22, 1862] *Rode over to see Sister Jane this afternoon.*

[Tuesday, December 23, 1862] *Finished my socks and pressed them out, ready to send off to the poor soldiers, a poor contribution when so much is needed. Only fifteen pairs, but then it is gratuitous.*

[Wednesday, December 24, 1862] *Franny, I can't manage. Went off and spent the night without my permission at Mrs. Moores and brought Miss Lewis home with her whilst I was immersed in cooking, soap making, and housecleaning. Was cooking my sweetmeats for our Christmas dinner tomorrow, finishing some soap to let the Negros have the pot, and I was most busy, too, as I wished* to go down and bring Misses Salmon and Rush home with me, and after all, only Miss Orpah came. But I feel I shall be amply repaid for my trouble.

Really, I don't feel like it's Christmas Eve. Oh, may our next be a pleasanter, if not a merrier one.

[Thursday, December 25, 1862] Today has been dull. A rainy day, or rather a misty day. A little sunshine now and then. Mr. Reuben, Sister Jane, and four smallest children spent the day. I fear Miss Orpah will not appreciate my motives, as we have seemingly made so little effort to entertain her. I have not felt well, and I never saw David half as dull in my life. He is habitually taciturn, but today he has been dumb. I am sorry not to have given him a nicer eggnog as he is so remarkably fond of it. Tomorrow I try to do better.

[Friday, December 26, 1862] Dr. Salmon came today at our dinner hour, bringing Miss Paralee. Mrs. Henshaw also came to see Francine. She has lectured her soundly on her ingratitude towards me. What I've already found out that she does not love to work and has her whole soul set on a dress.

Mr. Foster was drowned near Mr. Baker's, and Mrs. Foster frightened me dreadfully, galloping up in the rain without a shawl or bonnet, after David to get him out. He won't, though, without my consent, as he had fever [torn] the first of a new year, and what may it not [illegible]. I've made some high resolves today, though [torn] in cares—or would have been, had I yielded [illegible].[80]

[date illegible December 1862] This morning the first thing that greeted my ears was, "Miss Rachel, de lard all run out de barrel," and sure enough, when I went to see, the floor was white, and the barrel covered with frosty looking festoons. It was washday, and yet looked like rain and sleet or snow, and as Miss Larkin was looking for an escort to go home with her, and as I promised her one in case they should fail to come, I complied and David drove us in the carriage.[81]

Franny accompanied us and caused some unpleasant reflections on my part by my discovering one of the Negro's hoops on her just after we were seated in the carriage. I asked her immediately if she did not have some of the Negros' hoops on, and she replied in the negative, and as Miss Larkin was present, I said no more, but as soon as we left Dr. Salmon's, I insisted on knowing the truth, and she said, when pressed to do so, that she had borrowed a pair and acknowledged that she had done wrong.

How little has my caution about her intercourse with the Negros benefitted her. Poor child, she thinks of nothing but dress and her appearance. After all—and Mr. Connally's promises—I find but little good that is likely to accrue from them. His wife tells it publicly that she can't live with her, and he tells that why he is so anxious is because his wife wanted her! Why won't people be honest in their principles?

"Honesty is the best policy in all things."

We learned on reaching Dr. Salmon's that Mrs. Connally died this morning. Sad, distressing thought, she left five dear children who have lost what the world can never supply, a mother, one's own mother.[82]

[Wednesday, December 31, 1862] Another year has ended with no hopes of peace. War, bloodshed, and its concomitants are the only topics [illegible] we discussed. When? Oh! when will Peace wreath her chain around us? Oh, God, may this be the last day with us without hope, I hope for a speedy peace, a brighter hope of "yonder bright world."

"With hope-light, the true-light, we'll bound o'er life's billows."[83]

NOTES

[1] Laura Laffrado, *Uncommon Women: Gender and Representation in 19 Century U.S. Women's Writing* (Columbus: Ohio State University Press, 2009), 105.

[2] Lizzie Burnell, "Woman's Rights," *Mayflower*, May 1, 1861, 68.

[3] As late as 1981 the *Texarkana Gazette* featured an article on Baker, whom it hailed as the "favorite outlaw" of Bowie County. He is the hero of a highly fictionalized Louis L'Amour novel, *The First Fast Draw* (New York: Bantam Books, 1959). *Texarkana Gazette*, November 4, 1981, A-3; Barry A. Crouch and Donaly E. Brice, *Cullen Montgomery Baker: Reconstruction Desperado* (Baton Rouge: Louisiana State University Press, 1997); Yvonne Vestal, *The Borderlands and Cullen Baker* (Atlanta, TX: Journal Publishers, 1978), 55.

[4] Cordelia Ann "Dee" Rush was born in Alabama in September 1844. On March 31, 1868, she married Lloyd Samuel Wright in Cass County. She died in Clarence, Missouri, in 1907.

Sarah Salmon, a sister of Dr. George Hansel Salmon, was born in Missouri in 1846.

[5] Bone felon is a primary herpes simplex infection of the terminal segment of a finger, usually seen in those exposed to infected oral or respiratory secretions, such as dentists, physicians, or nurses. It begins with intense itching and pain, followed by the formation of deep coalescing vesicles. The process is associated with much tissue destruction and may be accompanied by systemic symptoms.

6 Orpha M. Salmon was born in Decatur, Alabama, on October 8, 1837, the daughter of Eliza Byrd Hansel and William H. Salmon. In 1860, she was a teacher in Lincoln, Tennessee.

7 Warren Hooks, a native of Wayne County, North Carolina, came, with his wife, Elizabeth Roberts, his family and numerous slaves, to Bowie County in 1848. The community of Hooks, Texas, located on Massack H. Janes headright in the Arthur Wavell Colony, grew up around his plantation. His son, James B. Hooks, was born in Tuscumbia, Alabama, on July 22, 1834. He was married to Mary Ann Rosborough in Cass County on October 9, 1861.

Mary Ann "Mollie" Rosborough Hooks was born on September 10, 1839, in Fairfield County, South Carolina, the daughter of Elizabeth Harrison Moores and James Thomas Rosborough. On October 9, 1861, she married James Blake Hooks. They became the parents of five children. James B. Hooks died on June 26, 1891, and Mary Ann Hooks died on August 15, 1899. They are buried beside one another in Rose Hill Cemetery. "Myrtle Springs" in Bowie County, Watlington Manuscript, *Texarkana USA Quarterly*, Texarkana USA Genealogical Society, http://files.usgwarchives.net/tx/bowie/history/myrtle.txt.

8 N. P. Willis (1806–1867), an American author, poet, and editor, was the highest-paid magazine writer of his day. He worked with Edgar Allan Poe and Henry Wadsworth Longfellow and was the employer of former slave and future writer Harriet Jacobs. His brother was the composer Richard Storrs Willis and his sister Sara wrote under the name Fanny Fern. "The Solitary," *Poems of Nathaniel Parker Willis: With a Memoir of the Author* (London: George Routledge, 1891), 278.

9 On November 8, 1861, the USS *San Jacinto*, commanded by Capt. Charles Wilkes, intercepted the British mail packet RMS *Trent* and removed two Confederate diplomats, James Murray Mason of Virginia and John Slidell of Louisiana, who were bound for Britain and France to present the Confederacy's case for diplomatic recognition and to lobby for financial and military support. The envoys were arrested, transported to Boston, and imprisoned at Fort Warren. In Union states, the general public celebrated the capture, while the Confederate States hoped that the incident would lead to a rupture in Anglo-American relations and diplomatic recognition by Britain.

The British were outraged by what they perceived as a violation of neutral rights and insult to their national honor. Queen Victoria's government demanded the release of the two envoys, along with an apology for the transgression of British rights on the high seas. The British began preparing for war, banning exports of war materials to America and sending troops to Canada. Plans were made to raise the blockade imposed on the Confederate coast, preventing southern cotton from reaching English textile mills and greatly impairing the British economy. Louis Napoleon of France also announced that his country was prepared to intercede on behalf of the Confederacy. The Lincoln administration wisely backed down—"One war at a time," the President said—and on December 27 the State Department informed British officials that the United States disavowed the actions of Captain Wilkes and announced that the envoys would be released.

Mason and Slidell were set free to continue their mission to Europe. Armed conflict with Great Britain was averted, but their mission was a failure as—due to Britain's staunch anti-slavery stance—they were unable to convince European leaders to support the Confederate cause.

10 *To Cuba and Back: A Vacation Voyage* (New York: Ticknor and Fields, 1859) is a travel narrative by Richard Henry Dana, Jr., the author of the more famous *Two Years Before the Mast*. Cuba in 1859 was an autocracy of the landed elite and a plantation society driven by slave labor. Dana admired the cultural and racial diversity of the working class but saw that power was concentrated in the hands of a small, racially homogenous elite.

To a great degree, the labor system in the American South informed his feelings about the land he visited, and his descriptions of Cuba are a reflection of those in the United States. "The African and Chinese do the manual labor; the Cubans hold the land and the capital, and direct agricultural industry."

Dana, a member of the Boston Brahmin elite, however, was not an Abolitionist and was not entirely unsympathetic to the plantation owners. "If the master of a plantation is faithful and thorough, will tolerate no misconduct or imposition, and yet is humane and watchful over the interests and rights, as well as the duties of his negroes, he has a hard and anxious life. Sickness to be ministered to, the feigning of sickness to be counteracted, rights of the slaves to be secured against other negroes, as well as against whites, with a poor chance of getting at the truth from either; the obligations of the negro quasi marriage to be enforced against all the sensual and childish tendencies of the race."

11 Eighteen-year-old Henry M. Connally served as a private in the Third Texas Cavalry.

12 Paralee T. Rush was born in 1836 and died in 1890. She is buried in the Courtland Cemetery, Queen City, Cass County, Texas.

13 In 1856, Rev. Nelson Porterfield organized the Antioch Baptist Church, some nine miles west of Queen City, Texas.

14 Rachel was presumably reading M. M. Henkle's *The Life of Henry Bidleman Bascom: Late Bishop of the Methodist Episcopal Church, South* (Louisville, KY: Morton and Griswold, 1854). Bascom (1796–1850) was born in Hancock, New York, and although with little formal education, he established himself as a circuit riding pastor in the Methodist church in Ohio. His style was said to have been too florid to suit many in Ohio, so in 1816 he was transferred to Tennessee and Kentucky where he achieved great popularity. According to Bishop Matthew Simpson, Bascom was "perhaps the most popular pulpit orator in the United States. . . . He was a man of remarkably fine personal appearance, and had a voice of great compass and power." In 1823, Bascom was appointed as chaplain of the US House of Representatives, where he served until 1826. In 1842, he was selected as president of Transylvania University in Lexington, Kentucky, serving until 1849.

When, in 1844, the Methodist church divided over the question of slavery and the church suspended Bishop James Osgood Andrew because he refused to manumit his slaves, Bascom wrote the "protest of the minority" of the Southern members, precipitating the denominational split out of which the M. E. Church, South, arose.

His 1845 book, *Methodism and Slavery; with Other Matters in Controversy between the North and the South; Being a Review of the Manifesto of the Majority, in Reply to the Protest of the Minority, of the Late General Conference of the Methodist E. Church, in the Case of Bishop Andrew*, was a defense of the Southern church, of which he was elected head in 1850. He was consecrated a bishop in May 1850, a few months before his death on September 8, 1850. The town of Bascom, Texas, was named in his honor. Matthew Simpson, *Cyclopaedia of Methodism* (Philadelphia, PA: Louis H. Everts, 1876), 92–93.

15 Elijah Johns was born in Alabama in about 1839, but by 1860 was living with his family in Courtland, Texas. On June 3, 1862, he enlisted as a private in Company I, Third Texas Cavalry. He was the brother of Agnes Johns.

16 John Baker was born in or about 1805 in South Carolina. He was the husband of Nancy Baker and the father of Eliza J. Baker, Hila J. Baker, and the notorious outlaw, Cullen Montgomery Baker.

17 Ulysses Scott Connally was born in 1835 in DeKalb County, Georgia, the son of Lucinda McConnell Montgomery and Dempsey J. Connally. He enlisted as a private in Company D, the "Star Rifles," of the First Texas Infantry. In January 1862, he was elected lieutenant of the company and detailed to recruiting service in Texas. On May 15, 1862, he was elected captain of his company but died of tuberculosis in Atlanta, Georgia, on November 20 [or 24,] 1862. Harold B. Simpson, comp., *Hood's Texas Brigade: A Compendium* (Hillsboro, TX: Hill Junior College Press, 1977), 33.

18 Francis Lister Hawks (June 10, 1798–September 26, 1866) was an American writer, historian, Episcopal priest, and the first president of the University of Louisiana (now known as Tulane University). His narrative of the Mathew Calbraith Perry expedition to Japan contains the first impressions of Japan and the Japanese presented to the American public. It was originally presented as a report to the United States Senate, then published commercially in 1856. Francis L. Hawks, *The Narrative of the Expedition of an American Squadron to the China Seas and Japan: Performed in the Years 1852, 1853, and 1854, under the Command of Commodore M. C. Perry, United States Navy*.

[19] The Battle of Mill Springs, also known as Fishing Creek or Logan's Cross Roads, was fought near current Nancy, Kentucky. Late in 1861, Maj. Gen. George B. Crittenden's division guarded the strategic Cumberland Gap, anchoring the eastern terminus of Gen. Albert Sidney Johnston's defensive line extending from Columbus, Kentucky. In November 1861, Crittenden moved into central Kentucky to strengthen Rebel control of the area around Bowling Green. Union Brig. Gen. George H. Thomas advanced against Crittenden's command, intending to drive the Confederates across the Cumberland River, arriving at Logan's Crossroads on January 17, 1862. There Crittenden attacked the federal force on January 19 and enjoyed initial success, but Union resistance stiffened, and Confederate Brig. Gen. Felix Zollicoffer was killed, sending the center of the Confederate line back in confusion.

A Union counterattack turned the Confederate left flank, causing Crittenden's troops to break and run back across the Cumberland as far as Murfreesboro, Tennessee.

As Rachel reported, casualties were relatively light, with Union losses amounting to thirty-nine killed and 207 wounded and Confederate casualties totaling 125 killed and 404 wounded or missing, as well as a dozen pieces of artillery, 150 wagons, more than 1,000 horses and mules. The Battle of Mill Springs, however, was a stinging Confederate defeat. Not only was it the first significant Union victory of the war and therefore much celebrated in the press, but it resulted in the loss of the vital state of Kentucky and laid open middle Tennessee to invasion by Union forces the following February. Kenneth A. Hafendorfer, *Mill Springs: Campaign and Battle of Mill Springs, Kentucky* (Louisville, KY: KH Press, 2001).

[20] Fort Henry, the principal Confederate stronghold on the Tennessee River, fell to Union forces under Brig. Gen. Ulysses S. Grant and Flag Officer Andrew Hull Foote on February 6, 1862. It was the first important victory for the Union and in the Western Theater.

On February 4 and 5, Grant landed two divisions north of the fort, planning to advance on the following day. Bombardment by Union gunboats, however, forced Brig. Gen. Lloyd Tilghman to surrender to Foote before Grant arrived. On February 12, Grant's army, again supported by the Union fleet, marched overland twelve miles to invest Fort Donelson on the Cumberland River.

[21] Henry Wadsworth Longfellow, comp. and ed., *Poets and Poetry of Europe, with Introductions and Biographical Notices* (New York: C. S. Francis, 1855).

[22] Scrofula or "cervical tuberculous lymphadenitis" is characterized by inflamed and irritated lymph nodes.

[23] Fort Donelson fell to the combined land and naval forces of U. S. Grant and Andrew Foote on February 16, allowing Union forces to move unopposed up the Tennessee River and capture the vital city of Nashville. Benjamin Franklin Cooling, *Forts Donelson and Henry: The Key to the Confederate Heartland* (Knoxville: University of Tennessee Press, 1987); Stephen D. Engle, *Struggle for the Heartland: The Campaigns from Fort Henry to Corinth* (Lincoln: University of Nebraska Press, 2002).

[24] "Ferrara, Prison of Tasso," Lord Byron (1788–1824).

[25] Titus Flavius Josephus, a first-century Romano-Jewish historian, was born into one of Jerusalem's elite families. During the First Jewish–Roman War he commanded the Jewish forces in Galilee until surrendering to Roman forces led by Vespasian after the six-week siege of Jotapata in 67 AD. Vespasian kept Josephus as a slave until Vespasian became Emperor in 69 AD, when he gave Josephus his freedom.

In 71 AD, he was granted Roman citizenship and became an advisor and friend of Vespasian's son Titus. While in Rome and under Flavian patronage, Josephus wrote all of his known works, which are major sources of modern understanding of Jewish life and history during the first century.

His most important works as an historian are *The Jewish War* (c. 75 AD) which recounts the Jewish revolt against Roman occupation, and the twenty-one volume *Antiquities of the Jews* (c. 94 AD) which is a history of the world from a Jewish perspective, outlining Jewish history beginning with the Creation, as passed down through Jewish historical tradition.

These books provide valuable insight into first century Judaism and the background of early Christianity and are the chief source next to the Bible for the history and antiquity of ancient Palestine.

Josephus's work was not available in English until Thomas Lodge published his translation in 1602. A new translation, published in 1732 by William Whiston, achieved great popularity, becoming—after the Bible—the book that Christians most frequently owned.

[26] Matthew 23:37.

[27] Luke 13:35.

[28] The exact identity of "Old Brown," as Rachel called him, cannot now be determined except insofar as he served as overseer for several Cass County plantations, including, for a time, that of the Moores. He proved to be not only unsatisfactory but a threat to their lives and property, however, and in 1865 Rachel referred to him as "the demon—the inhuman villain" and wrote that if she were a man she would "murder Old Brown in his tracks."

[29] The Battle of Pea Ridge or Elkhorn Tavern was fought northeast of Fayetteville, Arkansas, March 7–8, 1862. Federal forces under Brig. Gen. Samuel R. Curtis, moving south out of central Missouri, had driven Sterling Price's Missouri State Guard back into northwestern Arkansas. Maj. Gen. Earl Van Dorn launched a Confederate counter-offensive, hoping to recapture northern Arkansas and Missouri. The Confederate Army of the West outflanked Curtis's strong position on Little Sugar Creek and fell on his rear in two columns, one under Price and the other under Brig. Gen. Ben McCulloch. McCulloch was killed in the first day's action and his wing of the army fell into disarray. Price's troops pushed back the Union right wing but was driven from the field on the second day of fighting after the Union forces were reinforced by troops who had faced McCulloch's brigade on the previous day. Curtis's victory established federal control of Missouri and northern Arkansas. William L. Shea and Earl J. Hess, *Pea Ridge: Civil War Campaign in the West* (Chapel Hill: University of North Carolina Press, 1992).

[30] *Nathan the Wise* is a play published by Gotthold Ephraim Lessing in 1779. Set in Jerusalem during the Third Crusade, it describes how the Jewish merchant Nathan, the enlightened sultan Saladin, and a knight Templar bridge the gaps between Judaism, Islam, and Christianity. Its major themes are friendship, tolerance, the relativism of God, the rejection of miracles, and the need for communication.

[31] Cholera morbus is a gastrointestinal illness characterized by cramps, diarrhea, and vomiting.

[32] Eliza Bird Salmon, the wife of William H. Salmon, was born in Greenville County, South Carolina, on January 7, 1807. She died on November 19, 1872, and is buried in the Courtland Cemetery, Queen City, Texas. She was the mother of Rachel's friend Orpha M. Salmon.

[33] *Faust, the first part of which was published in 1808, is generally considered to be the greatest work of German literature. In this tragic play by Johann Wolfgang von Goethe, the* demon Mephistopheles lures the humanistic scholar Faust, God's favorite human being, into committing the sin of intellectual pride. Despairing at the vanity of scientific, humanitarian, and religious learning, Faust agrees to sell his soul in exchange for infinite knowledge.

[34] Thomas W. Cutrer, *Ben McCulloch and the Frontier Military Tradition* (Chapel Hill: University of North Carolina Press, 1993).

[35] This line is from American composer George Frederick Root's sentimental ballad, "The Hazel Dell," published in 1858.

All alone my watch I'm keeping
In the Hazel Dell,
For my darling Nelly's near me sleeping,
Nelly dear farewell.

[36] A Jonathan S. Carr was born in Tennessee in about 1825 but by 1860 was living in Cass County.

[37] A Martha Harper, who had been born in Maryland in or about 1838, was living in Cass County in 1862. In 1857, she had born a son named Tom H. Harper, Jr., but because no record remains of the birth of another

child in 1862, it is assumed to have died of its disease. The 1860 Federal census denominates her as a mulatto. A Martha E. Bell was married to B. Harper in Cass County on April 23, 1855.

38 Quoting American poet George P. Morris' 1826, "The Sweep's Carol."

A year, alas! had scarcely flown—
Hope beamed but to deceive—
Ere I was left to weep alone.
From morn till dewy eve!

39 New Orleans, the entrepot of the entire western Confederacy, was captured on April 25, 1862, by a naval expedition commanded by Flag Officer David G. Farragut. The loss of this vital port meant that the cotton planters of Louisiana and northeast Texas could no longer export their crops or import foreign goods.

40 Anderson Rochelle Moores' wife, Pauline Tucker Jarrett, had died on July 2, 1861.

41 Following the Union Army victory at the Battle of Shiloh, the Union armies under Maj. Gen. Henry W. Halleck—the Army of the Tennessee, the Army of the Ohio, and the Army of the Mississippi—set out to capture the strategically vital rail center of Corinth in northwest Mississippi. Halleck's advance was tediously slow, fortifying after each advance. At last, on May 25, 1862, having moved only five miles in three weeks Halleck began his siege of the town.

Gen. P. G. T. Beauregard, the commander of the Confederate Army of Tennessee, saved the greatly outnumbered garrison with an elaborate *ruse de guerre*. Under the shelter of so-called Quaker guns, the garrison cheered enthusiastically as trains from the Mobile and Ohio Railroad arrived in Corinth, as though they were being reinforced. During the night of May 29, with their campfires still burning and regimental bands still playing, the Confederate Army, including its sick and wounded, its heavy artillery, and tons of supplies, evacuated Corinth, withdrawing to Tupelo, Mississippi. When Union patrols entered the town on the following morning, they found the Confederates gone. Timothy B. Smith, *Corinth 1862: Siege, Battle, Occupation* (Topeka: University Press of Kansas, 2012).

42 Robert Pollok was born on October 19, 1798, in Renfrewshire, Scotland. While studying for the ministry at the University of Glasgow he anonymously published three poems: "Helen of the Glen," "The Persecuted Family," and "Ralph Gemmell." After his death, these were published together as *Tales of the Covenanters*.

In 1827, shortly before leaving the university, Pollok published what was to be his final and most famous work, *The Course of Time*, a poem in blank verse, which sold 78,000 copies and was popular as far away as North America.

Later that year, suffering from tuberculosis, Pollok was advised to travel to Italy. He left Scotland, but his health worsened rapidly and he died at Southampton on September 15 and was buried in the churchyard of St. Nicholas, Millbrook. A monument to Pollok in Newton Mearns, Scotland, bears the inscription, "He soared untrodden heights and seemed at home."

43 The first of these quotations is from the gospel of St. Matthew (26:40–41) rather than from the epistles of St. Paul. In the garden of Gethsemane, on the night before his crucifixion, Jesus returned to his disciples and found them all sleeping. "What," he asked Peter, "could ye not watch with me one hour? Watch and pray, that ye enter not into temptation: the spirit indeed is willing, but the flesh is weak." The second quotation is Pauline: "I find then a law, that, when I would do good, evil is present with me," he wrote to the church in Rome. (Romans 7:21). The third quotation is also from Matthew: "Enter by the narrow gate: for wide is the gate and broad is the way that leads to destruction, and there are many who go in by it. Because narrow is the gate and difficult is the way which leads to life, and there are few who find it." (Matthew 7:13–14)

44 Jaconet is a lightweight cotton cloth with a smooth and slightly stiff finish.

45 Reuben Harrison "Harry" and Judson Moores were sons of Jane Godbold and Reuben H. Moores.

[46] "Linsay" is possibly William Preston "Wild Bill" Longley, another Texas desperado who is said to have been a member of Cullen Montgomery Baker's gang. Dan Anderson and Laurence J. Yadon, *Ten Deadly Texans* (New Orleans: Pelican Publishing Company, 2009), 37, 41.

[47] Wesley Baily [or Bailey], a farmer, had been born in Tennessee in 1810, but moved to Texas after settling for a time in Alabama. Bailey had a wife, Louisa, and was the father of seven children, and owned $620 worth of real estate. The situation that led to his murder involved a perceived personal slight from an orphan boy named Stallcup on the street of Forest Home. Baker accused Stallcup of threatening to kill him. The boy told Baker that he did not intend to shoot anyone. Baker had "no inclination to believe it," reported one newspaper, but "fetched a long black snake whip from David Moores' store and preceded in front of several witnesses, to flog Stallcup almost to death." Wesley Bailey, one of the observers, served as chief witness against Baker, who was convicted of assault. Incensed at Bailey's testimony, Baker determined to seek revenge. On October 8, 1854, about one hour after the conclusion of the trial, Baker appeared at Bailey's home. Riding up to the barn, Baker accused Bailey of turning Stallcup against him, an accusation that Bailey "positively denied." Raising a double-barreled shotgun, Baker supposedly exclaimed, "I'll teach you or any other man to go into court and swear against me. Standout, damn you." When Bailey stepped out, Baker shot him in the hips and legs and then rode away. Bailey suffered for three or four days before dying. Crouch and Brice, *Cullen Montgomery Baker*, 35–38.

[48] This is further evidence of the systematic, often brutal, use of violence by women of the planter elite against enslaved women and helps to demolish the idea that gender solidarity was more important than race and class in plantation households. For an examination of this theory, see Thavolia Glymph, *Out of the House of Bondage: The Transformation of the Plantation Household* (New York: Cambridge University Press, 2008).

Elisabeth Félix, better known only as Mademoiselle Rachel, was a French actress. She became a prominent figure in French society, and was the mistress of, among others, Napoleon III and Napoléon Joseph Charles Paul Bonaparte. Madame Gassier was a well-known Spanish actress and vocalist, born in 1830.

[49] James Madison Lockett was born in Crawford County, Georgia, on December 28, 1830. By 1836 the family had moved to Crawford County, Arkansas, and in 1860 he was living in Cass County where, on April 24, 1862, he married Ellen Rand, who had been born in Franklin County, Alabama, on September 9, 1843. James Madison Lockett died in Texarkana on February 2, 1914, and is buried in the city's Rose Hill Cemetery.

[50] Lucinda Connally's son Charles W. Connally passed away in Cass County on April 1, 1860, at the age of thirty-one.

Three of Lucinda's sons died in the autumn of 1862: Pvt. J. R. Rhadamanthus "Ruddy" Connally of Company K, First Texas Infantry, was killed in action at the Battle of Sharpsburg, Maryland, September 17, 1862; First Lt. James M. C. Connally of Company H, Fourth Texas Infantry, was wounded at the Battle of Iuka, Mississippi, September 19, 1862, and died in Cass County sometime later that year; Capt. Ulysses Scott Connally died in an Atlanta, Georgia, hospital on November 29, 1862.

Rachel is quoting Matthew 24:21.

[51] These lines are from Thomas Moore's (1779–1852) poem, "Come, Rest in this Bosom."

[52] Historian David Hackett Fischer has observed that "the Puritan practice of will-breaking was not much practiced" in the South. Rather, boys were "compelled to develop strong and autonomous wills," and failure to develop a "boisterous disposition" was considered unmanly. David Hackett Fischer, *English Roots in American Soil: Four British Folkways in America* (New York: Oxford University Press, 1989), 311–12.

Emotional self-control was, to nineteenth-century Brahmins of decorum and propriety, a hallmark of good breeding, and was "the first element of a gentlemanly dignity." According to the 1855 *Illustrated Manners Book*, the man "who is liable to fits of passion; who cannot control his temper, but is subject to ungovernable excitement of any kind, is always in danger." Equanimity, however, "to an extraordinary degree," could be "acquired when it is wanting" by enforcing on ones' self "a steady effort to bear up against small annoyances." *Illustrated Manners Book: A Manual of Good Behavior and Polite Accomplishments* (New York: Leland Clay and Co., 1855), 205.

53 These lines are from Abby Hutchinson Patton's poem "Looking toward Sunset."

Oh, when the long day's work is done,
And we clasp hands at set of sun
Loved friends we meet,
In concourse sweet,
At even.

Abby Hutchinson Patton, *A Handful of Pebbles* (Privately printed, 1891), 57.

54 The sister in question was Jane Ross Moore, the wife of James C. Moore. She seems to have inherited the estate of Thomas Briggs Moore, who died in 1852. Fire in the Bowie County courthouse in January 1889, however, destroyed any record of the dispute.

55 John H. Graham, born in Tennessee in about 1830, was a surveyor in Linden, Texas, and was, according to the 1870 Federal census, a "mulatto," but this is unlikely as the 1880 census identifies him as white, and he served as the first lieutenant of Company D, Leonidas M. Martin's cavalry regiment, Texas State Troops, also known as the Fifth Partisan Rangers.

56 Elisha Kent Kane was an American explorer and a medical officer in the United States Navy. Kane organized and headed the Second Grinnell expedition which sailed from New York on May 31, 1853, in search of Sir John Franklin's lost expedition. Although suffering from scurvy and at times near death, he charted the coasts of Smith Sound and the Kane Basin, penetrating farther north than any other explorer had done up to that time. Kane finally abandoned his icebound brig, *Advance,* on May 20, 1855, and made an eighty-three-day march to Upernavik, Greenland. The party, carrying the invalids, lost only one man. Kane returned to New York on October 11, 1855, and the following year published his two-volume *Arctic Explorations. Elisha Kent Kane, The Far North: Exploration in the Arctic Regions* (Edinburgh: W. P. Nimmo, [1859?]).

57 "Nearly every one will concede that there is no greater tyrant than Fashion," wrote Baltimore physician Eugene Lee Crutchfield in 1897. "To please this goddess, men and women (even when possessed of intelligence) will endure any discomfort, distort the artistic proportions of the figure designed by Nature, sacrifice morality, and jeopardize health. The constricted waist of woman exhibited on all occasions and the decollete costumes generally worn when evening dress is required, attest the truth of this assertion. Both of these produce discomfort, rob the figure of its graceful outlines, suggest immoral thoughts and desires, and induce many serious maladies."

Victorian doctors believed that the uterus, in particular, suffered from the tightlacing of corsets, failing to develop properly due to the inactivity of the abdominal muscles or becoming prolapsed. Others believed that when the bladder or rectum emptied, the uterus was unable to lift back into place due to weak ligaments, causing head and back pain, inability to stand or walk, and improper menstruation. Valerie Steele, *Fashion and Eroticism: Ideals of Feminine Beauty from the Victorian Era through the Jazz Age* (New York: Oxford University Press, 1985); Valerie Steele, *The Corset: A Cultural History* (New Haven, CT: Yale University Press, 2005); Eugene Lee Crutchfield, "Some Ill Effects of the Corset," *Gaillard's Medical Journal* 67 (July 1897), 1–11; Hartland Law and Herbert E. Law, "Displacements of the Womb," *Viavi Hygiene: Explaining the Natural Principles upon Which the Viavi System of Treatment for Men, Women and Children Is Based* (San Francisco: Viavi Company, 1912), 258–271.

58 "Towel," in this sense, meant simply a strip of cloth, to be cut as needed.

59 William Henry Burkhalter, a Cass County farmer, was born in Green County, Tennessee, on February 18, 1820. He was one of the original trustees of the Enon Primitive Baptist Church, organized near Havana,

some eight miles west of Queen City, on June 7, 1845. He is buried in the Old Liberty Cemetery on the church grounds.

60 A slay or reed is the part of a weaving loom used to separate and space the warp threads, to guide the shuttle's motion across the loom, and to push the weft threads into place.

61 William M. McAdams was born in 1788 in Pickens, South Carolina. He married Cynthia Matthews Teague in North Carolina in 1806. The couple were the parents of ten children. He died in Bowie County in September 1860 and she in 1870. They are buried in the Sand Hill Cemetery, Simms, Texas.

62 Erysipelas, also known as St. Anthony's fire, is a bacterial infection characterized by an intense rash.

63 Kersey is a coarse ribbed woolen cloth.

64 Dr. Anderson Miles (March 8, 1808–November 21, 1900), a native of Milledgeville, Georgia, married Martha Ann Delilah Smith (July 5, 1835–September 13, 1868) in Cass County on August 17, 1862.

65 Blue mass was a medication based on mercury in its elemental state or in compound form, often as mercury chloride, also known as calomel. In common use from the seventeenth to the nineteenth centuries, it was a specific treatment for syphilis but was also prescribed as a remedy for tuberculosis, constipation, toothache, parasitic infestations, and the pains of childbirth. It was sold in the form of blue or gray pills, and the name probably derives from the use of blue dye or blue chalk in some formulations. William Frazer, *Elements of Materia Medica* (Dublin, 1851); John Marten, *A Treatise of the Venereal Disease* (London, 1711).

66 "Pygmalion" is a poem from William Cox Bennett's 1857 collection, *Queen Eleanor's Vengeance and Other Poems*.

67 Ananias Moores, the son of Jane Godbold and Reuben H. Moores, was born on September 19, 1862. He died on March 23, 1918, and is buried in the Fairview Cemetery, Memphis, Hall County, Texas.

68 Augusta J. Evans, born in 1835 in Columbus, Georgia, was one of the most popular domestic novelists of the latter half of the nineteenth century. Beulah Benton, the protagonist of her 1859 novel of the antebellum South, is a plucky, feminist, intellectual—but given to convoluted philosophical musings and, ultimately, acquiescent to women's traditional roles.

69 Mary Ann McCollum was born in Tennessee in or about 1848. She was married to John L. Daly of Camden, Arkansas, and they became the parents of one son, Richard Hugh Daly. Daly was elected lieutenant colonel of the Eighteenth Arkansas Infantry when it was organized at DeValls Bluff but soon acceded to command of the regiment, leading it at the battles of Iuka and Corinth where he was killed in action on October 4, 1862, in the ill-starred assault on Battery Robinette. In 1880, Mary Ann Daly was a widow living in Lafayette, Crawford County, Arkansas.

70 Jane Godbold "Janie" Moores, born in Cass County on January 4, 1856, was the daughter of Jane Godbold and Reuben H. Moores. On October 29, 1873, she married John Ewell Morriss, a merchant and lumberman, and was to become the mother of nine children. She died in Texarkana on February 19, 1912, and is buried in Rose Hill Cemetery.

She is not to be confused with Jane Ross "Janie" Moores, Rachel's niece and the daughter of Matilda Cooper and William Henry Harrison Moores, who was born on September 2, 1858, in Bowie County. She married John McElwee McGill on November 19, 1877, and became the mother of eight children. She died on June 2, 1937, and is buried in Oakland Cemetery, Dallas, Texas.

71 Pompholyx was defined in *Gould's Medical Dictionary* as "a rare disease, with bullas of the hands and feet." A bulla is "a bleb or large blister."

72 This is a verse from Johan Ludwig Uhland's poem, "The Passage," *Edinburgh Review* (October 1832).

73 *The Works and Life of Walter Bagehot*, ed. Mrs. Russell Barrington, 9 vols., *The Life in One Volume* (London: Longmans, Green, and Co., 1915).

74 Rachel's half-brother, William Johnson Godbold, was born in 1831 or 1832 in Monroe, Alabama, but moved with his family to Harrison, Columbia County, Arkansas. On February 27, 1862, he enlisted in Col. Thomas P. Dockery's Nineteenth Arkansas Infantry. He was elected as first lieutenant and was

subsequently promoted to captain of Company C. He was wounded and taken prisoner during the ill-fated Confederate attack on Corinth, Mississippi, on October 3, 1862, and died in captivity on the following day.

75 What is known of this shadowy Eilbeck Mason does not correspond to what he told Rachel of himself. He was born in Virginia in 1802—May 20, 1806, according to the date on his gravestone—and was, indeed, the brother of James Murray Mason, a former US senator from Virginia who became the Confederate envoy to Great Britain. He attended the College of New Jersey (now Princeton University) and by 1845 was practicing law in Vicksburg, Mississippi. On December 15, 1847, he married Virginia Magee of Vicksburg. In 1857, he purchased Limerick Plantation in Tensas Parish, Louisiana, where, by 1860, eighty-nine men and women were enslaved workers. An Eilbeck Mason died in Vicksburg on June 27, 1862, and is buried there in Cedar Hill Cemetery beside his wife, who died on September 9, 1863. This was, of course, before the appearance of the visitor, perhaps an imposter, appeared at the Moores' home. The Eilbeck Mason to whom Rachel refers as "our government agent" was in all likelihood a confidence man, a trickster preying upon a gullible public easily deceived by charlatans. This was a figure then common enough in American culture to have inspired Herman Melville's 1857 satirical novel, *The Confidence-Man: His Masquerade*. Robert W. Senator Young, *James Murray Mason: Defender of the Old South (Knoxville: University of Tennessee Press, 1998); Lydia Lasswell Crist, ed., The Papers of Jefferson Davis: 1880–1889*, vol. 14 (Baton Rouge: Louisiana State University Press, 2015), 170; Karen Halttunen, *Confidence Men and Painted Women: A Study of Middle-class Culture in America, 1830–1870* (New Haven, CT: Yale University Press, 1982).

The Trans-Mississippi Department did, indeed, contain great mineral resources, and on July 14, 1863, President Jefferson Davis instructed the newly appointed department commander, Lt. Gen. Edmund Kirby Smith, to "get iron, test its qualities, combine it into the best gun-metal, and cast ordnance." Cass County has valuable iron ore deposits, and during the 1860s and 1870s two foundries operated in the county, the one at Queen City, manufacturing hollowware, plows, and fencing material, but the lack of coal for fuel and the absence of railway transportation rendered the business unprofitable and it was abandoned.

This mine seems to have been located on the former estate of David Moores' brother, Thomas Briggs Moores, who had died in 1852 and which came into the possession of his sister Jane Ross Moores and brother-in-law James C. Moore. *OR*, 22 (2): 926; Ernest Francis Burchard, *Iron Ore in Cass, Marion, Morris, and Cherokee Counties, Texas* (Washington, DC: Government Printing Office, 1915).

76 From May to August 1861, the USS *Pawnee*, a sloop-of-war commanded by Commander Stephen Clegg Rowan, operated on the Potomac River, furnishing protection for surveying parties, bombarding Confederate shore batteries, convoying vessels, and performing general blockade duty. On May 24, a party from the ship demanded and received the surrender of Alexandria, Virginia. James L. Mooney, ed., *Dictionary of American Naval Fighting Ships* (Washington, DC: Naval History Division; Navy Department, 1981).

Elmer Ephraim Ellsworth was a close personal friend of Abraham Lincoln, who eulogized him as "the greatest little man I ever met." Before the war, Ellsworth had formed and led a popular drill team, the "Zouave Cadets of Chicago." Elected colonel of the Eleventh New York Infantry at the outbreak of the Civil War and was assigned to the defense of Washington. James W. Jackson was the proprietor of the Marshall House, an inn located in Alexandria, Virginia. An ardent secessionist, Jackson flew a large Confederate flag from his inn roof that was visible across the Potomac River. On May 24, 1861, less than twenty-four hours after Virginia seceded, Ellsworth led his regiment into Alexandria, resolved to remove the flag. Minutes after doing so he was killed by a shotgun blast fired by Jackson as he descended the stairs, the flag in his arms. Jackson was immediately killed by one of Ellsworth's soldiers. Both men gained instant fame as martyrs to their respective causes. Ellsworth was the first conspicuous casualty and the first Union officer to die in the American Civil War and his body lay in state at the White House. James G. Barber, *Alexandria in the Civil War* (Lynchburg, VA: W. E. Howard, 1988); George G. Kundahl, *Alexandria Goes to War: Beyond Robert E. Lee* (Knoxville: University of Tennessee Press, 2004).

77 The 1860 US census for Cass County records a J. Sager, the twenty-four-year-old wife of John A. Sager, age thirty-four, residing near Courtland. This couple were the parents of two boys, Charles Sager, aged ten or twelve, and M. C. Sager, age seven, and a daughter, H. Sager, age four. On March 30, 1862, the elder Sager enlisted at Jefferson in Capt. C. L. Marshall's Company D of Col. Richard Waterhouse's Nineteenth Texas Infantry. He rose to the rank of fifth sergeant.

78 Francine Henshaw Ironmonger was born in or about 1847.

79 Hila J. Baker married Elijah B. Turner on September 29, 1862, in Lafayette County, Arkansas.

80 Gideon Foster was born in Missouri in 1840, but by 1850 was a resident of Cass County.

81 Nancy Jane Larkin was born in Mississippi on August 29, 1854. She was married to John Wesley Graham and was the mother of one child, a daughter. She died in McLeod, Cass County, on November 26, 1948, and is buried there in the Good Exchange Cemetery.

82 Lucinda McConnell Montgomery Connally, the wife of Dempsey J. Connally, died in December 1862 and is buried in Courtland Cemetery, Queen City, Texas. She was the mother of nine children.

83 Rachel is here quoting from a popular song, "Trancadillo," the lyrics of which were written by Charlotte Howard Gilman. Of this song, Gilman wrote, "the following graceful harmony, long consecrated to Bacchanalian revelry, has been rescued for more genial and lovely associations. The words were composed for a private boat-party at Sullivan's Island, South Carolina, but the author will be glad to know that the distant echoes of other waters awake to the spirited melody." Helen Kendrick Johnson, comp., *Our Familiar Songs and those Who Made Them* (New York: Henry Holt and Company, 1885), 151.

chapter six

WHAT A HARVEST DEATH IS REAPING

Cass County, Texas
1863

T he war and natural disaster continued to disrupt the local economy. "The cut worm threatens our whole cabbage crop with death," Rachel wrote, and, worse, "the people here are nearly all out of corn." If the men who were not with the army, she wondered, could not grow sufficient corn, "then how is it to be expected the soldiers' wives, who were left upon the country, are to get it if not from the planters who are exempted, and yet they cry aloud against any exceptions of a planter. Strange inconsistency."

David was the only planter in northern Cass County who raised hogs, and Rachel had her "heart so set upon the army having it at half price." When her husband sold his pork to a better market, she felt that he would "regret not yielding to my wishes."

David was exempt from conscription because, she wrote, he was "not able to undergo the privations and fatigue of camp," and if he were to join the army, "the grand jury would find a bill against him for leaving his Negros without an overseer." But, feeling for the plight of the soldiers more than for their cause, she swore that "if I had a fortune, I would give it half to support the army."

Despite the war, however, Rachel's life remained largely uninterrupted. "Today has been one of constant labor to me, having lard dried up and put away and other etcs." Cooking was always to be done, even on the Sabbath, which she considered to be sinful. She writes of knitting socks for Uncle Edmund, the eldest and most trusted black man on the plantation, and she "worked most assiduously with Lizzie bedding the yard," planting roses and pomegranates. And, as always, read from the Bible "whilst resting today from my arduous tasks."

The principal deviation from the family's peace-time routine came with the opening of an iron mine and foundry near the Moores plantation. The shadowy Eilbeck Mason, at least claiming to be a "government agent," urged the local citizens to fund the operation as a stock company for the benefit of the Confederate arms manufacture. David Moores seems to have been among the principal stockholders and one of the most active corporate officials, and certainly Mason became a fixture in the Moores household, frequently making extended stays in their home, with Rachel cooking and sewing for him and nursing him through illness.

In April 1863, upon receiving word of her father's worsening condition, Rachel returned to her old home in Columbia County, Arkansas, as she frequently did until his death on May 27. "With each succeeding visit," she wrote, "I would grow so impatient to see him I could scarcely keep my seat and contain myself just before we would reach the old homestead."

Her father's passing left her "sick and broken spirited," a condition exacerbated by a growing estrangement from her sisters and a worrisome relationship with an orphan girl named Franny Ironmonger, who Rachel took in as a foster child. Franny, however, proved indolent and ungrateful. "She neither knits nor jots night lessons, and she is in great need of hose and knowledge." After weeks of moral and practical instruction, Rachel was forced to the conclusion that her ward was "slovenly with her needle, slatternly in her dress, and is certainly the most willful girl I ever saw." Worse, Rachel wrote, Franny would "not tell the truth if she imagines a falsehood will excuse her." She was expelled from school and often spent nights Rachel knew not where. Finally, Rachel sent the "poor, willful, wayward, unfortunate thing" away, declaring that "her character is gone."

By the end of the year, Rachel had begun to fear that "deserters will arrive any evening" as well as "Federal emissaries sent to plunder, burn, or tamper with the Negros." Worse, deaths, both civilian and in the army, were multiplying. "Our bereavements are coming so thick," Rachel lamented. In a year's time she recorded the deaths of two enslaved children of whom she seemed genuinely fond; her friends Sarah M. Salmon and Dempsey J. Connally; her favorite sister-in-law, Matilda Moores; her beloved half-brothers, Capt. William Johnson Godbold, killed at the Battle of Corinth, and Capt. Benjamin Franklin Godbold, killed at the Battle of Big Black River; and most painfully to Rachel, her father.

XXX

[from the Journal of Rachel P. Moores]

[January 2, 1863] *Have made extraordinary effort to get my ironing dune and put away, to do all my mending* [illegible] *renovate trunks and drawers, etc., and feel really fatigued.*

We have had a steady day's rain, an inclement day for poor Mrs. Connally's interment, but for which inclemency I should have attended.

[January 1863] *Though so much fatigued, slept but little last night, and from putting up window curtains and doing other such work. Riding over to Mr. Reuben's added. I feel exceedingly nervous tonight, though since supper I finished David a nightshirt.*

[Sunday, January 4, 1863] *Spent the morning in reading* The Life of General Marion, *the afternoon in reading my Bible and riding out. Rode as far as Mr. Turner's and Baker's.[1]*

Found a letter from dear Mat on my return. I wonder why my older sisters did not write to me. What is the matter? I'm sure I can't conjecture. It hurts me to have them treat me thus when I always direct my first to them after my return from home or their return from here.

[Monday, January 5, 1863] *Made a nightshirt for David today and superintended the making of my strawberry beds, and Lizzie has given me no little trouble. Made some quince preserves.*

[Tuesday, January 6, 1863] *Commenced another nightshirt, finished* The Life of General Marion, *than whom a more magnanimous general, statesman, patriot never lived. He was all that was noble and honorable. One of nature's true noblemen, and strange to say, patriotic South Carolina has never erected a monument to his memory, nor did she compensate him while living for spending a lifetime in her service. I think him nearer Washington's key in true greatness than any other man that ever lived. I cannot think him inferior either in "court or camp."*

I wish I could believe we had any is so true hearted patriots now in our field as Marion, as brave.

> *"The British soldier trembles*
> *When Marion's name is told."*[2]

[Torn] *David had hogs killed yesterday. Today has been one of constant labor to me, having lard dried up and put away and other etcs. attendant upon such occasions and, at the conclusion, a bath, or more strictly speaking, a wash, and, for the first time, with homemade soap. My stock of Castile and perfumed soaps are too much diminished for such a scrubbing as was necessary after such a day's work.*

I gave Franny a little talk about her indolence in study. She neither knits nor jots night lessons, and she is in great need of hose and knowledge.

[Thursday, January 8, 1863] *Mrs. Brown spent the afternoon here, and from her I learned that Franny had been kept in twice this week for imperfect lessons. It was painful news to me as Franny had told me voluntarily that she had never been kept in once since she started to school. I determined to ask Miss Lewis about it.*

After attacking Franny before Mrs. Brown was out was of sight, Miss Lewis rode up and sent for me to meet her at the gate, and on asking her whether or no Franny had been kept in, "Why, of course, three times," was her reply, and said she was constantly in the habit of telling untruths.

Now, I rather she was addicted to any vice but that vice, that of falsehood. Poor, poor child. Has her grandparents' course with her been such as to force the habit on her? Or can it be constitutional?

I came in and sent the servants out and gave her a most serious chat. Told her she was disgracing herself and entreated her to refrain, to desist. She wept long and silently, but insisted she had never told an untruth, and when I proved to her that she had, she still said she had not. Oh, Father in Heaven, help me to direct this willful, wayward child. What is to become of her if she continues in this wayward course? I'm sure I can't see nothing but destruction awaiting if she refuses all advice and follows her own inclination.

[Friday, January 9, 1863] *We drove down to Dr. Salmon's* **[torn]** *to get the mail matter but found none. David had not been to the office today but spent a few hours most agreeably with his family.*

[Saturday, January 10, 1863] *Sister Jane sent our mail matter over this morning—a letter to her from Sister Margaret and a letter to me from Mollie. I cannot imagine what makes Sister Margaret so vacillating in her feelings towards me. I wrote to her soon after my return from Arkansas and she has never replied to it nor sent me any message whatever in Sister Jane's letter, and when I reached Pa's last fall, she treated me very coolly for the first few hours. It hurt me much and it puzzled me too, somewhat.*

I know since Sister Jane's marriage, their meetings have been "few and far between." She shows a marked difference, and though it wounds me, yet I consider it a most flattering testimonial of my own merit. I had much rather we agree and live in perfect harmony with those with whom I have constantly to be in contact than with those I have constantly to meet. Most anyone, particularly if they are not very conscientious, can manage to please the casual, or otherwise purposed visitor, but it is quite a different affair to always give satisfaction to those with whom a large portion of your life is spent.

I know that there was far more compatibility, harmony, and confidence existing between Sister M[argaret] and myself before we left the paternal roof than between herself and Sister Jane. She knows it. Sister Jane knows it and all the family knew. She was several years older than myself and treated me, up to the time of my marriage, with the greatest deference and respect. My conduct was always flattering to her, my language dear, and when I grew up to woman's estate and thought and acted for myself, was more self-reliant, had other grown up sisters who claimed my respect as well as affection, Sister M[argaret] felt that her place was usurped. I know it is natural for an elder sister to feel thus sometimes. Sister acknowledged that she felt so when, after her marriage, how I confided in Sister Margaret and [illegible] been threatened with the same attack. And as for me, I cannot flatter. I cannot say what I do not feel.

Sister Jane can soothe Sister M[argaret] with the warmly expressed sympathy she feels. I cannot tell her how much I pity her. I know my actions show it, and I think that enough. God knows I do pity her and ever have flown to her in her moments of deepest affliction. When a girl, I never consulted my own feelings when she was in trouble, but she was so sarcastic to me on several occasions since my marriage that I cannot feel the same, and I suppose cannot act the same.

I cannot bear sarcasm, and yet it always calls it forth in me. I never could use it with anyone unless they attacked me, and then with shame. I confess I am inclined to fight with their own weapon. Sometimes, when I feel in unusually good health, I can sit still and bear it right patiently. But let me be in pain and I am morbidly sensitive. If I were a good Christian, I would not mind it, but I am sadly deficient then. Maybe after I study the New Testament more, I will be all right. Can be "reviled and revile not again."[3]

Spent the day as I usually do when Saturday's duties are on hand. I try to lessen Sunday's duties for the servants, but it seems there is always some cooking to be done, however. I may work then, and yet I think it sinful to do so. It is hard to break through long established customs, and I was raised to see cooking done on the Sabbath as was my husband. But that ought not to be an excuse for us. We have departed from many old family customs and set up ways of our own.

[Sunday, January 11, 1863] Surely there was never a [torn] than this blessed holy Sabbath. As I walked through the fields a few moments ago, I felt inspired by a new love of Him who created the outer blue, the bright sunshine, and every other beautiful thing that produces pleasurable emotions.

The buggy is ready, and I know I shall enjoy my ride. Franny is gone again, and I know not where to.

[Monday, January 12, 1863] *Doubled and had twisted some thread to make Uncle Edmund some socks, which I find is too fine. The remainder of the day. I worked most assiduously with Lizzie bedding the yard. Had our beds torn up and dug down.*

[Tuesday, January 13, 1863] *Fixed more thread this morning. Worked on the yard. Planted out a number of roses and some pomegranates. The sky looks like rain. Have begun Uncle Edmund's socks tonight. Read from Ezra whilst resting today from my arduous tasks.*

[Wednesday, January 14, 1863] *Last night the rain poured in torrents. The wind sighed a little and then roared. Today I sat out some twenty rose slips, which had just taken root, though it has rained incessantly. David finished setting his oaks, which he brought for the front windows last evening. Almost finished Jane Eyre whilst knitting today.*

[Thursday, January 15, 1863] *A real snowstorm today. Haven't seen such a thing in three years, though David killed hogs, and what a freeze tonight.*

[Friday, January 16, 1863] *The wind almost flayed me today whilst having the lard done up. But I am thankful it is all over for this season.*

[Saturday, January 17, 1863] *Had the last one of Uncle Edmund's socks finished today for is too cold to do anything but knit and read.*

[Sunday, January 18, 1863] *My husband's birthday. God grant he may live to see many happy returns. We celebrated by visiting poor old Mrs. Riley who has been an invalid for eighteen years, and now that her health is better, is bereft of all her children. Being boys and young, they are all subject to be conscripted and are all in the army save one, just now eighteen* [torn] *next week. May the Father of the* [illegible] *orphans shield them, is my prayer.*[4]

    [Torn] *home in the rain. Found Mr. Mason, our government agent, looking pleased as ever.*

[Monday, January 19, 1863] *A gloomy, gloomy day. Another government agent, and a sick one, too. Though it is getting late, I am not sleepy. Do not sleep well now. As I hear nothing worthy of record and the gentlemen are in the library room conversing, I will run into the parlor and practice a little.*

[Tuesday, January 20, 1863] *Have not been well and tried a ride, which helped me though only went as far as Mr. Reuben's. Found an old foolish German sitting with Mr. Mason on my return.*

[Wednesday, January 21, 1863] *Spent all the day until three in the afternoon stripping up and making into roles bandages for the hospitals or, rather, for the poor wounded soldiers.*
Sister Jane spent a few hours this evening with me, and as my husband is in Bowie tonight, I sent for them. Miss Lizzie with me. We made an effort to entertain Mr. Mason with some music tonight.[5]

[Friday, January 23, 1863] *Rolled bandages and assisted Lizzie in ironing. Feel too well to writeII Few things more laborious than stripping up and rolling bandages. To roll them sufficiently tight is exceedingly straining on my hands. My right thumb is almost out of joint. David got back from Bowie but brought but little news.*

[Saturday, January 24, 1863] *Our friend Mr. Mason left us today. I presume we will not see him anymore until he has consummated his contracts with the government. I think we will have him at no distant date for a neighbor as he has discovered an iron mine within two miles of here which he thinks superior to any he has seen and he is most anxious to engage in the iron business. From all my heart, I wish him success. He has been most unfortunate, to say the least.*[6]

I've been in bed all day and suffered much. Read Kings and Chronicles and a portion of Ezra. Nancy is sick.

[Sunday, January 25, 1863] *Rained incessantly* [torn] *most all day. Read Nehemiah and Esther. Finished* [illegible].

[Monday, January 26, 1863] *This morning, when breakfast should have been on the table, Louisa, who has been cooking in Nancy's stead, sent in her resignation, and so I rose and made biscuit while Lizzie prepared the other part of breakfast. Sewed on some night chemises that I had cut out some weeks ago. Rained all day.*

[Tuesday, January 27, 1863] *Sewed, made bandages, and done up some old shirts and linen cloths for hospital use, but really, it seems I cannot get* [anyone] *to carry them to Jefferson to the quartermaster or have an opportunity to send them. I will not risk them by a careless hand or what I consider an unsafe one.*

Two men here today looking to buy corn. If the men who stay at home cannot make corn, then how is it to be expected the soldiers' wives, who were left upon the country, are to get it if not from the planters who are exempted, and yet they cry aloud against any exceptions of a planter. Strange inconsistency.[7]

It has been bitter cold all day, but clear.

Mr. Hooper has come at last to do up the blacksmith work for the farm for the present year.

As Lizzie took to her bed today and the night duties are gathering thick, I must up and at it.

[Wednesday, January 28, 1863] *Have been unusually busy, though spent a few hours with Sister Jane this afternoon. Finished another Negro* [illegible]*.*

Franny chose to spend tonight with the Browns, and if she chooses to visit anywhere again without consulting me, she shall never come back here to live again.

[Thursday, January 29, 1863] *Lizzie still in bed, and I still a chambermaid. I ironed a little and finished another night chemise.*

[Friday, January 30, 1863] *Today was pleasant enough to spend some time in and on the yard.*

[Saturday, January 31, 1863] *Sister spent today with me. Dr. Salmon also dined.*

XXX

Enola, Texas

February 1, 1863

My dearest Miss Orpha,

I certainly do forgive and must excuse you for not visiting and not spending some time the latter part of last year with me as you oft promised to do. But, really, I doubt your present excuse being a legitimate one, for could I not have assisted you in accelerating your preparation for the important event? Most certainly it would have afforded me infinite pleasure.

I assure you, my dear friend, I am most highly sensible of the honor conferred on me (which I fully appreciate) by you. The kind and polite invitation contained in your affectionate letter of yesterday, and a thousand times I'm obliged to yourself and your good mother for the kind invitation extended on her behalf to spend the night of the second with her, did circumstances permit my going. I regret to say a multitude of them does not. I should be compelled to return the same day, as we cannot both spend the night away at once, and, of course, on an occasion like the present I should like no other escort than my husband.

Believe me, my dear Miss Orpha, when I tell you that there is no one whose nuptials I would go farther to see celebrated than yours, under ordinary circumstances. Nor is there one whom I wish a greater amount of earthly happiness nor for whom I would make greater sacrifice to make you happy were it in my power.

Yet, Miss Orpha, I was somewhat wounded at what I considered neglect on the part of yourself and sister during some of my days of deepest affliction and bitterness. In justice to you both, however, I must say I had less cause to be hurt with you than most anyone else. You were farther removed from the scene of my afflictions—mentally and bodily. And there may have been invasions of which I know nothing. I speak of the invasion on society—for when I was a young lady in society, it was considered a breach of etiquette not to visit occasionally socially those ladies who at times paid us marks of deference and

were always politely attentive, particularly when we had reasons to believe them to be persons of sincerity, and was willing to greet them at all as friends.

I pray you judge me not harshly for being thus communicative on a subject which may for a time seem unsuitable for the occasion, but it is strictly in confidence unless you wish to disclose it, for so much I never even said to my husband.

And I love you the same, my friend, as when first your noble course of conduct constrained me to love and admire all that was praiseworthy in you. And I must tell you that I do not wonder at Mr. Connell, as I know of no one so likely to perform the duties of the place he assigns you as yourself—no one on whom the honors of the place would grace more.

Nor do I wonder at you, Miss Oprah, for in these perilous times, as in all other seasons, you need "one who sticks closer to you than a brother," and such a one I would think you would find in Mr. Connell.

The place is a responsible one, but you are fitted for it, and great, oh, very great, will be your reward if true to the responsibility now committed to you.

May the God of Grace unite your hearts in love and holiness with more of the family to whom you are now about to unite your destiny. May all the temporal blessings be yours in this world, and everlasting joy await you in the world to come, is the sincere wish of your loving and affectionate friend,

R. P. Moores

XXX

[Sunday, February 1, 1863] *We had a much prettier day for church than the morning promised, though two disasters en route for which I was quite sorry as Miss Lewis accompanied us. The first was the choking down of one of the carriage horses, which we thought dead for a few moments, and then one of the carriage bolts gave way and came near breaking everything to pieces, as we drove several miles before we ascertained* [torn] *looking out to see* [illegible].

[Torn] *visited a few hours at Dr. Salmon, Senior, though the horses were sorely jaded now.*

[Monday, February 2, 1863] *Completed the bundling of my little parcel of socks, shirts, rolls of bandages, linen cloths, etc., which I designed sending to the quartermaster at Jefferson tomorrow to be sent to the Texas Hospital, now at Little Rock. I feel so proud that they are ready at last to send, and I felt so long that I was doing so little or nothing, I might say, but now I have knit eighteen pairs of socks (gave away four pair) and rolled up some hundreds of yards of bandaging, I am not so restless.*[8]

Mr. Wood[?], a government agent, dined with us today.

[Tuesday, February 3, 1863] *Though a bitter afternoon, I accompanied my husband to Mr. Powell's, who is to carry my parcel to Jefferson. Whilst we were there a soldier boy came for Mr. Powell to convey him to the post assigned him, as it is Mr. Powell's second destination. Poor young things. They "leap in the dark."*[9]

[Wednesday, February 4, 1863] *Oh, what a bitter day. It sleeted and snowed, both, last night. I nearly read one of the books I borrowed from good Mrs. Salmon the other day,* The Ways of this House. *I'm delighted with it, but somewhat disgusted with* Trial by Jury! *I am no monarchist, but assuredly not a black republican! Too much democracy is not a good thing. It breeds too many demagogues!*

[Thursday, February 5, 1863] *Finished my book this morning and began the other,* Queechy. *Am interested, though somewhat disappointed in it.*

[Friday, February 6, 1863] *Read, knit, and sewed. Followed "Fleda" from Paris to New York and then to Queechy,* **[Vermont,]** *where I leave her, the "angel in the house."*[10]

[Saturday, February 7, 1863] *My husband has been absent all day and will not return until tomorrow. To meet the enrolling officer in Linden. I find it a little lonely these perilous times when he is absent for a night.*

[Sunday, February 8, 1863] *Not well enough to* [torn] *this afternoon. Called on Mr. Turner a few* [illegible] *Reuben's. Found our old friend Mr. Mason awaiting our return, rather, he came a few moments after our return. Brought no news from the war department.*

[Monday, February 9, 1863] *A misty morning. Mr. Mason started several times to go up to Bowie County and returned each time dreading to get rained on.*

A real spring afternoon. I enjoyed a ramble down the road to meet my husband exceedingly, and then we ramble down to the sheep pasture to see two little tiny lambs skip and frolic. A most pleasing sight to me.

Little Lydia, poor little darkie, got her right eye burned badly a few moments ago.

[Tuesday, February 10, 1863] *Mr. Mason was detained until tonight on account of mist, but David, having sent on the other side of the river for a horse to meet him at noon today, he went "at all hazards" and he had a pleasant afternoon as my husband steered him through long ferriage safely.*

I cannot do much except attend to the curing of the meat. Finished Queechy this morning and am knitting me a comfort.

[Wednesday, February 11, 1863] *Sent thread by my husband this morning, who went to pay taxes and look up a weaver. Have done up all the rest I have ready to send to the loom.*

Feel miserably because I did not fix up some dinner for David. I cannot imagine how I forgot it unless, indeed, because I was so very busy fixing up the thread for him to carry and he hurried me so.

Here is some men coming in wagons for something.

Yes, for the first time in my life I went to the crib and measured corn. They said they engaged it this morning before Mr. Moores went off.

I went with Mr. Mason to look at the forge this morning and met Mr. Reuben coming and sitting a moment before they started. Mrs. Turner and her cousin Mrs. Foster spent the day. Mrs. Foster, poor young wife, does not look as if she had lost her husband since Christmas last, drowned at that.

Since supper, Mr. Mason, David, and I had a long and cozy chat. He explained to us how fish are caught in seins, etc.

[**Friday, February 13, 1863**] *Mr. Mason left today, taking my husband with him as far as Linden, and so I am alone in my room, Franny having retired for the night.*

I am worried tonight to know what to do with Mary Jane. She broke the reel a few days ago and has guessed at the cuts since, and because Louisa threatened to tell me when she next came up and bring her to me, she ran away and stayed in the woods all day for fear, she said, I would whip her when I found out she had ruined the hanks. Sometimes I really wish somebody's emancipation proclamation would take effect and rid me of the nasty, troublesome "Africans."

[**Saturday, February 14, 1863**] *A pretty business this. Mary Jane ran off this morning when Nancy told her to set the table and stayed until ten o'clock, and I sent Lizzie after her and she remained until this evening, and so I had all the housework to do this morning.*

David got home at two, wringing wet.

[**Sunday, February 15, 1863**] *We drove over to see Mrs. Haywood, who was confined a few days ago. Poor woman, her husband is in the army. Hasn't seen him for seven months.[11]*

Returned by Reuben's, but they were not there.

[**Monday, February 16, 1863**] *A drizzly, misty, gloomy day, and I'm almost sick enough to go to bed. Last night one of Mr. Reuben's men came at midnight and whispered very loud and said "Miss Rachel, Miss Rachel, wake up Marse Dave, wake Marse Dave! Three men atter Marse Reuben wid double barrel shot-guns!"*

"For mercy, Joe," said I, "what are they going to kill him for? What's the trouble? Who are they?"

"Don no-um. De ain't got dar yet. Mars' Brown overhear'd em say deys coming [torn] jump on dey horses and beat 'em dare and [torn] minute, and Miss Jane sent me to tell Marse Dave. [Illegible.] Dey knows it won't be long."

"Dey know it won't do for him to come," and so after further questioning Joe and getting the same replies every time, we decided to go with him. Leaving me almost frenzied and with an ague I

[illegible], I feel that I shan't have my bed. Soon as breakfast was over, we drove over in the rain to learn the particulars, but could get no clue, only Mr. Moores had heard of a threat some deserters had made because of his saying he could find them, and he was not long since accessory to the whipping of a horse thief.

[Torn] *suffered severely* **[illegible]** *knit today a little. Am weak and nervous.*

[Torn] *knit on my naboed[?] today. Had some leveling done on the yard.*

XXX

Mount Lebanon, Louisiana

February 19, 1863

Mrs. Jane Moores

Dear Auntie,

As an opportunity shows itself, with pleasure I will try and interest you with a few lines. I have been at the above named place near three weeks, going to school. We have a pretty good school. Some sixty-five students and accomplished teachers.[12]

Dr. Crane is president and Professor Shepherd is principal, and both very nice gentleman. Dr. Crane is a Baptist minister and we have preaching every Sabbath—also Sabbath school. The students are required to attend both.[13]

I am boarding at Dr. Crane's. He has a very nice family, indeed. Has a son about my age and a daughter about grown and four small boys. I am the only boy boarder he has. He has two young ladies boarding with him. There is a Female school here, too. They have about seventy students. Uncle Dan was speaking of sending Betty here to school. I do not know whether he will or not, as I have not heard from home since I left.[14]

Ma and Aunt Mollie came with me. They stayed two days and returned. I was not acquainted with but three persons when I came here. They were Mrs. Hartwell and her daughter Mrs. Gibbs and Mrs. Hay that used to live at Camden. You were acquainted with Dr. and Mrs. Hartwell. Mrs. Hartwell and Mrs. Gibbs told me to give their love to you and Aunt Rachel when I wrote to you. You will please tell Aunt Rachel. Tell her that I wrote to her just before I left home.

Oh, I would give a pretty to hear from home. It seems as though I've been here three or four months. I tell you, I'd never appreciated the kindness of my dear mother half so much as I do now. I think when I go home, I will be a great deal more kind to her than I ever was before.

I was sick last week. The neuralgia in my head and face. Suffered very much indeed. I thought of my dear mother a thousand times, though I'm in good health now.

I tell you, Auntie, boarding from home entirely among strangers is not of much pleasure to me, but I hope I will learn enough to pay for it. I'm studying Greek, algebra, Latin, and philosophy and how to speak every two weeks. We boys have a military company here. I think we drill very well.

I must end. Give my best respects to Aunt Rachel, Uncles David and Reuben. My love to all your children. I wish I could see my dear little brothers and sisters. Tell Charlie I will write to him and he must answer it. Direct to John C. Watts, Mount Lebanon, Bienville Parish, Louisiana. Write soon. It will be of great pleasure for me to get a letter. So, farewell from

Your Nephew,
John C. Watts[15]

XXX

[Friday, February 20, 1863] *Started with David to look for a new weaver, but as the weather was cold and I indebted many calls to Mrs. Brown, I stayed with her whilst David continued his unavailing search. Just before reaching home we met Sister Jane going to church to hear the new itinerant preacher, and had I not been so faint and weary, I would have gone over, but needed my dinner too much.*

We drove over since dinner and spent the afternoon at Mr. Reuben's. He seems much alarmed yet. Feels he is not safe. I was sorry to see them have the doors all bolted. I rather think that that course will invite danger when there might not be any near. In spite of all the argument to the contrary, he seems to think it possible that deserters will arrive any evening seeking his life. I suggested it might be Federal emissaries sent to plunder, burn, or tamper with the Negros.

Heaven defend them from all harm, I pray, and in future make them more prudent and aid them to steer clear of difficulties.

[Saturday, February 21, 1863] *Was sick and restless all night. All my old dyspeptic symptoms attacked me last night. I have tried exercise all day. I have been indefatigable. Made pastries all morning and part of the afternoon.*

Miss Lewis and Janie came over and spent an hour or two but could not be prevailed upon to spend tonight though it was almost dark when they left.

My husband and I have just come out on the portico where we had a lazy chat all alone. We find Franny such a restraint. It is a treat to get off to ourselves occasionally.

[Sunday, February 22, 1863] *Went out to Forest Home and heard a good sermon from Mr. Sheffield and was disappointed in not having him accompany us home to dinner.*

Since dinner, David and I rambled down through the orchard and meadows to the ewe lot and set us down on the serene site and watched the little lambs skip and frolic for several hours. I never saw a much more perfect picture of rural beauty. I do not **[torn]** shepherd to fill the Jewish throne. His **[torn]** have swelled hourly with interest **[illegible]** that the same time the most exalted. What so fit an emblem of the Son of God as a lamb? One who possesses the pen to portray—as I do not—the heart to feel, might fill a volume descriptive of my own emotion whilst rambling over these pleasant grounds. We, I and my husband, drinking such sweet draughts.

[Tuesday, February 24, 1863] *Miss Lewis and most of her little school spent last night with us. Had a candy stir, music, etc., etc. All of which seemed to delight the little folks.*

[Saturday, February 28, 1863] *Another day is past, and with me fraught with much anxiety. Franny Ironmonger, poor, willful, wayward, unfortunate thing, has been expelled from school. Her obstinacy and tongue will hurl her to destruction. I revisited her grandmother yesterday in hopes of bringing about a reconciliation. I pled eloquently and long and think I did soften the old lady's heart somewhat, but she is yet very bitter. I have been trying all the time to conciliate Franny. I believe I have nearly succeeded.*

I have witnessed enough to know if she finds a home elsewhere her character is gone, and, oh, it makes me miserable to think of it.

[Thursday, 5 March 1863] *Feel unusually sad and gloomy. Can't tell when I ever felt more dispirited. I feel as if some new trouble awaited me. I don't exactly know why, maybe that my digestion is weaker, liver torpid, or something of that sort, but yet in my secret heart I believe it is a failing to exercise that influence over my husband which I think is just and right.*

For a week or two I have been trying (more by insinuation than anything else) to induce him to go to a government commissary and offer his bacon at half the price it is selling at—twenty five cents—but he never gave me much satisfaction and last evening on our return from Dr. Salmon's we found Huey, a New Orleans commission merchant, Kentucky politician, a lawyer, Mississippi **[illegible]***, an ex-colonel, and I don't know what else, awaiting us* **[illegible]** *to buy meat for him and partners. Six hundred Negroes* **[illegible]** *they have bought and placed on a Red River plantation forty miles from us (I wish they were four hundred farther away!) and this morning David sold him five or six thousand pounds. It made me heartsick when he told me of it. What in the name of humanity is the army to do?*[16]

The people here are nearly all out of corn and David the only planter who raised meat in this vicinity, and I had my heart so set upon the army having it at half price. Do feel that my husband will regret not yielding to my wishes.

If I had a fortune, I would give it half to support the army as my husband is not able to undergo the privations and fatigue of camp, and then, the grand jury would find a bill against him for leaving his Negros without an overseer.

I have the satisfaction though, of occasionally supplying the soldiers some articles in which he stands in much need of. One poor unfortunate fellow who got burned out whilst home on furlough was here today, and I gave him a quilt, a pair of pantaloons, and a pair of socks, and today my good husband was kind enough to propose to carry Mrs. Haywood anything I might wish to send her, and hearing her say she was particularly in need of soap grease and potatoes, I sent her eighteen pounds of the former and David gave her one and a half bushels of sweet potatoes.

[Saturday, March 7, 1863] *A most charming spring day we have had—I might say inspiring, though the early morning was a little cloudy. Just as sun set I was walking around the front squares inhaling the perfume of the jasmine and jonquil when my attention was attracted by the noise of a flock of wild geese, and looking over head I was reminded of Bryant's beautiful lines:*

> *"While glow the heavens with the last*
> *Steps of day;*
> *Far, through their rosy depths, dost thou pursue*
> *Thy solitary way."[17]*

[Sunday, March 8, 1863] *Went this morning to hear a sermon on our National Calamity. I think to [torn] present, and I think to the edification of a few. He drew an analogy between Jewish and American history.*

After reading and lounging a while, my husband and self rambled over the green fields of wheat, rye, and oats, which in the distance presents a most pleasing aspect to the eye. My return by way of the front gate, we lingered long at the fragrant beautiful jasmine vine, now halfway up our pet oak. How many hallowed associations does a sight of it in bloom bring up. 'Twas in a little old field, covered with nature's greenest velvet and surrounded by festoons of yellow jasmine that some of the happiest moments of my checkered life was spent.

Then, with one whose blood now enriches the soil for which he died, did I wreath garlands of it, chase butterflies, and grasp at the tiny hummingbirds, whilst my dear lost one would ascend to the topmost boughs of the overspreading oaks in quest of the merry warbler who had just poured forth his sweetest strains.

Yes, we thought to have in our possession two living mockingbirds was all we needed just then to complete our bliss. Alas, how soon those joys were turned into sorrows, oftentimes, for much of the time I spent in my little paradise was stolen!

Notwithstanding I was a delicate child, I was early learned to sew, and when not engaged with my lessons, was closely—too closely—confined for any child, whether invalid or robust, and to this day do I feel the consequences and never shall I grow over it. Why is it that parents give the care of their children up to young and inexperienced hands is one of the greatest mysteries of life to me.

Their health and constitution is often impaired, sometimes entirely destroyed. If I could, I would speak in thunder tones to be heard this earth over and say to parents, "guard jealously, tenderly, religiously, carefully, and always guard, guard your offspring's health, for without it, then is little happiness and no comfort and little is the sympathy felt by the world for such unfortunates, and consequently there is many a bitter, mental pang combined with their other suffering."

[Monday, March 9, 1863] *Mr. Crawford Connally came here this afternoon by appointment. I requested an interview in order to get him to assist me in reconciling Mrs. Henshaw to Franny. I preferred that to have Franny go to his home to live,* [torn] *only read and knit.*

Was shocked and outraged at how badly the Negros acted Sunday whilst we were at church. Stealing best pair of wool cards out to use as general head combing, when cards are thirty-five cents a pair and not always to be found for that. I must conclude that the better you treat them, the worse they will treat you. I only found it out today and had all of them whipped who were concerned.

[Wednesday, March 11, 1863] *Went to the tanyard shoe shop and gave my measure for a new pair of shoes. I do not presume to find them so pleasant to wear as Howser and Sons, New York, or as Marshall, Lowell, Kentucky.*

Returned by and spent the afternoon at Dr. Salmon's, where I found for me two letters from my dear home. One was from dear Mollie who writes of my dear old father's continued ill health. Dear, dear Pa, how much you have to wear you out. How merciful our Heavenly Father has been to spare you thus long to your family. May I hope and pray to Him I may see you again, my only own dear parent.

[Sunday, March 15, 1863] *I have been confined in bed all day and read until I can read no longer. How much I miss my usual Sunday evening ramble with my husband among the green fields.*

I find but little worthy of record since laying down my pen Wednesday evening. The disposing of Franny is troubling me seriously. I can find people enough who will take her, but then, knowing her disposition as I do, I know they will not keep her. They want her services but will be disappointed, for unless to do some kind of work that is constantly changing and taking her hither and thither, she will not do anything. She has no system, no method about anything. Is slovenly with her needle, slatternly in her dress, and is certainly the most willful girl I ever saw. Worse than all, she will not tell the truth if she imagines a falsehood will excuse her or screen her. She does not wait to think, but tells the most unreasonable stories, all kinds of stories. It is truly distressing to hear her and see that she feels no compunction of conscience—is perfectly hardened.

When I first told her if she didn't change her conduct I should be compelled to send her away, she did not [illegible] who else [torn] and now that I have made preparation to take her to her grandmother she says she cannot go.

I sewed two days last week [illegible] took Betsy out of the field one day to assist me to make a dress for her whilst Franny, from Monday morning to Saturday night, only spun one hank—one day's work.[18]

But the above is a most unpleasant thought. Not so is the pleasant book I've just read, Reveries of a Bachelor. *Dr. Salmon loaned to me last Wednesday and I finished the last lines this morning.*[19]

[Wednesday, March 18, 1863] *Today I received letters from dear home. One from my dearest Pa, though he was only able to dictate it. Dear, dear Pa. I hope it is the will of the Father for us to meet again in this world. Poor Johnny* [John C. Watts]. *I received one from him. He is homesick—a bad disease, but not incurable.*

Wrote to Mollie and Sister yesterday, to John the day before. Yet, I'm not well enough to write to anyone. Sister Jane brought my letters this morning but did not tarry long. Both too melancholy to remain long together.

[Friday, March 20, 1863] *Today's toil being o'er. I seat myself by my window to muse on things, past, present, and future. "Who is to be benefited by my labor?" I often ask myself.*

But here comes the other half of my joys and woes, and here too is night, and so no jottings tonight.

[Sunday, March 22, 1863] *Heard a sermon from Dr. Salmon instead of Mr. Sheffield, who, though then was too indisposed to preach, had a larger congregation than usual. On yesterday, the new minister, Mr. Ervin, preached a most excellent sermon and accompanied us home to dinner. I walked over to Rueben's since dinner.*

Riding out to church today and yesterday has helped me very much. Oh, if I could only hear from my dear father tonight. I wrote him this morning—this morning before I went to church.

[Sunday, March 29, 1863] *Went to hear Mr. Cole preach today. As Mrs. Salmon was sick, called there a few hours, which I spent as I always do, most pleasantly.*

[Thursday, April 9, 1863] *My poor heart has been in two extremes of human happiness, and ever since I last resumed my pen. Two weeks ago, I was summoned to see my dearest father—perhaps for the last time. They did not tell me he was on a dying bed, but wrote his decline was so* [torn] *alarmed as Frank was at home on sick furlough though we* [illegible] *to see him anyway. When I met Johnson at the door I felt a kind of dread steal over me and was so surprised, too, that many moments elapsed e're I inquired after Pa, thinking in my bewilderment that Richard was just from the army.*

Though he assured me that Pa was not in imminent danger, yet I knew by his coming that he was unusually unwell and for a few moments I was half frantic. Went to tell Sister Jane, but was so overcome when I got there, could not utter one word for some minutes. Spent a sleepless, anxious night and started by sunrise the next morning, Sister Jane taking a seat with me.

We did not reach Pa's until noon the third day, the roads being miserable, but I learned at Falcon that he was much improved, and to our infinite delight we found it so. He was sitting up and some better but is still feeble. I never saw his face look so pallid before. Otherwise, he was looking well as is possible for one of his age and infirmities to look.

Dear, dear Pa, if it be the will of God, I hope to meet thee for many years at the old home. If He calls thee hence, may we "meet no more to leave" in the world of spirits.

I found dear Frank looking better than I ever saw him, his new honors sitting very gracefully on him. Dignity sufficient for a young captain. Not yet tired of the army—is more in love with camp life than anyone I've seen. He gave me some amusing anecdotes and graphic descriptions of his adventures as captain, or his impressions, whilst in the Federal lines, his interview with Federal officers, introduction to General Rosecrans, etc. His exceeding grief at the death of one brother and not obtaining his mortal remains.

I also met Mrs. McCollom, an old friend I had not met in years, and poor Mary Dealy in her widow weeds and her orphan boy, and Kate, too, was over, and Gusta[?] and Hugh.[20]

But really, Mary Dockery's marriage **[torn]** *created so much disturbance that everything else failed to make the impression it usually would have. I wonder if Heaven sanctions such* **[illegible]**. *Just to think of the base scamp being engaged to Allie until he was married to Mary Dockery, and Mary Dockery, too, knowing of Allie's engagement to him, her uncle Nick Gantt's confidante and repository for all his letters to Allie. I never can respect her any more than one of the basest of women who I now know to be a demon. Allie deserved punishment for ever engaging herself to such a knave.[21]*

I have today consummated a great task for me, put the finishing touch on a coat and pair of pantaloons for David—all since Saturday—only four days. They are of towel, dyed a beautiful lilac, and fit him to perfection, and now I'm feeling the effect of such close application to my needle.

Have been troubled with my bowels since I came home. They gripe me excruciatingly every day.

I have not neglected my housekeeping, either. Made soap and go to the fowl house ever so many times a day. I looked after my flowers, strawberries, etc.

[Saturday, April 11, 1863] *Cut out two dresses for myself, one a beautiful striped yellow calico and the other from a bolt of Negro handkerchiefs. If the war continues, I cannot imagine what I will next use for dresses—dyed towel, may be. Made the waists of my yellow today.*

I feel sad this evening. Would I could hear from my dear old home and know how my dearest father was.

[Sunday, April 12, 1863] *This morning I arose with lighter spirits.*

[Tuesday, April 14, 1863] *Still cloudy, windy, and unsettled* **[torn]** *out yesterday and looking lively enough, but the cut worm threatens our whole cabbage crop with death.*

Most of today has been spent imploring a kind Providence to guide me in this, one of my bitterest trials, one of the severest through which it has ever been my misfortune to pass, and, oh, Heavenly Father, save me from such another.

At times I almost regret the step I took, feeling that I have subjected my husband to a humiliation he ought not to bear, and then I chide myself for unchristian thoughts, remembering who has said "vengeance is mine. I will repay sayeth the Lord," and I have prayed for the last two days with all the fervency a spirit like mine is capable of to the Living God to be my husband's avenger.[22]

I do not ask human sympathy or will so long as the promise of a heavenly parent stands: "I will never leave thee nor forsake thee."[23]

William Moores came after late dinner, a most unexpected pleasure to me. Poor boy, I've not seen him before, since his great misfortune, for there is not many severer afflictions in this "vale of tears" than one must experience in losing a pure-minded, gentle, loving, affectionate wife as dear Matilda was, and most bitterly, too, does poor William feel it's biting effects. He can never love another as he loved her.[24]

[Saturday, April 18, 1863] *The week's toils and cares are o'er. Its toils, yes, and would I could say the same of its anxieties to me. The past week has been one of anguish, though much of my time has been spent supplicating the Throne of Mercy, and never, no never, will I ever feel myself so near the Majesty on High as for the last six days. I have not prayed for the forgiveness of the sin committed, but for the mercy my noble hearted husband showed to the most abject of his race, to be shown to him.*

That mercy I to others show
That mercy show to me.[25]

[Torn] *treacherous and bloodthirsty* [torn] *punished, but the task of the executioner is* [illegible] *a most painful one, and knowing my dear husband's tender heart as I do, I thought it best* [illegible] *to visit justice on the callous wretch though so greatly deserving it. I do, oh!, so earnestly pray that he will be spared the lowest—horrible task and that justice will be visited on all concerned.*

[Sunday, April 26, 1863] *My good husband received a letter from Mr. Mason this morning which called for him to meet him—Mr. Mason—yesterday on urgent business, and started forthwith in the hope of meeting him today, though it may be one day too late, and he should be in Linden today and return to Virginia to complete his government duties, and so I am left all alone so far as human companionship goes, but then, I never feel alone, particularly in spring.*

The whole premises is vocal with the sweetest strains the feathered tribes are capable of pouring forth, and they are sweet enough, and the yard is radiantly beautiful and fragrant enough to satisfy the demands of the most extravagant olfactories. Yes, growing before my windows are flowers whose beauty and fragrance would call forth the admiration and praise of the most fastidious.

There are fifteen varieties before me in full bloom of the best selection, some for beauty and others for fragrance, and for beauty and fragrance combined, the white tea rose is unsurpassed.

And leaving the flowers, God's sweetest messengers, and the birds, which thrill us with their melody—we are-ever feel, in the presence of Him who has promised to love us better than an earthly father. What protection and care do we feel, environed by the arms of the living God.

I shall have to conclude for this morning as the time for starting to church approaches, and I shall have to start a little earlier than usual having to drive myself with one of the maids in the buggy with me and the carriage driver on the horse to pilot me. What should I do without my best of husbands?

The evening shades appear, and long have I sat gazing at the scene before me. The human hive, buzzing and fluttering in the quarters, a constant parade from house to house, a distance of the [illegible].

[Torn] *after my return from church and then unpacking and then a kindling of fires to cook, all accompanied by bursts of merriment. Often, whilst watching their Sunday evening sports, I* have tried to concoct some plan to give them a taste for Bible reading or listening, rather, to its teachings. I've never seen any inclination whatever manifested on the part of the grown Negros to have a chapter from the Bible read to them. I have told some of them who were holding prayer meetings that they were groping in the dark, indiscriminately assisting at their prayer meetings, and I find the worst Negros of the place the most eloquent in prayer, their orgies of imitation being larger. They seem to think loud and long praying and singing is all that is necessary to be a Christian. In vain I tried to impress upon the older Negros the importance of learning and putting into practice the ten commandments.[26]

Oh, I shudder when I think of our responsibility as slaveholders!

I have walked around the flower beds and in the garden, poultry yard, eat my lonely supper, read and sung, and though quite dark, it is not bedtime, though not far from one's.

Another day is passed,
The hours forever fled,
And time is bearing us away
To mingle with the dead.[27]

I shall soon seek my lonely but peaceful couch after seeking the protection of Him who never sleeps. I hope my husband will get a good night's sleep after his hot, fatiguing ride and be back fresh and well tomorrow evening. Sorry he cannot be here by morning, as Mr. Sheffield sent an appointment by Dr. Salmon to fish tomorrow, and now it is too bad to have him disappointed.

[Monday, April 27, 1863] Mr. Sheffield came, accompanied by Dr. Salmon and Mr. Moores, and I insisted they should remain until after dinner [torn] here at eleven on their way to the river [illegible] they did not go at all. David came soon after dinner, failing to see Mr. Mason [torn].

Mrs. Haywood and I brought home a piece which [illegible] much needed as to force me to cut it half up this evening.

Hark! Here comes Colonel Huey, and I wish he had stayed away tonight as Lizzie has worried me so much today and supper is to get.

[Thursday, April 30, 1863] *Well, I have just achieved an extraordinary feat for me today—adjusted two rooms with my own hands, cooked dinner, and Mary Jane, Henry, Zilph, Uncle Charles, and myself have done the week's washing.*

Was hindered some hour and a half this evening by visitors—Mrs. William Haywood having the deplorable fate of being burned out yesterday, came to let us know that we might assist her. I will do all I can, but really, these calls come so often now, my wardrobe is getting low.

[Saturday, May 2, 1863] *Have had a wry neck Tuesday but have not given up for it, and though I have sewed very hard all day—made Mrs. Haywood a quilt—yet I am sick tonight. I cannot turn my head around at all and have fever. David went to Bowie and Mr. Mason started to Mr. Cole's, but it thundered and he returned.*

[Monday, May 3, 1863] *David returned yesterday a little after noon, bringing with him eight Negro men who he hired to assist in getting out the grass. I thought I was able to ride out, and got him to drive me as far as Mr. Bagenmeer's[?] to carry Mrs. Haywood a satchel of clothes, but I was not benefited by the ride and suffering very much today with my neck. Have been confined to bed all day. Dr. Salmon dined here, and Mr. Mason went to his house today. Went to Havana yesterday.*

[Torn] this week with Lizzie [Illegible] cook. I might say, for I have made all of the biscuit, waffle batter, muffins, etc. [Illegible] deserts, cakes, etc., but she makes the fire [Illegible] all mixing and I fear Mr. Mason thinks it but [Illegible] fare with so distinguished a cook presiding over cuisine department. I had but little time for reading this week, consequently the first volume of the Eastern Coolie[?] remains unfinished yet.

Spent yesterday with Sister Jane but had to run home to doctor sick darkies and make fresh cake for supper.

David goes out every morning soon as he dispatches his breakfast and only returns to dinner, and that devoured, I see him no more until dark, and yet he says his hired Negros won't near get him out of the grass. One is foundered from eating. The eight eat eight pounds of meat yesterday and half bushel of pears.

As I feel too weary with my day's task to read further of the week's events, I will stop and practice "Dixie." David brought it for me from Bowie.

[May 30, 1863] *Have been living over the past today. Yesterday I went fishing with the school children, and, oh, how vividly it brought to my mind my first adventure in that way.*

An older sister had me busily engaged in quilting when a little school friend was announced, and my kind sister released me for the day (it was Saturday) and away flew the hours like fairy bells. We roamed o'er hill and dale to gather the spring flowers. I well remember climbing the tallest magnolia tree in the grove and plucking two buds half blown with which to embellish the parlour vases. Anne Maria placed one in the vase and I placed the other and we carried them to Sister Margaret to say which looked the handsomest. I remember how much more prettily I thought A's looked than mine. I thought her my superior in everything. I almost worshiped her beauty [torn]. Sister very frequently asked me if [torn] to have an associate who surpassed me so far in personal charms and mental culture—but I did not envy my little playmate for all that I [illegible] she was wanting in one charm which I was pleased to know I possessed—to me dearer than all others—and we generally—or frequently—got our sums nightly together, and so that afternoon I asked my darling father's consent to go to the plantation.

Anne Marie, dear Brother, and myself wanted to go to Flat Creek, which ran through the plantation, and fish. I had never in all my life been a'fishing and as hooks were fixed up and we started, three lighter hearts ne'r tripped the same path bent upon the same pursuit, and soon we were seated upon the bridge angling for the poor little innocents. I might say learning to, for my little brother had to show me the use of the cork—put the bait on the hook. Not for any consideration would I touch a worm, and after we had fished an hour or so without any success on the part of Anne Maria and myself, we teased Brother William to let us take his hook. Still we caught none whilst he caught as readily with ours as with his own. At last we despaired and felt we must return home in disgrace—when he, dear, noble, generous creature that the always was, proposed to fasten a few on our hooks as he drew them from the water and let us put them in and draw them out and tell when we reached home how we drew out two, and next morning at the breakfast table he helped us to point out ours, and how it flattered us.

[Torn] feel less, less lone and sad—restless—[illegible] brought me a letter from the office [illegible] before we sat down to dinner containing [illegible] account of my dear, dear Pa's illness. [Illegible] like all the letters I receive, they say he was better when they wrote. Poor suffering

father. I have dreamed every night for two or three weeks that I was at his dying bed and then on my way to see him—after I had seen it all and was returning—I feel this evening like I had not heard the worst. Hope kindleth up and then dies out.

With the hot weather and training my new cook for the past two weeks, my habits have been quite desultory: knit, read, sewed, and lounged just as inclination prompted.

Mr. Mason has been with us all the time, pretty much, since April, and I devote more time to the culinary department when he is here as he is fond of food seasoned as people generally have it, somewhat different from the way we like it or it likes us.

[Sunday, May 31, 1863] All my forebodings are but [illegible] have been but torture. My dear precious father is no more of this world. I cannot think it, cannot realize the truth of it. Oh, my father, can it be that I never, no never in this world, can see you more? But I do pray, oh, so fervently, that I may meet thee in Heaven. Oh, Father, grant it, I do pray.[28]

I know it is best as it is, but how much I have ever desired to be with him in his last moments that I could have assisted in nursing, rendering some act of filial devotion and received from him one look of recognition, one of tenderness, and pressed his dear hand to my face once more. What a dear privilege it has ever been to me to serve him in sickness and how sweet the reflection that I did everything in my power to lessen his suffering, for since I was fifteen years old he has been a hopeless invalid and how he suffered no tongue can tell. In retrospecting my dear father [illegible] the week past, I'm inclined to believe at times all of his "afflictions were in mercy sent."[29]

He was at heart so [illegible] was the most exemplary man I ever knew, yet he [illegible] acknowledge before men! And I would fain hope that [illegible] his suffering was his punishment. It does seem to me it was enough to have expiated for a life of crime, and he, my good and noble father, was it not enough for him who only knew crime by name, and so benevolent, so charitable. Who in distress ever appealed in vain to his disinterested generosity? Such a careful, anxious father, and so kind a provider and Master.

I would not call him back to pain and anguish. If it was Thy will, oh, Father, I bow submissively, but, oh, the heartfelt pleasure it gave me to visit him and feel that I had a father good and kind left me so long. With each succeeding visit I would grow so impatient to see him I could scarcely keep my seat and contain myself just before we would reach the old homestead.

I wanted to see all, but, oh, my father was the chief attraction, and what joy that first long clasp and embrace would give me. I would often feel that it was more than I deserved to find him each time on my return, and now it is so sad, so sorrowful, to think of that pleasure never being mine again.

No father, no own mother, but one blessing is vouchsafed to me yet: my dear stepmother who has been ever affectionate to me. Though my darling Pa may have loved me more, he was never so affectionate to me.

But then, he was my own father and, oh, what a good, kind, and careful one. I believe I can say with truth that few ever had such a father. Justly proud we all were of him, and, oh, I wonder how mother is to get along without him. Never woman had a better husband, one more kind, careful, or provident, and I have seldom seen so anxious a father.

Oh, my father, dear darling father, can I give thee up **[torn]** *that I was going* **[torn]** *returned from the office* **[illegible]** *he said he had only two for me* **[illegible]** *and none for me, and when Mr. Moores came in, he* **[illegible]** *the earliest date, the one I spoke of on the* **[illegible]** *sheet, and at dinner I insisted that he should start in immediately and see my dearest, not just knowing the worst, and late in the afternoon David came in and said he had heard bad news from home but hoped I was prepared for it and would bear it with becoming fortitude, and then said he.*

"Your father is dead."

Can I ever feel thus again? No, never. I had not to give my mother up. She was taken before my eyes ever saw sun light and, ere I could remember, I was provided with a stepmother, but with my earliest recollections we knew a father's care. I always felt it a kind of care rather than affection. I was so frail as a child. I think he pitied more than loved me. I had a half-brother ere I ever lived at home, and my dearest Pa ever loved the youngest most tenderly—a natural feeling—but then, he was ever so careful of me.

I remember his sending my eldest sisters to examine Mr. Moores' **[illegible]** *closely one bitter cold day and see that I was more comfortably clad, and how grateful I felt though I said nothing, for I had suffered much for several days with cold and felt it most bitterly, and once when he was passing the schoolhouse just as the school was dismissed, he took me up behind him because I was the smallest and had a sore toe, and, oh, what a thrill of joy went to my little heart.*

I think had he known my temperament he would have always taken more notice of me. If he was unusually ailing, I would hide myself and weep all the time and would creep to mother when she was out of the room and ask her if he were not going to die. And, oh, it is such a heartfelt comfort [torn] attentively I nursed him all my life. I can put my hand on the Bible before the living God and say the only real satisfaction I have ever felt through life has been in regard to my conduct as wife and daughter! If I had been as perfect in my deportment in every other relation in life as in those, I would be a [illegible], a happier woman.

My dear father never knew how hard I strove to please him—what a comfort I tried to be to him. I was indefatigable in my endeavors, and yet I felt all the time conscious of falling far short. It seems to me that to have given him perfect satisfaction would have completed my own happiness. But he is gone, gone from earth, from us, from all he held dear on earth, I trust, I hope, I pray, to join my sainted mother in the realms of the blessed.

Oh, my father and mother, are you united in that world of spirits? Do you watch over the destiny of your erring children? Spirit of my departed parents, are you near me? My murdered darling brother, can I believe your spirit commingled with theirs? Oh, Heavenly Father, grant that we may all, all be reunited around Thy throne.

I often grieve that there is much dissension here below, that we as brothers and sisters differ so in sentiment. Not that so much, as the want of understanding each other's disposition and mistakes. I feel that Sister Jane ought to know me best, and yet she seems to understand me less. Sometimes I feel that I shall have to drop all intercourse, I am so little understood, my best actions misconstrued. What a world for sensitive people, a continual jar. Oh, for a preparation for that world of rest beyond the Jordan "where the weary be at rest."[30]

[Torn] not been in the most of [illegible] sickness in ten years. Eight of our Negros are down and have been for a week. One little Negro sweetly died in the night—less with [torn] caused, we think, from worms. She died so suddenly. I had been in bed for the two days previous to her death, but the woman who nursed her told me she had no fever and was but little sick, and the day following her death I had vermifuge given all of them and I never saw such quantities come as came from each and all of them.[31]

Dear Mrs. Connally has been to see us. Spent a day and night. Mr. James Moore has been over twice to stockholder meetings and spent the night with us, the first time he has been here since the year after we were married.[32]

Today has been most chilly. A large fire has been most comfortable all day. The rainfalls like an autumnal shower, in drizzles, and on my spirit time falls heavily. I'm alone, alone I live now. Since the middle of July, I have rarely **[illegible]** *with my husband and often do not see him for three or four whole days together. I must think he does the riding for all concerned. I see nor hear of nobody else making a single trip. For the past two nights he has been too tired to sleep and told me when he started this morning, ten o'clock, it would be late in the night before he returned. I had to go twenty-five or thirty miles, and what a day I have had, toothache and colic, but toothache all day.*

Oh, me, what sad news David has brought from Mr. Whitaker. He went down today. Mrs. John Salmon died last Sunday. Only taken sick on Friday. Poor little orphan children. How distressing to think of your bereavement. Who will ever love you as well?[33]

[Wednesday, July 26, 1863] *Enjoyed the horseback ride with my husband this afternoon. He came from the fields to accompany me to Mr. Reuben's. I feel that it has done me so much good. I've been at home so closely the last six weeks, and for the past three weeks waiting upon the sick has been my sole occupation.*

[Thursday, July 27, 1863] *David started to Bowie this morning to be gone four days. Since he accepted the position of caterer for the iron foundry, he has not been at home two days at one time, engaging in purchasing food, stock, wagons, utensils, hands, etc., etc. He finds a sore job in a community where such things were always scarce. Hands is all that can be had without very great expense and inconvenience. I had as well submit kindly to my fate of loneliness as to murmur. But it is exceedingly unpleasant at times, and then it deprives me so long of the pleasures of visiting my dear mother, brothers, and sisters.*

Seven of my first patients are doing very well, one of them not so well. My **[illegible]** *last are not doing so well.*

I took a ramble for the first time down in the peach orchard this afternoon. It has jaded me considerable. I hardly feel like I could set up until Mr. Mason and Doyle come to supper. It is now one hour after dark every night before they come.

[Saturday, July 29, 1863] *Have been confined to my bed most of the time since Thursday, though have made Mr. Mason a pair of pantaloons with Mary Jane's assistance. David came home this morning and did not take time to rest a moment. Sent out to the "works" for hands and returned to the river once before dinner, twice since. He is killing himself, and yet he won't let me say one word. He was too much fatigued to sleep until I gave him a toddy sometime after he had been in bed tonight, and tomorrow morning he has to start to Fulton—forty-five miles. Has to reach there or the probability is Mr. **[torn]** since I made a record **[illegible]** much longer, so much, so many **[illegible]** of such importance.*

Our old neighbor and friend, Mr. D. J. Connally has sickened and died, and many others whose names have not appeared in this Journal.[34]

Alas! What a harvest death is reaping. A week after my loved Pa's death, I went to Bowie at the earnest solicitation of Lenie and Frankie to see them all examined. Mrs. Hathaway entertained us most pleasantly for one day. Had a most interesting examination and concert, and I enjoyed as much as I could anything now.[35]

A week afterwards, Mrs. Hathaway, her son Lenie, Frankie, and Jenny all came over and spent two weeks, only leaving yesterday, and how changed our little home looks. When of late all was noise and bustle, now the buzz of an insect could be heard. I enjoyed their visit very much.

Mrs. Hathaway, I found most companionable. At times she is decidedly the most intellectual woman I've met in Texas. Lenie and Frankie, dear children, what a pleasure, what a comfort they were to me with their warm loving hearts and bright sunny faces. I look forward to the time when I shall derive immense pleasure from their visits. Not that I shall ever love them more, but as they grow older, they will be more companionable.

Mr. Chappell and Mason came in just after supper last evening. I had just got through with the house, which was in sad plight, and had gone out on the front portico to enjoy the blues when they rode up, and so "the spirit of my dream was changed." As my best of husbands was gone, I had to entertain his friends. Mr. Chappell asked many questions about the deer.[36]

[Friday, July 24, 1863] *Dear [illegible] what have [torn] is making of my happiness. David was gone the latter part of last week, left home Thursday and did not return until Sunday. Went yesterday to a meeting of the stockholders and did not return until tonight when he tells me he has to leave for Little Rock tomorrow morning and will not return for two weeks. I'm so afraid it will make him sick, and then to be alone. Mr. Mason is here, but then I'm alone in a great measure.*

[Saturday, July 25, 1863] *Went to Courtland to church today. There was a larger audience in attendance, and I suppose it will be larger tomorrow as two funeral services will be preached. Doctor Salmon, Senior, and Mr. Connally. Left at nine this morning and only returned to supper. Did not sit down all day. Came straight to bed. Came by Mr. Reuben's and insisted on Miss Lizzie's coming with us. Mr. Mason and I both insisted, but she refused. I feel badly to be here alone with Mr. Mason, but I will make the best of it.*

[Sunday, July 26, 1863] *Am too tired to hold my pen. Have been up all day. Did get a little nap in the carriage yesterday, but now, today, two long funeral sermons and two besides. I went by and carried Mrs. Salmon with me, or else she could not have heard her husband's funeral preached!*

Mr. Mason has been quite sick for a few days past. Miss Lewis spent yesterday and last night with me. Have been most busy all the week dying some dresses, hanks, and [torn].

[Illegible] who accompanied David to Little Rock returned today without him, and, oh, how [illegible] frightened until I learned the cause of his delay, which was because of his horse being stolen near Washington, Arkansas. Oh, I feel so thankful he is not sick.

Our bereavements are coming so thick, I shall always think the worst. Since I took up my pen before, another dear one has been launched into eternity. Yes, Frank, darling Frank, can it be that you are gone from us forever—gone?[37]

Oh God, help us to be reconciled to his untimely end. Oh, the cruel thought of his meeting such a fate. Oh, to think, my loved brother, of your dear, precious body lying in the watery deep, to think of you crying for assistance and none rendered, to think of the demons shooting at a drowning man! Oh, Father, have mercy on us all!

All my cherished hopes, where are they? So much pleasure I promised myself with thee, darling Frank, when from the wars you came, crowned with laurels, manly, able brother, how proud

I was of you! What a stay, a joy, a comfort I thought dear Mother would have in thee. Dear widowed mother, poor brokenhearted mother, how you will mourn for long years to come and then not cease to mourn when e'er the thoughts of your darling murdered sons arise. Oh, it seems a bitter fate for you, but maybe good will come. God permitted it. He did not will it. Maybe he has been "taken from the evil to come."

Oh, Frank, have you joined the spirits of departed friends? Was you, oh, was you, prepared to welcome that dear father to the home of the blessed? Have you changed the warrior's wreath for the Christian's hallowed crown?

Oh, Father, grant it. "Forgive my grief for one removed, Thy creature, whom I found so fair. I trust he lives in Thee, and there I find him worthier to be loved."[38]

It seemed one of the merciful dispensations of an All-Wise Providence [illegible] met for the last time around the dear [illegible] of—or what proved soon to be the deathbed—of our dear father. Dear Frank, coming home [illegible] on so short a furlough.

[Torn] to purchase will [illegible] could be there. Oh, it is the most distressing [torn] thing I have endured in a long time to [illegible] so utterly indifferent about life and health [illegible] Doctor Salmon remarked whilst here this afternoon to see [illegible] how badly I looked and how much I needed a trip [illegible] thought if he knew but half I suffered here in my loneliness he would not have been surprised at seeing me looking thin and wan, pale and listless.

Last night I could not sleep. Thoughts of my poor drowned brother so distressed me, and whenever I awoke the name of Franklin was sounding in my ears or dying on my lips. Yes, Franklin, my sweet brother, thy name, thy image, haunts me in my dreams, in my awakenings, in moments of unrest and in solitude.

[Sunday, July 30, 1863] *In spite of my remonstrances, David would go to Fulton today, or started. I feel so thankful to have all the sick except Harrison get their allowances today. Henry and Wanda are a little sick and Genrice is lying down, but nothing that I can discern is the matter with her.*

My head is still confused and aching at times, feet and hands cold, and liver torpid.

I read Ephesians, Philippians, Galatians, Thessalonians, Timothy, Titus, and a portion of Hebrews. Wrote a letter and read some of Hamilton on Metaphysics.[39]

[Monday, July 31, 1863] *Again, most suddenly and without warning has death visited us. Another little servant, poor little Genrice, expired this morning at eleven o'clock. Her mother came up after breakfast and told me she wished I would go and look at her. Said she was heaving and looked very badly. I told her I did not feel hardly like walking then, but would be down soon, and just as I arose to go Nancy came and said Eliza had sent for me. I went down, but as I had the doctor sent for, did not give her anything. I saw, or thought, death stamped on every feature. I remained three quarters of an hour down there and returned to lie down* **[torn]** *down more than one quarter of an hour.* **[Torn]** *came and said she was dying, and when I arrived she was dead.*

Leaves have their time to fall,
And flowers to wither at the north wind's breath,
And stars to set; but all,
Thou hast all seasons for thine own, O Death![40]

Oh, how sad and lone I feel. I do wish my husband would come. Mr. Mason and Doyle will not return tonight.
There he comes!!

[Tuesday, September 1, 1863] *Three more sick Negros and Charles reported Mason abed and David drove down to bring him home. For the sake of the ride, I accompanied him, though we found Mr. Mason up and going around. Returned by Mr. Reuben's. Feel better tonight.*
Dr. Salmon says none of his sick are dangerous. He visited them all whilst here this morning.

[Wednesday, September 2, 1863] *Packed up my trunk today to start to my dear old home Friday next. I much fear sickness among the Negros will prevent. Had more come in this evening.*
Spent the remainder of the day arranging the house so as to give my dear husband as little trouble as possible during my absence.

[Thursday, September 3, 1863] *My husband returned home this evening with a fever. The doctor being here to see the Negros, gave him an emetic. It hadn't any other effect, though, than a very sick stomach. I give my trip up for the present.*

[Friday, September 4, 1863] *David feeling better this afternoon, we drove over to Reuben's. Met the new teacher, Miss Boykin, with whom I was very much pleased. Found J. C. Moores alighting from his buggy just as we rode up.*

Such a pain in my back as I rarely ever felt. Soon as I make David pills and give Lizzie, who has just been taken [torn] *passed through that scourge.*

[Torn] *I never rose from my bed until a few minutes ago. Now I can walk to the garden. Whilst I regard* [illegible].

The Monday after I was taken, David's stomach [illegible] *became congested and he commenced vomiting blood at about eleven o'clock and about one blood began to flow from his bowels. It was the most trying ordeal I ever passed through. He seemed in the very agony of death for six or more interminable hours. Soon as he vomited the blood, I sent for Dr. Salmon, who had left in the morning to return in the afternoon. Not knowing where he was, I had four Negros in different directions, one for Dr. Miles, and sent to Bowie for Mr. and Mrs. Moores and other relatives and for the most skillful physician they know in Bowie County.*

But before Dr. Salmon arrived, we checked both vomiting and purging by cold applications to the throat, stomach, and bowels. Kept one Negro bringing cold water from the well and one changing the cloths all the time. With every breath he asked for water, water, and someone was constantly pouring it down his throat.

Oh, the anguish I endured that ever-to-be-remembered afternoon, laying in a bed in the same room and not able to give him one sip of water. Mr. Reuben, Sister Jane, and Miss Lizzie were here, and all as kind as could be, but still I knew my nursing would have been more soothing, and, sick as I was, I could not desist from tottering to his bed occasionally to feel his hands. They looked death like.

I felt all that time that God would raise him from that spell and felt then and feel now that it was a warning to him to prepare for a dissolution that will e'er long take place. Oh, he is so frail, so feeble, and no one will appreciate his danger but myself. When I speak of his shattered nerves and frail health, I'm scoffed at. God alone knows what I endure since the [torn] of this foundry. He has done hard riding and labor enough for five stout men, and yet he would put five times more on him if he could, and he already does more than everybody concerned put together.

Twice this week he got out of bed and measured up wagonloads of corn—once in a shower of rain. I know a camp life would kill him, but no faster than this, and but for his being where I can see him occasionally, I would prefer his going into the army. Oh, what is life now? A train of trouble, trials, and vexations. Oh, that we may be fitted for the life to come. "If in this life only we have hope in Christ, we are of all men most miserable."[41]

[Monday, September 21, 1863] Last evening David received a note from Mr. Mason which has caused him to think very hard things of him (Mr. Mason). It is evident he does not mean for David to rest one moment as he urges the necessity of David going to Larey's sawmill, as the Negro who went for the planks could not carry the money. Oh, I verily believe they mean to kill him, and he went off and cannot return tonight! And I wish he was here as I am sick tonight. I have a sour stomach every night and never have had an action from the bowels except by enema in twelve days.

[Tuesday, September 22, 1863] David reached home tonight just as I was concluding my supper, completely exhausted. He brought a verbal invitation to Dr. Larey's wedding, which takes place in two weeks, and his wife died in July last. Oh, the inconsistency of men![42]

[Wednesday, September 23, 1863] Alone again all today. David heard Mr. Baron was going to run away today and has gone to try to collect a debt. It was gold borrowed by Mr. Baron before this ever began, and David saw him yesterday and he told him he would be here Sunday to pay him, and a few hours after the above mentioned invitation he saw a man who told him Baron was all ready to start today.

[Torn] he had, for Mr. Crawford [Connally] sent me word that David would not be at home tonight but was well. Poor dear, [illegible] he has so many trials and vexations for one in such frail health. Oh, Heavenly Father, turn his heart to Thee, and be with him in every trial. Be his shield, his staff, through all of life's rugged paths.

Miss Lewis and Sister Jane came over this afternoon and Miss Lewis kindly consented to spend the night.

Had to have a wagon loaded with corn for the iron works. Sent Mr. Mason a jar of citron.

[Thursday, September 24, 1863] Miss Lewis left quite early this morning and I've spent another day all alone and as the "dim grey twilight" approaches I feel lonely and anxious about my dear husband who has not yet arrived, but Mr. Moores, I see, is coming from the direction of the foundry and maybe he can get me some tidings of him.

[Friday, September 25, 1863] My dear husband came after dark last night and my spirits are considerably lifted, but I'm not getting well. Liver still torpid and bowels inactive. Stomach sour and appetite distressingly good.

[Saturday, September 26, 1863] Feel sick and broken spirited tonight. Have fever. I tried to work in the garden today and perhaps did too much. Mrs. MacAdams brought some cloth home today—eighteen yards.

XXX

Davis County, 12 miles west
Linden
October 7, a.d. 1863

Mr. D. H. Moores
Dear Brother, I bought a buggy of Mrs. Cooper, and she became dissatisfied from some cause and sent for it a day or two since. Consequently, I am under the necessity of asking the loan of your buggy a few days.[43]

I am having mine repaired in Linden, which will be completed in a couple of weeks.

I wish to go to Smith County to visit my wife's relations. If you can spare your

buggy until I can make that trip, I will be much obliged to you and I'll return it in

as good condition as I receive.

Tell Rachel we will be up to see her as soon as we return from Smith.

Yours respectfully,

W. H. H. Moores

XXX

NOTES

[1] John Frost, *Pictorial Life of General Marion; Embracing Anecdotes, Illustrative of His Character* (Philadelphia, PA: Lindsay and Blakiston, 1847). John Frost was born in Kennebunk, Maine, in 1800 and educated at Bowdoin and Harvard. Frost produced hundreds of books for the popular market, including a novel, travel accounts, captivity narratives, ancient histories, a great number of biographies, and titles such as *The Wonders of History*, "comprising remarkable battles, sieges, feats of arms, and instances of courage, ability and magnanimity, occurring in the annals of the world, from the earliest ages to the present."

Frost advanced an agenda of unabashed nationalism, with the goal of providing a vision of the American past to inspire readers to act in responsibly "American" ways.

[2] These lines are from William Cullen Bryant's poem, "The Song of Marion's Men."

[3] Rachel refers to 1 Peter 2:23: "Who, when he was reviled, reviled not again; when he suffered, he threatened not; but committed himself to him that judgeth righteously."

[4] Catie Riley, the wife of Henry Riley, lived near Courtland, Texas, in 1863. A native of Georgia born in about 1810, she was the mother of four sons: Jud Riley, age twenty-four; William F. Riley, age twenty-two; James Franklin Riley, age twenty-one; and S. J. Riley, age eighteen.

[5] "Miss Lizzie" is not to be confused with "Lizzie," an enslaved black woman who worked in Rachel's kitchen.

[6] Sulfur Iron Works Company, Cass County Genealogical Society, Cass County, Texas, Records of 1890 Abstract number, 1025; certificate number 74 (Atlanta, Texas).

[7] The "Twenty Negro Law," enacted by the Confederate Congress as part of the Second Conscription Act in 1862, exempted from military service one white man for every twenty slaves on a plantation. The law was designed to ensure a steady supply of agricultural products to the army and the people and also addressed Southern fears of a slave rebellion while so many white men were absent from home, serving in the Confederate army. The legislation met with considerable resistance, however, from non-slave owing whites who resented fighting for slave-owners' property while the masters were themselves exempt from conscription. A common response to the law was the belief that the Civil War was "a rich man's war and a poor man's fight." Colin Edward Woodward, *Marching Masters: Slavery, Race, and the Confederate Army during the Civil War* (Charlotte: University Press of Virginia, 2014); John M. Sacher, *Confederate Conscription and the Struggle for Southern Soldiers* (Baton Rouge: Louisiana State University Press, 2022).

[8] By 1862, Little Rock had become "a hospital city," to which wounded and ill Confederate soldiers were sent from the entire state. Two hospitals had been established there: one occupying the buildings of St. Johns College and a second in the former Rock Hotel. Cynthia DeHaven Pitcock, "Gunpowder, Lard and Kerosene: Civil War Medicine in the Trans-Mississippi," in *The Earth Reeled and Trees Trembled:" Civil War Arkansas, 1863–1864*, edited by Mark K. Christ (Little Rock, AR: Old State House Museum, 2007); Cynthia DeHaven Pitcock and Bill J. Gurley, eds., *I Acted from Principle: The Civil War Diary of Dr. William M. McPheeters, Confederate Surgeon in the Trans-Mississippi* (Fayetteville: University of Arkansas Press, 2002), 55–56.

[9] William M. Powell was born in Alabama on October 25, 1828. He died on January 20, 1911, and is buried in the Powell/Jones Cemetery, Douglasville, Texas.

[10] *Queechy* by Elizabeth Wetherell, the pen name of Susan Bogert Warner (1819–1885), is a domestic novel focusing on gender dynamics. Fleda is the book's central character.

"The Angel in the House" is the title of Coventry Kersey Dighton Patmore's vastly popular 1854 poem, a guide in verse to the wife's proper behavior in a marriage.

[11] Eliza Jones Haywood was born on March 22, 1820, at Plevna, Madison County, Alabama. William H. Haywood, Jr., a tinner by trade, was born in North Carolina on April 13, 1810. On 27 March 27, 1836, the two were married in Hardeman County, Tennessee. He died on January 29, 1877, and she in Texarkana, Texas, on September 8, 1908. Both are buried in the Oakwood Cemetery, Jefferson, Texas.

[12] Mount Lebanon was founded by a community of Baptists from South Carolina in what is now Bienville Parish. In 1853, they established a school known as Mount Lebanon University. The university closed during the Civil War but continued to serve as a high school and as a Confederate hospital. The school reopened after the war and in 1906 consolidated with Louisiana College in Pineville in Rapides Parish. Gerald Pollard, "The History of Mount Lebanon University, 1852–1912," M.A. thesis, Louisiana State University, 1971.

[13] William Carey Crane was born in Richmond, Virginia, on March 17, 1816. He attended Mount Pleasant Classical Institute in Amherst, Massachusetts, Virginia Baptist Seminary (now Richmond College), Hamilton Literary and Theological Institute, and Madison (now Colgate) University. In 1834, he entered Columbian College (now George Washington University), from which he received an A.B. degree in 1836 and an A.M. in 1839. While teaching in Georgia from 1837 to 1839 he was ordained into the Baptist ministry in 1838. In March 1839, he accepted a pastorate at Montgomery, Alabama. Crane married Jane Louisa Wright, also of New York, in 1841. In 1845, he married Catharine Jane Shepherd of Mobile, Alabama. The couple had nine children, eight of whom lived to maturity. During the 1840s Crane held pastorates in various communities in Mississippi and served as president of Mississippi Female College (1851–1857), Semple Broaddus College in Mississippi (1859–1860), and Mount Lebanon College in Louisiana (1860–1863). At Mount Lebanon he was also co-editor of the *Mississippi Baptist*.

In 1863, Crane moved to Texas where he accepted the presidency of Baylor University, effective January 1, 1864, serving until his death on February 27, 1885. He was originally buried in Independence, Texas, but in 1937 the Texas Centennial Commission had his body reinterred in the State Cemetery at Austin. Crane County is named in his honor. James Milton Carroll, *A History of Texas Baptists* (Dallas, TX: Baptist Standard, 1923); Lois Smith Murray, *Baylor at Independence* (Waco, TX: Baylor University Press, 1972); E. Bruce Thompson, "William Carey Crane and Texas Education," *Southwestern Historical Quarterly* 58 (January 1955).

[14] Betty was Margaret Johnston Godbold, the daughter of Daniel Perry and Lucretia Collins Godbold.

[15] John Comer Watts, Sr., Rachel's nephew and executor of her estate, was born on July 22, 1846, in Lowdnes County, Alabama, but moved as a small child with his parents, Elizabeth Evans Godbold Watts and Thomas Jefferson Watts, Sr., to a location near the present town of McNeil, Nevada County, Arkansas. During visits to his aunts, Jane Godbold Moores and Rachel Godbold Moores, he met and courted their niece, Nancy Harrison Moores, the daughter of Eli and Minerva Ann Janes Moores. After

serving as third sergeant of Company G, Ninth Arkansas Infantry, during the Civil War, he returned home to marry "Nannie" at the home of her parents in Texarkana, Texas, on February 13, 1884.

Nancy Harrison Moores was born in Bowie County on October 28, 1859. The couple lived in "Watts Hill," the old Moores home at 1609 Old Boston Road where, according to family lore, "no smoking or dancing was allowed." They became the parents of eight children: Eli Moores Watts; Elizabeth "Lizzie" Watts; John Comer Watts, Jr., who was killed in action at the Battle of Saint Mihiel, September 12, 1918; Thomas Jefferson Watts; David Moores Watts; Minerva James Moores Watts; Monroe Perry Watts; and Nancy Harrison Moores Watts.

Watts was prominent in early Texarkana affairs, serving as city treasurer, president of the school board, and deacon of the First Baptist Church, and is said to have laid the first brick for the First Baptist Church at Fourth and Pine Streets, built in 1898.

Watts died on July 7, 1912. His pastor, Dr. William M. Harris, called him "one of the truest and best men that ever lived. If required to select the best man in Texarkana, I would have chosen John C. Watts without hesitation." Nancy Harrison Moores Watts died in Texarkana on September 24, 1931. Both are buried in the Rose Hill Cemetery. Walter W. Thornton, *History of the First Baptist Church*, (1952), 71; Nancy Moores Watts Jennings, comp., *Texarkana Pioneer Family Histories* (Texarkana, Arkansas–Texas, 1916).

[16] James K. Huey was born in Livingston County, Kentucky, on March 27, 1827. He was admitted to the bar and in 1857 was elected as a Democrat to the state legislature, serving for a single term. At the beginning of the Civil War he raised and was elected as captain of a company of cavalry. He and his men escaped from Fort Donelson with Bedford Forrest's command, fought largely as partisan rangers for the remainder of the war, and he eventually rose to the rank of colonel. Unable to resume his law practice at the end of the war, he became a commission merchant in New Orleans. In 1872, he returned to Livingston County where he was elected county judge in 1874. His father-in-law, Robert Powell, is said to have been one of the largest planters of the South. J. H. Battle, W. H. Perrin, and G. C. Kniffin, *Kentucky: A History of the State* (Louisville, KY: Battey, 1885), 823–24; New Orleans *Times Picayune*, December 13, 1870, 7.

[17] These lines are from William Cullen Bryant's poem, "To a Waterfowl."

[18] Franny F. Ironmonger was married to Richard Knight, a Cass County resident, in Lafayette County, Arkansas, on October 23, 1864.

[19] *Reveries of a Bachelor; or, A Book of the Heart*, by American author Donald Grant Mitchell was published in 1850 under the pseudonym Ik Marvel. The novel explores the themes of boyhood, country life, marriage, travel, and dreams.

[20] For Mary E. Dealy [or Daly], see chapter five, note number sixty-nine. Mrs. McCollom was her mother.

[21] Mary Ann Dockery (July 11, 1839–January 19, 1938) was the sister of Confederate Brig. Gen. Thomas Pleasant Dockery and was the niece of Dr. Thomas Pleasant Mask, the husband of Rachel's younger half-sister, Martha A. "Mat" Godbold. She married Nicholas Jordan Gantt in Columbia County, Arkansas, in 1865. He had been appointed postmaster at Lamartine, Ouachita County, Arkansas, on February 18, 1852, and was, at the time of his marriage, serving as captain of Company G, Sixth Arkansas Infantry. The couple had one child, a daughter named Anna Nicholas Gantt, born on March 6, 1866. Following the death of N. J. Gantt in November 1865, Mary Ann Dockery married William Hardy Browning on March 24, 1870, in Columbia County.

[22] "Dearly beloved, avenge not yourselves, but rather give place unto wrath: for it is written, Vengeance is mine; I will repay, saith the Lord." Romans 12:19.

[23] Hebrews 13:5.

[24] On April 25, 1863, less than a year after the death of his wife Matilda, William Henry Harrison Moores married Maria Louise Adams Ross (September 11, 1838–March 19, 1875). The couple were to have four children. She is buried in the Harrison Chapel Cemetery at Redwater. The year after Maria's death he married Mary Lunsford Douglass (born May 5, 1833, in Blackstock, Chester County, South Carolina) on

April 20, 1876. This, his third wife, died in Texarkana on October 12, 1900, and is buried beside him in the Rose Hill Cemetery.

25 "Teach me to feel another's woe, to hide the fault I see, that mercy I to others show, that mercy show to me," is from Alexander Pope's 1738 poem, "The Universal Prayer."

26 From a more positive point of view, abolitionist Harriet Beecher Stowe averred that what she called "the negro mind" was "impassioned and imaginative" and thus "always attaches itself to hymns and expressions of a vivid and pictorial nature." Harriet Beecher Stowe, *Uncle Tom's Cabin* (Boston, MA: John P. Jewett, 1852), 51.

27 Anne Steele was born at Broughton, Hampshire, in 1717. Her father officiated as the lay pastor of the Baptist Society at Broughton. Her mother died when she was three. At the age of nineteen she became an invalid after injuring her hip. At the age of twenty-one she was engaged to be married, but her fiancé drowned on the day of the wedding. On the occasion of his death she wrote the hymn "When I Survey Life's Varied Scenes." Steele never married but assisted her father with his ministry and, in in 1760, published a volume of poetry, *Poems on Subjects Chiefly Devotional*, under the pseudonym "Theodosia."

28 Samuel A. Godbold died on May 27, 1863, in Columbia County, Arkansas, and is buried in the Watts Cemetery, Willisville, Nevada County, Arkansas.

These lines are from Michael Frost's poem, "The Captive Spirit," published in *Poetic Fragments* (London: Houlston and Wright, n.d.), 27.

30 "There the wicked cease from troubling; and there the weary be at rest." Job 3:17.

31 Vermifuge is an anthelmintic agent that destroys or expels parasitic worms.

32 The operations of the iron mine and foundry that Eilbeck Mason opened near the Moores' plantation were funded by the sale of shares. The land on which it was located seems to have belonged to James Moore, inherited from Thomas Harrison Moores, but David Moores seems to have been among the principal stockholders and one of the most active corporate officials.

33 John H. Salmon, born in South Carolina in about 1831, lived near Boston, Texas, but owned land in Bowie and Davis Counties valued in 1860 at $25,000. He served as a private in Company F, Nineteenth Texas Infantry. He was married to Sarah M. Salmon, who the 1860 federal census classified as a "lady" who had three children under the age of seven.

34 According to the inscription on his gravestone in Courtland Cemetery, Queen City, Texas, Dempsey J. Connally died on July 6, 1863.

35 H. W. Hathaway, a Bowie County school teacher, was a native of the state of Maine, born in or about 1825. In 1860, she was living in Lewisburg, Conway County, Arkansas. At that time, she had a six-year-old son named Arthur.

36 An A. H. Chappel was on the Davis County tax rolls in 1863.

37 Rachel's half-brother, Capt. Benjamin Franklin Godbold, the commander of Company B of Col. Thomas P. Dockery's Nineteenth Arkansas Infantry, was killed at the Battle of Big Black River, Mississippi, May 16, 1863, in the opening phase of the Siege of Vicksburg. Lt. Col. William H. Dismukes, who then commanded the regiment, was mortally wounded and most of the regiment was captured. Pvt. A. H. Reynolds, in his memoirs, describes returning from his imprisonment at Fort Delaware: "When I returned to my command I found Colonel Dockery promoted to Brigadier General, promoted for bravery at Champion Hill, Farmington, Corinth, Hatchey Bridge, Iuka, all of which battles were inscribed on our battle flag. It found a watery grave in the hands of Captain Godbold who perished with it in the Big Black River on the morning of May 17, 1863, as our command was falling back into Vicksburg. No officer was truer or braver than Captain Godbold, and he sacrificed his life rather than see his colors in the hands of the enemy. Heaven bless that noble soldier!" A. H. Reynolds, "Vivid Experiences at Champion Hill, Miss.," *Confederate Veteran*, 18:1 (January 1910), 21.

38 These lines are from "In Memorium," Alfred, Lord Tennyson's, 1849 elegy for his friend Arthur Henry Hallam.

39 Sir William Hamilton (March 8, 1788–May 6, 1856) was a Scottish philosopher and metaphysician, perhaps best remembered for his recognition of the importance of German philosophy, especially that of Immanuel Kant. His most important work was "Philosophy of the Unconditioned," in which he developed the principle that the human finite mind can have no knowledge of the infinite. Rachel was most likely reading from his four-volume *Lectures on Metaphysics and Logic*, posthumously published between 1858 and 1860.

40 These lines are from Felicia Dorothea Hemans' (1793–1835) poem, "The Hour of Death."

41 1 Corinthians 15:19.

42 John M. Larey, a physician, was born in or about 1825 in Autauga County, Alabama. On July 13, 1847, he married Mary Kelly in Lafayette County, Arkansas. They were the parents of five children. In October 1863, he married Annie T. Roach, and they were to become the parents of ten additional children. Larey died in Cass County in 1895 and is buried there in Queen City.

43 Hodges Cooper was W. H. H. Moores' former mother-in-law.

chapter seven

YOU ARE AMONG A HANGMAN'S SET

October–December 1863

I n March 1862, David H. Moores and a number of his neighbors formed an independent company to serve as home guards. On March 1, 1864, Texas reorganized its militia into brigade districts, with Bowie, Cass (Davis), and Marion Counties as the base of the Seventh Militia Brigade, Texas State Troops. Brig. Gen. Marion DeKalb "M. D. K." Taylor, a former speaker of the Texas house of representatives, was the brigade's commanding officer.

On March 18, 1864, David Moores enlisted for a six-month tour of duty as a private in Capt. James Morgan Nelson's mounted company of the Seventh Brigade at Camp Cusseta, located in the Cusseta Mountains, a range of low, stony hills in the western part of Cass County, some five miles east of Marietta.[1]

Rachel was distraught at the thought of her husband leaving home and going into harm's way. "A lonely lot will mine be, and for protection dependent upon the mercy of Negroes." She was deeply concerned about her inability to manage the plantation in his absence. "I do not see how I am to do what little I have undertaken without my dear husband," she wrote. Much worse, she thought, "We may meet and soon or, oh bitter agonizing thought, it may never be."

Prior to his departure she worked on accoutrements and food for her husband; clothing, bedding, provision bags, and haversack. This effort proved too much for her "weak nerves and already prostrate body to stand, and it is not surprising I sunk under it." Unable to set up to eat, she suffered through two days that she "thought would be my last," she wrote. "My suffering was such I thought I greatly preferred death."

In 1844, attorney R. K. Clark wrote to his sister in Tennessee that "society is bad here at present," and that "a great many mean people" were then living in northeast Texas, for such was the case in all frontier communities.[2]

Indeed, the presence of the likes of Montgomery Cullen Baker bore out Clark's observation, and although the horrors that Rachel envisaged did not come to pass, with almost all of the area's white men absent on military duty, many of the enslaved men and women on plantations and farms began self-liberating or committing acts of sabotage and defiance. In Rachel's dairy, for example, they removed and threw away the bungs from the vinegar barrel. "Another month's labor lost and not three gallons of vinegar and the house!" she lamented. "Everything else upside down!" With "no protector and entirely in their power," the "self-willed Negroes," she wrote, seemed "determined at times to run roughshod over me, defy my authority." And to her horror, she discovered "tracks coming in from towards the bottom. I suppose they are our Negros that are in the woods, and how unsafe it makes me feel."

David, writing from his company's camp on the Red River where it was attempting to round up deserters from the Rebel army in Indian Territory, reported that he was "standing the service very well." In response to Rachel's complaints about the behavior of their rebellious enslaved, he pledged that "when I come home, I will make them sore." But, somewhat condescendingly, he told her that "you must try and do the best you can as there are thousands in the same fix as yours and a thousand times worse. So Darling," he sanctimoniously advised, "you must cheer up." Rachel, however, was not to be consoled, still longing for the safe and familiar antebellum world that had been ripped away from her.

XXX

[from the Journal of Rachel P. Moores]

[Thursday, October 8, 1863] *The first day I've sat up since Sunday week, and never have I suffered more, and some of the time all alone. David went to camps to get permission to remain at home until he was a little recovered in health and he was detained three days and nights and I was not able to set up to eat my meals, and two days I thought would be my last, and the week before Brother went, and my suffering was such I thought I greatly preferred death.*

[Friday, October 9, 1863] *Worked some outdoors in* **[torn]**. **[Illegible]** *I made last winter. Dr. Salmon and wife came and spent the afternoon.* **[Illegible]** *cent. I do not see how I am to do what little I have undertaken without my dear husband.*

[Saturday, October 10, 1863] *Made a very neat haversack for David today of a piece of oilcloth I was fortunate enough to have on hand. But ache so terribly I can't finish the stays.*

Got Sister Jane to make the overshirt. I had one on hand Mother let me have. Must go to bed and leave undone what can't be done. Had eight towel provision bags made and a single mattress and small pillow.

[Sunday, October 11, 1863] *How strangely, how different this has been spent to any other Sabbath in my life. Finished knitting the straps to the haversack, filled the provision bags, and had cake, tarts, and soda biscuit made, and though I have violated the sacred day thus, much more remains to be done than I can possibly do in time tomorrow morning e'er the dreaded farewell takes place.*

Mr. Reuben's family, Miss Lewis, Miss Boykin, and Mr. Mason took tea with us. Mr. Mason spent the day and will remain until morning.

My poor husband, too, has been most busy all day and is out giving orders for the gathering of new crops, paying out allowances, etc., etc.

XXX

October 13th, 1863

My Dear Wife,

I hope that you feel much better today than you did yesterday when I left you. I send Charles for the basket and the axe that you have in the house and a piece of oil cloth to wrap up my meat in and one pound of 6-p[enny] nails and some leather which he will get at the foundry.

I don't know when we will leave here. I hope that I will get to come home before we leave.

I slept very comfortable last night in the old hack. I hope that you had as comfortable a night's rest.

Good bye, my Darling wife. I hope I see you in a few days.

D. H. Moores

XXX

Mr. Mason,

Please [send] some leather by the boy Charles—I told him what kind I want—and you will oblige yours,

D. H. Moores

XXX

[Saturday, October 17, 1863] *Too much for my weak nerves and already prostrate body to stand, and it is not surprising I sunk under it. Just before the dreaded leave taking, a high fever laid me again upon my bed, which I never left until today, after putting the cooked things in the little division assigned for them in the provision box, mending Charlie's suit and pistol belt, etc., and gave up, and on bended knee I was clasped to the bosom where "my head so oft hath lain," perhaps for the last time, though I can't believe it.*

I feel in this that God will be merciful, ache my poor heart ever so much and flow my tears as raindrops at the thoughts of his dear face, form, or kindness.

I've been just as sick as I could and live this week. Same nauseated stomach, chills, and fever. There!! He comes!!

[Torn] up asking to this. Oh! The first parting would be brief, though I had no particular reason, or rather, very good reason for it. But now [illegible] that all is uncertain. We may meet and soon or, oh bitter agonizing thought, it may never be. Oh, my husband dear and kind, tried and true, may Our Father in Heaven grant us reunion on earth, and may we gain strength from this one greatest earthly affliction. Those who suffer severe afflictions here must sink under them or grow stronger.

Oh, fear not in a world like this,
And thou shalt know ere long—
Know how sublime a thing it is
To suffer and grow strong.[3]

May I, oh, may I, Gracious Heavenly Father, gather strength, Christian strength, courage, and fortitude. A lonely lot will mine be, and for protection dependent upon the mercy of Negroes. Their master gave them a long lecture a few minutes before he started in regard to their behavior to me.

[Saturday, October 24, 1863] I could not help [torn] my dear husband only because he came [illegible] evening. I presume, for I had no reason whatsoever to look for him. He told me when he left it might be months ere we met again. But such were my feelings I had cake, tarts, etc. made and tongue boiled and other little etc. and etcs. I usually have fixed up on Saturdays.

I do not feel quite so well as I could wish. Am too cold and ache a little. I do not know whether my disappointment has anything to do with my feelings physically or not. But, oh, how infinitely delighted I would have been to have heard the dear familiar steps. Alas, I may listen long and in vain. Here I have sat thus for the nights since he left, all alone, no one to exchange one thought with.

I've been most busy all the week when well enough, making him a comfort. It is only one and a half yards, but it is so wide and heavy I can scarcely hold it in my hands. I knit of a morning whilst it is too cold to go out. Then walk around and attend to the household affairs. Knit again until near dinner and then broil my steak over the coals, eat my dinner in my rocking chair by the fire. Afterward I walk a little and lay down. Knit and walk until supper and then knit, walk the floor, and read my Bible until bedtime, and here I am tonight in my chair, candle stand beside me. Mary Jane and Lizzie before the fire knitting. Nightgown and chemise in the other corner, warming foot brick ready on the hearth. Knitting put up. My five hundred steps taken all between my hearth and the dining room hearth. Two chapters read in the Bible, and though not sleepy suppose I must go to my lonely couch in order to dismiss these mooning maids.

Mr. Mason was here last evening. Said he saw my husband the day before at camp, and never saw him looking better.

[Torn] but heard [illegible] no preaching, the preacher failing to come, and I regretted it much for I feel the need of religious instruction very much at present. Rode over to Mr. Reuben's [illegible] my watch this afternoon. I wrote Sister Mat since my return.

[Monday, October 26, 1863] That "coming events cast their shadows before" is, I believe, conceded to most of us. I felt so much like I should see my husband at home soon that when I started to church I left lunch on the table for him, and today, just as Mary Jane and I were getting dinner (Lizzie and Nancy washed) he came up and gladdened my poor heart. But it pained me so to see him so worried about the way things were getting along—fences down, gates broken, sheep, cows, and hogs all in one place. No more than I expect, though. No Master.[4]

XXX

Lonely Fireside
Monday night
November 9, 1863

I am in a most perplexing dilemma, my dearest husband: about one of the clock today—Sam, I suppose was his name—brought Nathan here. Took him *up near Mr. Richard Sam's and supposing him to be run away—and I presume he was correct for he has no pass, yet persists in saying he had one given him but lost it.*

The young man stopped at Mr. Scott's on his way and told Mr. Scott as Nathan was in the Government's employ, he had best not bring him home, and Mr. Scott told the man that you had a boy run away and Nathan spoke up and said he was the very one, and had run away two months, and had a wife and children at home.

They are rather inconsistent, aren't they? Some running away from home and some running away to get home—but to precede and give you all the particulars, I told him I could not let him stay at all here though he had a severe cold and says he has rheumatism badly—told the young gentleman Mr. Reuben Moores was going to Linden tomorrow for the purpose of delivering one of his, (Jess,) and probably he would take charge of him—he seemed not to know what to do with him. To ask him anyway, and if he would not, he must take him to the proper authorities, and he went to Reuben's. Did not find him home and Sister Jane suffered him to leave Nathan chained there.

You think he did not bring him back to me? I was angry and told him if he would not take charge of him one night I would send to the foundry get Mr. Mason, Moores, or someone there to take him for me, but he said Mr. Mason was not there, "nor nobody else."

I told him both those men had kindly proffered me any assistance I might need during your absence—particularly if I was troubled in any way with Negros—but he said if I would send him over riding early tomorrow morning, and I suppose I will have it to do, and Dan behind him to bring the mule back.

It may not meet your approbation, My Dear, but I'm afraid to have him here.

I look every day for all the rest except Uncle Edmund, and if he is talked to here, he too will go with them. He has a considerable cough and says he suffers very much for want of bedclothes, and I am going to make him take a comfort.

I presume you will get the letter containing Ollie's exit the same time you get this, though it was written Saturday night. I have not heard one word from him yet. One of his little children was with me in my room about half an hour and I asked her what her daddy ran away for.

"Cora said he ran away because my master whipped him," said she, and she said Henry said Eli was sitting under the gin one day when he went to carry off the cane. But I asked him nothing about it, for you cannot rely on one word they say.

I'm afraid Edmund is sowing the wheat too thin, and I told him so. He is still sowing that from [remainder of letter missing.]

XXX

16 November 1863
David H. Moores, Esq.
Camp L[ane's] Ferry,[5] *Texas*

Dear Husband,
Charles said you said nothing to him about moving me down to your encampment today; therefore, I conclude my going would not prove agreeable to you and so I decline to do so. Else I would make Kemp or Uncle Edmund drive me, as Charles says you paid him carry a load of fodder this morning and return for the hack tomorrow.

I had you a nice dinner cooked but see no way to send it on the fodder—will endeavor, though, to get something to you.

I marked all your clothes that came in the satchel and transferred them to the trunk as you desired. I also put your overcoat in. The socks I found very troublesome to mark. They stretch so badly, and only part of a "D" on all except one pair. Marked D. H. M. I hope they will suit you. You will find every article in the trunk that was in the satchel.

I have fixed up a sweet potato pie since Charles has put the fodder in and a cake of butter underneath the biscuit—enough for your supper and breakfast.

Take good care of yourself, my Dearest—know and keep a strict watch. You are among a hangman's set.

I will not detain Charles, for he has a miserable late start. I wrote my note before he went after the fodder but did not know whether he could carry the bucket or not.

Come when you can to [illegible] *your sad and lonely Wife.*

Rachi

XXX

[Monday, November 23, 1863] [torn] *My thirty-third birthday passed and no husband near to give the accustomed* [illegible] *no father, no mother, but all, all alone in my home do I call to mind, but not celebrate, the thirty-third anniversary day of my mother's death!*

There was lamentation instead of thanksgiving at my birth, grief instead of joy, for as I came into the world, my dearest of mothers passed from its checkered scene. I can but hope to meet her where the "weary are at rest."[6]

Oh, could you, my precious, sainted mother, have but known what the future had in store for your early-orphaned child, your afflicted child, your now desolate child, I could almost say, your deserted child, for since my husband left, with one or two exceptions, I've been entirely so. But he was fortunate enough to be sent home on business, a blessing to me, and for four days he was encamped at Lane's Ferry, and I went down and spent one day with him and he came home and spent two days and nights, but, alas, is gone to Clarksville. I know not for how long nor when he will be called from there. Oh, it did seem Saturday when he left. I should be crazier for a while. My poor heart ached until it was sore.

It is well, perhaps, I've so many other cares and anxieties, as it somewhat diverts my mind from the ever-present pain of absence—"absence that makes the heart grow fonder."[7]

Byron said he went to bed with regret on his thirty-third birthday at having lived so long to so little purpose, regretted more for what he had left undone than for what he had done.

I differ much with him, for I regret more of the things done than of those left undone. Most of all, I regret abusing my constitution as I did by sedentary habits, by tight clothing, by intemperance in eating, too little sleep etc., etc.

[Torn] *this morning* **[illegible]** *sunny* **[illegible]** *I was kept from enjoying by a basket full of* **[illegible]** *Sister Jane spent this afternoon. Mr. Mason spent last night with me. Received, or rather, read a letter from home addressed to Sister Jane. All well. No news.*

XXX

*I enclose a little tribute of affection to you. Some lines on "My Birthday Night."
They are mere outpourings of a fond and faithful heart—no other merit they
claim, no other wished by your fond and faithful wife.*

*To My Husband
On My Birthday Night
November 23, 1863*

1. *My heart is sad and lone tonight,
   No husband near my side,
   To greet with tender smiles and kiss
   Me on this birthday night.*
2. *For hours I've sat and pondered
   Upon the drear fate
   That bears him to the tented fields
   And leaves me here bereft.*
3. *And 'tis a sore bereavement, too,
   For though my life art spared
   'Tis taken upon thy country's alter
   That life, oh, me, how dear, how dear.*
4. *I can but mourn and weep tonight
   Though know 'tis much against thy will*

But, oh, to me thou cannot know how drear

To live without thy loving care.

5. Thy tender care, through years of pain,

'Twas music to know it's soothing spell.

And though 'twas like my burning love,

It made my world an Eden bright.

6. But now, alas, **[illegible]** a joyful bliss

Of thy dear presence once **[illegible]** cause:

Thine earnest look, of melting tenderness.

The soft pressure of thy hand.

7. But more than this, than these, I miss

The magic of thy caress.

I miss thy clear protective power,

I suffer so alone.

8. But me, I'm not alone tonight,

For He who answers prayer

Has promised that He shall be found

If we but ask aright.

9. And each night on my bended knees

In silent prayer I bow

And Him to guard and keep me safe,

To protect thee while away.

10. And hasten soon the day, when thou

In peace shall be restored

To bless thy wife, thy loving wife,

Who mourns thy loss this birthday night.

XXX

[Tuesday, November 27, 1863] *Suffered the pain of parting again, today noon, but with strong hopes of meeting again soon. At least a chance for it, as David thinks they will be placed upon the eastern boundary of the State. Regretted so much I could not finish his comfort before he left. Knit until my hands were swollen and then could not finish.*

Miss Lewis and Mrs. Boykin came to spend the night. We had music and cheerful converse since supper, and I feel much benefited by their presence.

I ache badly and feel badly from the effects of the quinine I took this afternoon to keep off chills.

After I finished David's comfort I went into the milk house, and, oh, horrors. What confusion! The bungs taken out of the vinegar barrel and thrown away! Another month's labor lost and not three gallons of vinegar and the house! Everything else upside down!

[Monday, November 31, 1863] *Received a letter from my dear husband. He is well and stationed at Clarksville for he knows not how long. Oh, I was so delighted to hear from him. God protect us while apart, I pray.*

Sent to mill today and from twelve bushels of wheat only received one barrel of flour.

XXX

Camp Clarksville, Texas[8]
December 2/[18]63

My Darling Wife,

I wrote you a few days ago by Samuel Watkins. We're still here, and our captain thinks we will remain here this winter. I am enjoying fine health and weigh one hundred and fifty.[9]

We are guarding the roads here. We sent off this morning ten men to the mouth of Kiamisha to guard the ferry.[10]

We have glorious news from Bragg's army. General Thomas has surrendered his whole army. We hear so much, I don't believe anything I hear.[11]

I want you to have the hogs fed and fat by Christmas so you can have them killed. I hope you have an overseer before this. If not, you must try and get some one to hire you one. I would like to come home Christmas if I could get a furlough. I may get to come sooner, or I may not get to at all.

Darling, you have a harder time than I have, but you must try and do the best you can as there are thousands in the same fix as yours and a thousand times worse, so Darling, you must cheer up. When you get an overseer, I will send Charles down for you and you can come and see me.

Carrol is waiting and I will have to close. So, kiss and goodbye until next week and I will write you again.

D. H. Moores

XXX

[Sunday, December 6, 1863] *But little has transpired since my last record worthy of note. Oh, last week and this week, I have been troubled with these self-willed Negroes, but none have run away as did Lizzie and Louisa last week. But every few days, and, oh, it does make me so miserable to think of no protector and entirely in their power.*

Have been so busy sewing all this week. I finished my dress I began last week and made my cloak and ripped up [illegible] *to dye.*

Agnes spent Tuesday and Wednesday night with me. Mrs. Boykin spent yesterday afternoon and last night and today with me. I enjoyed her society so much. She is so ladylike, genteel, and refined, so respectful of other people's rights.

We took a nice ride. Uncle Edmund drove us halfway to the foundry. I thought it would be beneficial to both. Mrs. Boykin is convalescing, and I am threatened again—chills. I suffered more with my throat last night than ever I suffered with it, and ache again tonight. Feel exceedingly feverish.

Mr. Doyle and Bowers dined here today. I sent a letter by Mr. Doyle to my dear husband [torn].

XXX

Camp Clarksville, December 11, 1863

My Darling Wife,

This is the third letter that I have wrote to you. I have not received the first scratch of the pen from you, Darling. Do write once a week if you don't write but two or three lines. I have but little news to write. I went last Friday over the Indian Nation to carry a dispatch to Brigadier General Hawes and returned day before yesterday.[12]

I seen Dike Rochelle and the Moores of Boston.[13] *Dike looks very well, but William Moores looks like he was dried up to a crackling, and he is very low spirited. He wants a furlough to go home and he can't get it. I feel very sorry for him and he is dressed badly. It looks hard that he can't get a furlough to go home, and his command is twenty miles of home. The whole brigade, which is about two thousand men, is at Lane's Port, which is about forty-five miles from my house. I think we will be ordered there in a few days.*

It was all false about Old Blunt being killed. It was reported here last week that he was at Fort Smith on his way to Red River by way of the line road. That is, the road between the Nation and Arkansas. That was the contents of the dispatch that I carried over last week. But the Feds come down as far as Walden and their heavy wagons has turned back to Fort Smith. There is about fifteen hundred or two thousand Federals at Walden.[14]

I had the pleasure, when I was over in the Nation, of being at General A. Pike's camp. What do you think he is doing over there—writing the history of this war. He has two or three Negros and a white women keeping camp for him. His family is in Little Rock. He has a fine time with the woman he has there. He told me that there was a good many good-looking squaws near camp.[15]

I've seen Mr. Anderson once since I've been here. He asked me home with him, but I never have been yet. I was out at preaching last night and heard an eloquent speaker.

Darling, make Old Edmund make a hog pen where it was last year to pen the hogs in, and have wood and rock hauled up so you can have the hogs butchered by the last of this month.

I am heavier now than I have been in fifteen years. A kiss, Darling, goodbye 'til next week.

Your husband, D. H. Moores

P.S. I will send this by Mr. Haskin and to be mailed at Camden.
D. H. Moores

XXX

[Saturday, December 12, 1863] [torn] *busy week* [illegible] *unusually ill today! Have suffered most acutely with my old disease, or rather symptoms of uterus disorder. Have been unable to sit up, only a few moments at a time. I began to suffer severe pains just as I rose from my bath.* [Illegible] *uterus and abdomen, back, etc.*

Altered, or commenced altering, the bombazine dress I got in exchange from Mrs. Moore. I had no trouble in piecing up the waist but can't get sleeves unless I use some other material to trim them with.

Knit me a small black worsted comfort for my throat and also one for Mr. Moores and have had Nancy spinning some very fine thread all the week to knit as a moble, mist, or whatever you may call it. Today I tried to bleach it over sulfur smoke but was unable to attend to it properly.

Mr. J. C. Moore spent Tuesday night here and Mr. Mason, Wednesday and Friday night. No other company. Only a short call from Sister Jane. I wrote to my husband tonight and I am sick and tired.

[Sunday, December 13, 1863] *Another lonely Sabbath has passed, and I suppose another and another "will be numbered with the things that were" ere I am permitted to see my darling husband. He speaks of sending for me as he cannot come home, provided I can get an overseer, and that is most uncertain.*

I rode around a portion of the farm and saw considerable signs of tracks coming in from towards the bottom. I suppose they are our Negros that are in the woods, and how unsafe it makes me feel. Such evidence of their proximity. But I do try more each day to put my trust entirely in my Creator, "in whom there is no variableness, neither shadow of turning." [16]

Oh, how entirely dependent I feel upon Him for life, health, and happiness. No one around except the maids who are pinching each other silly. Each one wants to arrange my hair, both are **[illegible]** *the week before last was spent, one day in knitting a mariposa and comfort, one in carrying yarn to the looms and looking for an overseer, in which journey I have the very good luck of meeting my husband's captain who tells me he is well.*

Wednesday in cooking.

Mr. J. C. Moore and Col. Mason spent that night here, and from them I hired foundry hands (eight) to assist in hog killing, which was done Thursday. Mr. Morrison, their overseer, superintending from noon until night, and during that time I was most busily engaged in making "all things ready" for the cutting up. But as they were so very late in coming up with the hogs, I got only sixteen cut up before supper, which was exceedingly late and then I had a roomful of company to wait on at supper which consumed much time and so I thought it too late to go out again, but was up and out and have all weighed before breakfast and a number cut up.

All the gentleman who spent the night here said it was so excessively cold as to freeze the meat very hard if left out, and so they urged me to put it in the meat house, and Morrison was commissioned to put it in a little after eight, and thinking he would know better than to pile them all together I let him go out and put them in without saying one word, but what was my consternation next morning at beholding smoke issue for each hog as they were butchered!

But all the gentlemen, when I came into breakfast, said that made no difference. But I do and will have my own way again and will have the meat sliced before night and have it **[torn]** *day after. It was put into the meat house* **[illegible]** *against my will and better judgment, for the gentleman said if the hogs were left out they would freeze so hard as to render them unfit to be cut* **[illegible]**.

The next two days were, of course, spent by myself in attending to lard, sausages, etc., etc., and in suffering from the effects of eating brains, sausage meat, spareribs, etc. Mr. Mason came again on Saturday night and remained until Monday morning and came again Monday evening last by engagement with Mr. Moores who had very kindly brought Janie who has been with me since.

We knit, sewed, and read until last evening—her breaking the monotony a little by practicing and I somewhat by cooking. but last evening, a few more moments after Agnes Johns left, (who accompanied Sister Jane over Friday afternoon,) we had a drive over to see my old friend, Mrs. Connally, who, together with Mrs. Watson, her daughter, and Mrs. Crawford Connally, her daughter-in-law, is moved home to reside permanently until the war is over, at least. I know not how much longer. I was quite sick a few moments whilst there, and, indeed, have been ill since yesterday morning.

I returned by Mr. Reuben's gate and left Janie to spend the night and went home. Wrote some pages of a letter to my husband.

It started raining—had rained all day—but today, Sunday, it is windy, cold, cloudy, and damp. Rode over and brought Janie home a few moments ago.

They have talked so despondently to her at Mr. Moores about bad political prospects that her spirits are below zero tonight. When the war began, I made up my mind to subjugation and seldom does hope revive **[illegible]** *feelings* **[torn]**.

This morning I proposed Janie should pay Agnes Johns a visit, which she did, and a few minutes after she started, I lay me down to recover my shattered nerves, having been ill since Saturday and just about died. So, Nancy came running to tell me that Harrison had found Nathan in his house and wished me there. I ran and tried, but in vain, to make him come out to me. He would not, but got out at the backside and ran off at full speed, Harrison after him. He did not catch him though, but Mr. Reuben Moores was out hunting and found him and brought him in, but himself had a spell from his chase after Nathan, and, as he could not whip him, I sent him to jail.

Whilst we had his pockets emptied of their contents, which consisted of onions, tobacco, needles, thread, and a conjure bone, which truck he said he used as an antidote against Negro dogs! I was no little angry with him and pelted him with Lizzie's catch stick for not pulling out from under the cabin and coming to me and running from me.

Janie has returned and I am weary enough of our day's excitement to go to bed. Janie is looking brighter for her bracing view. Dear child, what a comfort she has been these past weeks to me. I shall hate for the time to arrive in which I shall have to give her up. I will be glad when her school days are over and she can stay more with me. I hope she will not marry soon. She comes from her practice [torn]

My mind has been disturbed all day [illegible] *Mr. Crawford Connally has taken Nathan to Courtland instead of sending him to Jefferson. I'd much rather he was at Jefferson if the proceedings are legal, but I fear he will fail to appraise the proper authorities of his whereabouts. I must see him. Will dispatch a note to him before I sleep.*

So many cares, so many perplexities, for a poor invalid like me. If I had no care to do what was right, these matters would not disturb my mind the least. But having to exercise my own judgment in matters wherein I am no judge, and have no expertise, worries me too much at times.

XXX

Enola, Davis County, Texas
Saturday night
December 13th, 1863

One week since I last wrote you, My Dearest Husband, and it seems two at least, though this time has been made considerably shorter by my reception of a letter from yourself handed me last Tuesday by Mr. J. C. Moore but brought over from Clarksville by Carrol.

I'm sorry to tell you, My Love, that as yet I've got no overseer—and I fear but little prospect of one. Mr. Moores says he has tried in Bowie and he'll try again. Since you wrote you would send Charles after me soon as an overseer was procured, I am more anxious than ever to get one. I know, as you say, thousands are in a worse situation than myself, yet it does not mitigate my anxiety any to see and be with you! I shall be very loath to spend my Christmas at home without you. I could have company, but as I will be looking for you to send for me, I will not be in a hurry to invite anyone. I could also go home to Arkansas, soon, if anyone was here to take care of the house.

Mr. Moores is going to send Mr. Mason to Camden soon, and I could go in company with him. Mr. Moores ordered him to start last Monday and Mr. Mason spent that night here on his way, but told me it was too soon—that Mr. Moores was doing wrong. He told him so, but it did no good, and by the time Mr. Mason reached his house he had reconsidered the matter and concluded himself it was too early and sent Mr. Mason back. He spent the night here on his return and was regretting that your brother was not a man of more reflection and stability.

Of course, this was said in strict confidence, and you warranted the liberty by speaking of Mr. Moores careless way of doing business in his presence.

Last Friday or Thursday Mr. John White caught Ollie in a camp a few miles from Mr. Moores' and carried him there. Mr. Moore whipped him and handcuffed him until Saturday, and Ollie begged he would let him loose. Said he would not run away again and, as there was no one to bring him home that way, Mr. Moore turned him loose and he, Ollie, ran off straight way. I asked Mr. Moore what made him turn Ollie loose.

"Why," said he, "I knew you would have to turn him loose as soon as he got home, and I knew he would run away again."

"Why," said I, "David ordered he should be turned over to the Government."

He said you gave him no instructions to that effect, and I remember it was so. That you would not say a word to Mr. Moore about either he or Eli. What a pity, my dear, that there is so little friendly intercourse, so little understanding, between members of your family.

If I had been in your situation, had brothers and a brother-in-law in Bowie, where all Ollie's and Eli's relatives were, I should have asked them to have looked out for him and told them what I wished done with them when caught.

Uncle Edmund is sick today or I should probably have gone and seen Pratt. He has been spoken highly of as an overseer. The same I presume that you once tried to get.[17]

I'm suffering considerably myself lately and have been in bed most of the day. I'm afraid dyspepsia is getting a strong hold on me again, and several other things most painful and disagreeable. It is late, and yet I pause to say goodnight, Dearest.

December 13, Sunday night. Though it is late, bedtime, yet there is a few things I wanted to ask you, My Dear, whilst I think of it, and one is—Mr. Moores thinks that all overseers whom we might chance to get would object to putting their families in such quarters as ours where there is so little shade, comfort, etc., where the Negros would be in front of them, and the carts passes through, and you know, Dear, it lowered Brown in our estimation because he was willing to put his family in such a place.

I told Mr. Moores I could sit in my sitting room and give Mason my new dining room, fasten up my doors there, and the hall door that goes into the dining room. I know it would be unpleasant, but I find many things in life very unpleasant to bear; it would render the house safer and give me some leisure to walk out and go off occasionally. I know I am confined far too closely for my health, but I'm afraid to leave the house one hour. Write me soon as you get this what I must do.

Tuesday night, December 15. I went today to Mrs. Salmon's for my cloth. She did not have it quite out, and I left another piece with her and went on to see Mrs. Pratt, but she had "quit the loom." I asked her husband if he could be employed to attend to your business. No, said he, had considerable stock around him and it would be sacrificing too much of his own interest. Of course, I said no more and started on to Watkins, but Mrs. Watkins would only weave for special [illegible].

I saw your captain on my way, Uncle Edmund fortunately driving up then for Watkins. No, Captain Nelson told me, you were very well but absent when he left, and he gave me the blues by telling me he was ordered not to furlough any of his men for more than twenty hours, and seems to think you would not get home unless he got orders to remove down in this county to remain a while, and I trust that you will all be permitted to do so.[18]

For, oh! My Husband, you can't think how much I want to see you—to sit on your knee and fold my arms around your dear neck and be pressed to your heart—your loving heart.

Oh, when shall it be? Now I sit on this cold, stormy night by a comfortable fire, whilst you, My Darling, may be lying on the cold earth and the rain pouring in your face. The very thought is agony at times. It is well I do not always feel so, for if I did, I never would be well again. My Heavenly Father gives me strength to submit—and I try to, cheerfully, though it is not without a severe struggle at times.

Mr. Reuben told us yesterday to send to Mr. Armsworthy for your leather, as the men were afraid it would be stolen, so I came by there this evening and Mr. Armsworthy made many inquiries about you. Seemed very glad to hear from you. He told me that just before you left me he had sent two undressed calf skins to you and he had charged you twelve dollars (his usual price for his portion) and there was one left as it was too heavy for your shoes. He sold your part of it for twelve dollars and that made you even. He told me to tell you they gave two rolls of leather. I've not counted my pieces yet, but never put them away.

Am too tired to write more tonight, dearest, so I commend you to our Heavenly Father for this night and ask His blessings to rest on you.[19]

[Wednesday, December 16, 1863] *I forgot to mention to you in my last letter, Dear, that Mr. Moores told me about the hog cholera. He said, as many people were losing their hogs with it, that everybody was killing, and advised me to*

REGULAR PACKET
FROM SHREVEPORT TO FORT TOWSON, AND ALL INTERMEDIATE LANDINGS IN LAKES AND RED RIVER.

The fast, new, light draught Steamboat FRONTIER. CHEATHAM Master, will run regularly between the two above named places.

The steamer FRONTIER is an entirely new boat throughout, strong and of the best materials, built by G. K. Cheatham, at Louisville, Ky., the dimensions to suit the navigation of upper Red River and Bayous from Lakes to the River; and will ply regularly between Shreveport and the head of navigation, meeting the South Western at Shreveport. Both boats owned by G. K. Cheatham. No boat has yet entered the trade, so thoroughly adapted to it. For freight or passage, for which the boat has superior accommodations, apply on board.

Clarksville, January 6th, 1844   9—tf

Advertisement for the steamboat *Frontier* that traveled on the Red River.

do so forthwith. I told him you wrote to kill about Christmas. On yesterday they were killing at every house I passed or cutting up. All of them said the cholera had frightened them. Said it had got in the neighborhood, and so on my return home I told Uncle Edmund to get everything ready, or have it done so—for he has a bad cold and says he is sick all the time. And this evening it is turning very cold, it is bitter now.

Mr. Moores told me he would be here tonight. The stockholders have a meeting tomorrow and he said he would bring company, and I just finished some preparation I was compelled to make. Louisa is grumbling and Mr. Mason will probably be here tonight, having business with Mr. Moore, or he said he wanted to see him the day before; and it rained this morning, so Mr. Moore could not, I know, get to come by the foundry.

Did you get my letter I sent last Sunday week by Mr. Doyle? He told me yesterday he did not get off but sent it by a cousin. I saw the Telegraph moving to his Webster place yesterday.[20]

I hear Mrs. Connally has moved home for the duration of the war.

Crawford says he will probably live at Courtland. Has been offered quartermasters commission at that place—is going to get Mr. Castle or Mr. Allers to oversee for him.[21]

Hark! There is Mr. Mason--will write again tonight, my Darling.

By the time Mr. Mason got here last evening it was freezing cold and he advised me by all means to kill hogs, and I concluded to do so. It is a week today until Christmas, but all things considered I think it for the best. And do hope it will meet your approval.

As there is only three men here besides Uncle Edmund, and he so much complaining, Mr. Mason proposed to get eight hands from the foundry and to pay them in meat and be done with it. I was very glad he proposed it.

I told Uncle Edmund to start them several hours before day, and it was broad daylight before one of them left the house.

When Mr. Moores and Mason got to the foundry, they sent Morrison to attend to it. I am going to have it cut up and salted as it is so cold I'm afraid it will freeze by morning. Mr. Moores don't want me to have them cut up, but I know 'tis best.

Friday morning. I could only get sixteen hogs cut up last night. Mr. Moores is going to [illegible] I am rendering by now lard, pork, and ham [illegible] by daylight. Came up to have hogs weighed and cut up [illegible].

Mr. Mason, Mr. Moody, and Mr. Chappell spent last night here.

Most fondly, your wife

Rachel

Camp Clarksville

Tuesday, December 29th, 1863

My Darling Wife,

I have just returned from a scout from the Fork of White Oak and Sulfur, hunting deserters, but we did not find any. I received a letter today from you and one last week you sent by Doyle. I would've wrote sooner but there is a probability of our company being sent back to Davis. If we are sent back, we will start the last of this week.[22]

I was sorry to hear that your health was so bad, Darling. You are trying to do more than you are able to do. Must not confine yourself so close at home. You must ride about over the neighborhood and make Old Edmund drive you.

You wanted to know if you could give up the dining room to the overseer. Of course, My Darling, and do everything that you think best. You did right by having the hogs killed. How many was killed?

Your birthday poetry was very pretty.

I was very sorry to hear what troubles you had with Louisa and Lizzy. When I come home, I will make them sore. I think I will get a furlough in ten or twelve days.

You wanted to hear if I had met with any of your acquaintances. I have not, and only three of my mine, Mr. Anderson, Morgan, and Epperson. I have some of the apples, cake, and all of the butter. We have no mess, and to put it out I would not get any of it.

Darling, you think that I treated you so bad the morning I left by saying before the servants I did not want any overseer. I did not mean to hurt your feelings in the least, nor I would not do anything to wound your feelings for every darkey that I own. So, Darling, if I did, forgive me. I did not do it intentionally.

I think James Moore did very badly by turning Ollie loose. I did not give him any instructions about my affairs, only to hire an overseer. I asked Moore's son, if they should be caught, to brand them and put them in the army. I would have asked J. C. M., but I knew he would not attend any thing.

I'm standing the service very well. I hope these few lines will find you in good health. I send this letter by Dr. Nelson's boy, so a kiss and goodbye until next week, and I will write again if I don't get to come home.

Your husband,

D. H. Moores

XXX

[Wednesday, December 30, 1863] *A cloudy, a gloomy, rainy day. Has been so the entire day. Mr. [Crawford] Connally came and went before breakfast and, I trust, will arrange this affair. Oh, these Negroes. They harass one's soul out of oneself!*

[Thursday, December 31, 1863] *The heavens have been pouring out snow, sleet, and rain. The ground was almost white when we arose this morning. I never saw so cold a snow. No walking out. Janie practiced and read. I knit and read.*

NOTES

[1] Texas Adjutant General's Department, Civil War military rolls. Archives and Information Services Division, Texas State Library and Archives Commission. Texas, Muster Roll Index Cards, 1838–1900.

[2] R. K. Clark to Mrs. Harriet Stephens, J. E. Price, ed., "A Letter from Lamar County in 1844," *Southwestern Historical Quarterly*, 53 (July 1949), 66–67.

[3] These lines are from Henry Wadsworth Longfellow's poem, "The Light of Stars," first published in 1838 in *Knickerbocker's Magazine* and reprinted in his 1839 anthology, *Voices of the Night*.

[4] This proverb is from Thomas Campbell's "Loichiel's Warning." A wizard foretells the decisive victory of the English over Prince Charles Stuart's Scottish army at the Battle of Culloden in 1746, warning Sir Donald Cameron of Lochiel to . . .

> *. . . beware of the day,*
> *For, dark and despairing, my sight I may seal,*

But man cannot cover what God will reveal.
'Tis the sunset of life gives my mystical lore,
And coming events cast their shadows before.
I tell thee Culloden's dread echoes shall ring
For the bloodhounds that bark for thy fugitive king.

5 Lane's Ferry spanned the Red River, connecting northeast Bowie County with southwest Little River County, Arkansas. It was located near the site of the present town of Lanesport, Arkansas.

6 *"For now should I have lain still and been quiet, I should have slept: then had I been at rest,*
With kings and counsellers of the earth, which built desolate places for themselves;
Or with princes that had gold, who filled their houses with silver:
Or as an hidden untimely birth I had not been; as infants which never saw light.
There the wicked cease from troubling; and there the weary be at rest." Job 3:14–17.

7 The Roman poet Sextus Propertius gave us the earliest form of this proverb in *Elegies*: "Always toward absent lovers love's tide stronger flows." But Thomas Haynes Bayly published the first modern version of the epigram in his poem "Isle of Beauty," which appeared in *Songs, Ballads, and Other Poems* in 1844.

What would not I give to wander
Where my old companions dwell?
Absence makes the heart grow fonder,
Isle of Beauty, fare thee well!

8 Clarksville is the seat of Red River County, fifty-eight miles northwest of Texarkana in the northern-most part of the Piney Woods region of East Texas. At the time of the Civil War, Clarksville was the most important trading center in northwest Texas, with steamboats bringing goods up from New Orleans by way of the Red River and delivering them to Rowland's Landing fifteen miles to the north.

9 Samuel Watkins was born in South Carolina in or about 1815 but by February 1860 was living near Courtland in Cass County. He died in 1871 and is buried in Lafave, Scott County, Arkansas.

10 The Kiamisha River, now Bois d'Arc Creek, a tributary of the Red River, rises in southeastern Grayson County, runs northeast across Fannin County, and forms the 1863 boundary between Fannin and Bowie counties. In 1863, Camp Kiamisha was located at the mouth of the river.

11 The Battle of Chickamauga was fought on September 18–20, 1863, between the Union Army of the Cumberland under Maj. Gen. William S. Rosecrans and the Confederate Army of Tennessee under Gen. Braxton Bragg.

Rosecrans, having maneuvered the Confederates out of Chattanooga, followed Bragg's retreating army, but on September 17 the reinforced Confederates turned and attacked Rosecrans' isolated XXI Corps. On the morning of September 19, the Rebels assaulted but could not break the Union line behind Chickamauga Creek. The following morning, however, Rosecrans, fearing that Bragg would turn his left flank and cut his line of retreat toward Chattanooga, inadvertently created a gap on the front of Lt. Gen. James Longstreet, whose corps had been detached from the Army of Northern Virginia. Maj. Gen John Bell Hood's Texas Brigade sliced through the Union line, isolating the Union right wing, including Rosecrans himself.

One third of the Union forces were routed but rallied under Maj. Gen. George H. Thomas, who formed a defensive line along Snodgrass Hill. In Rosecrans' absence, Thomas assumed command of the Army of the Cumberland and held until evening when he retired into Chattanooga.

The subsequent Confederate Siege of Chattanooga was broken when U. S. Grant, fresh from his victory at Vicksburg, reinforced the Army of the Cumberland with divisions from his own Army of the Mississippi and with Maj. Gen. Joseph Hooker's corps from the Army of the Potomac.

12 James Morrison Hawes was born on January 7, 1824, in Lexington, Kentucky. He was graduated twenty-ninth in the West Point class of 1845 and was posted to the Second US Dragoons as a brevet second

many people were "as black hearted and evil as ever disgraced the revolutionary pages of Seventy-Six." The danger from bushwhackers and deserters with which his company was sent to deal was real enough. As early as 1840, historian Mark E. Nackman noted, northeast Texas was populated by "appalling numbers of adventures, desperados, and bankrupts." It was the "dumping ground of the States" and "a refuge of all the bold and lawless spirits of the entire frontier." Added to this volatile mix, during the Civil War large numbers of deserters from the Confederate army, local Unionists, and—most fearsome in the minds of the area's citizens—formerly enslaved men who had taken advantage of the chaos of war to liberate themselves from bondage, but who had no place to go and no means of support other than the farms and plantations on which they had formerly toiled, the region became subject to fearsome depredations. Rachel Moore lamented having to live, in the absence of her husband, with so many outlaws "plundering and marauding about over the premises, and not one effort made to put them down."[2]

As the war progressed, and with her husband away, Rachel spent increasing time and energy dealing with runaways. She was increasingly convinced that the "loyal" slaves on her plantation were harboring fugitives, and she vowed that, if she were master of the place, she "would take them up—the last one on the place—and punish them until they told me where they were."

XXX

[from the Journal of Rachel P. Moores]

[Friday, January 1, 1864] *Today has been almost too cold to put into practice all, or hardly, any of the good resolutions one has made for the New Year. Oh, that I can live nearer to my God than ever I have done. May, oh, may He help me to "fight the good fight" and "keep the faith," that there may be "laid up for me a crown of righteousness."[3]*

I never felt a more bitter cold day than this has been. The ice in the tubs, water buckets, etc., is one solid piece, and yet it seems to grow colder [torn] over one quarter around the lanes.

[Illegible] *the hogs had been fed, and all the ground was frozen and covered with snow, not one ear of corn in the pen though two grown men had just returned from there when I started, and on my return I had Uncle Edmund summoned and asked him if the hogs had been fed.*

"Oh, yes, Ma'am," said he.

"Do you know it?" said I.

"Oh, yes 'um. Indeed, I does know."

"What evidence have you."

"Why, Henry and Harrison just come from there."

"Call them up here!"

And what will it avail that I lecture them about starving the hogs this bitter cold weather when they ought to be fattened? Not one thing will they do but harbor those runaways.

David will find out when too late that they are harbored here. If I were master of the place, I would take them up—the last one on the place—and punish them until they told me where they were. I cannot believe, like my husband, they—Eli ad Ollie—have gone to the Federals. Would to Heaven they had!

What a time trying to get wool spun. Have just reeled and not three cuts apiece today. I shall never try to get any more work out of that worthless no-account Mary. It wears out my life to make her take the exercise that is essential to keep her alive!

I never felt so keen, so penetrating, a cold in all my life. As Janie is about through her practice, I will go in and we will have a cozy tete-a-tete on the rug before the fire.

Dear [torn] *companionship—sick and alone I must pour out all my love, my griefs to thee* [illegible] *out and off to camps again—*[torn]*, snatched from me, darling husband. This is the third time* [illegible]*. "How long till we shall meet again?" Alas . . . it may be many a day, and it may be forever. Still, I am hopeful to a degree and that saves me from despair. How it made my poor heart ache to see him leave, and so illy able to perform camp duties.*

I shall feel a little desolate after having a whole house full for the last week, and such a cold, cold time I never in all my life experienced. Such an intense cold spell, and of such duration.

The day after the great change in the weather, my dearest husband came home, beard and outer garments frozen, boots stiff. Frozen two days after Mr. Moody's two daughters, Miss

Nesmith, and Mr. Mason came and remained one week, until the change was over, three days ago, and now "my own good hall seems deserted."

No kindly voice to greet my dear
With dear and cheering tones
To softly whisper when I'm sad
To smile when I am gay.

And I shall miss it unusually much, for in laughing and rejoicing and talking, the days have been happily spent since dear husband came home, and in the evening Miss Sally entertained us delightfully with such good music, and each morning before the guests came down we would enjoy the luxury of a good tete-a-tete in the parlor, entirely free from intrusion as the breakfast was the summons that first brought them down. And that one-hour talk was always such a solace to me though I sometimes got a scolding for want of management, yet I would get an affectionate number of caresses for "doing more than any other woman would do."

[Torn] David found out [illegible] Thursday and a dispatch awaiting [illegible] who was at Courtland, and so Friday he came [illegible] Courtland with it and there found a letter from my brother, Mr. D. P. Godbold, requesting him to come or send for "Willis," a boy, since his late father's decease belonging to us.

Today David brought Mrs. Henshaw, who is to keep house for us, as he wishes me to accompany him. Much as I wish to see my dear relations, I do not wish to go. In the first place, I should be hurried too much, and then, I have a presentiment that the trip will be attended with disaster of some kind. Much rather have someone to go, but David insists that if I don't go, he won't, and says he would never any way. Says his furlough is only given on condition of and to attend to the business of getting the Negro home. I agreed, though most reluctantly, and so to bear.

[Monday, February 8, 1864] Spent part of today in the garden planting cabbage seed. Read some and knit some.

Rachel Moores, ca. 1900,
Moores Collection,
Wilbur Smith Archives,
Museum
of Regional History,
Texarkana, Texas.

[Tuesday, February 9, 1864] *Betty and I spent today quite pleasantly at Mrs. Connally's with one or two exceptions. Not, however, on Mrs. Watson's and Connally's account, who were always deference personified to me.*

[Torn] my cabbage today "Man of [illegible]. Though it remained yet unfinished [illegible] moments since Betty was playing "Come Dearest the Daylight is Gone." and how its congenial melody awakened all the tender feelings of my heart.[4]

Yes, yes; I fear many a daylight will dawn and dim ere my dearest comes, should he be ever so fortunate, which I can and will but hope. Oh, could I but soothe that aching frame and troubled mind this night, for well I know thou wert weighed down by fatigue, worn in body and mind.

[Thursday, February 11, 1864] *Have been no little disturbed today by depredations the foundry Negros are committing. Week before Christmas they stole the gin band, and now they have stolen the mill band, and it is potatoes every week, hogs, etc., and no accusation is ever made. Betty and I walked over to Mr. Moores' to get him to report to the overseer.*

Two women, strangers, dined here today—came for potatoes—three bushels each—Miss Mayfield and Mrs. Wilkins.

[Friday, February 12, 1864] *But little occurs worthy of record. Finished a pair of gloves. Finished reading* **[Illegible]***, but he was too much of an egotist to enlist much admiration from me.*

Sister Jane rode over and was thrown from her pony by the horse block and much bruised by the fall.

Two men—Mr. **[Edward B.]** *Castel and Mr. Wilkins—came for and got Mrs. Wilkins' six bushels of potatoes and Mr. Castle, five. Mr. Castel also took up a note the amount of which was twenty-one dollars, interest and all, twenty-seven and fifty cents.*

Here I am, transacting business from which my natural inclination shrinks as well as my capacity. Dear husband, I at least will be faithful to your interest and faithful, oh so ever faithful, to thee in love, duty, in all a wife should be in.

Betty is complaining, and so to bed with her.

[Torn] *transpired* **[illegible]** *made a pot of dye to dye my dearest* **[illegible]** *was troubled again with potato seed* **[illegible]** *Mr. Barnes and a Mrs. Castle. Commenced reading Wordsworth poems. "The Excursion"—but another* **[illegible]** *too tired and stupid and sleepy to do aught but go to bed and rest my weary limbs.*[5]

Good night, dearest husband. God bless you now, bless you forever. Amen.

[Wednesday, February 17, 1864] *Put a quilt in today and have concluded to write some three or four young ladies and the young Captain Connally. I know he is fond of such, and Nellie, poor child, I know, must long for some change. The weather "cold as charity in war times!"*

[Thursday, February 18, 1864] *Joy fills my heart tonight. My precious husband has been furloughed in common with all the company, but, oh, he looks so pale and thin.*

[Sunday, February 21, 1864] *Yesterday Mrs. Watson, Mrs. John Connally, Miss Paralee Rush, Miss Orpha Salmon, and Miss Fannie Norwood came to quilt. We were all favored with Captain*

Nelson's presence, whom David sent for yesterday morning. But little quilting was done, but I am repaid as the young folks all seemed to enjoy themselves much.

I'm sick tonight and never suffered more than last night in my life, though Paralee and Orpha and Miss Fannie Norwood spent last night with us, and Dr. Nelson escorted them home today. David, Betty, Miss Lewis, and myself took a ride.

[Monday, February 22, 1864] We rode to the tan yard today, calling on Mrs. Salmon on our way. Feel weary enough to sleep well tonight.

[Tuesday, February 23, 1864] Another horse stolen tonight and yet the alarm was [blotted] as Mr. Moores sent Dick over [torn] and one [illegible] I [illegible] I cannot live among the [illegible] I would expect were protection [illegible] yet. Here I have lived for five months thus, with runaway Negros, deserters, and jayhawkers plundering and marauding about over the premises, and not one effort made to put them down. I do not expect anything but for them to attack me in my room or bed. I never saw such a set of cowards as are in this community. They will see whether or not these thieves and murderers will let them off as easily as they are letting them off!

I have every right to believe that the perpetrators of these outrages are men, some of whom have lived on the place in the capacity of overseers. Thrice on my return from driving out on business I saw the infamous Old Brown near the gate, once dodging from me when he knew I saw him, came up and pretended to be catching a hog near the gate and had the impudence to ask me to let him go into the lot with it—the demon—the inhuman villain to be trying to turn our very own servants against us that they may play into his own hands and steal for him, help him to conceal the vagabonds that lie around me and be fed from my poor harassed husband's crib, meat and potato houses.

Oh, if I was a man, as poor Marie Antoinette said, "I would show myself." I would murder Old Brown in his tracks or I would make him keep away from our Negro quarters. I see and know [torn] on them [illegible] here and the chamber [illegible] [the Negros] between themselves [illegible]. I know he would murder me in my bed for 50¢ if he thought I had it in gold or silver. I candidly believe he is trying to put the Negros and other people up to it, for I have heard of his saying that he thought we had boxes of **[illegible]** full, when he knew we had not enough to defray my medical bills and that we borrowed for that purpose since the last crop was sold.

I believe I'm half crazed. I feel that this life will miss me without the intercession of a higher power, and I've prayed, oh so fervently, for help, for deliverance.

[Sunday, January 31, 1864] In two instances have my forebodings in regard to our trip to Arkansas been realized. My husband was attacked most violently the night before we reached home and has been confined to his room ever since, and whilst in Arkansas we purchased a young mare of mother for a thousand, to ride to the surrey, and she was stolen out of the horse barn last night. Betty Johnson (who accompanied us home) and I walked out after the Negros saying they could find no tracks and found the lot fence had been taken down and carefully put up again, and also where she was led through the rye field and the outside fence put up again, after leading her out.

She was mounted and rode in the direction of Mr. Baker's. I tracked her to the creek and there so many other tracks came into the road I lost the track.

[Torn] so changed. At my first **[illegible]** my dear father's chamber I was **[illegible]** at the site of his vacant chair **[illegible]** the place where he was wont to **[illegible]** on the bed at night. All, all in his hallowed chamber told to me that he was gone from whence there is no return. There was no pipe upon the hearth, no carefully folded paper in the same dear old quarter, no cloak lay upon the lounge ready to be thrown on his shoulders, no blanket for his feet, none of the little appurtenances for his comfort that I have been accustomed from childhood to survey hung around his room. No dear voice to say, "is that you child?" "I cannot see you, my site is so dim."

And then that solitary walk to the church where first I saw my father's grave, when only the cold wood should meet my nervous grasp, when the earth, the cold damp earth, lay heaped between me and that dear form that I had for years so tenderly nursed.

Oh, my father, you never knew how deep the devotion, the affection I felt for you, but the half was returned. I do not think that for worlds would I have it reversed—not ever. Before heaven can I say that my conscience can smart above my deportment to my dear father. I know I seldom ever gave him pleasure, but I can endeavor to Dear Mother. She looks so desolate, so bereft, the house so **[torn]**.

[Torn] *enough to* [illegible] *constitution. When I beheld my brother's door and Lucretia* [illegible] *to me she did not for a full minute recognize me, and all in a breath and exclaimed "how changed: what's the matter?" And so, mutation as the song goes, is written on all things, on all we have and are.*

I was gratified to find Mother having taken as a boarder so nice a gentleman as I take Mr. Byrel to be. He seems so kind and unassuming. And dear Sister, too, has such a polished officer. I've not been so much pleased with any military gentleman I've met since the war as Colonel Kelly. He must be a great protection, and so entertaining, too.[6]

That night we spent at sister's, a band came out from Price's army and serenaded us, rather a poor entertainment I must say, particularly the vocal part of it.[7]

We did not, on account of the roads, come by Falcon and spend the night, as usual, with Mat, which I regret very much, but I revisited poor little Charlie's grave and, oh, my heart ached so for Mat, for, oh, I know what it is to be childless, and instead of the sympathy of the world it is jeers and scoffs. Strange the world should consider it a crime to be unfortunate. I pray if it be the will of God, Mat may again be blessed with offspring.[8]

I see their unborn faces shine
Beside the never-lighted fire.[9]

[Torn] *alone, or rather bereft* [illegible.] *My darling husband left again for camp* [illegible]. *I cannot help it, but Mr. Pitts* [illegible] *most heavily upon me. Had he remained at home I think he might have leave for* [illegible]. *But, oh, how destructive is camp life to diseased lungs, liver, etc. Oh, Father, spare my husband if it be Thy will. Thou alone knowest the bitterness of my soul. Oh, to see my dearest husband go from me to buffet with the hardships of camp life, and so illy able for the conflict, is more than at times than I can well bear, or bear it with the fortitude I should.*

I can do very well when he is looking well, but to see him looking wan and pale, so emaciated as he looked when he left this time. How could he stand such a life? When he can barely live surrounded by a luxury [illegible] *and, I will add, nursed by the most devoted of wives. You have most of my thoughts, dear old Journal, and I've no one else to talk to now. I mean, I haven't thee, my dear husband, and that is all to me.*

Betty is kind and attentive. I mean assiduous, in her endeavors to make me forget that I'm alone, bereft of my dearest husband, for one of her age and experience, but then, she cannot supply the place of protector, and that I need so much. May the Ruler of the Universe ever watch over and keep thee, dearest.

[Thursday, February 25, 1864] *David, Mr. Crawford, and George Connally tracked their horses to the river Tuesday evening, and David was decidedly in favor of crossing as he heard the neighing of their horses over in Mush Island, but that Mr. Connally opposed the steps as being rash and bitter in the extreme, and so tomorrow Mr. Connally says the minute men will be here to join them in further pursuit. But—pooh—the thieves will exchange camps in that time and so such tracking ever ends!*[10]

[Friday, February 26, 1864] *Just as I predicted, some eighteen men are here tonight from the chase and no vestiges of the scamps. Our gin and mill bands, or rather what remained of them, in the deserted camp.*

[Torn] *spent last* **[illegible]** *came over this* **[illegible]** *discoursed so much* **[illegible]** *between two opinions. Some are in favor of pushing further pursuit, some for resorting to the authorities at headquarters, some for going to the houses of disloyal citizens and make them accessories for the depredations committed, etc., etc.*

George Connally dined and spent the afternoon with us.[11]

XXX

[Thursday, May 19, 1864] *Colonel Austin, a gentleman who came here at Dr. Salmon's suggestion to recuperate some two months since and remained a few days came back three weeks ago and asked for board for himself and wife. "I would take the best of care for her until he could provide a suitable nest!" Poor deluded pair. An old dilapidated man, a blooming, vigorous young girl. Oh, the end, the end, the terrible end of all such injudicious connections.*

[Sunday, May 28, 1864] *This morning I heard a good sermon* **[illegible]** *before preaching to us* **[illegible]** *she has been sick some days, and then* **[illegible]** *poor Mrs. Watson and Mrs. Connally.*

Poor Mrs. Watson, I cannot look at her in her widow's weeds without feelings of deepest emotions. How soon like her I may mourn the loss of my dearest on earth? Through all the week of storm and rain he has been engaged in the most arduous, most dangerous of all the duties that devolve on the poor soldier, and yet they have to bear their toils in secret yet. And yet I'm constantly asked, "what are the conscripts doing?" "They'd better be at home, etc., etc."[12]

A hard rain has just fallen—the sixth or eighth this week.

My dear David returned on business today. Will go again tomorrow. Has consented for me to go to Linden with poor Mrs. Watson to hear the funeral of her husband, so came and spent last night with her and insisted on my accompanying her—poor afflicted woman. May the Father of Widows help her to bear more resignedly her great grief.

Oh, my soul! How deeply hast thou been bathed in the floods of bitterness since I last closed these pages. Surely, I thought I should be overwhelmed and sink forever beneath them!

But Thy mercy, oh God, has sustained me and it may be for yet more heavy afflictions that I have been spared. Tribulations such as I have never known before. For daily I am passing through new trials such as I never in former years even dreamed of.

For could I, even one short year ago, have dreamed that a servant of our household would have committed a crime who's just [torn] and it is ever [illegible] expiated some of his sins upon the gallows. I returned home quite sick and prostrated with a [illegible] and found my poor, careworn, harassed, perplexed husband on a bed and poor [illegible] being, whose earthly career was so soon to close [illegible] ignominiously reclining nearer, nearer not only in the "gall of bitterness and bonds of iniquity," but in the galling fetters of the hopeless criminal —in chains.[13]

I had heard of David preceding me at Mrs. Griffin's, some five miles distance, and sank almost under the conviction of what I thought must be the sentence, for a jury, I felt convinced, must try him, and I knew the opinion of the community—and then captured, as he was, on a gentleman's horse—having his bridle and saddle.

David was so incensed at his own confession of crimes that verily I believe he would have made the Negroes hang him without any trial whatever, but, oh, I could not bear to think of his taking the whole responsibility in his hands, and now his spirit is having meted to it its final reward.

I do pray he felt truly penitent in his last moment. I wanted much to read to and admonish him, but he looked so surly and defiant I felt I would not. Perhaps it would be a mockery. I saw no earthly power could convince him that in reality he was going to be hanged, and therefore I did not exchange one word with him. I may have done wrong. If so, I earnestly pray to be forgiven.

I have not set up for several days and therefore must rest my poor body. My mind is too much disturbed for much repose and I have not been able to write one line to those [illegible] *many other things having absorbed my time, among which has been almost constant attendance upon my husband's sickbed* [illegible] *week after my last record he was taken ill in camp near DeKalb, and thither I went for him and found him much improved from a sudden and violent attack of fever, but a few days after his return he relapsed again and continued vacillating until the middle of the week when he had a severe spell of congestion from which I thought he could not possibly recover, but since he rose from that he continued to improve but is still subject to fever occasionally but his liver.*

Sister Jane's long spell of fever, from which she has just recovered, has tended to divert my mind from writing, too, for when David was so I could leave him, I would go to see her, and when my brother and family visited us I had what would have been, apart from her illness, all the pleasure of their company. It was painful, it is true, to see dear Brother Dave suffer as he did from a slight attack of fever, but to have Allie, dear Lucretia, and her—or a portion of her—little family with me a few weeks was so dear a pleasure.

My trip to Shreveport and the ordeal through which I had to pass in order to obtain my husband's detail, who was detained at home from indisposition.[14] *The pleasure of meeting my dear family! The polite attention of Colonel Wascome* [?] *and family—all interesting events to me, which but for the constant attendance on David I should have descanted upon, particularly, my interview with General Boggs and Colonel Williamson of headquarters.*[15]

[Torn] *left us today after* [illegible] *Tillman was unfortunate to lose his horse and fortunate in obtaining another so easily. David sold him one for a Navy pistol. Poor Hannibal* [illegible]*.*

[Wednesday, October 19, 1864] *Clear and bitter cold. Went down to the weaver's—Mrs. Smith's— for the cloth I carried the thread for a month ago. Very tired, but cut out a number of garments since my return.*[16]

[**Tuesday, November 15, 1864**] *They came a few days since—the poor, weak, decrepit man* [**Colonel Austin**], *not able to get upstairs without assistance, and the fresh, rosy young bride, looking so comfortable, so unconcerned for the future, alas, so sorely perplexes me for them. It is so difficult to hope, even, to influence for good, the men and women, the people among whom you live, when your standards are so different from theirs.*

XXX

[January 1865]

Miss Orpha M. Salmon,

As I told your brother George, Miss Orpha, that most probably I would be in attendance on the second, I now deem it proper to state I did not change my mind until, upon a second perusal of your letter, which was not concluded before your brother left.

After which perusal, I found I could not, consistently with my views of the rules of propriety, accept your invitation, though so kind and affectionately given, and by me prized above every other demonstration of your affection for me.

From you, it was both cordial and affectionate, and again, I thank you, for these new proofs of esteem.

Mr. Moores, who has just come in from a ride to the foundry, says "present my compliments, and tell Miss Orpha I have read the book of Genesis and shall expect her, as a Bible reader, to be faithful in fulfilling all the commands found therein."

Also, he adds in his congratulations to yourself and Mr. Connell and says we shall expect that visit you promised to be multiplied by two and not deferred, as the calf is fatted "and all things are ready."[17]

As the rain is falling heavy and fast this afternoon, I shall have to defer sending my letter and a bunch of white lilies which I took from my summer hat to dress your hair, as your brother said you had not prepared any—though desired to—for the occasion. If it is not raining tomorrow morning, I will send them early with a "tiny gift," the only one I could find at all suitable after a rummaging my drawers for some time. One has but little now that don't feel its age "from wear and tear."

Again, the warmest wishes of my heart, for you know of the happiness.

Rachel

XXX

NOTES

[1] An expedition of some 30,000 Union troops commanded by Maj. Gen. Nathaniel Prentiss Banks, supported by a massive naval flotilla commanded by Rear Admiral David Dixon Porter, attempted in the spring of 1864 to seize control of the Red River, capture Shreveport, and occupy East Texas, confiscating along the way as much as a hundred thousand bales of cotton and the organization of Unionist state governments in Louisiana and Texas.

On April 8, however, Banks's juggernaut was checked at Pleasant Hill, Louisiana, by Maj. Gen. Richard Taylor and fewer than 10,000 Confederates, ending the threat of Union occupation of northeast Texas.

Ludwell H. Johnson, *Red River Campaign: Politics and Cotton in the Civil War* (Baltimore, MD: Johns Hopkins Press, 1958); Gary D. Joiner, *Through the Howling Wilderness: The 1864 Red River Campaign and Union Failure in the West* (Knoxville: University of Tennessee Press, 2006).

[2] Mark E. Nackman, "Anglo-American Migrants to the West: Men of Broken Fortunes?: The Case of Texas, 1821–1846," *Western Historical Quarterly*, 5 (October 1974), 452.

[3] "Fight the good fight of faith, lay hold on eternal life, whereunto thou art also called, and hast professed a good profession before many witnesses." 2 Timothy 6:12.

"Henceforth there is laid up for me a crown of righteousness, which the Lord, the righteous judge, shall give me at that day: and not to me only, but unto all them also that love his appearing." 2 Timothy 4:8.

[4] "Come, Dearest, the Daylight Is Gone" was a popular parlor song, written in 1853 by Brinley Richards.

Come dearest the daylight is gone,
And the stars are unveiling to thee,
Come wander my lov'd one alone,
If alone thou can'st call it with me
Let us go where wildflowers bloom,
Amid the soft dews of the night,
Where the orange dispels its perfume,
And the rose speaks of love and of light.

[5] William Wordsworth's *The Excursion*, published in 1814, was to have been one part of a longer poem, never finished, called *The Recluse. The Excursion* consists of nine long philosophical monologues, one of

which, "The Ruined Cottage," is considered among his finest work. It is the tragic narrative of the slow, sad decline of a woman whose husband—a soldier—was lost in the Napoleonic wars.

6 John H. Kelly was the colonel of the Eighth Arkansas Infantry. He was killed in action at the Battle of Franklin, Tennessee, September 4, 1864. Maud McLure Kelly, "Gen. John Herbert Kelly: The Boy General of the Confederacy," *Alabama Historical Quarterly,* 9 (spring 1947): 9–12.

7 Following the repulse of Lt. Gen. Theophilus H. Holmes's attack on Helena on July 4, 1863, Maj. Gen. Sterling Price was elevated to command of the Confederate army in Arkansas. Price fortified and attempted to defend Little Rock, but after the city fell to Union forces on September 11, 1863, he and his command fell back on Arkadelphia and then to Washington and Camden where they went into winter camp. Camden fell to Union forces under Maj. Gen. Frederick Steele on April 12, 1864. Albert Castel, *General Sterling Price and the Civil War in the West* (Baton Rouge: Louisiana State University Press, 1968); Robert Shalhope, *Sterling Price: Portrait of a Southerner* (Columbia: University of Missouri Press, 1971).

8 Charles Mask was born in 1859 but died in infancy.

9 These lines are from Alfred, Lord Tennyson's, "In Memorium: A. H. H."

I seem to meet their least desire,
To clap their cheeks, to call them mine.
I see their unborn faces shine
Beside the never-lighted fire.

10 George Anderson Connally was born in Georgia on January 11, 1837. During the Civil War, he served as a captain in Col. Elkhana Greer's Third Texas Cavalry. Douglas Hale identifies James Connally, one of the regiment's lieutenants, as a former sheriff of Cass County, but seems to confuse him with Crawford Connally, who did serve as sheriff but not as a Confederate soldier. Douglas Hale, *The Third Texas Cavalry in the Civil War* (Norman: University of Oklahoma Press, 1995), 44.

Mush Island, bounded by the Sulfur River and Elliott Creek, was according to the memoirs of Robert H. Wadlington, an early Bowie County teacher, "a desolate jungle of vines, briars and dense cane brakes, rarely, if ever fully explored by the white man." During the Reconstruction era, "the notorious outlaw Cullen Baker with his clansmen, when hard pressed, would find safe refuge in the lonely jungles of this desolate island." Robert H. Wadlington, typescript of personal memoir, Wilbur Smith Research Archive, Texarkana Museum of Regional History.

11 George Anderson Connally, the son of Lucinda and Dempsey Connally, was born on January 11, 1837. On May 15, 1860, he was appointed postmaster at Courtland, and on September 25, 1866, he married Mary Ella Christopher in Cass County. He died on December 28, 1880, and is buried in Linden, Texas.

12 John R. Watson was born in Georgia on March 20, 1826. He was married to Lucinda Clementine "Clemmie" Connally and the couple had one child, a son named Robert J. Prior. In 1850, his family moved to Linden, Cass County, Texas, where he practiced law and served as deputy clerk of court. On April 2, 1862, Watson enlisted in Col. Thomas Ochiltree's Eighteenth Texas Infantry and was elected captain of Company B. He was promoted to major on February 23, 1863, and to lieutenant colonel on August 10, 1863. Watson was promoted to colonel of the Eighteenth Texas on April 9, 1864, but was killed in action only twenty-one days later, April 30, 1864, at the Battle of Jenkins' Ferry, Arkansas.

13 Rachel is quoting from the *Book of Mormon.* "My soul hath been redeemed from the gall of bitterness and bonds of iniquity. I was in the darkest abyss; but now I behold the marvelous light of God. My soul was racked with eternal torment; but I am snatched, and my soul is pained no more." Mosiah 27:29.

14 Shreveport, Louisiana, was the political capital of the Confederate Trans-Mississippi Department and the headquarters of its commander, Gen. Edmund Kirby Smith and the Army of the Trans-Mississippi.

15 William Robertson Boggs was born in Augusta, Georgia, on March 18, 1829. In 1853, he graduated from the United States Military Academy at West Point. As a junior officer, first as a Topographical Engineer

and later as an ordnance officer, he saw duty at the Watervliet Arsenal in Troy, New York; at the United States Arsenal at Baton Rouge, Louisiana; at Port Isabel, Texas; and at the Alleghany Arsenal at Pittsburgh, Pennsylvania.

With Georgia's secession, Boggs resigned from the US Army and accepted a commission in the Confederate army as an engineer and ordnance officer, working on the fortifications of Charleston, South Carolina, and Pensacola, Florida. He served on Edmund Kirby Smith's staff during the invasion of Kentucky in 1862 and in the spring of 1863 followed Smith to the Trans-Mississippi Department as chief of staff with the rank of brigadier general.

Boggs resigned after a quarrel with Smith, and for a short time commanded the District of Louisiana before being superseded by Brig. Gen. Harry T. Hays.

After the war, Boggs returned to civil engineering, participating in railroad construction in the West. In 1875, he was appointed Professor of Mechanics in the Virginia Polytechnic Institute at Blacksburg, Virginia. General Boggs died in Winston-Salem, North Carolina, on September 11, 1911, and is buried in Salem Cemetery.

George McWillie Williamson was born on September 22, 1829, in Shreveport. A distinguished attorney, he represented Caddo Parish in Louisiana's secession convention and was a signer of the ordnance of secession. In 1864, he was serving as Gen. Edmund Kirby Smith's adjutant general in the Confederate Department of the Trans-Mississippi with the rank of lieutenant colonel.

He was later appointed by President U. S. Grant, May 17, 1873, as minister to Honduras, El Salvador, Guatemala, Nicaragua, and Costa Rica, concurrently until his retirement in 1880. On January 29, 1882, Williamson "died suddenly of apoplexy on board the steamer *Jesse K. Bell* near Baton Rouge" and is buried in Shreveport's Oakland Cemetery. *Lafayette* [Louisiana] *Advertiser*, February 4, 1882, p. 2; *Claiborne Guardian, Homer, Louisiana*, February 8, 1882.

[16] A W. F. Tillman was born in Hardeman County, Tennessee, in 1833. He died in Bowie County, Texas, in 1921 and is buried in the Redwater Cemetery.

[17] William Fort Connell was born on September 14, 1826, in Robertson, Tennessee. On February 2, 1865, the couple were married in Cass County, Texas. David Moores' allusion seems to be to God's command in Genesis 1:28 that Adam and Eve "be fruitful and multiply."

AFTERWORD

The end of the Civil War brought what Rachel Moores called "a grand and gloomy time." The Reconstruction era saw wrenching changes in the economic foundation of northeast Texas. While the end of slavery meant freedom for enslaved blacks, to white slaveholders it presented a serious loss of capital. In 1859, Cass County slaveholders had paid taxes on 4,697 enslaved persons valued at $2,387,500, equaling 60 percent of all taxable property in the county. Bowie County slaveholders had paid taxes on 2,269 enslaved persons appraised at $1,167,139, a sum that represented 64 percent of all taxable property. The loss brought about by emancipation, together with the uncertain status of the South in the nation, caused property values to plummet in 1865.

Economic loss, coupled with the widespread belief that free blacks would not work, led to the abandonment of many of the region's plantations. Consequently, following the Civil War agriculture became of less importance than the region's timber industry, and livestock raising also assumed greater economic significance. Between 1860 and 1870, Cass County's assessed valuation fell to $761,809, but by 1881 it had rebounded to $1,612,881.

The general population of Bowie County maintained a slow growth to 8,875 in 1870; to 16,724 in 1880; to 22,554 in 1890; and to 22,841 in 1900, due in large extent to Texarkana's railroad boom.

For David and Rachel Moores, financial recovery seems to have come relatively quickly, for both were careful managers and less heavily invested in cotton than most Southern planters, and soon Rachel was again traveling extensively—her "first object," she protested, being the restoration of her health "when all the other means fail to prolong life"—but also out of what seems to have been a natural wanderlust. "I've seen much of the world that would have remained unknown to me," she proudly wrote.

Her first post-bellum trip was to New Orleans, seeking treatment from two eminent physicians and founders of the Medical College of Louisiana, now Tulane University. Augustus Henry Cenas was a professor of obstetrics the Medical College of Louisiana and Warren Stone was also the founder of the Maison de Sante (later Stone's Infirmary) in New Orleans, one of the earliest private hospitals in America.[1]

As had been the case in Brandon, New York, and Louisville, Rachel's treatments in New Orleans were unavailing, but until the end of her life she

Dr. Warren Stone, the founder of the Maison de Sante (later Stone's Infirmary) in New Orleans, one of the earliest private hospitals in America.

continued to travel, visiting her sisters and their families and touring for pleasure. David, as usual, remained at home.

On February 6, 1879, David and Rachael Moores celebrated their silver wedding anniversary. "This happy couple, who for a quarter of a century have stood shoulder to shoulder in loving unison of purpose, sentiment and joy," said the *Texarkana News*, are known and respected throughout North Texas." Attending the ceremony were "an army of friends and a regiment of relations," among whom were representatives of the Whitaker, Rosborough, Moores, and Hooks families. The newspaper trusted that "their diamond wedding will be attended by the same parties."[2]

Twelve years short of their fiftieth anniversary, however, David Harrison Moores passed away in Texarkana on January 18, 1892—the sixty-fifth anniversary of his birth.[3] After her husband's death, Rachel sold their Cass County plantation and moved to 302 Spruce Street in Texarkana, Texas, then a rapidly growing railroad hub. Most of the plantation's acreage was subsequently sold to the federal government, and in 1953 was inundated with the damming of the Sulfur River and the impoundment of what was to become Wright Patman Lake. In 1895, Rachel built and was living at 802 State Street (now the corner of Martin Luther King Boulevard and Main Street). This two-story, neo-classical home, locally known as "the Mansion on Main," was designed by architect Henry Koerner, and featured decorative fish scale shingling and elegant parquet flooring.[4]

"Aunt Rachel," as she had come to be called by Texarkana friends as well as by her nieces and nephews, died on April 21, 1904, and, as she and David had long desired, was buried beside him. Rachel's last will and testament reveals that she died possessed of thousands of dollars in cash and many luxury items, which she bequeathed to her church, her family, and friends. In accordance with that will, her body was "suitably prepared in a white silk or worsted robe for internment as near as possible beside the sacred

Rachel Moores' last home, locally known as "the Mansion on Main," was designed by architect Henry Koerner.

relicts of my dear husband (in the vault prepared for them)" in Rose Hill Cemetery. She left five hundred dollars "to keep said lot where we are buried in good condition; I desire that a holly tree be kept growing on each side of monument where they are now planted, to be kept in good, healthy condition, and all else connected with the said lot, to be well cared for, the walks to be covered with shells."[5]

NOTES

[1] "Dr. Stone's infirmary, or Maison de Sante, corner Canal and Claiborne streets. This institution under the direction of Dr. Stone, has been completely reorganized, and is ready for the reception of patients. The building is spacious and airy, and has undergone complete repairs. The wards are arranged in such a manner as to render them equally pleasant and comfortable in every season. The terms of admission are as follows: private room on the first floor, per day $5.00. Wards on the second floor, per day $3.00. Ordinary wards on the third floor, per day $1.50. Slaves, $1.00. These charges include all medical attendants, nursing, etc. All capital surgical operations charged for extra. All persons on admission are required for security, to give satisfactory city references or to make a cash deposit. For admission apply at the infirmary or to Dr. Warren Stone, 124 Canal Street." New Orleans *Daily Picayune*, January 7, 1850, p. 6, column 6.

2   *The* [Texarkana, TX] *News*, February 7, 1879.

3   The "Last Will and Testament" of David Harrison Moores, witnessed and filed on September 23, 1871, and probated on February 26, 1892, specified that his entire estate, estimated at a value of $10,000, become the property of his wife, Rachael P. Moores. Cass County, Texas, Probate Minutes, Vol. G, 1889–1899. James Tennison, "Mysteries Surround Ante Bellum Moore Home," *Texarkana Gazette*, March 22, 1986.

4   Upon Rachael Moores' death, the house was purchased by Robert Emmett Burke, and in 1978 the Texas Historical Commission designated it as a Texas Historic Landmark. "Moores-Burke-Ragland Home," Landmark Buildings file, Museum of Regional History, Texarkana, Texas.

5   Her will also included a bequest of $2,000 to the First Baptist Church of Texarkana, prompting the church's historian to refer to her as "that sainted woman. . . . Only God can properly appraise the true value of her benefactions." Walter W. Thornton, *History of The First Baptist Church, Texarkana, Texas. Commemorating its Semi-Sesquicentennial*" (Texarkana, TX: 1952), 74.

BIBLIOGRAPHY

Manuscripts

Austin Statesman, December 5, 1921.

Book of Texas: A Newspaper Reference Work (Houston: Houston Chronicle et al., 1914).

DAR Library, Austin.

"Diary of Rachel Godbold Moores, Wife of David Moores." Museum of Regional History. Texarkana, Texas.

Fort, Dr. Josiah W., Individual file. This is a copy of a letter written from the Republic of Texas in 1837. The letter written by Diane C. Fort implies that her husband established a town on the present site of Texarkana in about 1837.

Last Will and Testament. Eli H. Moores. Courtesy of Mr. Bill Watlington, Texarkana, Texas.

Log of Moores' family on journey from South Carolina to Texas by Anderson Rochelle Moores, courtesy of Mrs. Mattie Lee Montague, Cleburne, Texas.

Moores Papers, Barker Texas History Center, University of Texas, 2R121.

Texarkana Public Library vertical files.

"Thomas Sheldon Maxey Papers, 1868–1933," Barker Texas History Center, University of Texas at Austin.

Primary Sources: Books

Boswell, Angela, and Deborah M. Liles, eds. *Women in Civil War Texas: Diversity and Dissidence in the Trans-Mississippi.* Denton, TX: University of North Texas Press, 2016.

Cass County, Texas, Records of 1890. Atlanta, TX: Cass County Genealogical Society, 1998.

Jenkins, John Holmes, ed. *The Papers of the Texas Revolution, 1835–1836.* Austin: Presidial Press, 1972.

Kemble, Frances Anne. *Journal of a Residence on a Georgia Plantation in 1838–1839.* New York: Harper and Bros, 1863.

Menn, Joseph Karl. *The Large Slaveholders of Louisiana, 1860*. New Orleans, LA: Pelican Publishing Co., 1964.

White, Gifford, comp. *First Settlers of Bowie and Cass Counties Texas, from the Originals in the General Land Office and the Texas State Archives*. St. Louis, MO: Ingmire Publications, 1983.

Secondary Sources: Books

Adam, Louis A. *Adam's Directory of Points and Landings on Rivers and Bayous*. New Orleans, LA: np, 1877.

Ammer, Christine. *Unsung: A History of Women in American Music*. Westport, CT: Greenwood Press, 1980.

Augustin, George. *History of Yellow Fever*. New Orleans, LA: Searcy and Pfaff, 1909.

Bailey, Candace. *Music and the Southern Belle: From Accomplished Lady to Confederate Composer*. Carbondale, IL: Southern Illinois University Press, 2010.

Beecher, Catherine E. *Letters to the People on Health and Happiness*. New York: Harper and Brothers, 1855.

Biographical and Historical Memoirs of Southern Arkansas: Comprising a Condensed History of the State, a Number of Biographies of Its Distinguished Citizens, a Brief Descriptive History of Each of the Counties Mentioned, and Numerous Biographical Sketches of the Citizens of Such County. Chicago, IL: Goodspeed Publishing Company, Southern Historical Press, 1890.

Boswell, Angela. *Her Act and Deed: Women's Lives in a Rural Southern County, 1837–73*. College Station, TX: Texas A&M University Press, 2001.

Boswell, Angela. *Women in Texas History*. College Station, TX: Texas A&M University Press, 2018.

Bowie County Historical Commission. *Bowie County, Texas, Historical Handbook*. Texarkana, TX: Smart Printing Company, 1976.

Brecken, Dorothy K., and Maurine W. Redway. *Early Texas Homes*. Dallas, TX: Southern Methodist University Press, 1956.

Campbell, Randolph B. *A Southern Community in Crisis: Harrison County, Texas, 1850–1880*. Austin: Texas State Historical Association, 1983.

_____. *An Empire for Slavery: The Peculiar Institution in Texas, 1821–1865*. Baton Rouge: Louisiana State University Press, 1989.

_____., and Richard Lowe. *Planters and Plain Folk: Agriculture in Antebellum Texas*. Dallas, TX: Southern Methodist University Press, 2015.

Chandler, Barbara Overton, and J. E. Howe. *History of Texarkana and Bowie and Miller Counties, Texas–Arkansas* (Texarkana, Texas–Arkansas, 1939).

Chase, Harold, et al., comps., *Biographical Dictionary of the Federal Judiciary*. Detroit, MI: Gale Research, 1976.

Cheatham, Belzora. *The History of Whitaker Memorial Cemetery, Cass County, Texas*. Chicago, IL: 1996.

_____. *Slaves and Slave Owners of Bowie County, Texas, in 1850: 1850 Bowie County Slave Census with Information from the 1850 Free Census*.

Clinton, Catherine. *Fanny Kemble's Civil Wars*. New York: Simon and Schuster, 2000.

———. *The Plantation Mistress: Woman's World in the Old South*. New York: Pantheon Books, 1982.

———, and Nina Silber. *Battle Scars: Gender and Sexuality in the American Civil War*. New York: Oxford University Press, 2006.

———, and Nina Silber. *Divided Houses: Gender and the Civil War*. New York: Oxford University Press, 1992.

Cooling, Benjamin Franklin. *Forts Donelson and Henry: The Key to the Confederate Heartland*. Knoxville: University of Tennessee Press, 1987.

Corrigan, John. *Business of the Heart: Religion and Emotion in the Nineteenth Century*. Berkeley: University of California Press, 2002.

Crouch, Barry A., and Donaly E. Brice. *Cullen Montgomery Baker: Reconstruction Desperado*. Baton Rouge: Louisiana State University Press, 1997.

Cutrer, Thomas W. *Ben McCulloch and the Frontier Military Tradition*. Chapel Hill: University of North Carolina Press, 1993.

David, Deirdre. *Fanny Kemble: A Performed Life*. Philadelphia: University of Pennsylvania Press, 2007.

Dearborn, R. F. *Saratoga and How to See It: Giving Information Concerning the Attractions and Objects of Interest of the Fashionable Watering Place with the History Analysis and Properties of the Mineral Springs*. Saratoga, NY: C. D. Slocum, 1872.

Doyle, Mary Ellen. SCN. *Pioneer Spirit: Catherine Spalding, Sister of Charity of Nazareth*. Lexington: University Press of Kentucky, 2006.

———. *Catherine Spalding, SCN: A Life in Letters*. Lexington: University Press of Kentucky, 2016.

Dudden, Faye E. *Serving Women: Household Service in Nineteenth-Century America*. Middletown, CT: Wesleyan University Press, 1984.

Ellis, Summer. *Life of Edwin H. Chapin, D.D.* Boston, MA: Universalist Publishing House, 1882.

Engle, Stephen D. *Struggle for the Heartland: The Campaigns from Fort Henry to Corinth*. Lincoln: University of Nebraska Press, 2002.

Faust, Drew Gilpin. *Mothers of Invention: Women of the Slaveholding South in the American Civil War*. Chapel Hill: University of North Carolina Press, 1996.

Fischer, Gayle V. *Pantaloons and Power: Nineteenth-Century Dress Reform in the United States*. Kent, OH: Kent State University Press, 2001.

Forester, A. A. *DeKalb and Bowie County History and Genealogy*.

Fox-Genovese, Elizabeth. *Within the Plantation Household: Black and White Women of the Old South*. Chapel Hill: University of North Carolina Press, 1988.

Fuller, Robert C. *Spiritual, but Not Religious: Understanding Unchurched America*. New York: Oxford University Press, 2002.

Goodell, William. *Biographical Memoir of Hugh L. Hodge*. Philadelphia, PA: Philadelphia County Medical Society Collins, 1874.

Gould, George M. *Gould's Medical Dictionary*. London: P. Blakiston's Son & Co., 1927.

Hafendorfer, Kenneth A. *Mill Springs: Campaign and Battle of Mill Springs, Kentucky*. Louisville, KY: KH Press, 2001.

Hartley, Florence. *The Ladies' Book of Etiquette, and Manual of Politeness: A Complete Hand Book for the Use of the Lady in Polite Society.* Boston, MA: G. W. Cottrell, 1860.

_____. *The Ladies' Hand Book of Fancy and Ornamental Work.* Philadelphia, PA: J. W. Bradley, 1859.

Haskins, James. *Scott Joplin.* Garden City, NY: Doubleday and Company, 1978.

Hendler, Glenn. *Public Sentiments: Structures of Feeling in Nineteenth-Century American Literature.* Chapel Hill: University North Carolina Press, 2001.

Hilde, Libra R. *Worth a Dozen Men: Women and Nursing in the Civil War South.* Charlottesville: University Press of Virginia, 2012.

Jennings, Nancy Moores Watts, comp. *Texarkana Pioneer Family Histories-Texarkana, Arkansas–Texas.* Texarkana, Ark./Tex., Roark Printing Co., 1961.

_____, and Elizabeth Edwards Varner, comps. *Bowie County, Texas, Historical Handbook.* Texarkana, Texas: Bowie County Historical Commission, 1976.

_____, and Mary Lou Stuart Phillips, comps. *Texarkana Centennial Historical Program, 1873–1973.* Texarkana, Texas: Texarkana Centennial Association, 1973.

Johnson, Frank White. *A History of Texas and Texans.* Five volumes. Chicago, IL: American Historical Society, 1914.

Jones-Rogers, Stephanie E. *They Were Her Property: White Women as Slaveowners in the American South.* New Haven, CT: Yale University Press, 2019.

Kendall, John. *History of New Orleans. Chicago, IL: Lewis Publishing Company, 1922.*

Kilgore, Nettie Hicks. *History of Columbia County.* Magnolia, AR: Magnolia Printing Company, 1947.

Klotter, James C. *The Breckinridges of Kentucky, 1760–1981.* Lexington: University Press of Kentucky, 1986.

Laffrado, Laura. *Uncommon Women: Gender and Representation in Nineteenth-Century U.S. Women's Writing.* Columbus: Ohio State University Press, 2009.

L'Amour, Louis. *The First Fast Draw: A Novel.* New York: Random House, 2003.

Levy, Jo Ann. *Unsettling the West: Eliza Farnham and Georgiana Bruce Kirby in Frontier California.* Berkeley, CA: Heyday Books, 2004.

Lindsley, Philip, and Luther B. Hill, eds. *A History of Greater Dallas and Vicinity.* Vol. 2. Chicago, IL: Lewis Publishing Company, 1909.

Lloyd, James T. *Lloyd's Steamboat Directory, and Disasters on the Western Waters, Containing the History of the First Application of Steam as a Motive Power.* Philadelphia, PA: Jasper Harding, 1856.

McCaslin, Richard B. *Tainted Breeze: The Great Hanging at Gainesville, Texas, 1862.* Baton Rouge: Louisiana State University Press, 1994.

Marks, Paula Mitchell. *Hands to the Spindle: Texas Women and Home Textile Production, 1822–1880.* College Station, TX: Texas A&M University Press, 1996.

Massey, Mary Elizabeth. *Women in the Civil War.* Lincoln: University of Nebraska Press, 1994.

Meadows, Emma Lou. *DeKalb and Bowie County.* DeKalb, TX: DeKalb *News*, 1968.

Miyoshim, Masao. *As We Saw Them: The First Japanese Embassy to the United States (1860).* Berkeley: University of California Press, 1979.

Moores, Merrill. *Moores, Harrison, Ross, Conger,… : Watts, Godbold, Jones, McGill, Cooper and Allied Lines.* Indianapolis, IN: 1913.

Nissenbaum, Stephen. *Sex, Diet, and Debility in Jacksonian America: Sylvester Graham and Health Reform.* Westport, CT: Greenwood Press, 1980.

Palmer, Phyllis. *Domesticity and Dirt: Housewives and Domestic Servants in the United States, 1920–1945.* Philadelphia, PA: Temple University Press, 1985.

Philbrick, Nathaniel. *Bunker Hill: A City, A Siege, A Revolution.* New York: Viking, 2013.

Ranck, James B. *Albert Gallatin Brown: Radical Southern Nationalist.* New York: D. Appleton Century Company, 1937.

Rinn, Joseph F. *Searchlight on Psychical Research.* London: Rider and Company, 1954.

Rollins, Judith. *Between Woman: Domestics and Their Employers.* Philadelphia, PA: Temple University Press, 1985.

Russett, Cynthia Eagle. *Sexual Science: The Victorian Construction of Womanhood.* Cambridge, MA: Harvard University Press, 1989.

Ryan, Mary P. *Cradle of the Middle Class: The Family in Oneida County, New York, 1790–1865.* New York: Cambridge University Press, 1981.

Sacher John M. *Confederate Conscription and the Struggle for Southern Soldiers.* Baton Rouge: Louisiana State University Press, 2022.

Scheffelin, J. J., comp. *Bowie County Basic Background Book.* Texarkana, TX: 1980.

Shea, William L., and Earl J. Hess. *Pea Ridge: Civil War Campaign in the West.* Chapel Hill: University of North Carolina Press, 1992.

Silverthorne, Elizabeth. *Plantation Life in Texas.* College Station, TX: Texas A&M University Press, 1986.

Simpson, Harold B., comp. *Hood's Texas Brigade: A Compendium.* Hillsboro, TX: Hill Junior College Press, 1977.

Simpson, Matthew. *Cyclopedia of Methodism.* Philadelphia, PA: Louis H. Everts, 1876.

Smith, Catherine, and Cynthia Greig. *Women in Pants: Manly Maidens, Cowgirls, and Other Renegades.* New York: Harry N. Abrams, 2003.

Smith, Timothy B. *Corinth 1862: Siege, Battle, Occupation.* Topeka: University Press of Kansas, 2012.

Smith-Rosenberg, Carroll. *Disorderly Conduct: Visions of Gender in Victorian America.* New York: Oxford University Press, 1985.

Stampp, Kenneth M. *Peculiar Institution: Slavery in the Ante-Bellum South.* New York: Alfred A. Knopf, 1956.

Steele, Valerie. *The Corset: A Cultural History.* New Haven, CT: Yale University Press, 2005.

———. *Fashion and Eroticism: Ideals of Feminine Beauty from the Victorian Era Through the Jazz Age.* New York: Oxford University Press, 1985.

Strasser, Susan. *Never Done: A History of American Housework.* New York: Pantheon Books, 1982.

Szczesiul, Anthony. *The Southern Hospitality Myth: Ethics, Politics, Race, and American Memory.* Athens: University of Georgia Press, 2017.

Thornton, Walter W. *History of The First Baptist Church, Texarkana, Texas, Commemorating its Semi-Sesquicentennial.* Texarkana, TX: 1952.

Veblen, Thorstein. *The Theory of the Leisure Class*. New York: The Macmillan Company, 1899.

Vestal, Yvonne. *The Borderlands and Cullen Baker*. Atlanta, TX: Journal Publishers, 1978.

Weiner, Marli F. *Mistresses and Slaves: Plantation Women in South Carolina, 1830–80*. Urbana: University of Illinois Press, 1998.

White, H. Loring. *Ragging It: Getting Ragtime into History (and Some History into Ragtime)*. Bloomington, IN: iUnivesrse, 2005.

Woodward, Colin Edward. *Marching Masters: Slavery, Race, and the Confederate Army during the Civil War*. Charlotte: University Press of Virginia, 2014.

Wright, Ann Mims. [Annie Julia Mims]. *A Record of the Descendants of Isaac Ross and Jean Brown and Allied Families*. Jackson, MS: Consumers Stationery and Printing Co., 1911.

Wyatt-Brown, Bertram. *Southern Honor: Ethics and Behavior in the Old South*. New York: Oxford University Press, 1982.

Young, Elizabeth. *Disarming the Nation: Women's Writing and the American Civil War*. Chicago, IL: University of Chicago Press, 1999.

Young, Robert W. *Senator James Murray Mason: Defender of the Old South*. Knoxville. University of Tennessee Press, 1998.

Essays and Journal Articles

Amsler, Robert W. "General Arthur G. Wavell: A Soldier of Fortune in Texas." *Southwestern Historical Quarterly*. 69 (July 1965), 186–209.

Barker, Eugene C. "General Arthur Goodall Wavell and Wavell's Colony in Texas." *Southwestern Historical Quarterly*. 47 (January 1944), 1–21.

Burnell, Lizzie. "Woman's Rights." *Mayflower. May 1, 1861*.

Carrigan, Jo Ann. "Impact of Epidemic Yellow Fever on Life in Louisiana." *Louisiana History*. 5:2 (Spring 1964), 5–34.

_____. "Privilege, Prejudice, and the Stranger's Disease in Nineteenth-Century New Orleans." *The Journal of Southern History*. 36:4 (Summer 1970), 568–78.

Crutchfield, Eugene Lee. "Some Ill Effects of the Corset." *Gaillard's Medical Journal*. 67 (July 1897), 1–11.

Ellwood, Robert. "How New is the New Age." In *Perspectives on the New Age*. Edited by James R. Lewis and J. Gordon Melton. Albany, NY: SUNY Press, 1992.

Everett, Donald E. "The New Orleans Yellow Fever Epidemic of 1853." *Louisiana Historical Quarterly*. 33:4 (October 1950): 380–405.

Faust, Drew Gilpin. "Alters of Sacrifice: Confederate Women and the Narratives of War." In *Divided Houses: Gender and the Civil War*. Edited by Catherine Clinton and Nina Silber. Oxford University Press, 1992, 171–99.

Herbert, Thomas. "Hugh Lenox Hodge: A Master Mind in Obstetrical Science." *American Journal of Obstetrics and Gynecology*. 33:5 (May 1937), 886–92.

Kearney, Reginald. "Reactions to the First Japanese Embassy to the United States." *Hitotsubashi Journal of Social Studies*. Vol. 26:2 (December 1994), 87–99.

Kelly, Howard A., and Walter L. Burrage, eds. "Charles Delucena Meigs." In *American Medical Biographies*. Baltimore, MD: Norman, Remington Company, 1920.

Lintz, Bernadette C. "Concocting *La Dame aux camélias*: Blood, Tears, and Other Fluids." *Nineteenth-Century French Studies*. 33:3–4, (2005), 287–307.

"Our Daughters." *Harper's New Monthly Magazine*. 16:91 (1857), 72–77.

Smith-Rosenberg, Carroll. "The Female World of Love and Ritual." *Signs: Journal of Women in Culture and Society*. 1:1 (1975), 1–30.

Strong, Melissa J. "'The Finest Kind of Lady': Hegemonic Femininity in American Women's Civil War Narratives." *Women's Studies*. 46:1–2 (2017), 1–21.

Tompkins, Kyla Wazana. "Sylvester Graham's Imperial Dietetics." *Gastronomica: The Journal for Food Studies*. (Winter 2009), 9:1, 50–60.

Verbrugge, Martha H. "Women and Medicine in Nineteenth-Century America." *Signs*. 1:4 (Summer 1976), 957–72.

Watlington, Robert Herman. "Captain Jack." *Reminiscences of Bowie County and East Texas*. 1921.

Welter, Barbara. "The Cult of True Womanhood: 1820–1860." *Locating American Studies: The Evolution of Discipline*. Edited by Lucy Mattox. Johns Hopkins University Press, 1999, 43–66.

Winfrey, Dorman H., ed., "Diary of Major John Pollard Gaines: March of First Regiment of Kentucky Volunteer Cavalry, from Memphis, Tennessee, to Mexico, during the War with Mexico in 1836." *Texana*. 1 (Winter 1963), 20–41.

Wood, Ann Douglas. "'The Fashionable Diseases': Women's Complaints and Their Treatment in Nineteenth-Century America." *The Journal of Interdisciplinary History*. 4:1 (Summer 1973), 25–52.

Yanaga, Chitoshi. "The First Japanese Embassy to the United States." *Pacific Historical Review*. 9:2 (June 1940), 113–38.

Theses, Dissertations, and Unpublished Typescripts

Chandler, Barbara S. Overton. "A History of Bowie County." M.A. thesis, University of Texas, 1937.

Jaynes, Nita Mac, and Willard Jaynes. "Cass County, Texas: Short Sketches of its History and People." Unpublished typescript: Linden, Texas, 1972.

Lutz, Sibyl Harlalson. "A History of the Anglo-American Settlement and Development of Bowie County, Texas," M.A. thesis, East Texas State University, 1965.

Pollard, Gerald. "The History of Mount Lebanon University, 1852–1912." M.A. thesis, Louisiana State University, 1971.

Strickland, Rex W. "Anglo-American Activities in Northeastern Texas, 1803–1845" (Ph.D. dissertation, University of Texas, 1937).

Wagy, Tom, comp. *An Historical Bibliography of Bowie County, Texas and Miller County, Arkansas*. East Texas State University at Texarkana, 1987.

Government Documents

Burchard, Ernest Francis. *Iron Ore in Cass, Marion, Morris, and Cherokee Counties, Texas*. Washington, DC: Government Printing Office, 1915.

Texas Adjutant General's Department Civil War Military Rolls. Archives and Information Services Division. Texas State Library and Archives Commission.

Patman, Wright. *History of Post Offices and Communities, First Congressional District of Texas, Cass County.* 1946.

Newspaper Articles

Abeles, Neil. "Plantation Gives Peek at Past." *Texarkana Gazette.* July 27, 2016.

"Eli Moores, Bowie County Pioneer, Owner Land Where City of Texarkana Now Stands." *Four States News.* December 2, 1923.

"Famous Home Destroyed." *Texarkana Weekly News.* March 10, 1981.

Mchaffey, J. Q. "Pride in a Good Name." *Texarkana Gazette.* June 10, 1947.

"Outlaw Used Ferry in Quest for Vengeance." *Texarkana News.* February 13, 2013.

Tennison, James. "Mysteries Surround Ante Bellum Moores Home." *Texarkana Gazette.* March 22, 1986.

Turner, Annie May. "To Attract Relatives from Near and Far, Direct Descendants of Charles Moores, and Allied Families, to Have Gay Reunion Sunday." *Texarkana Daily News.* June 26, 1958.

INDEX

B

Bacon, (Mrs.), 59

Baker, Cullen Montgomery, 61, 62, 186–87, 221, 262, 264, 267–69, 318, 360

Baker, Elizabeth J. "Eliza," 61, 186, 208, 211, 216, 228, 234, 259, 264

Baker, Hilda J., 49, 52, 54, 61, 62, 186, 206, 208, 211, 228, 234, 264, 272

Baker, John, 52, 54, 61, 62, 193, 206, 261, 264, 275, 353

Baker, Nancy, 40, 61, 62, 220, 239, 264

Baldwin, Joe, 46

Balfe, Michael William, 178

Banks, Nathaniel Prentiss, 359

Barnes, (Dr.), 101

Baton Rouge, Louisiana, 361

Bayless, Dezzina Brown, 93

Bayless, Eugenie E. Brown, 93

Bayless, Samuel H., 66, 93

Bede, Adam, 139

Bedford County, Tennessee, 3

Beecher, Catherine Esther, 27

Bell Buckle, Tennessee, 3

Bell, J. H., 96

Bell, John, 173, 181

Bell, Nancy, 82, 96

Bennington, Vermont, 97

Benton, Louisiana, 48

Betsy (enslaved woman), 116, 145, 148, 193, 210, 227, 229, 293

Beverly, Massachusetts, 99, 107

Bible, 20, 25, 36, 51, 55, 124, 128, 139, 151, 193, 195, 196, 198, 201, 202, 239, 266, 274, 275, 297, 298, 303, 322, 358; Book of Acts, 201; Book of 1 Corinthians, 178, 316; Book of Hebrews, 314; Book of Job, 315, 342; Book of 1 Peter, 312; Book of Romans, 314; Book of 2 Timothy, 359; Book of Titus, 307

Bienville, Louisiana, 288, 313n

Blacksburg, Virginia, 361

Blain, Francis, 62

Blain, John Stephen, 62, 78, 94

Blain, Martha McRoberts, 49–50, 62

Blain, Mary, 62

Blacksford, South Carolina, 32

Blackstock, South Carolina, 60

Blevis, (Mrs.), 59

Blind Asylum, New York, New York, 88

Bloom, 42

Bloomer, Amelia, 96

bloomers, 64, 96n

Blue Ridge Mountains, 3

Blunt, James Gilpatrick, 343

Boggs, William Robertson, 360n, 361n

Bois d'Arc Creek, 342

Bonham Landing, 62

Book of Mormon, 360n

Boston, Massachusetts, 90, 93, 95, 98, 99, 106, 107, 108, 111, 135, 174, 175, 179, 180, 181, 330

Boston, Texas, 182

Bowie County, Texas, 4–9, 31, 32, 33, 40, 61, 78, 82, 92, 93, 96, 135, 172, 174, 175, 178, 179, 181, 182, 183, 198, 242, 280, 285, 299, 304, 305, 309, 334, 335, 342, 363–364

Bragg, Braxton, 342

Brandon, Mississippi, 20, 21, 23, 28, 56, 61, 63, 364

Breckinridge, John Charles, 173, 181, 343

Breckinridge, Robert Jefferson, 165, 181

Bright Star, Alabama, 180

Brontë, Emily, 177

Brown, Albert Gallatin, 28, 33

Brown, John, 1, 35

Brown, Tily, 188, 199

Browning, Elizabeth Barrett, 29, 30, 42

Browning, Rebecca Ann Rives, 62

Browning, William Daniel, 62

Bryant, William Cullen, 291, 312, 314

Buchanan, James, 183

Bullock County, Alabama, 179

Bunn, Alfred, 178

Burke, Robert Emmett, 367

Burnell, Elizabeth R., 185

Burns, (Mr.), 46

"Bury Me Not on the Lone Prairie," 97
Bush, (Dr.), 129, 163, 164
Bush, (Mrs.), 46
Butler, Frances Anne "Fanny" Kemble, 17, 23, 25, 33n
Butler, Pierce Mease, 23

C

Caddo Bell (steamboat), 42–43
Caddo Lake, 44, 48, 62
Caddo Parish, Louisiana, 62
Camden, Arkansas, 10, 95, 270
Camille, 30
Campbell, Thomas, 341
Cass County, Texas, 4–10, 32n, 61, 62, 63, 92, 98, 132–133, 135, 146, 169, 171–172, 174, 183, 186–187, 273, 317, 363, 365
Castel, Edward B., 351
Cauthen, James M., 63
Cauthen, Lucinda Clementine Connally Watson "Clemmie," 62n, 63n, 78, 90, 360n, 395n
Cenas, Augustus Henry, 364
Center Ridge, Arkansas, 114
Central Park, New York, New York, 98, 104, 110n
Chappell, Archer H., 42, 180, 315
Charles Town, Virginia, 35
Chattanooga, Tennessee, 342
Chesnut, Mary Boykin, 25
Chester County, South Carolina, 60
Clarence, Missouri, 262
Clarendon Hotel, Quebec, Canada, 111
Clarksville, Arkansas, 32
Clements, Sarah B. "Sallie" Moores, 93
Cole, Pulaski DuBose "Tip," 179
Collum, Minerva Ann Janes Moores, 92, 93, 313
Columbia, Arkansas, 60, 94
Columbia County, Arkansas, 9, 10n, 60, 76, 94, 98–99, 177, 274, 314
Columbia County, Alabama, 110, 315

"Come, Dearest, the Daylight Is Gone," 359
Conecuh, Alabama, 179, 180
Confederate Army, 32, 194, 197; Army of Northern Virginia, 342; Army of the Trans-Mississippi, 266, 360; Eighteenth Arkansas Infantry, 270; Eighth Arkansas Infantry, 360; Nineteenth Arkansas Infantry, 180, 270, 315; Ninth Arkansas Infantry, 314; Sixth Arkansas Infantry, 314; Texas Brigade, 342; Thirty-Second Texas Cavalry, 32
Congress Spring, New York, 105
Connally, Charles W., 278n
Connally, Crawford, 233, 302, 320, 344, 349, 351
Connally, Dempsey J., 52, 59, 62, 63, 64, 66, 67, 71n, 73n, 75, 144, 146, 157, 179, 196, 244, 268, 272, 282n, 285, 315, 316 325n
Connally, George Anderson, 360, 361, 365, 370n
Connally, Henry M., 199, 201, 274n
Connally, J. R. Rhadamanthus "Ruddy," 278n
Connally, James M. C., 278n
Connally, John, 180, 189n, 361
Connally, Lucinda McConnell Montgomery, 47, 49, 51, 52, 59, 61, 63n, 64, 67, 71n, 88, 90, 127, 144, 146, 179, 180, 197, 198, 199, 201, 210, 216, 233, 234, 252, 264, 268, 272, 282n, 285, 360
Connally, Ulysses Scott, 216, 264n, 268n, 361
Connell, William Fort, 293, 368, 371n
Conway County, Arkansas, 315
Cora (enslaved girl), 131
Corn production, 7, 11, 82, 86, 103, 113, 132, 134, 143, 185, 211, 219, 257, 273, 281, 285, 290, 311
corsets and corseting, 29, 64, 269n
Cotton production, 2, 7, 11, 24, 39, 76–78, 83–84, 86, 113, 131, 132, 134, 136, 144, 153, 163, 171–173, 175, 184, 227–228, 238–241

Godbold, Gasaway, 15

Godbold, Harriet A., 62, 120–22, 126, 134, 135, 137, 140, 147, 148, 154, 155, 160, 163, 164, 165, 169,

Godbold, Lucretia Collins Johnson, 63, 94, 110, 114, 116–17, 177n, 357

Godbold, Margaret "Mat," 5, 59, 65, 90, 187, 209, 244, 255, 275, 322, 354

Godbold, Margaret (or Margrett) "Betty" Johnston, 5, 94, 287, 313n, 350, 351, 352, 353, 355

Godbold, Mary A. "Mollie," 62, 94n, 101–102, 110, 140, 160, 176, 245, 277, 287, 292–93

Godbold, May Hardin, 94, 110

Godbold, Rachel Perry, 63

Godbold, Samuel Ananias "Pa," 9, 60, 62, 63, 109, 127, 144, 179n, 270n, 292, 293, 315

Godbold, Samuel Ananias R., Jr., 9, 62, 109n, 152, 244

Godbold, Thomas, 99, 115

Godbold, Virginia, 15, 31n, 62, 63, 136, 152, 170, 174, 176, 209

Godbold, William Johnson, 62, 66

Godbold, William Nathan, 94

Goldsmith, Oliver, 179

Gordon, (Dr.), 76, 79, 80, 85, 88, 176

Gordon, (Mrs.), 75, 80, 85, 89, 104

Grand Union Hotel, 111

Grant, Ulysses S., 265, 342, 361

Great Britain, 184

Griffin, B. M., 61

Griffin, L., 61

Grigsby, Justin M., 63

Grigsby, Nancy A. Brantly, 63

H

Hallam, Arthur Henry, 315

Halleck, Henry W., 267

Harper's New Monthly Magazine, 27

Harrison, (Agent), 168

Harrison, Anne Perry, 181

Harrison, Arkansas, 63, 94, 177

Harrison Chapel Cemetery, Cass County, Texas, 5

Harrison, Lucy, 72, 87

Harrison, Mary Virginia, 31

Harrison, William Henry, 173, 181

Harrit (enslaved woman), 35, 53–54, 57

Hartley, Florence, 13, 26, 33n, 178n

Harvard College, 99, 107, 312n

Hathaway, Arthur, 315

Hathaway, H. W., 315

Havana, Cuba, 14, 103–104, 110

Havana, Texas, 174, 190, 233, 269, 299

Hays, Harry T., 361

Haywood, Eliza Jones, 313n

Haywood, William H., Jr., 313n

Hempstead, Arkansas, 177

Henry (enslaved man), 233

Hobson, John Samuel, 63

Hobson, Sarah A., 57, 63n, 72

Hodge, Hugh Lenox, 100, 109n

Holmes, Henry, 28–29, 119, 125

Holmes, Oliver Wendell, 29

Hood, John Bell, 342

Hooks, James B., 182, 263

Hooks, Mary Ann "Mollie" Rosborough, 174, 182, 263

Hooks, Robert W., 179

Hooks, Texas, 182

Hope, Arkansas, 93

Hovey, Daniel, 179

Howells, William Dean, 27

Hoyt, Alice Louise, 180

Hoyt, Mary Harrison, 180

Hoyt, Thomas Alexander, 178, 180

Huckleberry Finn, 14

Hydropathic and Physiological School, New York City, 69–71, 74, 127

Hydropathy ("water cure"), 74

I

"I Dreamt I Dwelt in Marble Halls," 178; see also "The Gipsy Girl's Dream"

Illinois, 95

Independence, Texas, 313

Indiana, 94, 198

Indigenous peoples, 343; Cherokee, 343; Choctaw, 343; Creek, 343; Indian Territory, 318, 330, 343

"In Memorium: A. H. H.," 315, 360

Ironmonger, Francine Henshaw "Franny," 257, 272n, 274, 290, 314

"Isle of Beauty," 342

J

Jane Eyre, 225, 279

Jarrett, Pauline Tucker, 31, 267

Jefferson County, Arkansas, 180

Jefferson Medical College, Philadelphia, Pennsylvania, 109

Jefferson, Texas, 39, 42, 43, 46, 48, 49, 78, 91, 125, 235, 248, 281, 313n, 334

Jenkins Ferry, Arkansas, 63, 360

Jennings, Nancy Moores Watts "Nannie," 31, 32, 34

Jesse K. Bell (steamer), 361

Joe Baldwin (steamboat), 46

Johns, Agnes T., 39, 61, 63, 192, 218, 235, 236, 240, 264, 329, 333

Johns, Elijah, 264

Johnson, A. (Miss), 152

Johnson, Allie, 63

Johnson, Elizabeth B., 9, 60n, 63n

Johnson, Francis P., 63

Johnson, Samuel J., 63

Johnson, Samuel M., 63

Johnson, William Dickey, 63

Johnston, Albert Sidney, 265, 343

Joplin, Giles, 1

Joplin, Scott, 1

Josephus, Titus Flavius, 265

K

Kane, Dr., 232

Kansas, 343

Kant, Immanuel, 316

Kennebunk, Maine, 312

Kentucky, 32

Key West, Florida, 74

Kiamisha River, 342

Kittrell, Margret Talbot, 30–31

L

Lafave, Arkansas, 342

Lafayette County, Arkansas, 179, 180, 272, 314, 316

Lamartine, Arkansas, 314

L'Amour, Louis, 262

Lane, Joseph, 173

Lane, William, 31

Lanesport, Arkansas, 342

Larey, Ann T. Roach, 180, 316

Larey, John Michael, 180, 316

Larey, Mary M. Kelly, 180

Law of April 6, 1830, 5

Leake's Store, Arkansas, 76, 77, 94, 102

Le Jan, Francis, 24

Lewisburg, Arkansas, 315

Lexington, Kentucky, 342

Lincoln, Abraham, 181, 183, 271

Linden, Texas, 39

Little River County, Arkansas, 342

Little Rock, Arkansas, 3, 284, 306, 313n, 330

Long Island Sound, 99, 105

Louisiana, 48, 92, 263, 288, 313n, 343, 361; State of, 92

Louisville, Kentucky, 91, 94

Lousia "Lizzie" (enslaved house servant), 23–24, 117, 131–32, 140–41, 195, 281, 286, 312n, 329, 338, 340

Lowdnes County, Alabama, 313

M

Madison County, Alabama, 313

Maine, 99, 107, 108, 312, 315, 343

Maison de Sante, New Orleans, Louisiana, 376n. Also known as Dr. Stone's Infirmary.

Mary Ann, 85

Moores, Maria Louise Adams Ross, 314

Moores, Martha M., 31

Moores, Mary Jane, 31

Moores, Mary Lunsford Douglass, 314

Moores, Mary Virginia Harrison, 1, 4, 31, 93n, 182n

Moores, Matilda, 314

Moores, Mattie Lee, 31

Moores, Pauline Tucker Jarrett, 267

Moores, Perlina A., 31

Moores, Rachel Perry, 9–26, 28–31, 35–36, 64, 71–72, 76, 92n, 94n, 96n, 98–99,109n, 111n, 112–113, 124, 146, 165, 167, 177–182n, 183–187, 250, 261, 264–266n, 273–274, 286, 288, 312–314n, 316n, 317–318, 339, 345–347, 359, 360, 363–365; femininity, 15, 21, 185; illness, 4, 29, 60, 79, 130, 320–321, 331; Victorian ideals, 11–12, 14, 20–21, 25, 29, 183, 186

Moores, Reuben Henry Harrison, 2, 4, 5, 10, 37–38, 60n, 113, 134 136, 143–144, 152–153, 172, 174, 188, 190, 192, 203, 210, 215, 219, 220, 222, 229, 233, 236, 238, 241, 244, 246, 252, 255, 259–261, 270, 275, 280, 285–286, 288–289, 304, 306, 308–309, 319, 322–323, 333, 337

Moores, Ruth, 41, 51, 60n, 62n, 82, 200, 206, 216

Moores, Thomas Briggs, 3, 4, 32, 93, 182

Moores, Virginia, 31

Moores, William "Buck" Massack, 93

Moores, William Henry Harrison, 2, 199, 247, 296, 314, 330

Mooresville, Texas, 4, 10, 31, 179n

Morris County, Texas, 6

Mosquito, *Aedes aegypti*, 96

Mount Auburn Cemetery, 107

Mount Pleasant Classical Institute, Amherst, Massachusetts, 313

Mount Vernon, Virginia, 256

Mount Washington, Maine, 108

Museum of Regional History, Texarkana, Texas, 30–31

Mush Island, 355, 360n

N

Nancy (Moores' cook), 22, 83, 102, 103, 116, 117, 188, 195, 198, 199, 201, 206, 221, 227, 280, 281, 286, 308, 322, 331, 333

Nevada County, Arkansas, 9, 63, 66, 94, 177, 313, 315

New Albany, Indiana, 94

New Hampshire, 99, 107

New Haven, Connecticut, 98, 105

New Orleans, Louisiana, 2, 10, 14, 26, 35–36, 38–40, 42, 45, 48, 62n, 73, 75–78, 81, 89, 91, 94, 95, 96, 97, 98, 101, 104, 116, 131, 143, 152–153, 167, 170, 184, 214, 267, 290, 314, 342, 364

Newport, Rhode Island, 98, 105

New York, New York, 10, 11, 14, 26, 64–98, 104, 105, 110, 181, 184, 237, 254, 269, 284, 292, 313

Norvelle, John, 3, 15

Norvelle, Sarah Margaret, 15

North Carolina, 263, 313n

O

Oakwood Cemetery, Jefferson, Texas, 61, 187

"Ocean Burial," 97

Ocean House hotel, 111

Ochiltree, Thomas, 360

"Ode to a Nightingale," 28

Ogle, (Miss), 120, 124, 126, 127, 138, 159

Ohio, 85, 119, 136, 198, 264, 343

Olmstead, Frederick Law, 110

"On My Birthday Night," 326–327

O'Neill, Hugh, 92

Ouachita County, Arkansas, 10, 33, 63, 94, 314

Ouachita River, 66, 168

Frontier, 343; Army of the Mississippi, 267, 342; Army of the Ohio, 267; Army of the Potomac, 342; Army of Tennessee, 32, 267, 342; Eleventh New York Infantry, 271

United States Arsenal, Baton Rouge, Louisiana, 361

United States–Mexican War, 6

United States Military Academy at West Point, 360

Universalism, 64, 90, 97

USS *Pawnee*, 271

USS *San Jacinto*, 263

V

"Vain and Fleeting All Things Here Below," 96

Van Dorn, Earl, 266

Vaughn's Saloon, Camden, Arkansas, 10

Vermont, 97, 284

Vicksburg, Mississippi, 72, 73, 177, 271, 315, 342

Victorian ideals, 11–12, 14, 20–21, 25, 29, 183, 186

Vinning, Elizabeth "Betty" Perry Harrison, 172, 181

Vinning, Wade H., 172, 181

Virginia, 35, 62, 63, 78, 182, 255, 256, 263, 271, 297, 313, 361

Virginia Polytechnic Institute, 361

W

Waddle, William Henry, 182

Warner, Susan Bogert, 313n

Warren, Joseph, 111

Washington, Arkansas, 306

Washington, DC, 110, 256

Washington, George, 106, 108

Washington, Texas, 145

Waskom, Mary Elizabeth Lary, 179

Waskom, Sanctus Emmett, 144, 179

"Water cure," 74

Watervliet Arsenal, 361

Watson, John R., 63

Watson, Lucinda McConnell Montgomery, 56, 57, 63n, 333, 350, 351, 355, 356

Watson, Robert J., 63

Watts Cemetery, Willisville, Arkansas, 177n, 315n

Watts, David Moores, 314

Watts, Eli Moores, 314

Watts, Elizabeth Evans Godbold, 177, 313n, 314

Watts, Elizabeth Eva "Lizzie," 177, 178

Watts, Isaac, 96

Watts, John Comer, Jr., 314

Watts, John Comer, Sr., 34, 93, 177n, 178n, 209, 288, 293, 313n

Watts, Minerva James Moores, 314

Watts, Monrow Perry, 314

Watts, Nancy Harrison "Nannie" Moores, 93, 314

Watts, Thomas Jefferson, Sr., 34n, 78, 178, 313n, 314

Wavell, Arthur Goodall, 5, 6, 93, 263

Wayne County, North Carolina, 263

Weakley County, Tennessee, 186

Westerly, Rhode Island, 111

Wetherell, Elizabeth, see Susan Bogert Warner.

Wharton, Grace, see Katherine Byerley Thomson.

Wharton, Philip, see John Cockburn Thomson.

"What Can the Matter Be?," 179

"When I Love You," 94

Whitaker family, 1–3, 48, 50, 61n, 141, 143, 150, 163

Whitaker, Elizabeth Harrison, 61

Whitaker, Harrison Ross, 62

Whitaker, Sarah Harrison Moores, 61, 226, 236

Whitaker, Willis Loundes "Willie," Jr., 37, 42, 48, 50, 61, 136, 141, 142, 143, 150, 226

White Mountains, New Hampshire, 99, 107

White Sulphur Spring, New York, 111

Whitman, Walt, 95

Wilbur Smith Archives, Texarkana, Texas, 2, 5, 23, 350, 360
Willis, N. P., 263
Willis, Sara, 94
Willisville, Arkansas, 63, 94, 177, 315
Winchester, Tennessee, 136, 142, 178
Winn, Robert Nicholas, 178
Wisconsin, 74
Woodlawn, Arkansas, 94, 132
Wooten, Francis G., 62
Wright, Cordelia Ann "Dee" Rush, 262
Wright, Lloyd Samuel, 262
Wuthering Heights, 177
Wyatt-Brown, Bertram, 18

Y

Yale College, 98, 105
yellow fever, 28n, 89, 96–97n
York, South Carolina, 182
Young, Overton C., 343

Z

Zollicoffer, Felix, 198, 265